Critical Advances in Reminiscence Work

From Theory to Application

Jeffrey Dean Webster, M.Ed, has been an instructor in the Psychology Department of Langara College, in Vancouver, Canada, since 1987. He was co-editor, with Barbara Haight, of *The Art and Science of Reminiscing: Theory, Research, Methods, and Applications* (1995). He has presented at the annual gerontological meetings of the American, British, and Canadian societies and his published work has appeared in journals such as *The Journals of Gerontology: Psychological Sciences, Journal of Aging Studies, Journal of Adult Development, Canadian Journal on Aging,* and the *International Journal of Aging and Human Development.* He is a founding member of the Society for the Study of Human Development (SSHD) and the International Institute for Reminiscence and Life Review (IIRLR) where he is currently serving as President-Elect. In addition to his interests in reminiscence, he is currently involved with projects on attachment styles in elderly adults and the development of a wisdom scale.

Barbara K. Haight, DrPh, is a tenured professor of Gerontological Nursing at the Medical University of South Carolina in Charleston. Dr. Haight is a fellow in the American Academy of Nursing, the Gerontological Society of America, and the Florence Nightingale Society and has presented and published nationally and internationally on life review and reminiscence. She was co-editor with Jeffrey Webster of the *Art and Science of Reminiscing: Theory, Research, Methods, and Applications.* Recipient of a variety of service awards, Dr. Haight also was named the South Carolina Career Woman of the Year for 1989. In 1990, she was honored by the Health Science Foundation of the Medical University of South Carolina as one of three developing research scholars. She is a founding member of the International Institute for Reminiscence and Life Review where she is currently serving as President.

Critical Advances in Reminiscence Work

From Theory to Application

Jeffrey Dean Webster, MEd
Barbara K. Haight, RN, DrPH, FAAN
Editors

 Springer Publishing Company

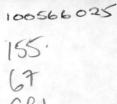
j

Springer Publishing Company, Inc.
536 Broadway
New York, NY 10012-3955

Acquisitions Editor: Helvi Gold
Production Editor: Jeanne W. Libby
Cover design by Joanne Honigman

02 03 04 05 06 / 5 4 3 2 1

Library of Congress Cataloging-in-Publication Data

Critical advances in reminiscence work : from theory to application / Jeffrey Dean Webster, Barbara K. Haight, editors.
　　　p. cm
　　Includes bibliographical references and index.
　　ISBN 0-8261-6992-9
　　1. Reminiscing in old age. I. Haight, Barbara K. II. Webster, Jeffrey D.
(Jeffrey Dean)

　BF724.85.R45 C75 2002
　155.67'1312—dc21

　　　　　　　　　　　　　　　　　　　　2001057821

Printed in the United States of America by Sheridan Books.

To Shirley, Troy, and Ryan, with all my love—JDW

*To my mentor and teacher, Sister Rose Therese Bahr.
Without her faith and support, my work in life review
would never have begun—BKH*

Contents

Part V   Clinical Applications

Contributors

Nicole Alea, Institute on Aging and Department of Psychology, University of Florida, Gainesville, Florida.

Lisa A. Barker, Counselor, Private Practice, Vancouver, British Columbia.

James E. Birren, Associate Director, Center on Aging University of California at Los Angeles, Los Angeles, California.

Susan Bluck, Institute on Aging and Department of Psychology, University of Florida, Gainesville, Florida.

Joanna Bornat, Open University, Milton Keynes, England.

Philippe Cappeliez, Department of Psychology, University of Ottawa, Ontario.

Sally Chandler, Department of English, Wayne State University, Detroit, Michigan.

Peter G. Coleman, Department of Psychology, University of Southampton, Southampton, England.

Robyn Fivush, Department of Psychology, Emory University, Atlanta, Georgia.

Prem S. Fry, Department of Psychology, Trinity Western University, Langley, British Columbia.

Tilmann Habermas, Institute for Psychoanalysis, Johann Wolfgang Goethe Universität, Frankfurt, Germany.

Joyce L. Harris, College of Communication, The University of Texas at Austin, Austin, Texas.

Airi Hautamaki, University of Helsinki, Helsinki, Finland.

Shirley Hendrix, Department of Gerontological Nursing, Medical University of South Carolina, Charleston, South Carolina.

Barbara Keller, Department of Psychology, Dresden University of Technology, Dresden, Germany.

Gary M. Kenyon, Gerontology Programme, Saint Thomas University, Fredericton, New Brunswick.

John A. Kunz, Department of Continuing Education, University of Wisconsin-Superior, Superior, Wisconsin.

Toyoko Nomura, Department of Social Work, Iwate Prefectural University, Takizawa, Japan.

Michele L. Norman, College of Health Professions, Medical University of South Carolina, Charleston, South Carolina.

Christine Paha, Institute for Medical Psychology, Free University, Berlin, Germany.

Susan Perschbacher Melia, Department of Sociology, Assumption College, Worcester, Massachusetts.

Andrei Podolskij, Moscow State University, Moscow, Russia.

William L. Randall, Gerontology Programme, Saint Thomas University, Fredericton, New Brunswick.

Ruth Ray, Department of English, Wayne State University, Detroit, Michigan.

Elaine Reese, Department of Psychology, University of Otago, Dunedin, New Zealand.

Robert L. Rubinstein, Department of Sociology and Anthropology, University of Maryland Baltimore County, Baltimore, Maryland.

Muriel E. Shaw, Department of Counselling Psychology, University of British Columbia, Vancouver, British Columbia.

Brian Schiff, Department of Psychology, Saint Martin's College, Lacey, Washington.

Marvin J. Westwood, Department of Counselling Psychology, University of British Columbia, Vancouver, British Columbia.

Paul Wink, Department of Psychology, Wellesley College, Wellesley, Massachusetts.

Foreword

Here is a contemporary book in the fullest sense. It comes at a time of great interest on the part of the general public and academics in the personal accounts of the experiences of life. In many countries there is a growing contemporary interest in the stories of life, and reflections about events in life and their meaning. Personal narratives afford insight into the different ways life is experienced. Increasingly, academics have become interested in the content and processes of reminiscence as part of the domain of the social and behavioral sciences.

Many new and important questions are being raised as researchers and scholars look seriously into the growing volume of personal accounts of life. One of these questions is why there is so much interest on the part of the general public in reviewing their lives and perhaps preparing an autobiography. Another question is whether the drift of the information age is toward a busy and efficient but impersonal lifestyle. One motive, among others, may be the need to establish a clearer personal identity in societies where there is little opportunity for sharing memoirs. Finding the answers to such questions will advance our knowledge about the various ways life is experienced.

Other important questions touch upon basic matters of life. Thus, answers to questions about the similarities and differences in the ways men and women interpret their lives can contribute to reducing the uncertainties of contemporary marital life and relationships. The accounts of siblings growing up and growing old can also provide insights into the differences in interpretation of family experiences and, thereby, reduce problems in relationships. How people extract meaning from their lives is a broad question of considerable importance. Insights into the process of finding meaning in life are accessible through the study of personal narratives. This is one of the many windows on life this volume offers the reader.

A related issue to meaning in life is how people interpret causality in their lives—external events, self actions, or divine powers. The development of interpretations of causality underlies motivation and the extent to which individuals feel responsible for making decisions and initiating actions. Many more significant topics arise in the chapters of this book when reminiscence about the life is pursued further.

Of particular interest is the narrowing gap between the laboratory studies of memory and its real life use by individuals. In accounting for the ways memories of life events are stored, recalled, and reinterpreted, this book cannot provide an encyclopedia of established facts. That is for the future. This book is a map that directs us toward future territories that call for exploration of the many ways we recall the facets of human life lived under greatly differing conditions. It points to ways of improving the quality of life by encouraging the processes of reminiscence and thereby enlarges our understanding of the ways human behavior is interpreted and organized. This book is therefore a mind opener to many important issues of human behavior.

JAMES E. BIRREN

Preface

Life Is story. *

The new millennium has been heralded by an energetically expansive investigation of all things biographical. Autobiographical memory, life stories, narrative therapy, life review, guided autobiography, and oral history are only a few examples of this narrative focus. Reminiscence work, as an integral component of many biographical approaches, has continued to develop in exciting and productive ways as well. The major purpose of *Critical Advances in Reminiscence Work: From Theory to Application* is to present examples of cutting-edge treatments of reminiscence work which, we believe, will shape the direction of the field for at least the near future.

Reminiscence, the process of recalling personally experienced episodes from one's past, has received steadily increasing attention since Butler's (1963) seminal article. In his pivotal paper, Butler emancipated the concept of reminiscence and life review from the shackles of a medical model which perceived the reminiscences of older adults as harbingers of mental decline or imminent dementia. Instead, Butler averred that life review was "universal" and "natural," a process with the power to provide a sense of meaning and purpose in life, and an opportunity for older adults to achieve a sense of closure, psychological well-being, and positive personality reorganization in the face of their own mortality. These were liberating and compelling ideas which set off a chain of empirical enquiry.

Subsequently, reminiscence has been both hailed as a panacea and denigrated as an ersatz religion (Moody, 1988). Between these extremes, researchers and practitioners have struggled over the past forty years

---

* Birren & Cochran, 2001, p. 10.

to strike an empirically grounded balance between unbridled enthusiasm and mainstream neglect. Recently, exciting progress has been made in the theoretical, empirical, and clinical aspects of reminiscence and life review, particularly within the past half decade or so.

Dimensions of reminiscence and life review are currently seen as crucial elements in many facets of contemporary social science. Examples range from neuroscience (e.g., the neuroanatomy of autobiographical memories) to health care delivery (e.g., life review interviews as patient intake measures). This burgeoning interest is evident in the proliferation of internet sites devoted to the topic, recent workshops and conferences such as the one sponsored by the American Society on Aging (San Diego, March, 2000) and the 17th World Congress of Gerontology (Vancouver, July, 2001), the European Reminiscence Network, the Reminiscence Interest Group of the Gerontological Society of America, and the recently founded International Institute for Reminiscence and Life Review.

Critical Advances in Reminiscence Work: From Theory to Application examines progress in the field of reminiscence, focusing on what we consider to be key areas. The "critical" in our title does not refer to a specific epistemological or philosophical position; rather, it reflects two basic concerns. First, critical means those theoretical/conceptual, empirical, and applied areas which are necessary to move the field forward. Much of the research in the field has traditionally been gero- and ethno-centric, conducted primarily with elderly, white participants. This focus is changing, as is clearly reflected in the present volume. Second, critical refers to an evaluative lens which focuses attention on the need for increased rigor in the substantiation of claims for the putative benefits of reminiscence. In this regard, certain "sacred cows" are explicitly tested and found wanting. As one example, Butler's universality claim is challenged by empirical results presented by Wink and Schiff in the opening section of this volume.

Critical Advances in Reminiscence Work: From Theory to Application is a multinational and multidisciplinary effort reflecting remarkable diversity in methods, aims, and implications. Contributors represent Canada, Finland, Germany, England, Japan, New Zealand, Russia, and the United States; in terms of disciplines, gerontology, nursing, social work, audiology and speech-language pathology, psychology, continuing education/extension, sociology, anthropology, and English departments, as well as private practice claim authors. As a result, the present volume can serve as a valuable resource to many persons interested in the relationship between reminiscence processes and a host of potentially adaptive outcomes. Researchers, practitioners, and senior undergraduate/graduate students will benefit from the chapter information, particularly since many of the contributing authors are internationally acclaimed. We are particularly fortunate and honored to have contributions from stellar pioneers in the field; we hope we will not slight others if we name in particular Peter Coleman, Joanna Bornat, and Jim Birren.

Moreover, we have intentionally included chapters from contributors whose main allegiance is not reminiscence per se, but conceptually related domains. These authors explicitly examine how reminiscence is both similar to, but unique in some ways from, their particular field. Bluck and Alea's chapter on autobiographical memory and reminiscence and Bornat's chapter on oral history and reminiscence are two examples.

Content Overview

The volume is divided into five parts. Part I comprises a single chapter in which Shirley Hendrix and Barbara Haight provide an invaluable foundation and orientation for the work to come in their review of the literature. Chapters in part II address important conceptual and theoretical issues in the field. Joanna Bornat describes similarities and differences between reminiscence and oral history. By explicitly linking these conceptually related domains, Bornat articulates ways in which each field can benefit from the findings of the other. Paul Wink and Brian Schiff discuss several factors which mitigate the "universal" assumption of life review. Their elegant case studies illustrate that life review is not a necessary, but can be a sufficient, condition for achieving successful aging. Susan Bluck and Nicole Alea bring together two relatively separate research domains which can benefit from the insights of each other. Specifically, they compare functions of reminiscence and those postulated for autobiographical memory. Sally Chandler and Ruth Ray's chapter expands the focus on intrapersonal, psychological dimensions of reminiscence to the broader issues of social construction and power relations in reminiscing. Joyce Harris and Michele Norman note how reminiscence is often manifested in language and examine this important relationship between cognitive-linguistic and memory processes.

Articles in part III coalesce around the interrelated dimensions of development and sociocultural contexts of reminiscence behavior. Robyn Fivush and Elaine Reese provide an excellent bridging chapter which will prove very provocative for gerontologists, namely, the notion of reminiscing styles and emotional bonds in childhood. There exists almost no crossreferencing between researchers interested in reminiscence either at the beginning or end of life and this chapter will

be an important stimulant to interdisciplinary discussion. Tilmann
Habermas and Christina Paha describe the importance of souvenirs in
the transition to university in young adults as triggers of reminiscence
in the aid of identity issues. Jeff Webster's research provides some of
the first evidence concerning race/ethnic differences in reminiscence
functions, an important yet neglected topic. Robert Rubenstein examines the home environment of elders as a cultural/contextual prism
through which the meanings of personal memories are refracted.
Barbara Keller extends these developmental and contextual concerns
to the broader social/cultural and historical arenas. She asks how reminiscences are shaped by one's cohort and the types of profound historical events which we may experience.

The focus of part IV is on underrepresented groups or special populations in reminiscence research. Susan Perschbacher Melia introduces
the concept of spiritual reminiscence in elderly nuns which serves to
foster connection and growth. This links reminiscence to emerging
research in the area of late life spirituality. Little has been written about
the relationship between reminiscence and victims of abuse. Prem Fry
and Lisa Barker address this limitation in their chapter on the potentially adaptive, as opposed to obsessionally neurotic, nature of reminiscence in this group of individuals. Peter Coleman and his colleagues
Airi Hautamaki and Andrei Podolskij explore dimensions of reminiscence and life review in groups of Finnish and Russian war veterans.
Themes of reconciliation and generativity are addressed and the
power of memory in the service of these positive psychosocial goals is
poignantly described. Finally, tacit links between reminiscence and
wisdom are made explicit by William Randall and Gary Kenyon. Using
the perspective of "narrative gerontology" they explore how reminiscence helps explicate the story of one's life, the examination of which
can foster what they term "ordinary" wisdom.

Part V remains faithful to the clinical roots of much reminiscence
and life review research. Muriel Shaw and Marvin Westwood detail the
life review program for Canadian veterans who, for the most part, have
not had the opportunity to integrate the war experience into their broader
life stories. John Kunz illustrates the therapeutic benefits of integrating
reminiscence and life review techniques with the well-established intervention of brief cognitive behavioral therapy. Toyoko Nomura describes
a unique program for using reminiscence with dementia patients in
Japan. Finally, Philippe Cappeliez demonstrates how specific reminiscence types and functions have specific corresponding outcomes in
treating depression in older adults in long-term care.

Webster (2001) recently stated that reminiscence work is at an
important crossroads. The chapters in the present volume lead us down

a path of increased sophistication in the conceptualization of reminiscence as a multifaceted, ecologically valid form of episodic memory. By contrasting reminiscence with related domains we improve conceptual clarification. We also broaden the potential appeal of reminiscence work to others in similar areas. Further, by identifying relatively neglected research areas we extend the scope beyond the original gerontological, and often institutional, emphasis.

Paradoxically, this may in fact help us to understand the sometimes conflicting findings reported in the clinical gerontology literature. The chapters dealing with development/sociocultural issues, for instance, illustrate that age per se is a poor predictor of reminiscence in later adulthood. Rather, context, culture, family dynamics, and reminiscence "styles" are probably more direct indices of reminiscence behavior throughout the lifespan. Finally, a more differentiated approach to therapy allows clinicians to "match" reminiscence styles or functions with particular outcomes (e.g., the use of instrumental reminiscence to increase self-efficacy).

By viewing reminiscence in this light, we hope readers will gain an appreciation for the complexity and interconnectedness of this natural process and make their own contributions to this vibrant and expanding field.

JEFFREY DEAN WEBSTER
BARBARA K. HAIGHT

I

Overview

1

A Continued Review of Reminiscence

Shirley Hendrix and Barbara K. Haight

This chapter continues the integrative reviews of reminiscence that were begun in 1991 (Haight) and continued in 1995 (Haight & Hendrix). Because of the many favorable comments we received for the past reviews, particularly by doctoral students, we will continue in the same format with the same key words. Remaining with only the original key words is a difficult thing to do because we see such growth and widening of the field. Interestingly the term life review is now used much more widely than the term reminiscence, as many theorists, researchers, and practitioners look at the phenomena of reminiscence within a more total life span approach. In doing this review we again felt we left out an enormous amount of important work that also uses reminiscing as a method, such as autobiography, oral history, narrative, and biography. Only if the search engines picked up one of our keywords as being an important part of a document was the document included. Our apologies to anyone we have slighted, particularly the author of our foreword who has done groundbreaking and early work in autobiography, and whose work we greatly respect. Finally, we have not included books in this review but have again confined ourselves to peer reviewed publications.

Now to the criteria for this review. To build upon the prior reviews that went as far as 1993, this review covered the years 1994 to 2000. International peer reviewed journals were searched for the following keywords: reminiscence, life review, life story, and remembering the past. An article sometimes contained a key word in the title but only had one of the concepts as a major part of the article and so was brought up in the search. For example, *A narrative approach to quality care in long term care facilities* is about the life review, and so part of this review. Though the terms reminiscence and life review are not used interchangeably as they were six years ago, there is a new generation of terms often used interchangeably with the life review. They include life history, life line, narrative and autobiography. These interchangeable terms are not an issue unless one is conducting a search. The search engines used in this review were CINAHL, Medline, PsycInfo, and Current Contents. Additionally many reference lists in articles were hand searched to look for additional and related articles not picked up by our search engines.

DATA COLLECTION

This field that used the words reminiscence and life review is said to have begun in 1963 with a seminal article by Dr. Robert Butler. Though we know others have mentioned similar topics in earlier times, such as Socrates who said, "the unexamined life is not worth living," Butler's description was timely as nations became focused on aging and gerontology. These modalities were seen as related phenomena and were used mostly with older people. In the 30 years between 1960 and 1990 there were 68 published articles, most of which reported serendipitous results as clinicians observed the way people responded to reminiscing. The research was exclusively with older adults and often flawed by small samples and a confusion of terms.

In the last ten years alone, there have been over 150 new publications. The last decade of publications in the area showed increased rigor in the area of research and a more scholarly approach to the phenomena of life review and reminiscence. There is wider use of reminiscing with different age groups and in a wider variety of ways. The new psychology of narrative therapy may have grown from this field. Recent publications show growth in scholarly thought, creativity, and an increased curiosity about the phenomena itself.

To give order to the growth, we will again divide the manuscripts into four sections: The first, Scholarly discussion, looks at the thinking pieces, theory, and discussion. The second category addresses Research, both quantitative and qualitative, and the third category, Methods, again looks at suggestions and instructions for the use of reminiscence. Finally, Applications consists of reports of use, usually by practitioners and clinicians in the field.

SCHOLARLY DISCUSSION

There is never enough scholarly discussion. Researchers need to spend more time sharing their thoughts that rarely get included in the research articles. From these discussions we generate new hypotheses and are exposed to different ways of interpreting the same phenomena. Discussions are illuminating and many times prime the thinking pump. Webster (1999) demonstrates the value of a thinking piece as he argues for a contextual metamodel and a life span perspective for future research, introducing a new way to look at an old topic. Coleman (1999) also makes a significant contribution to our thought processes in describing the four elements that constitute a good life review. He suggests this be a beginning framework to guide the work in telling the life story. Soltys and Coats (1994) join Coleman and offer a model to facilitate reminiscence, especially with those who are terminally ill.

An interesting approach to looking at a life was offered through narrative intelligence. Narrative intelligence is a core component of biographical aging. Randall (1999) submitted that perhaps the novelty of the lived life required new theories to enlarge our understanding of the way people live their lives.

Andrews (1997) reasoned that a life must be examined within the prevailing social structure as that would affect what is viewed as memorable in one's life. Her thoughts are supported by Levine (1996) who described the importance of younger therapists understanding the social as well as the personal history of their older clients. In this context there is a need for interventions to have personal relevance for individuals from culturally and linguistically diverse backgrounds (Habermas & Bluck, 2000).

Cohen and Taylor (1998) critically evaluated what other scholars had written about reminiscence and concluded that no one method of studying reminiscence is satisfactory and that there are numerous factors other than age that contribute to the initiation of reminiscence. Silver (1995) talked of the need for someone to listen to the life review and recommended that knowledge of developmental theory would illuminate the story for the listener and in turn would help older people find meaning in their memories.

Two authors suggested theories for guiding reminiscence. The first, Parker (1995), discussed the application of continuity theory to the study of reminiscence. The second, Tornstam (1999), argued that the theory of gerotranscendence was a better way of studying reminiscence, because he posits that gerotranscendence and reminiscence functions were intertwined. Tornstam suggested that reminiscence rather than just contributing to stabilizing an already established identity can contribute to the reconstruction of identity and one's perception of the world.

RESEARCH

Research on reminiscence is prolific and there is use of both qualitative and quantitative paradigms. Since the last review, we have found more qualitative work, more work with individuals, and more work over time using the entire life story instead of a moment of remembering. Researchers are fully defining their process, using larger sample sizes and diverse ways of looking at functions, processes, and outcomes.

Many authors used case studies as jumping off places for a scholarly discussion or to illuminate a particular idea. The subject numbers in the case studies range from 1–3 and offer rich discussion. Sokolovsky (1996) discussed the case study as a research method and said that the analysis of interviews could offer differing interpretations of the case, while Rubinstein (1995) commented on the fact that interviewer and informant were sometimes at odds and illustrated this fact with a case history. White (1995) reported a life review done while writing an autobiography, and Tabourne (1995b) reported the use of a life review program with a newly relocated nursing home resident that decreased depression and increased orientation. Using a similar case study approach, Brown-Shaw, Westwood, and de Vries (1999) showed how one person reframed an experience from the past to facilitate meaning. Again using the case study approach, Hirsch and Mouratoglou (1999) described an older adult with memory difficulties whose ego integrity continued to improve after the life review, as did Mills and Coleman (1994) who reported it was meaningful for older adults with dementia to reminisce. Finally, Kropf and Tandy (1998) described a case where the use of the narrative by an older woman created an alternative story of survivorship rather than depression and fear.

Many studies looked at aggregate outcomes as a result of using a life review intervention. Tabourne (1995a) studied three groups of people with Alzheimer's disease and showed significant decrease in disorientation and improvement in social interaction. Haight, Michel, and Hendrix (1998, 2000) conducted a longitudinal study with 256 newly admitted nursing home residents and found therapeutic outcomes increased over time for at least two years in those receiving a life review. Differences between those who experienced the presence of a life review in a near death event and those who did not experience the life review in a near death event showed a vast variety of outcomes (Stevenson & Cook, 1995).

Webster conducted several quantitative studies to examine reminiscence predictors and functions. In 1994 he examined predictors of reminiscence across the life span with 94 adults divided into three different age groups. He found personality traits significantly predicted reminiscence. With McCall (Webster & McCall, 1999), he replicated and extended results from a 1993 study with a group of 268 subjects to look at age and gender differences, and in 1998, he examined reminiscence functions and attachment styles. His scale has been widely used by others in this review and is a major contribution to the field. One study by Blankenship, Molinari, and Kunik (1996) found trends in all factors of the Reminiscence Function Scale except for Bitterness Revival.

Both Weiss (1995) and Watt and Cappeliez (2000) looked at cognitive therapy and life review as a way of treating depression. Both found the modalities successful but the outcomes difficult to measure. Watt and Cappeliez discussed a more effective way to analyze clinical outcomes that would provide information for other clinical outcomes researchers. Ashida (2000) used reminiscence music therapy sessions to effectively decrease depressive symptomatology in patients with dementia. McDougal, Blixen, and Lee-Jen (1997) reinforced the use of a life review modality for depression by retrospectively analyzing 80 home health nurses' notes on people discharged with the primary diagnosis of depression. They found that those who life reviewed experienced a positive increase in overall well-being.

In research done in long-term care settings, Goldwasser and Auerbach (1996) found that a reminiscence intervention with staff present improved the residents' feelings toward the staff. Weiss (1994) describes group therapy with two groups of cognitively intact older people in a long-term care setting and found that the treatment group showed a significant increase in sense of purpose and meaning in their lives. Brooker and Duce (2000) also found more improved well-being in their reminiscence group of dementia patients, as did Cook (1998) in life satisfaction.

During the last decade, qualitative research has taken hold and seems to be the most effective and natural way to measure factors in the life story. One can pose a question and then look for the answer in a set of transcribed life histories. An example of this approach is in the article by Johnson, Ball, Haight, and Hendrix (1998). They were curious about what older people thought of their parenting skills in the context of their present child/parent relationships. They and another doctoral student analyzed transcribed life reviews of people who had children and revealed interesting connections. Again using transcribed life reviews, Haight and Hendrix (1998) looked for differences in life patterns between suicidal and satisfied women. They found the suicidal women were exceptionally lonely and isolated throughout their lives compared with satisfied women who had wide social networks. In a secondary analysis of published interviews, McAdams, Diamond, de

St. Aubin, and Mansfield (1997) used the same technique to determine differences between adults who were generative and those who
were not.

Qualitative analysis is an excellent way to study peoples' experiences to determine what makes them who they are. Heliker (1997), on
a topic of life in a nursing home, used hermeneutical methods to analyze the data. Melia (1999) used grounded theory to analyze thirty-five
interviews of sisters in a religious community to determine differences
in developmental stage between the young-old and the old-old. Note
the chapter by Fivush and Reese in this book which offers insight into
childrens' reminiscences. Stewart and Vandewater (1999) also used
reminiscence to determine whether or not women made mid-life review
corrections. Still another form of looking back, a life line, enabled
Boyd, Hill, Holmes, and Purnell (1998) to study a stress model in
women who smoke crack to determine if childhood stress influenced
future drug use behaviors.

Scholars are beginning to look at ethnic and cultural differences in
the use of reminiscence functions. Atkinson, Kim, Ruelas, and Lin
(1999) found that older Chinese-Americans, Mexican-Americans, and
European-Americans shared many of the same reasons for reminiscing with a facilitator and no group was found to be less willing to reminisce about difficulties they or their families experienced. In fact,
Mexican-Americans were perhaps more inclined to resolve problems in
life review therapy than the other two groups. Related findings are reported by Webster in this book looking at Chinese-Canadians. Perhaps in
the future we can explore background issues that might account for
similarities and differences in various ethnic groups.

APPLICATIONS

Applications are sometimes a result of research as people tell us the
uses of life review that they have experienced that have been helpful.
Much of the reported literature in applications lies between a case
study approach and an application as some authors describe the use in
one person. Others discuss their applications in a more nebulous way
as a result of their practices and offer rich discussion. Andrews (1997)
sees the life review as helpful in cases of social transition. It is reported
that life review is useful in a visual format with end-of-life AIDS patients
(Weishaar, 1999), even though others (Vaughn & Kinnier, 1996) warn
against using the life review with this population because of problems
they encountered. McGowan (1994) talks about the mentoring role of

reminiscence between elderly people and college students, and Draucker (1998) sees the narrative as a potentially useful tool for women who have experienced violence or have been victimized throughout their lives. This use is further elucidated by Fry and Barker (this volume) and supported by McInnis-Dittrich (1996) who uses the technique for elderly survivors of childhood sexual abuse and believes the technique empowers women.

Family therapists employ the life review or a reminiscence modality to foster better relationships and coping skills in families under stress. Porter (1998) applies the technique with developmentally disabled adults themselves by creating life story books. A similar utilization is sanctioned by Hussain and Raczka (1997) who engage in life story work with people with learning disabilities and believe it gives them an opportunity to talk about themselves in a safe environment, resolve past issues, and become more known to others who live and work with them. Sandberg (1999) believes the life review which includes family members along with an older person fosters forgiveness in families through shared understanding of past difficulties. Still focusing on families, Sukosky (1994) sees the life review as a useful tool for family and marriage therapy.

These are all differing and special problems which make one believe reminiscing modalities that are guided are excellent for therapy. For example, Rife (1998) used life review techniques with unemployed older workers to establish work histories, identifying successes and sad times in their work lives. This was also seen to assist them to cope with the depression that often accompanies job loss. Social reminiscence as a therapeutic intervention to teach effective communication skills to nursing students is advocated by Puentes (2000), and Weishaar (1999) examined the effectiveness of Visual Life Review with an end-stage AIDS patient.

METHOD

Method consists of instructive pieces that help others employ the same method or at least offer an understanding of the technique that was used. Often method and application become confused and in this review there are only a few method pieces. The first is offered by Davis-Berman and Berman (1998) and describes a model for therapy based on storytelling in a group. Many of the method pieces speak to the use of the story and the importance of the therapist's understanding of the story. Kennedy (1999) also reinforced the importance of the therapist paying attention to the context of the story and discussed the therapist's involvement in the story. The need to understand the teller's story is reinforced by Boldt and Mosak (1998) who offer implications for therapy.

In instructions for students of the life review, Beechem, Anthony, and Kurtz (1998) offer a life review interview guide that adds a great deal to the field, especially when cross referenced with Birren's themes for autobiography (1996) and Haight's life review and experiencing form. Brown-Shaw, Westwood, and de Vries (1999) described a process model combining methods of life review and autobiography in the context of group psychodrama.

This method section may be short, because there is a greater understanding of our processes. Also because the processes are better explained in the research articles attesting to our growth as a discipline.

SUMMARY

Much has happened in a decade—we have evolved into a more orderly and understandable discipline. Our research has become more sophisticated. There is an increased use of case studies and qualitative descriptions to describe our process and outcomes. There is an increased curiosity about what actually happens during the process of recall. And finally more of us are using longer interventions to gain better outcomes. The growth for this decade makes us curious about the next. In the next we will have to include the work in narrative therapy and oral history to better understand ourselves and each other.

SCHOLARLY DISCUSSION

Authors	Journal Title	Journal Citation	Write-Up of Article
Andrews, M.	Life review in the context of acute social transition: The case of East Germany.	*British Journal of Social Psychology* (1997) 36(3), 273–290.	Examination of the relationship between the personal life review and the social structure, that may affect what is viewed as memorable in one's life.
Bluck, S., & Levine, L.	Reminiscence as autobiographical memory: A catalyst for reminiscence theory development.	*Aging and Society* (1998) 18, 185–208.	Examination and discussion of reminiscence as form of autobiographical memory. Suggests this is a first step to tie together several approaches to help understand significance of contemplation of past by people.
Cohen, G., & Taylor, S.	Reminiscence and aging.	*Aging and Society* (1998) 18, 601–610.	Discussion of the literature on reminiscence, including definitions, different functions, and distinction between reminiscence and autobiographical memory. Types and amount of reminiscence are also discussed.
Coleman, P.	Creating a life story: The task of reconciliation.	*The Gerontologist* (1999) 39(2), 133–139.	A discussion of four elements that constitute a good life review. Suggests greater attention to the processes involved in telling one's life story may give therapists a framework to assist older people reviewing their lives.
Coleman, P. G., Ivani-Chalian, C. & Robinson, M.	Self and identity in advanced old age: Validation of theory through longitudinal case analysis.	*Journal of Personality* (1999) 67(5), 819–847.	Five case studies drawn from a a 20-yr longitudinal study of aging to examine support for two theoretical viewpoints of self in later life; management of self-esteem and development of identity as story.

SCHOLARLY DISCUSSION (*Continued*)

Authors	Journal Title	Journal Citation	Write-Up of Article
Habermas, T., & Bluck, S.	Getting a life: The emergence of the life story in adolescence.	*Psychological Bulletin* (2000) *126*(5), 749–769.	Outline of a conceptual framework for the development of life story in adolescence to fill the gap between research on childhood autobiographical remembering and adults' autobiographical remembering and recounting of their lives.
Levine, L.	Things were different then.	*Social Work Health Care* (1996) *22*(4), 73–88.	Stresses importance of younger therapists understanding the social and personal history of older women clients and the use of life review to achieve this. Discusses impact of women's movement in clinical practice.
Parker, R.	Reminiscence: A continuity theory framework.	*Gerontologist* (1995) *35*(4), 515–525.	Discussion of application of continuity theory as a way to understand reminiscence carried out across the life span.
Randall, W.	Narrative intelligence and the novelty of our lives.	*Journal of Aging Studies* (1999) *13*(1), 11–28.	A discussion of narrative intelligence, its changing form throughout our lives, and posits it being a core component of biographical aging. Speculates this may be a framework to explore and better understand life stories (life review, guided autobiography, reminiscence), particularly in later life, as there's a need for theories outside of normal gerontological ones to enlarge our understanding of aging lives.
Rubinstein, R.	The engagement of life history and the life review among the aged: A research case study.	*Journal of Aging Studies* (1995) *9*(3), 187–203.	Discussion of how the purposes of the interviewer and the informant may be at odds in the process of collecting a life history.

Author	Title	Source	Description
Silver, M.	Memories and meaning: Life review in old age.	*Journal of Geriatric Psychiatry* (1995) *28*(1), 57–73.	Discussion of need for listener with subjects of life review to have an understanding of the process in order to participate with the reviewer. Suggests that knowledge of developmental aspects and theory of life review by listener may assist the older person find meaning in their memories.
Sokolovsky, M.	Case study as a research method to study life histories of elderly people: Some ideas and a case study of a case study.	*Journal of Aging Studies* (1996) *10*(4), 281–294.	A case study of a case study to describe the use of theory to make data reliable and valid, but also states that different interpretations of data would always be possible according to analysis of interviews.
Webster, J.	World views and narrative gerontology: Situating reminiscence behavior within a lifespan perspective.	*Journal of Aging Studies* (1999) *13*(1), 29–42.	Article identifies three "world hypotheses" or metamodels and suggests that reminiscence research has only been conducted under the rubric of one metamodel. Discusses what reminiscence looks like under each and argues the advantage of a contexual metamodel and lifespan perspective for future research.
Weiss, J.	Cognitive therapy and life review therapy: Theoretical and therapeutic implications for mental health counselors.	*Journal of Mental Health Counseling* (1995) *17*(2), 157–172.	Discussion of the synergistic effect of combining these two therapies in assisting older adults to redefine their sense of identity and resolve conflicts.

SCHOLARLY DISCUSSION *(Continued)*

Authors	Journal Title	Journal Citation	Write-Up of Article
White, M.	Historical narrative or life review? The role of interpretation in Wallace Stegner's *Angle of Repose.*	*Journal of Aging Studies* (1995) 9(2), 175–186.	Examines life review done through writing a grandmother's biography. States that novel and life review interpretations are partial but no less valuable because of that.
RESEARCH			
Ashida, S.	The effect of reminiscence music therapy sessions on changes in depressive symptoms in elderly persons with dementia.	*Journal of Music Therapy* (2000) 37(3), 170–182.	Research in a residential care facility with four groups of older adults diagnosed with dementia. Paper tests and video taped analysis were used. There was significant decrease in depressive symptoms after five days of reminiscence focused music therapy. N=20.
Atkinson, D., Kim, A., Ruelas, S., & Lin, A.	Ethnicity and attitudes toward facilitated reminiscence.	*Journal of Mental Health Counseling* (1999) 21(1), 66–81.	Senior centers primarily serving Chinese-American, Mexican-American, and European-Americans were asked to participate in having clients voluntarily fill in a four part Reminiscence and Life Review Questionnaire. One finding was more positive attitudes toward facilitated reminiscence of the Chinese-American and Mexican-American elders than expected. N=80 Chinese-Americans, 68 Mexican-Americans, and 70 European-Americans.

Authors	Title	Citation	Description
Blankenship, L., Molinari, V., & Kunik, M.	The effect of a life review group on the reminiscence functions of geropsychiatric inpatients.	*Clinical Gerontologist* (1996) *16*(4), 3–18.	Ongoing structured life review groups met three times weekly and patients were encouraged to join in as part of their standard treatment plan. The Reminiscence Functions Scale showed nonsignificant positive trend in all factors except Bitterness Revival, and total reminiscence were significantly greater than in the normal elderly geriatric sample. N=25 veterans over the age 65.
Boyd, C., Hill, E., Holmes, C., & Purnell, R.	Putting drug use in context: Lifelines of African-American women who smoke crack.	*Journal of Substance Abuse Treatment* (1998) *15*(3), 235–249.	Exploratory study using interview data to create retrospective lifelines. Focused on extraordinarily disturbing events or usual but often stressful events, and periods of drug use. N=25 randomly selected from 208 stratified interviews with African-American women who smoke crack.
Brooker, D., & Duce, L.	Well-being and activity in dementia: A comparison of group reminiscence therapy, structured goal-directed group activity and unstructured time.	*Aging and Mental Health* (2000) *4*(4), 354–358.	Within-subject design to compare levels of well-being of people with mild to moderate dementia. Relative well-being was measured using Dementia Care Mapping after one of three types of activity. There was greater well-being during Reminiscence than Group activity. N=25.
Cook, E.	Effects of reminiscence on life satisfaction of elderly female nursing home residents.	*Health Care for Women International* (1998) *19*, 109–118.	Experimental design with over age 65 female nursing home residents. Randomly assigned to a reminiscence group, current events discussion, or no treatment group. Results showed significant increased life satisfaction in the reminiscence group. N=36.

RESEARCH *(Continued)*

Authors	Journal Title	Journal Citation	Write-Up of Article
deVries, B., & Watt, D.	A lifetime of events: Age and gender variations in the life story.	*International Journal of Aging and Human Development* (1996) 42(2), 81–102.	Lifelines created by individual life story revealed differences by age and gender in life events related. The subjects were divided into three age groups of young, middle-aged and older adulthood. N=60.
Goldwasser, A., & Auerbach, S.	Audience-based reminiscence therapy intervention: Effects on the morale and attitudes of nursing home residents and staff.	*Journal of Mental Health and Aging* (1996) 2(2), 101–114.	Nursing home residents were interviewed with and without staff present and in either a reminiscence/life review or present-focused format. Residents were viewed more positively when staff were present at interviews. Attitudes of residents toward staff improved with reminiscence and with staff presence at interview. N=36 Residents, N=27 Staff.
Haight, B., Michel, Y.,, & Hendrix, S.	Life review: Preventing despair in newly relocated nursing home residents. Short and long term effects.	*International Journal of Aging and Human Development* (1998) 47(2), 119–142.	Experimental study using Solomon Four design with newly relocated nursing home residents to examine using life review for prevention of clinical depression. Significant results were shown in the experimental group for depression at short term testing with an additional decrease in depression and hopelessness at one year. N=256.
Haight, B., Michel, Y.,, & Hendrix, S.	The extended effects of the life review in nursing home residents.	*International Journal of Aging and Human Development* (2000) 50(2), 151–168.	Three year follow-up of newly admitted nursing home residents to examine effect of life review over time. Half received life review and half in control group. Revealed efficacy of life review over time. N=52.

Author	Title	Journal	Description
Haight, B., & Hendrix, S.	Suicidal intent/life satisfaction: Comparing the life stories of older women.	*Suicide and Life Threatening Behavior* (1998) 28(3), 272–284.	Secondary analysis of life review transcriptions with women newly relocated to a nursing home to examine differing themes in their lives. Selected by their scores on life satisfaction and suicide ideation. N=12.
Hargrave, T.	Using video life reviews with older adults.	*Journal of Family Therapy* (1994) 16(3), 259–268.	Description with aging families using life review format in producing a video taped life vignette with a therapist assistance. Relates individual and family impact of these videos and includes discussion of future use. N=15.
Heliker, D.	A narrative approach to quality care in long-term care facilities.	*Journal of Holistic Nursing* (1997) 15(1), 68–81.	Study using a modified life review with volunteers over age 75 living in long-term care facility. Interview analyzed using seven-step hermeneutical method. Indicates revelation of personal and shared meaning may guide new, innovative patient care interventions. N=5.
Hirsch C., & Mouratoglou, V.	Life review of an older adult with memory difficulties.	*International Journal of Geriatric Psychiatry* (1999) 14(4), 261–265.	A case study that illustrates the efficacy of life review with a cognitively impaired person whose ego integrity continued to improve after the therapy.
Johnson, M., Ball, J., Haight, B., & Hendrix, S.	A life history perspective on parenting.	*Narrative Inquiry* (1998) 8(1), 113–149.	Secondary analysis of life review transcriptions of older women. Line by line content analysis extracted themes related to this study. Their early experiences were found to be linked with their parenting and relationships with their adult children. N=18.

RESEARCH *(Continued)*

Authors	Journal Title	Journal Citation	Write-Up of Article
Klausner, E., Clarkin, J., Spielman, L., Pupo, C., Abrams, R., & Alexopoulos, G.	Late-life depression and functional disability: The role of goal-focused group psychotherapy.	*International Journal of Geriatric Psychiatry* (1998) 13, 707–716.	Pilot study using goal-focused group psychotherapy or group reminiscence therapy with older depressed adults who continued to report symptoms after remission with either medication or psychotherapy. N=13.
Kropf, N., & Tandy, C.	Narrative therapy with older clients: The use of a "meaning-making" approach.	*Clinical Gerontologist* (1998) 18(4), 3–16.	Case study which described use of narrative therapy with older woman who created an alternative life story of survivorship from earlier one of fear and depression.
Lie, M.	Two generations: Life stories and social change in Malaysia.	*Journal of Gender Studies* (2000) 9(1), 27–43.	Analysis of life stories studying effects of change in lives of women and daughters to determine whether ideals and values tend to change or remain the same. Study conducted at two times seven years apart.
McAdams, D., Diamond, A., de St. Aubin, E., & Mansfield, E.	Stories of commitment: The psychosocial construction of generative lives.	*Journal of Personality and Social Psychology* (1997) 72(3), 678–694.	Qualitative study of life-story interviews to determine how highly generative adults differ from their less generative counterparts in the ways they make sense of who they are and who they may be in future. N=70.
McDougall, G. J., Blixen, C., & Lee-Jen, S.	The process and outcome of life review psychotherapy with depressed homebound older adults.	*Nursing Research* (1997) 46(5), 277–283.	Retrospective analysis of notes from 80 patients over age 65 who were discharged home from psychiatric hospitals with primary diagnosis of depression. Use of psychosocial intervention was found to have a positive impact on their overall well-being and facilitated their ability to live at home and remain independent. N=80.

McGowan, T.	Mentoring reminiscence: A conceptual and empirical analysis.	*International Journal of Aging and Human Development* (1994) 39(4), 321–336.	Examined the ego-supportive role of mentoring-reminiscence project between college students and homebound elderly. N=12.
McInnis-Dittrich, K.	Adapting life-review therapy for elderly female survivors of childhood sexual abuse.	*Families in Society* (1996) 77(3), 166–173.	Discusses four case studies that used specific adaptations of the life review process. Described as a valuable tool to empower these women even to be able to reject the process.
Meddin, J. R.	Dimensions of spiritual meaning and well-being in the lives of ten older Australians.	*International Journal of Aging and Human Development* (1998) 47(3), 163–175.	Secondary analysis of published interviews with prominent older people about their sense of meaning in life. This analysis looked at how aging persons maintain or establish a viable sense of meaning in the face of societal and personal changes. N=10.
Melia, S.	Continuity in the lives of elder Catholic women religious.	*International Journal of Aging and Human Development* (1999) 48(3), 175–189.	Qualitative research study in grounded theory tradition analyzed taped life review interviews with sisters of three religious orders to examine the question of whether the old-old undergo additional developmental stages after reaching ego integrity when they are young-old.
Mills, M., & Coleman, P.	Nostalgic memories in dementia: A case study.	*International Journal of Aging and Human Development* (1994) 38(3), 203–219.	A case study that demonstrates it is possible for older people with dementia to reminisce and that this is meaningful for them particularly, in the face of the losses associated with dementia. Use of counseling skills to assist recall and support subject when/if painful memories arise and benefits to health care workers to better know their patients are addressed.

RESEARCH (*Continued*)

Authors	Journal Title	Journal Citation	Write-Up of Article
O'Connor, P.	Salient themes in the life review of a sample of frail elderly respondents in London.	*Gerontologist* (1994) 34(2), 224–230.	Qualitative research analyzing taped life reviews of independent living people over age 65 who received home help or social services. The pervasiveness of unresolved grief and loss was found rather than the assumed state of acceptance or resolution of these losses. N=142.
Parker, R.	Reminiscence as continuity: comparison of young and older adults.	*Journal of Clinical Geropsychology* (1999) 5(2), 147–157.	Study examining the difference in amount, life-time of and satisfaction with reminiscence between younger and older adults. N=43 younger adults and N=47 older adults.
Ray, R.	Social influences on the older woman's life story.	*Generations* (1999) 23(4),.56–62.	A qualitative study on the social dynamics of writing groups and how this influences the telling of one's life story. Rather than analyzing life stories from these groups for recurring themes or coping strategies the stories are viewed as acts of language. The ways in which gender influences power relations in a writing group, and how the writing group serves as a microcosm of the larger society, creating social norms to be adhered to or ignored at risk of exclusion, are examined. This study is from a feminist-gerontology and a social constructionist viewpoint.

Reis-Bergan, M., Gibbons, F., & Ybema, J.	The impact of reminiscence on socially active elderly women's reactions to social comparisons.	*Basic and Applied Social Psychology* (2000) 22(3), 225–236.	Study to look at impact of reminiscence on older women's social comparisons of themselves to women in an upward, a downward and a younger comparison situation. Reminiscence appeared to have an impact. N=105 independent-living, older women.
Rennemark, M., & Hagberg, B.	Sense of coherence among the elderly in relation to their perceived life history in an Eriksonian perspective.	*Aging and Mental Health* (1997) 1(3), 221–229.	Sample to represent Swedish population was recruited and participated in a individual life history interview, some self-evaluations and a structured questionnaire. Self-evaluations of the life history were generally related to the Sense of Coherence strength. N=58.
Rybash, J., & Hrubi, K.	Psychometric and psychodynamic correlates of first memories in younger and older adults.	*The Gerontologist* (1997) 17(5), 581–587.	Report on two studies to examine how cognitive and psychodynamic processes influence the recall of the earliest experience of their lives by older and younger adults. Study I N=96, Study II N=68.
Sherman, E.	The structure of well-being in the life narratives of the elderly.	*Journal of Aging Studies* (1994) 8(2), 149–158.	Qualitative analysis of taped interviews to determine if there was a relation between how older people told their stories and late life adjustment, determined from scores on well-being from an earlier study. N=40.
Stevenson, I., & Cook, E.	Involuntary memories during severe physical illness or injury.	*Journal of Nervous and Mental Disease* (1995) 183, 452–458.	Report on near death events with people who experienced a life review and people who did not experience life review during the event. There was wide variety in the experience of the life review, and several outcomes as a result of this experience are discussed. N=108.

RESEARCH *(Continued)*

Authors	Journal Title	Journal Citation	Write-Up of Article
Stewart, A., & Vandewater, E.	"If I had it to do over again": Midlife review, midcourse corrections, and women's well-being in midlife.	*Journal of Personality and Social Psychology* (1999) 76(2), 270–283.	A study that examines whether a mid-life review takes place among women. Also, if making desired life changes at this time were related to personality characteristics of rumination or to effective instrumentality. N=83.
Stuber, S.	The interposition of personal life stories and community narratives in a Roman Catholic religious community.	*Journal of Community Psychology* (2000) 28(5), 507–515.	Study to examine the interplay of individual and community stories in a religious community. Thematic similarity and the stories generated about each other was seen as reflecting strong sense of community.
Tabourne, C. E. S.	The effects of a life review program on disorientation, social interaction, and self-esteem of nursing home residents.	*International Journal of Aging and Human Development* (1995a) 41(3), 251–266.	Study using life review with three groups of people with Alzheimer's disease. Assigned to control or life review in groups randomly as were third group who had prior experience with life review. Results showed significance for life review groups in decreased disorientation and improvement in social interaction. N=32.

Author	Title	Source	Description
Tabourne, C. E. S.	The Life Review Program as an intervention for an older adult newly admitted to a nursing home facility: A case study.	*Therapeutic Recreation Journal* (1995b) 29(3), 228–236.	Case study examining use of Life Review Program with newly relocated nursing home resident to decrease depression, increase orientation, perceived competence, and social interaction.
Tornstam, L.	Gerotranscendence and the functions of reminiscence.	*Journal of Aging and Identity* (1999) 4, 155–166.	Mail survey of 3000 with a 67% response rate. Aim was to elaborate if the functions of reminiscence are related to gerotranscendence process.
Vaughn, S., & Kinnier, R.	Psychological effects of a life review intervention for persons with HIV disease.	*Journal of Counseling and Development* (1996) 75(2), 115–123.	Special problems were encountered using life review groups with this population and the hypothesis was not supported. A discussion of how these problems may be addressed in future studies as well as participants feedback suggest that it remains a promising intervention for this population. N=27.
Watt, L., & Cappeliez, P.	Integrative and instrumental reminiscence therapies for depression in older adults: Intervention strategies and treatment effectiveness.	*Aging and Mental Health* (2000) 4(2), 166–177.	Twenty-six older adults with moderate to severe depression were part of an integrative or instrumental reminiscence group, or the control, active-socialization group. Significant clinical improvement in depression was found in both treatment groups. N=26.

RESEARCH *(Continued)*

Authors	Journal Title	Journal Citation	Write-Up of Article
Webster, J.	Predictors of reminiscence: A lifespan perspective.	*Canadian Journal on Aging* (1994) 13(1), 66–78.	Study with subjects divided into young adults, middle-aged adults, and older adults completing an eight-item assessment of reminiscence. Age differences in reminiscence frequency were not found but personality traits were significant predictors for all four reminiscence dimensions. N=94.
Webster, J., & McCall, M.	Reminiscence functions across adulthood: A replication and extension.	*Journal of Adult Development* (1999) 6(1), 73–85.	Study with subjects completing RFS, MUNSH, and a single item importance of shared family memory question. The primary purpose was to replicate findings on age and gender differences in reminiscence functions from earlier study. N=268.
Webster, J.	Attachment styles, reminiscence functions, and happiness in young and elderly adults.	*Journal of Aging Studies* (1998) 12(3), 315–330.	Study with community living older adults and younger adults to specifically study attachment styles of older adults and their internal model of self. Scales of health, attachment styles, reminiscence function, and happiness completed by the participants were analyzed. N=195.
Webster, J.	The Reminiscence Functions Scale: A replication.	*International Journal of Aging and Human Development* (1997) 44(2), 137–148.	A replication and validation study of the Reminiscence Functions Scale. N=399 ages 17–45 with M age of 22.7.
Weishaar, K.	The visual life review as a therapeutic art framework with the terminally ill.	*Arts in Psychotherapy* (1999) 26(3), 173–184.	A Case Study examines the effectiveness of Visual Life Review with an end-stage AIDS patient.

Author	Title	Citation	Annotation
Weiss, J.	Group therapy with older adults in long-term care settings: Research and clinical cautions and recommendations.	Journal for Specialists in Group Work (1994) 19(1), 22–29.	Research study with two groups of cognitively intact, age grouped older people in a long term care setting. Cognitive therapy group, life review group or control group. Eight weekly 90 minutes sessions with pre-test, post-test and six week follow-up. Two treatment groups were significantly different from control group showing increased sense of purpose and meaning in their lives. N=48.
Whitbourne, S. K., & Powers, C. B.	Older women's constructs of their lives: A quantitative and qualitative exploration.	International Journal of Aging and Human Development (1994) 38(4), 293–306.	Quantitative and Qualitative examination of life construct drawings to a subgroup of older women from larger study. The Locus of control and Bradburn Affect-Balance scales were administered. Also discussed was what played role in maintaining a positive sense of identity. N=78.

METHOD

Author	Title	Citation	Annotation
Beecham, M. H., Anthony, C., & Kurtz, J.	A life review interview guide: A structured systems approach to information gathering.	International Journal of Aging and Human Development (1998) 46(1), 25–44.	A clinical project to study the use of a structured interview guide to assist in a methodological systems approach in conducting life reviews with older people by baccalaureate students interviewing older adults residing independently and in nursing homes. Well-being, self-control, addressing loss/grief issues and cultural-social benefits were examined.
Boldt, R., & Mosak, H.	Understanding the storyteller's story: Implications for therapy.	Journal of Individual Psychology (1998) 54(4), 495–510.	Understanding the life story can change the therapeutic conversations to conclude the Problem/therapeutic chapter. Discussion of use of early recollections to determine personality types and explain behavior.

METHOD (*Continued*)

Authors	Journal Title	Journal Citation	Write-Up of Article
Brown-Shaw, M., Westwood, M., & de Vries, B.	Integrating personal reflection and group-based enactments.	*Journal of Aging Studies* (1999) *13*(1), 109–119.	A process/model combining methods of life review and Guided Autobiography in the context of group psychodrama. A case study is presented and discussed in the context of facilitation of meaning and the ability to reframe an experience from the past without the necessity of taking action.
Burnside, I., & Haight, B.	Reminiscence and life review: Therapeutic interventions for older people.	*Nurse Practitioner* (1994) *19*(4), 55–61.	This paper describes the differences between life review and reminiscence as therapeutic modalities for older people. Protocols for one-to-one reminiscence therapy, group reminiscence and one-to one life review are presented to improve the effectiveness of each specific intervention.
Davis-Berman, J., & Berman, D.	Life stories: Processing experience throughout the lifespan.	*Clinical Gerontologist* (1998) *19*(3), 3–11.	Describes a model for encouraging older adults to confront losses and deal with death related issues through a three phase telling of their stories.
Soltys, F., & Coats, L.	The solcos model: Facilitating reminiscence therapy.	*Journal Gerontological Nursing* (1994) *20*(11), 11–16.	Discussion of reminiscence literature and presentation of a model to facilitate reminiscence with older people individually, in groups, and with those who are terminally ill.

APPLICATIONS

Draucker, C.	Narrative therapy for women who have lived with violence.	*Archives of Psychiatric Nursing* (1998) *12*(3), 162–168.	Discusses narrative therapy as a potentially useful approach for women who have been victimized throughout their lives.

Author	Title	Citation	Description
Frank, G.	Life histories in occupational therapy clinical practice.	*American Journal of Occupational Therapy* (1996) 50(4), 251–264.	Describes need to use one of six types of life histories to reconstruct and interpret the lives of ordinary people. Also as method to facilitate positive changes in patients' lives.
Gatz, M., Fiske, A., Fox, L., Kaskie, B., Kasi-Godley, J., McCallum, T., & Wetherell, J.	Empirically validated psychological treatments for older adults.	*Journal of Mental Health and Aging* (1998) 4(1), 9–46.	Review of literature reporting outcomes of psychological treatments for older adults. Includes life review as treatment for depressed persons or those at risk for depression.
Harris, J.	Reminiscence: A culturally and developmentally appropriate language intervention for older adults.	*American Journal of Speech-Language Pathology* (1997) 6(3), 19–26.	Describes multiple factors that make reminiscence a good tool to use with older clients as well as some sample clinical activities.
Hussain, F., & Raczka, R.	Life story work for people with learning disabilities.	*British Journal of Learning Disabilities* (1997) 25(2), 73–76.	Use of Life Story Work to ease stress of transition for people with learning disabilities discuss value of a person-centered approach to enable the person to develop a sense of identity by talking in a safe environment about their ideas, thoughts and feelings about their life.
Jones, D., & Churchill, J.	Archetypal healing.	*American Journal of Hospice and Palliative Care* (1994) 11(1), 26–33.	Description of five methods of psychospiritual methods of pain relief or archetypal healing. Life review is the first mentioned.

APPLICATIONS *(Continued)*

Authors	Journal Title	Journal Citation	Write-Up of Article
Kennedy, S.	Life review and heroic narrative: Embracing pathology and attention to context.	*Australian and New Zealand Journal of Family Therapy* (1999) 20(1), 1–10.	Discusses ways a therapist should be involved in facilitating the process of an ongoing life review. This is illustrated in the context of a published autobiography by a homosexual couple who were personal friends of the therapist.
Porter, E.	Gathering our stories; claiming our lives: Seniors' life story books facilitate life review, integration and celebration.	*Journal on Developmental Disabilities* (1998) 6(1), 44–59.	Describes use of life story as method of life review to construct a life history book with people who have developmental disabilities. Describes variety of sources to obtain the life story and methods of assembling the book used with L' Arche Daybreak Seniors Club.
Puentes, W.	Using social reminiscence to teach therapeutic communication skills.	*Geriatric Nursing* (2000) 21(6), 315–318.	Describes social reminiscence as a teaching tool for enhancement of nursing skills in communication.
Rife, J.	Use of life review techniques to assist older workers in coping with job loss and depression.	*Clinical Gerontologist* (1998) 20(1), 75–79.	Clinical comment about benefit of a work life review strategy to assist unemployed older clients and the therapist to understand their skills.

| Sandberg, J. | "It just isn't fair": Helping older families balance their ledgers before the note comes due. | *Family Relations* (1999) *48*(2), 177–179. | Essay recommending need for life review and forgiveness in family therapy that includes older adults. |
| Sukosky, D. | Life review in family psychotherapy. | *Journal of Family Psychotherapy* (1994) 5(2), 21–39. | Explores the relevance of life review for family and marriage psychotherapy. |

II

Conceptual Issues

2

Reminiscence and Oral History: Comparisons Across Parallel Universes*

Joanna Bornat

For the last twenty years or more I have occupied a position which, as far as I am aware, has not been shared by anyone else. I am an oral historian who also writes and researches issues relating to reminiscence and life review. It is paradoxical that many of the debates and discussions developed in oral history and reminiscence and life review research are so similar, while conducted in quite separate universes, often with a singular lack of awareness of the other's existence, concerns, or expertise. Issues such as contexts for remembering, the effect of trauma on remembering, storytelling, the interview relationship, ethics, the nature of memory, the role of remembering in establishing identities, and finally, outputs and dissemination are all typical of debates in each domain.

An outsider might find it difficult to distinguish the two areas. Each is concerned with recall of the past and, in the main, this involves communication with older people. However, things feel quite different when viewed from the inside, and it is this difference which I explore here. In part the differences are rooted in differing disciplinary origins and in part in the distinctive aims and objectives of the two approaches. From a British perspective, this chapter offers some comments on the key distinguishing characteristics of oral history and reminiscence and life review while pointing out what is shared. In covering two areas, each

* An extended version of this chapter was published in *Ageing and Society,* 21(2), 2001, pp. 219–241.

with rich and active populations of researchers and students, I have made some selections and some necessary omissions. I may also be guilty of misrepresentation in my attempt to portray similarity and difference. For these decisions I apologize in advance. The chapter is structured around two key areas of work: context, i.e., partnerships in the interpretation of memories; and presentation, i.e., the ownership and control of personal memory.

In reviewing these differences and similarities I ask the question: Can the two universes afford to be unaware of each other?

Defining Difference

Oral history in the U.K. and elsewhere draws on the disciplines of history and sociology for its origins. However, as Thompson (2000) argues, the origins of oral history lie in a particular understanding of what history is. His argument that "all history depends ultimately upon its social purpose" points to an instrumental role for history and its making. The social purpose of history may, in some cases, be the maintenance of the status quo or to support divisions within and between societies. However, history can take a quite alternative stance, challenging and revising what is accepted. It is within this tradition that oral history developed in the late 1960s. History as a critical endeavor, undertaken as an activity with a view to bringing about change and to validate the testimony of witnesses to the past, features strongly in the writings of many oral historians though, as Thompson also points out, the extent to which change is invoked ". . . depends upon the spirit in which it is used."

In terms of disciplinary base, reminiscence has deep roots within psychology (Butler, 1963). While this has determined the pattern of research, it has not had such a strong influence on practice outside those clinical settings where reminiscence is used as the basis for therapeutic intervention (Bender, Bauckham, & Norris, 1999; Burnside, 1990; Garland, 1993; Norris, 1989). In work with older people, reminiscence and life review tends to draw on an eclectic mix of nursing and social care practice, gerontology, psychology, counseling, the creative therapies, and adult education skills. Such a mix leads to a diversity of approaches and a lack of professionalization which is an encouragement to inventiveness and a discouragement to routinization and exclusivity on the part of practitioners. Reminiscence work is still very much open to experimentation and development, with particular challenges thrown up as what I have elsewhere described as a "social movement" (Bornat, 1989) and has extended to include people who are cognitively impaired through dementia or learning disability (Atkinson, 1997; Gibson, 1993).

These contrasting disciplinary starting points continue to influence the direction in which each has developed. However, as I will demonstrate, evidence from recent debates suggests that within their separate universes, similar issues are being raised. This also suggests that, between them, the two approaches occupy more common ground than might previously have been considered. Each is addressing similar questions but their differing focus leads to the possibility of creative problem solving. In what follows I look in more detail at the parallel universes and shared endeavor of these two approaches to memory in late life, drawing on an example of work from each area in relation to contexts and presentation.

Context: Partnerships in the Interpretation of Memories

By focusing on context I want to shift the discussion towards a comparative positioning of oral history and reminiscence in relation to their relative contributions to supportive strategies in work with older people. Within oral history circles (in the U.K. and Australia at least, if not elsewhere), a burning issue persists. This is the question of how a method whose purpose is to *give voice* to people out of the mainstream of history can ensure that its practice matches this ideal? Is it possible to work in partnership so that the narrator is not alienated from his/her own story by the analytical skills of the researcher. Early on in oral history little attention was paid to this issue. For some researchers, their own purpose and political stance seemed good enough as a guarantee of shared objectives. People's willingness to be interviewed, to make their story available to others, setting records straight and providing a challenge to the status quo meant that issues of partnership felt irrelevant. And it is still the case that to hand back a transcript so that someone might alter or change their words is still more a feature of archive work than of research or publication. Oral history's origins within the discipline of sociology pull it in the direction of academic research and the norms of academic life tend not to recognize partnership with subjects as a necessary part of the research process.

The result is that examples of partnership tend to be developed in areas of work which are focused more on practice than research. Government funded programs rarely include budgeting or scheduling for any form of partnership model of research and publication. Models of partnership in oral history projects range from handing back transcripts for checking to full-blown collaboration. In some cases, collaboration stems from inequality. So, for example, colleagues at the Open University, working with people with learning disability in the production of oral histories, have developed collaborative strategies which enable people without written communication skills to produce narrative accounts (Atkinson, 1977; Walmsley & Atkinson, 2000). This more "bottom-up" model of production has also become commonly practiced in community projects where Frisch's idea of "shared authority" (1990) has been embodied within oral history practice. How this works in practice is detailed in the account of an oral history of the closure of an American poultry processing plant in Maine. Here one woman's story was developed in close collaboration with an interviewer and a photographer. At the end of the process, Alicia Rouverol, the interviewer, wrote up her account of what she had learned from the experience:

> If oral history challenges historical generalizations, collaborative oral history . . . challenges our generalizations as historians and folklorists. It complicates our analyses when our interviewees disagree with our interpretations; it forces us to re-think our stance, to consider the critiques and suggestions of our narrators whose stories we seek to tell. We may not agree with their interpretations; and that isn't our obligation. It is our obligation, though, to present multiple and contradictory perspectives when and if they arise within the same body of testimony; to offer in our analyses conflicting interpretations, or what may seem to be paradoxical reflections or assessments. (Rouverol, 1999, p.76)

Rouverol's position challenges the basic conventions of academic writing, in placing the interviewee, the "subject," on a par with the researcher, and suggesting that the object of research may not necessarily be a tidy categorization or the derivation of comparative constructs.

Feminist oral historians had earlier faced the dilemma of being both subject and researcher, noting the uncomfortable reality that the interview may be both a positive and a negative force, with subsequent analysis driving a wedge between those who should have been experiencing solidarity (Gluck & Patai, 1991). Who exercises interpretive powers is at the nub of this ethical dilemma. Borland, whose grandmother challenged the feminist interpretation she drew from her interview, concludes:

> . . . we might open up the exchange of ideas so that we do not simply gather data on others to fit into our own paradigms once we are safely ensconced in our university libraries ready to do interpretation. (Borland, 1991, p. 73)

The possibility that interpretation might itself be a dialogic power struggle is suggested by Portelli, when he describes the experience of feeding back his account of a student occupation of 1990 in Rome. Drawing on interviews with students who had taken part, he and his student group presented their interpretation to one of the leaders whom they had interviewed. He rejected their interpretive use of metaphor. As Portelli explains:

> . . . interpretation is always part of a power relationship: to interpret is one thing; to be interpreted is another. (Portelli, 1997, p. 270)

He suggests that the interviewee's "counter-interpretation" is itself a contribution to an interpretive process which he describes as being part of the "endless spiral of the search for a necessary and unattainable meaning" (Portelli, 1997, p. 272).

What Portelli and Frisch are pointing to is the need to find some way to establish partnership in the interpretive process, a partnership which both includes, and controls, academic powers. Indeed Frisch, in a review of Studs Terkel's *Hard Times,* criticizes those who take a "no-history" approach. By this he means the idea that testimony requires no interpretation, that it speaks for itself with ". . . self-evident and unequivocal significance." Against this, he argues for the role of "the historian" in asking the questions and introducing insights which both challenge and situate the "documents of oral history" (Frisch, 1998, p. 36).

The search for an interpretive method which is both reliable and recognizable, has led to the development of a method in biographical research which distinguishes the "lived life" from the "told story." This is achieved by undertaking two contrasting analyses drawn from the text of one interview. By this means a "biographical data analysis" and a "thematic field analysis" are derived with a view to understanding the interviewee"s own theory of action and expressed identity (Rosenthal, 1993; Wengraf, 2000). The biographical interpretive method (BIM) aims to forge conceptual links between the events described in individual life stories and such broader structural issues as class and power. At present such a strategy seems some distance away from partnership or shared authority, given that those who undertake the analysis of the interview data will not necessarily have taken part in the interview. One option to be explored is the possibility of developing the method as a training tool for social care workers. In this way the practice of interpretation is itself opened up to critical review while the words in the interview transcript help to develop understanding and suggest new insights to particular dilemmas in social welfare.

Ethical issues concerning partnership in the process have also exercised reminiscence workers. Concern over the content of sessions, and the question of the extent to which it is representative and therefore equally facilitative of people from different backgrounds persists (Harris & Hopkins, 1993). Partnership is perhaps most easily guaranteed and sustained where older people are able to take part in the shaping of the process with a view to agreed outcomes. A reminiscence theater production clearly cannot emerge without the collaboration of the players. People are not likely to want to portray themselves or events in ways that they find unacceptable or unrecognizable. For this reason, producing a play could provide a helpful model in other settings and for other interpretive processes.

Concern has developed in recent years both in oral history and reminiscence and life review over how to respond when painful emotions are evoked and how to handle interactions when memories of past trauma are evoked (Hunt, Marshall, & Rowlings, 1997; Rogers, Leydersdorff, & Dawson, 1999). Such concerns serve as a reminder of the social purpose of oral history and, coupled with ideas of reconciliation and acceptance drawn from clinical work with older people, it seems that both approaches have much to contribute to each other's understanding and practice. These issues are too broad for detailed discussion here; rather I consider evidence from research into reminiscence as an intervention in care settings. In drawing on this I want to suggest that, in responding to expressions of painful emotion, it is important to consider context and circumstances.

Questioning care staff about their experiences of reminiscence work in residential and nursing settings, two separate examples were obtained where, unexpectedly, older people had reacted with extreme emotion (Bornat & Chamberlayne, 1999). We were offered interpretations by staff of what ensued. We were told that a man disliked having cot sides on his bed due to his second world war experiences, and that a woman had difficulties about bathing because of her personal history. While not wanting to deny that these people had endured genuinely traumatic and abusive experiences, evoking uncontrollable emotions in their recall, there is a possibility that, by ascribing these episodes solely to past trauma, present abusive or insensitive care practices and interpersonal actions are ignored. So, for example, it might be proper to ask if anyone, whether or not they had been a prisoner of war should be placed in a cot bed against their wishes and that, if someone is expressing fears about bathing, then this might be an outcome of insensitive handling of intimate care. Incidents such as these not only point to a need for care workers and those interacting with older people to have interpretive skills of a high order including an informed understanding of the history of the last eight or so decades and a need to locate reminiscence within the present and to enable this process to highlight the quality of such interactions (Adams, Bornat, & Prickett, 1998). What older people do not require is any kind of denial or censorship resulting from a misplaced search for protective practice.[1]

I have focused on contexts for interpretation in order to draw attention to the structures and norms in which oral history and reminiscence and life review operate. Looking at practice in each other's universes, both good and bad, can be instructive and perhaps support the process of learning about issues which are both shared and distinctive.

Presentation: The Ownership and Control of Personal Memory

Reminiscence and oral history share a number of different approaches to presenting outcomes, and it is in relation to this stage that the most self-critical debates have taken place, amongst oral historians at least. Phrases such as "giving back" or "giving voice" are used to establish the provenance of forms of presentation, and the credentials of promoters. Similarly, where reminiscence and oral history lay claims to contributing to advocacy and empowerment, then who owns the spoken words becomes highly significant.

Debates within oral history center on separation between the subject and the researcher and the additional separation where presentation involves the mass media or public settings such as museums and exhibitions. While these boundaries can lead to feelings of loss of control by the person whose story has been told, it is worth noting that ownership of the words spoken has a legal basis in some countries. U.K. law (1988 Copyright Act), for example, now gives separate ownership to the words spoken and to the recording of those words. This means that the owner of the copyright in the words is the speaker, while the copyright in the recording belongs to the person or organization who arranged the recording.

Legally, any further use made of the words means that permission must be sought from the copyright owner, the speaker, although, alternatively, copyright can be assigned to the interviewer. At one level this may all appear as an administrative obstacle in the process of presentation, but the law does help to clarify and emphasize the point about

---

[1] An example of this is the website "Oldfarts," targeted at older people. This includes a discussion list whose moderator describes the "purpose" in the following way: We want you to enjoy this list . . . (their parenthesis) tell as many friends as you would like about it. Bear in mind, we are trying only the "OVER 50" crowd. Do not introduce religion (in any form) or politics to the discussions (http://www.topica.com/lists/oldfarts/).

ownership in words, stories, and narratives which are usually given quite freely. "Giving back" is thus a redundant concept as, under U.K. law at least, ownership cannot be alienated in the first place.

How people's words are used and the extent to which they are able to determine their further use, is an issue which has been subjected to much debate within oral history circles. I have already outlined the idea of "shared authority" in relation to community-based projects and publications (Frisch, 1990; Rouverol, 1999). This type of approach is more likely to be followed where questions of witness and authenticity are highly politicized as, for example, in contests over land rights (Goodall, 1994) and refugees (Westerman, 1998). Amongst archivists, academics, museum staff, radio and television researchers, community workers, and educationalists, different strategies tend to be adopted and much critical attention has been given to ethical practice. Signing off ownership or imposing restrictions as to who may have access to tapes and transcripts and when; adopting a protocol for sharing the production process; abiding by such basic rules as naming interviewees as authors or editors; all these are approaches which have been taken up. However, practice is variable and standards can often leave much to be desired. Moreover, as I have already suggested, some contexts are less open to ideals of partnership than others. Academic practice in the U.K. is only recently, under pressure from recipients of services, changing to include the notion of partnership in areas such as research into health and social care provision.

In other disciplines, the traditional role of the researcher, presenting the product of a research process which may involve a mass of interviewees, is one which is difficult to conceive as developing on a partnership basis. Issues such as confidentiality and sensitivities around categorization and comparability of evidence, might rule out a collective approach to involving interviewees in all stages of writing and presentation. It may be that in these circumstances the protection of subjects' interests is better protected by researcher training in ethical principles and, in particular, in the legal rights of the interviewee.

Oral history practice has produced some useful pointers to how such training might be focused. One possibility (as some feminist oral historians have argued) is to identify topics which have immediate relevance to the wider public. This could be the public which makes up communities local to academics, or the public in the wider world. So, for example, the history of a local industry may have relevance not just for those who work in it, but also as an example of industrial change generally. Another strategy is to create alternative formats so that the published academic article is accompanied by an informal talk, a publication written in a more popular form, or a museum display (Olson &

Shopes, 1991). Of course, such developments are more likely within institutions where there is a commitment to outreach and to developing learning opportunities for members of local communities. Even so, as Olson and Shopes (1991) suggest, the role of the interpreter in presenting the experiences of interviewees will still involve intervention and decision-making and the possibility that quotations may be taken out of context.

Within reminiscence and life review, appropriation and control are equally possible, despite the fact that the role of the facilitator is likely to be more personal, ongoing, and immediate. Indeed the very informality of some reminiscence exchanges opens up possibilities of misrepresentation, mishandling, or inaccurate reporting of personal accounts and the details of private disclosures. Here again, existing protocols relating to client and service user privacy, disclosure, and confidentiality should guard against bad practice. However, given the vulnerability and high dependency of many of those involved in reminiscence activities, there is a certain element of risk involved, particularly where facilitators or group leaders have not had access to basic training in communication skills.

There is an additional problem. Such training is unlikely to include reference to history as a discipline or to the varied social contexts in which people have lived out their lives. Care staff are often forced to rely on popular histories, local experts or whatever resources they have access to in the contexts in which they live and work. The result is that the way reminiscences are communicated and presented may depend on the energy, resources, and enthusiasms of those engaged as facilitators. Inevitably this means that the curriculum is likely to be highly idiosyncratic.[2]

To what extent this particular approach is socially, politically, and culturally inclusive is debatable and, indeed, awareness of diversity amongst groups of older reminiscers is an issue which reminiscence research has tended to neglect up to now. In this respect it is interesting to reflect on the comments of an older African Caribbean man:

> People cannot reminisce here in Britain, which is very important . . . by the time I reach 60 I will revert back to talk about family history and importance of childhood in the Caribbean, you cannot have those reminiscences in old people's home in this country. The people in these homes never talk to you. People are not going to listen to you. (Plaza, 1996, p. 16)

---

[2] A reminiscence worker described a session which included hand-clapping, singing, classical music, a video of the 1953 coronation, the music of Elgar and Wagner, Handel's *Water Music* and *The Messiah,* all with a view to evoking memories of classical music and royalty (Personal Communication, October 19, 2000).

In considering the range of possible forms for presenting reminiscence, then it seems likely that drama is the best guarantee of control by participants over any presentation. Reminiscence theater, where older people act their own words and the process of presentation involves them in discussing and devising both form and *content* is one example. However, these older actors are very much a privileged group of reminiscers, and their form of presentation is not one which can easily become universal practice. Even so, the apparent purity of the process is compromised to an extent by the role of the director without whose skills no play is likely to be possible.

How oral historians and reminiscence workers tackle issues of ownership of words and memories is instructive and each could learn from each other. Where oral history has placed emphasis on ownership of the spoken word, reminiscence tends to emphasize control in the process and awareness of vulnerability and risk. Perhaps each might learn from each other's reflection on practice.

CONCLUSION

I began this article by pointing out the differences between oral history and reminiscence and life review. In the argument which followed I have touched on a number of areas and have had to leave out many more. In reviewing their parallel universes I have suggested that there is much that is similar. There is the influence of context on how accounts are developed and responded to. Again, when it comes to presentation, the issue of ownership of the product is equally an issue of concern for oral historians and for reminiscence workers.

There may be shared endeavor; there are also differences within the two universes. Oral historians have deliberated issues of ownership and control in relation to their own and participants' contributions to the process, coming up with models of partnership and experimenting with equality in the production and presentation of memories. Reminiscence work has focused more on group processes and the influence of present situation and life stage on remembering. For oral history, the older person has been viewed *as* the source of evidence; for reminiscence and life review the older person, who they were and who they are now, *is* the evidence. This more holistic approach to remembering in the life of older people is one which might benefit oral history, introducing more interpretive layers once "the person who is" comes to be valued as much as "the person who was." For reminiscence, the bonus to be gained from oral history is recognition of the significance of the told story and its place in the history of a particular life, community, and society.

ACKNOWLEDGMENT

Thanks to Al Thomson, University of Sussex, England, and to Pam Schweitzer of Age Exchange Theater, London, for their helpful and supportive criticisms of this chapter.

3

To Review or Not To Review? The Role of Personality and Life Events in Life Review and Adaptation to Older Age

Paul Wink and Brian Schiff

Butler's (1963) concept of the life review provides contemporary gerontology with a new and powerful paradigm or myth (Moody, 1988). The notion that a time of transition is conducive to self-exploration and reintegration of the self is, however, not new. It is not accidental that both Butler and Erikson (Erikson, Erikson, & Kivnick, 1986) were attracted to Isak Borg, the protagonist of Ingmar Bergman's film, *Wild Strawberries.* Confronted with signs of mortality explicit in his nightmares and implicit in being awarded a prestigious award for lifetime achievement, Dr. Borg reviews his life and in the process overcomes some of his lifelong narcissism. In doing so he becomes more vitally engaged in life, compassionate, and wise. The need to reorganize the self in response to a life transition is also a central tenet of Jung's theory of individuation. According to Jung (1965), midlife, rather than old age, serves as a trigger for a shift in psychological energies from a preoccupation with external success to an emphasis on the process of inner growth and self-integration (Wink, 1999a). For Butler, Erikson, and Jung, the act of reorganizing the self offers a promise of successful adaptation to the demands of the aging process, including an acceptance of one's mortality. A failure to do so, on the other hand, threatens the individual with the prospect of despair, depression, and turmoil. At best it may result in a foreclosed pattern of adaptation characterized by behavioral rigidity and emotional constraint (Clayton, 1975; Whitbourne, 1986).

In recent years, an alternative to this psychodynamic view of adaptation to aging has emerged from a number of empirical studies of the life review and more general models of the self. Dating back to the early 1980s, a number of interview-based studies have cast doubt on the proposition that life review is a necessary condition for the acceptance of past and present in older age (Coleman, 1986; Lieberman & Tobin, 1983; Lowenthal, Thurnher, & Chiriboga, 1975; Merriam, 1995; Sherman, 1991a). Although in each of these studies a significant proportion of well-functioning older adults reported having reviewed their life, an equal, if not larger, number of individuals appeared to achieve high levels of life satisfaction and self-acceptance without showing evidence of life review. Presumably under the influence of Erikson's and Butler's theories, the latter group has been variously labeled as foreclosed (Whitbourne, 1986), engaging in flight from the past (Lieberman & Tobin, 1983), or defensive (Coleman, 1986). Their presence, nonetheless, seriously questioned the necessity of life review for successful adaptation to old age. Merriam (1995), for example, raised the possibility that the participants in her study who did not review their lives in old age might have simply felt no need to do so. Lieberman and Tobin (1983) argued that because the process of sorting and restructuring the past demands high levels of inner skills requiring a lifelong habit of introspection, most people may never review their lives. Coleman (1986) interpreted his findings as suggesting that we should not lightly dismiss the views of those who deny the importance of reminiscence as (over) defensive. Most participants in Coleman's study who accepted their past without having reviewed it had understandable reasons for doing so such as the emergence of new opportunities in old age (especially in the case of women), or being simply too busy and active to reminisce.

A more theoretically grounded argument against the necessity of life review for successful adaptation to old age can be derived from Atchley's continuity theory. Despite changes in the lives of many older individuals, such as retirement, relocation, or changes in physical appearance, Atchley (1999) argues that ruptures are rarely associated with a redefinition of identity. Rather, internal (to the self) and external (environmental) processes work together to assimilate change by reinforcing the perception that the self is consistent and coherent over time. Atchley does not dispute that change is a part of adult life. Rather, he argues that transitions are usually assimilated using preexisting patterns of self-understanding. Atchley's view on how individuals deal with transitions finds support in Greenwald's (1980) theory of the totalitarian self which, as suggested by Bluck and Levine (1998), implies that the window of opportunity for self-change should be fairly infrequent. Even in the case of trauma and life transitions the function of reminiscence may be more to reaffirm the current view of self than to promote radical change. Although Atchley (1999) does not directly address the issue of life review, Parker (1995) used continuity theory to make the argument that undertaking life review in old age may be more of an exception than a rule. According to Parker, it may be primarily confined to individuals who feel adrift, exhibit a lower level of functioning, or confront a crisis.

In this chapter we address a central question in gerontological research: Does successful adaptation to older adulthood require psychological work aimed at reorganization of the self (life review), or can this process be achieved as smoothly by relying on preexisting psychological resources? Our argument is based in part on the already existing evidence that although many older adults who are highly satisfied with life appear to have reviewed their lives, an equal, if not higher, number have not. We contend that it is a mistake to portray those who are life reviewers as isolated exemplars of individuals who have somehow managed to escape from the clutches of a "totalitarian ego," and it is equally unjust to label those who are not life reviewers as foreclosed or engaging in flight from the past. Following Coleman (1986) we would like to argue that the question of whether reminiscence (life review) promotes adjustment in later life is too simplistic. We need rather to determine the conditions under which life review and reminiscence are adaptive and the conditions under which adaptation is achieved without embarking on the process of life review.

This chapter considers the role played by life review, personality, and negative life events in generating two distinct patterns of adaptation to older age. We will first describe our data source which comes from the Institute of Human Development Longitudinal Study. We will next summarize quantitative findings on the life review in old age and its current and longitudinal predictors. Finally, we will use two life narrative case studies to explore and document the differential role played by the life review in adaptation to older age contingent on personality style and life events.

The Institute of Human Development Longitudinal Study

Sample.   The data for our research comes from a longitudinal study established by the Institute of Human Development (IHD) at the University of California, Berkeley in the 1920s. The original sample was a randomly generated representative sample of newborn babies in Berkeley in 1928/29, and of pre-adolescents (ages 10–12) selected from elementary schools in Oakland in 1931 (and who were born in 1920/21). Both cohorts were combined into a single IHD longitudinal study in the 1960s. The participants were studied intensively in childhood and adolescence, and interviewed in depth four times in adulthood: in early adulthood (30s), middle adulthood (40s), late middle adulthood (mid 50s/early 60s) and in late adulthood (late 60s/mid 70s).

A total of 293 participants took part in at least one of the first three assessments in adulthood. In late adulthood, this number decreased to 172 because of death (25% of the sample), refusal to participate (6%), and being lost to follow-up (10%). In other words, 90% of available participants (neither dead nor lost) took part in the last assessment. Attrition analyses comparing those participants who took part in the assessment in late adulthood with those who declined to participate or who were lost to follow-up showed few differences. The main difference was that those who refused to participate were significantly less socially poised or extroverted than those who consented to be interviewed.

The 172 participants in the IHD study who were assessed in late adulthood were differentiated by cohort: 37% were born in the early 1920s and 63% in the late 1920s; and gender: 53% are women and 47% are men. With the exception of four African-American members all the remaining participants are White. At the time of the interview in late adulthood, 71% of the participants were living with their spouse or partner. The median household income for the sample was $55,000. 40% of the sample reported their general health as good and a further 49% reported it as moderately good. (For a further description of the sample see Wink & Dillon, in press).

Summary of Quantitative Findings
on Life Review and Its Predictors

The life review was scored in the IHD study using portions of the interview transcript from the assessment in late adulthood (Wink, 1999b). In keeping with the format of earlier adult interviews, the assessment in late adulthood included in-depth interviews with the participants that on average took three and a half hours to complete. The interviews covered all of the main aspects of current and past psychological and social functioning. The interviews were structured, but the interviewers were free to follow up any ambiguities and issues that they found clinically and psychologically interesting.

Two independent judges rated the participants on a measure of the life review using portions of the transcript that dealt with self-description and life review. In these segments the participants were asked to rate their life satisfaction, describe themselves in terms of their personal strengths and weaknesses, discuss whether they reminisced about their past and whether this has changed over the years, whether they evaluated the past in order to get a new picture of themselves, to talk about their regrets and the high and low points of their lives, and to provide an example of a past experience that had the most influence on their life.

The life review was rated using a 5-point scale adapted from the work of Sherman (1991a). A score of 4 or 5 was assigned to individuals who used their reminiscences to reach a new level of self-understanding (depending on the level of emotional involvement and evidence of perspective taking). The tone of the reminiscences might have been positive or negative depending on whether the process of life review was completed or not. A score of 3 was given to persons who showed evidence of emotional involvement in the process of reminiscence but where doubt existed as to whether the reminiscences were used to gain a new level of self-understanding. A score of 1 was reserved for individuals who reported not reminiscing at all, and a score of 2 was given to those whose reminiscences were restricted to a description of personal events and behaviors without including feeling states, evaluations, or elaboration. The Kappa coefficient of agreement between the two sets of ratings was .59.

As reported by Wink (1996b), 22% of the total sample were rated as high on the life review (an average score across the two raters of 3.5 or above); 20% were moderate (an average score of 3); and 58% were rated as low. In other words, 42% of the sample showed clear or marginal evidence of the life review, and 58% appeared not to use their reminiscence in any way that would lead to the development of a new level of self-understanding or integration. Women scored significantly higher on the life review than men. There were no significant differences between the younger (late 60s) and older (mid 70s) participants. In late adulthood scores on the life review were not associated with observer based ratings of acceptance of the past or self-report ratings of life satisfaction. Life review was, however, positively related to questionnaire based ratings of openness to experience, creativity, personal growth, and generativity.

Longitudinal analyses showed a significant, positive relation between life review in late adulthood and an observer-based index of introspection and insight scored from the interview transcripts in early, middle, and late middle adulthood. This predictive association between life review in older age and antecedent personality characteristics was significant for the whole sample and for the women participants but not the men. Life review in older age was also positively related to a global measure of past negative life events including an off-time death of a relative, major illness of self or a family member, personal crisis as reflected in seeking psychotherapy, major family conflict, and financial strain. Once again this relation was significant for the whole sample and for the women but not for the men. In the case of the women participants there was a particularly strong relation between life review in older age and the experience of negative events between early (30s) and middle (40s) adulthood.

Finally, scores on the measure of the life review and a 5-point observer-based measure of acceptance of the past were used to group the participants into four quadrants. 18% of the total sample were classified in the high life review and high acceptance category and 52% were placed in the low life review and high acceptance group. Members of both groups showed high levels of satisfaction with the present and acceptance of the past either, as was the case with the first group, because they had used life review to come to terms with past disappointments or, in the case of the second group, because they had experienced relatively few conflicts or negative life events in their life. Of the remaining participants, 14% fell into the high life review, low acceptance category and 15% showed signs of low life review and low acceptance (see Wink, 1999b).

The Case Studies

In this section we explore the relation between life review, personality, and negative life events with two case studies. Both cases were drawn from the group of participants who in late adulthood were rated as high in acceptance of the past. Melissa who received the highest possible score of 5 on the measure of life review is a member of the high acceptance, high life review quadrant. In contrast, Frank who received a low score of 2 on life review represents the largest quadrant of individuals who were high in acceptance but low in life review.

Melissa

At the time of the last interview, Melissa, age 69, was living alone on a six and a half acre property located on the California coastline. Although retired from teaching arts and crafts six years ago, Melissa continues to be a productive artist whose days are filled with various activities. She has recently started doing senior peer counseling which involves seeing clients and attending weekly supervision sessions. Ever since her retirement, Melissa goes square dancing twice a week. In addition, she is a member of various support groups and is involved in the environmental movement. She is also an avid gardener.

Melissa maintains a close relationship with her daughter and son. She divorced her husband over twenty years ago and is not currently involved in a romantic relationship, a fact that she regrets. Melissa does, however, have a group of close friends with whom she goes out to lunch and shares other activities on a daily basis. In view of her active involvement in life, her exceptionally good health, and lack of financial worries, it is not surprising that Melissa rates her current life satisfaction as very high. In response to a question asking which life period brought her the most satisfaction, Melissa said: "Well it's kind of a toss up between working, and now being retired."

Melissa's life could be construed as an unending struggle to pierce through the veil of maya, or, to paraphrase her, to "push the screen in front of my eyes further and further back." She has used a number of approaches to further her process of self-understanding. Among these activities she has used Jungian psychology and therapy, keeping a diary of her dreams, meditating, and sporadically embarking on shamanic journeys. Because of Melissa's penchant for self-exploration, it is not surprising that she answered the question whether or not she had undertaken a life review with a resounding "Yes, I have!" To understand the nature of this life review we will give an overview of the main themes from Melissa's past.

Betrayal.   When interviewed for the first time in adulthood in 1958, Melissa, then 29 years of age, was estranged from her parents and her brother. Her marriage was rapidly disintegrating. Her relationship with her two children Carolyn and Adam was strained. Suicidal and incapable of seeing a way out, Melissa had begun psychotherapy a year earlier.

At that time, the prevailing theme in Melissa's life story was one of betrayal and a feeling that she was barely alive. It is striking, in fact, that in all four of her adult interviews, Melissa recounts a pivotal scene. This scene involves Melissa as a college student coming back home from a date and being locked out of the house by her mother who saw and disapproved of her daughter kissing her boyfriend good night. Melissa's boyfriend had to help her to climb up a trellis onto the balcony of the house. The strong emotion evoked by this episode even 50 years after it occurred reflects the fact that in Melissa's mind it was the final act in a series of betrayals. Melissa dates the beginning of her troubles to the time when she was in sixth grade and her family moved from Berkeley to San Francisco. At that time, Melissa's father, confronted with a new job that appeared to exceed his competency became even more hostile and demeaning of his daughter than before.

"He was so angry; I always felt that he might murder me on the spot
. . . He would clench his fists all the time. I would always plan what to
do if he came after me" (Melissa at age 29).

Melissa's mother responded to the new neighborhood by becoming
even more concerned than before with decorum, manners, and doing
"the appropriate thing at the appropriate time." Her message to Melissa
was be a lovely girl and do what other people think you should do. In
practice this meant that Melissa was prohibited from ever closing the
door to her room. She was forbidden to decorate the walls of her room
in case she did damage to the wallpaper. Her budding sexuality was
denied. Before the family's move, Melissa found an ally in her younger
brother, but now he also betrayed her trust by not wanting to play with
her. He began to side with the parents.

Shortly after the episode of being locked out of the house, Melissa
moved out, got pregnant, and married the man who so gallantly helped
her climb the trellis. At the time, Melissa had deep reservations about
marriage. She felt inexperienced, was scared of sexuality, and was
uncomfortable with men. However, Harry, her future husband, attracted her because of his sensitivity. Before marriage he gladly played the
role of Melissa's "psychotherapist." After marriage, not unexpectedly,
the would-be therapist turned out to be at least as emotionally needy as
his wife. Gradually, he became more and more controlling, insensitive,
and abusive. Harry blamed all the marital problems on Melissa and
accused her of lacking in willpower. This revived in Melissa past experiences of caring, being rejected, and then going to pieces.

Melissa's feelings of depression were compounded by her guilt over
the negative effect that the marital problems were having on the children. In particular, Melissa's trouble with Harry tended to get displaced
onto Carolyn, their daughter. This led Melissa to realize that she was
repeating in relation to her daughter a pattern of behavior that she
associates with her own mother. With this insight (offered at age 29)
Melissa showed an awareness that she was no longer just the betrayed
party but had herself become an instrument of betrayal.

In spite of her marital problems, Melissa did not make the decision to
divorce Harry lightly. Melissa tried going to therapy, assuming that the
problem was with her, and even attempted to ignore her disappoint-
ment and anger with Harry, but this only worked for a short time. The
couple eventually separated in 1969 when Melissa realized that Harry
had no intention of changing and had refused to acknowledge any
faults or shortcoming of his own. They were finally divorced in 1977.
As recounted by Melissa at age 54, after the divorce Harry started to
smoke increasing amounts of marijuana, lost his job, squandered an
inheritance, and died the death of a destitute street person.

Gradual, radical change.   When asked at age 69 about periods of radical change in her life, Melissa answered by saying that she had experienced "gradual radical change." It is clear that Melissa at age 69 is a very different person to what she was at age 29. It is also quite evident that this process of change was indeed a gradual one, requiring a lot of hard work, painful choices, and adjustments. There is little doubt that starting with early adulthood Melissa began to review and evaluate past experiences in order to find insight into herself and others, a process that would culminate in later adulthood. Therapy played a vital role in helping Melissa to transform from a passive, confused, self-blaming, and frightened young adult to an assured and vitally involved older person.

In her struggles, Melissa was helped by her ego strength, psychological perceptiveness, and a unique ability to combine her interests in inner reality with a very practical, matter of fact, goal-directed orientation to the external world. This is a strength of character that Melissa reports she inherited from her mother who was very good at taking care of business and an efficient problem solver. For example, although early on in her marriage Melissa did not entertain the idea that she had any personal rights, she acted very quickly once provided with this insight and confronted her husband with his physical abuse of her. When confronted with the prospect of a failed marriage, Melissa not only sought out therapy but she also enrolled in courses, got credentials as an art teacher, and became financially self-sufficient. When Melissa found it scary to be physically alone she went to a martial arts studio, put on boxing gloves, and learned to defend herself. It is this ability to become financially and emotionally independent of others that not only enhanced her self-esteem but also provided her with the necessary space to grow. In other words, Melissa made sure that she developed personal resources that safeguarded her from drifting into another relationship based on codependency.

The circle becomes complete.   Melissa's claim at age 69 that she had been a reflective person all her life is well supported by the material we have cited from earlier interviews. From the perspective of the life review the question is whether there is something qualitatively different about Melissa's process of reflection as she approaches her 70th birthday compared with her past reminiscences? We would argue that there is.

As we have already documented, Melissa has grappled with feelings of betrayal all of her adult life. While the story of being locked out of the house played an important part in all the interviews with Melissa, there were other instances of betrayal such as having her furniture appropriated by her mother, or being abandoned in front of others by her brother.

It is only in the last interview at age 69 that Melissa pinpoints her sense of betrayal to being sexually abused by her father at the age of 3 or 4, a fact that she believes was subsequently covered up by her mother. Prior to the abuse, Melissa says that her father thought she was "cute and cuddly." After her early childhood, and the episode of abuse, Melissa's father became hostile and rejecting. Father and daughter hardly exchanged a word again until the years before his death in 1985. In view of these circumstances, it is not surprising that Melissa never confronted her father about her sexual abuse. However, she describes a cathartic scene where she shook her father with rage and yelled at him to behave. Following this confrontation which took place in a convalescent hospital shortly before the father's death, Melissa suffered a panic attack in her car and thought that she was going to die.

The memory of incest reported in the interview at age 69 and the ability to express at least some of the resulting anger seem to have played a critical role in allowing Melissa to come to terms with her past in a new and more integrated way. She can now understand the hostility of her father, the ambivalence of her mother, and even begin to comprehend her longstanding problems in relationships with men. When asked to interpret her past pain and suffering, Melissa responds:

> Well it's all a learning experience . . . I guess I go with the idea that maybe you chose your parents. So I can say that you, in this philosophy anyway, that you set yourself these, parameters, or the difficulties, and then see what you can do with them. I've just sort of gone on that philosophy. So that is what I've been doing (age 69).

While later in the interview Melissa interprets "choosing your parents" in terms of her views on reincarnation, to us it seems to offer a perfect illustration of what Erik Erikson (1963) means by accepting the inevitability of one's life cycle in old age. Melissa has finally come to terms with her past and she has integrated her parents into a cohesive life story. We believe it is not accidental that Melissa has reached this new level of understanding in late adulthood. Perhaps the death of her parents has contributed to this process as well as the fact that Melissa herself must now address issues of her mortality.

Melissa's new level of acceptance of her past does not mean that she is left without regret or anger. Melissa is still angry with her parents for betraying her trust, and she feels sorry that she was not a better mother to her children, although both Carolyn and Adam have turned out to be well-functioning adults. Melissa continues to work on her negative attitude toward men and she still has hopes that maybe some day she will find a new partner. We believe that she does so as a wiser person.

Frank

Frank was interviewed in the elegant study of his Californian home. Now age 76, Frank has been retired for nearly 20 years from a highly successful career in banking. He decided at age 58 to leave the hurried life of travel, board meetings, and cocktail parties to take up writing, a passion that he left behind in college. Though he has not found the same level of public affirmation in writing literary criticism as he did in banking, Frank is very satisfied with his past and present. He narrates his life story with humor and in a lively and engaging manner.

Frank and his wife of 51 years, Elaine, share a wide range of activities from the instrumental to the adventuresome, including a passion for the outdoors and wildlife. Elaine has also learned to enjoy Frank's interest in collecting first editions of books by prominent Victorian writers. Both are closely involved in the lives of their son, Ian, daughter-in-law, and two grandchildren. It is obvious that Frank is very proud of Ian, who is well launched in life and in a career in business. Father and son have lunch together about once a month, which gives them an opportunity to "bounce decisions off one another." Frank described the relationship as one based on equality and respect.

After retirement, Frank, who describes himself as "kind of a loner," severed most of his contacts with past business associates. He hardly ever attends functions at the bank where he used to work. Instead, Frank devotes himself to research in literary criticism and history and the related hobby of book collecting. Frank's investment in writing is so strong that he calls it an "avocation." In the past 20 years, he has published several essays and has written a book which remains unpublished. The book length manuscript titled "Poison Pens" describes arguments between literary people including Dickens vs. Thackeray, Fielding vs. Richardson, and Amy Lowell vs. Ezra Pound. "There were two duels fought in it, there was a rape, there was all sorts of salacious stuff." Frank concludes that the difficulty in finding a publisher for the book is due to the fact "it [the book] wasn't really any good—at least in the publishing sense. But I had a lot of fun. I learned a lot doing this." Frank is bemused by the fact that his literary efforts over the last 20 years have brought in a grand total of $265!

Although in excellent health and full of energy, Frank has been forced to deal with changes in his appearance and physical functioning. Frank copes with these changes with humor and understanding. When asked, "What signs of aging do you see in yourself?" Frank responds, "When I was born, the nurse said to my father, 'He looks just like a prune.' I think I look like a prune now. (Laughter) I'm all wrinkled up and saggy. (Laughter) That doesn't particularly bother me." Frank also employs various compensating strategies to continue leading an active life. For instance, he now uses a staff when fishing in stronger currents to steady himself. Because of Elaine's discomfort with strenuous, physically demanding trips, Frank has abandoned his plans of traveling to the remote Arctic island of Spitsbergen, Antarctica, and the heartland of Papua/New Guinea. Instead, the couple is planning trips to less exotic places. In order to keep himself mentally alert, Frank tries to learn new things with, at times, self-surprising results. Recently, he took up modern poetry, something that he previously "would not touch with a ten-foot pole," only to find that this has opened up a whole new field of interest for him. Frank feels that he has become more mellow and open minded. He is content to sit in his study and to read a good novel listening to Sviatoslav Richter play the preludes and fugues of Bach. At age 76, Frank is not approaching death with strong emotions, either positive or negative; he simply accepts the fact that it will arrive.

In spite of his deep intellectual interests, Frank states that he is not interested in introspection or self-reflection. Frank described his life at age 76 in a manner that reveals no evidence of an attempt to achieve personal integration, develop a consistent life history, or carry out a life review. While Frank does reminisce, these memories are not used to gain insight into the past or present. The reminiscences are used in a more interpersonal way to relive with Elaine some of their past travel experiences and to tell the grandchildren "some of the goofy things that happened to us . . .". It is not surprising, therefore, that Frank responds with a clear "no" to the question as to whether or not he has ever undertaken a life review. He has never thought of writing an autobiography. As Frank comments: "In autobiographies nobody ever tells the whole truth. I have passed on some genealogical kind of stuff to my son." It is not the case that Frank does not value personal honesty because he obviously does. Rather, Frank simply does not feel the need for self-reflection.

Choosing a career.   Frank was not predestined for a career in business. As a child, his imagination was captured by the exploration of the natural world and this became his first career dream. "When I was growing up I wanted to be an ornithologist because I was very interested in the outdoors, and birds and stuff, and biological sciences." Years later, in college, Frank discovered another possible path, "I really wanted to teach English literature." But the war was imminent. The day I started classes, September 1939, Hitler marched into Poland." Frank decided to major in economics at the University of California at Berkeley, while reading literature and learning literary theory on his own. He used the library extensively and read widely outside his major.

Though Frank's desires led him to literature and writing, his parents counseled him to find a stable occupation in which he would earn a high salary and provide a comfortable life for his future family, especially during the uncertain times of the 1930s and 40s. Frank chose stability over uncertainty and completed his degree in economics. Barely finished with his BA, Frank left for the war in the Pacific where he served in the infantry and took part in the battle over Saipan. While in the army, Frank met his future wife who lived in Honolulu. The couple got married just after the end of the war. At the time, Frank, who needed money but was quite uncertain what to do, took up a job as a clerk at the Bank of Hawaii. Career opportunities in Honolulu, however, were not very promising for "mainlanders" like Frank who did not have any backing or contacts. Frank and Elaine decided to move to California where Frank became a clerk in a small, one-branch bank. Wittingly or not, he was now following in his father's footsteps. Frank's father, who like his son had strong literary interests, spent his entire adult life working in a bank.

Decision to retire.   Frank entered the banking business as an ambitious young man full of great expectations. Yet the odds of success seemed to be stacked heavily against him. Here was an introvert with a passion for the outdoors and strong literary aspirations, who had only a basic degree in economics, did not have contacts in the world of high finance, and lacked knowledge of the corporate boardroom. Yet, by the time Frank retired at the age of 58 he was a vice-chairman of a major bank with over 16,000 employees.

Although Frank started his career as a clerk in a small one-branch bank, the institution was a "silk stocking, blue chip kind of a place." The bank had a very high caliber clientele consisting of large corporations and affluent individuals. Frank, who intentionally endeavored to advance himself, moved from being a clerk to the position of an assistant cashier in six years. By the time his bank merged with a very large retail bank in 1960, Frank was vice president and corporate secretary.

After the merger, Frank adapted quickly to the new organization and, unlike many of his old colleagues, he "refused to roll over and play dead." He also had the good fortune of working with the man who eventually became president of the bank. The two of them got along very well together and when his friend was promoted, Frank was given the responsibility of managing all the branches of the bank. Subsequently, Frank himself was promoted to the position of vice-president in charge of branches, and international and big corporate domestic accounts. From then on, Frank and his two colleagues managed the day-to-day affairs of the bank.

At the age of 57, while at the height of his power, Frank astonished his friends and colleagues by announcing his decision to retire. Frank gives a very similar account of his decision to retire when interviewed at both age 61 and age 76.

> Well my wife and I were fishing in Idaho, when I was still working, and we were admiring the beauty of the outdoors and so on. So we said, "Why don't we just throw this other thing over and do this?" And we did. I went back and I told the guy that I was working for that I'm going to retire in September and that was it (age 76).

Although there appears to be little doubt that the actual decision to retire was a spontaneous one, it is an idea that Frank has mulled over throughout his adult life. When interviewed at age 38, Frank described a plan, which never came to fruition, to enter academia and teach literature to business students. An additional incentive to retire was provided by the fact that while working in the bank, Frank developed a hobby of collecting first editions of the work of Dickens, Trollope, and Scott. He did not, however, have the time to write or to engage in serious literary scholarship. It may also be the case that in deciding to retire Frank had in mind his father who worked in a bank until old age, never fulfilling his literary interests. Frank's father, although not an alcoholic, became a problem drinker.

Living life in reverse.   It is obvious that Frank is a psychologically complex individual. Here is an introvert and a loner who achieved great success in the extroverted world of business; a man who takes pride in his rational and practical self but who also has an interest in reincarnation and who used ESP and intuition in making banking decisions; a member of the famous, London-based, Roxborough Club of book collectors who loves the rugged outdoors. In spite of these complexities, it is also quite clear that Frank is not prone to self-reflection. He shows no evidence of undertaking a life review in older adulthood or at any other stage in his life. Although throughout his adult life Frank had to contend with negotiating three quite disparate interests in the outdoors, literary history and criticism, and business, he never made an attempt to integrate them in his professional life. As a young adult, Frank abandoned ornithology and literature by making a conscious decision to embark on a career in banking. In middle adulthood, he gave up his banking career completely in order to pursue his passion for the outdoors and writing. At age 61, Frank comments "we retired early to just live my life in reverse." This is a very apt description of Frank's strategy of living his life serially without ever attempting to fuse his interests into a cohesive whole. There is also no evidence that Frank has ever attempted to integrate the various aspects of his psyche. Throughout his life, Frank has been content to rely on his intellect as a primary mode of adaptation and to seek emotional catharsis by reading Dickens, Trollope, and Scott. Emphasizing reason and practicality, Frank relegates his exceptional intuitive abilities primarily to the realm of the exotic and the quirky.

In older adulthood, Frank exudes a strong sense of satisfaction with his past and present life. He is accepting of old age and has no desire to live his life over again. We have no evidence to suggest that things will change as Frank grows older. In other words, Frank has managed to avoid despair without ever striving for psychic integration. He exemplifies, in fact, that an unexamined life may be worth living after all.

In Review

We believe that the case studies of Melissa and Frank illustrate well the quantitative findings from the IHD study showing a relation between life review, personality, and life experiences. Although both Melissa and Frank show high levels of acceptance in their lives, they have reached this state following very different paths. Melissa entered her adulthood as a dispirited, angry, and highly disappointed young woman. By a process of introspection and psychotherapy, beginning with great intensity in early adulthood and then continuing gradually later on in life, she managed to overcome many of her conflicts and to radically change her way of being in the world. Life review was an essential part of her struggle for acceptance. Frank's life progressed with less turmoil. Despite a seemingly abrupt decision to retire, Frank shows a strong sense of continuity of the self throughout his life. There is no place in his mind for the kind of reflections required by a life review. Although Frank made a radical life-style change in late middle age, he did so without reworking or altering his basic sense of self-understanding. In fact his decision to retire parallels in its rationality his earlier decision to seek employment in a bank The changes following retirement are perceived by Frank as returning to a self that was temporarily lost, suspended, or compartmentalized.

There is no doubt that Melissa and Frank possess very different personality styles. Melissa has shown interest in introspection and things psychological throughout her adult life. She clearly exhibits these characteristics in the first adult interview at age 29, providing insightful, if incomplete, observations on her family life and marriage. Melissa has also been able to direct her well-developed intuitive skills in the service of getting in touch with unconscious processes. This has served her well in psychotherapy and in her career as an artist. Melissa is also a highly spiritual person.

Although Frank shares Melissa's deep interest in the inner world, his mental energy is invested differently and for different purposes. Frank is not prone to self-reflection or psychological thinking. Even when alone, Frank prefers to keep himself occupied with something concrete, something that can be analyzed or studied, such as literature or music. The focus of his reflections remains on things outside of himself. He does not use his private time, normally several hours a day, to allow his mind to reflect on emotions, relationships, or the past. Frank's interests are much more intellectual and tangible. He likes to read novels, to write about intellectual arguments, and to listen to Bach fugues which "might sound like pure scales to other people." Frank's way of approaching the world is evident in all four adult interviews. It is just not his style to dwell on emotions or to review the past.

Melissa and Frank also differ in terms of their life experiences. Melissa's life has been one of conflict and pain. Abandoned and abused by her father, betrayed by her mother, and rejected by her husband, Melissa had to deal throughout her life with conflicting feelings of love, hate, anger, guilt, and the need for reparation. Her life resembles a rich text full of mystery and drama that cries for self-interpretation and understanding. In this sense she illustrates well Schopenhauer's contention that "for man to acquire noble sentiments . . . pain, suffering and failure are as necessary to him as weighty ballast is to a ship, which attains no draught without it" (Safranski, 1990, p. 198). In contrast, Frank's rich and interesting life has been relatively conflict free. Even though Frank faced the problem of choosing a profession, he virtually submerged his inclinations toward literature, put his head down, and strove for the top of the corporate game. It is hard to regret a choice of vocation that brings with it wealth, power, and prestige. Frank's successes allowed him to pursue his life interests in ornithology, literature, and business serially without any regret or the need to confront personal demons.

It is common to think of life review as a purely psychological phenomenon that is solely a function of one's personality and immediate life experiences. Our interview data suggest that the process of life review may also be facilitated or inhibited by the larger historical and cultural contexts for one's life. In discussing Melissa's life review as an older adult, we raised the possibility that Melissa's acceptance of her present and past life was, in part, associated with her ability to remember being sexually abused by her father. We further speculated that Melissa's ability to gain this insight might have been influenced by her age and the death of her parents. It is also possible that Melissa was able to remember her abuse and thus complete the process of life review because we now live in an era where there is a public vocabulary for talking about sexual abuse without feelings of stigmatization. After all, memory, and by implication life review, is inherently context dependent. In the case of Frank, one could argue that his tendency toward self-reflection was inhibited by the fact that he grew up in an era when there was a strong adherence to traditional sex roles. Men were supposed to adopt the instrumental, and women the expressive, role. Upon marriage, it was expected that the wife would adapt her personality to fit with that of her husband. It is possible that this traditional patterning of personal and social expectations made it harder for Frank to experience other ways of being in the world than his own. While this obviously did not reduce Frank's level of self acceptance in old age, it made it less likely that he would be drawn to the type of self-reflection that is triggered by the need to deal with resistance offered by the "other."

In conclusion, the life stories of Melissa and Frank exemplify two different paths to adaptation in older age. Melissa's story, with its high drama, suspense, working through of traumatic events, and final reconciliation, has all the characteristics of a Dionysian or Romantic epic. In this sense it meets all the criteria of a good life story based on the life review (Coleman, 1999). In contrast, Frank's tale is much more refined, calm, stylized, and steeped in tradition. Devoid of high drama, extremes of passion, and intoxication, it exemplifies an Apollonian or Neoclassical tale. Nonetheless, both life stories allow the narrator to accept the past, enjoy the present, and look forward to the future.

4

Exploring the Functions of Autobiographical Memory: Why Do I Remember the Autumn?

Susan Bluck and Nicole Alea

This is rather a wistful title to begin a theoretical chapter on memory. Then again, memory sometimes brings up wistful feelings, reminds one of happy times or opportunities missed, of how things once were. The focus of this chapter is to examine the functions of autobiographical memory (AM), that is, to ask *why* humans remember so much of what has happened in their lives. The title's poetic reference to autumn is intentionally provoking. A common image in literature is the first signs of autumn: the turning of the leaves, that smell in the air that brings back to mind the first day of school, or Thanksgiving with family. How does it serve us to remember these things? In this chapter, we do not seek to understand why we remember autumn particularly, but in a larger sense, what functions AM serves. Of course, huge amounts of information are also forgotten, but why do humans remember so much of their lives?

Autobiographical memory is viewed here as including event-specific details and images, complete memories for particular events (*personal memories,* Brewer, 1996), life-time periods and life themes, and one's entire life story (Bluck & Habermas, 2000). That is, there are many levels of specificity of autobiographical memory (Conway, 1992).

Reminiscence is one particularly interesting form of autobiographical remembering: we view reminiscing as an activity in which personally significant autobiographical memories are accessed. These memories are then mulled over, repeated, or interpreted, and then often shared with other people. Different from some other types of AM that may serve largely informational needs, reminiscence may serve primarily psychosocial needs (Wong, 1995).

This distinction between reminiscence and autobiographical memory is not one that is only definitional. The two literatures have quite distinct roots. Reminiscence work is based in the tradition of psychodynamic theory (e.g., Butler, 1963) while autobiographical memory research comes out of an everyday approach to cognitive psychology (e.g., Neisser, 1978). A few papers have already been written that attempt to bridge these substantively similar but traditionally different literatures (Bluck & Levine, 1998; Fitzgerald, 1996; Webster & Cappeliez, 1993). These papers have had some impact and one now sees researchers in the reminiscence literature referring to memory concepts and processes, and those in the AM literature referring not only to basic memory processes, but also to interpretation and meaning-making (e.g., *autobiographical reasoning,* Habermas & Bluck, 2000). This is a cautious step forward: in viewing reminiscence as a type of autobiographical memory, it is crucial not to simply reduce it to cognition.

Though some interaction between these fields can be seen, there are still basic differences in the two approaches. Coming from a primarily cognitive perspective, research on AM has largely been concerned with understanding the organization of, and processes related to, storing and retrieving memories. Research in this area does however move beyond basic cognitive models to embrace emotion, self, and personality (e.g., Levine, Stein, & Liwag, 1999; Singer & Salovey, 1993; Rubin, 1986, 1996; Thorne & Klohnen, 1993). On the other hand, reminiscence research and practice has traditionally focused on the use of reminiscence groups and techniques of various sorts (e.g., Birren & Deutchman, 1991) as informal interventions, particularly in later life.

We believe that the issue of memory functions is a crucial one for identifying the similarities of reminiscence and autobiographical memory work. That is, an important link between these two areas is that each requires the understanding of the functions of remembering and thinking about the past. Despite the different aims and goals of the researchers and practitioners in these two areas (e.g., building models of how memory is organized versus developing effective reminiscence practice techniques), we believe that they are faced with a common substantive problem that must be resolved for either of these fields to develop productively. More modestly, we suggest that consideration of the functions of AM could greatly enhance the theoretical conceptualizations and empirical agendas of those working in either area. AM researchers stand to benefit from an understanding of the functions of AM because this is a crucial part of elucidating the organization and processes of the memory system (which are most likely guided by the function of the system). Researchers and practitioners who develop, use, and evaluate reminiscence techniques need to understand function so as to be able to understand or predict the types of outcomes that thinking about the past might have for participants (e.g., see Bluck & Levine, 1998). In sum, benefits for each of these two areas derive from making the functions of autobiographical memory a centerpiece of research. Of course, another underlying benefit is that these two areas are, by this common agenda, brought into closer relationship.

Before proceeding further, let us clarify the use of the term *function*. Function can have at least two meanings, connoting either *use* or *adaptive function* (i.e., functional versus nonfunctional). These two meanings are related, but for now we take the simpler definition of function, that is, what do individuals *use* their memory of their life for? A later development in any program of research dealing with function would be to also focus on the latter meaning of function: to identify the adaptive and nonadaptive ways in which memory is used in everyday life.

In this chapter we briefly review the existing work on the functions of remembering and thinking about life both from the reminiscence and from the AM literature. Next, we point out the overlap and distinctiveness in the hypothesized functions of AM and reminiscence. Finally, considerations for future investigations of function for researchers in both domains are highlighted.

The Functions of Autobiographical Memory and Reminiscence

Autobiographical remembering, or reminiscing, implicitly involves thinking about the past in the present. A number of theoretical writings suggest the importance of temporal perspective, the expansion of one's perspective through an extended temporal view of self and life (e.g., Lewin, 1926; Neisser, 1988a; Neugarten, 1979). More specifically in both the AM and the reminiscence literature researchers have addressed why remembering and thinking about the past occurs in everyday life. Due to the different traditions or roots of these two research areas, as previously discussed, the nature of this work provides different angles of insight. We review work first from the AM and then from the reminiscence literature.

Functions of Autobiographical Memory:
Theory and Empirical Evidence

Various researchers have described the benefits of a functional approach to memory (Baddeley, 1987; Bruce, 1989) and outlined the theoretical functions of the human ability to contemplate the past. While different researchers have focused on different particular functions, or different subsets of functions, most hypothesized functions fit into one of three categories. These categories are well represented in Pillemer's (1992) formulation of AM as having self (self-continuity, psychodynamic integrity), directive (planning for present and future behaviors), and communicative (social bonding) functions. While these three functions (self, directive, social) have discrete labels they do not necessarily represent discrete categories in everyday behavior or mental life. For example, one may remember a past success (e.g., a public speaking engagement) in order to serve the directive function of preparing for an upcoming engagement. At the same time, however, that memory may serve a social function in reminding one of acceptance within a group. For simplicity, however, and to mirror the way that most formulations have appeared in the literature, functions are reviewed here largely in discrete categories.

Many theoretical formulations emphasize the function of AM in the continuity of the self. While these share a similarity to Pillemer's (1992) "psychodynamic function" which emphasizes the psychological and emotional importance for the self of recalling one's own past, other researchers have not necessarily embraced the psychodynamic aspect of the self function. Knowledge of the self in the past, and as projected into the future, has been seen as one critical type of self-knowledge (Neisser, 1988b). Conway (1996) claims that the adequacy of autobiographical knowledge depends on its ability to support and promote continuity and development of the self. Similarly, a hypothesized function of the personal past is to preserve a sense of being a coherent person (Barclay, 1996), and Fivush (1988, 1998) describes how this coherent sense of self-over-time develops in young children. Autobiographical knowledge may be especially important when the self is in adverse conditions requiring self-change (Robinson, 1986). Other self functions such as mood-regulation, and self-concept preservation and editing have also been suggested (Cohen, 1998). In short, autobiographical memory has been viewed as serving self functions. While most researchers agree that self-continuity is maintained through the interdependent relation of self and autobiographical memory (Bluck & Levine, 1998; Brewer, 1986), the directive function of AM is also seen as important. For example, Cohen (1989, 1998) has described the role of AM to solve problems as well as in developing opinions and attitudes. AM allows us to ask new questions of old information in order to solve problems in the present, and to predict future events (Baddeley, 1987). An hypothesized function that may be seen as both directive and social, is to use our own past experience to construct models that allow us to understand the inner world of others, and thereby to predict their future behavior (Robinson & Swanson, 1990). Similarly, Lockhart (1989) has argued that the major function of AM is to provide flexibility in the construction and updating of rules that allow individuals to comprehend the past and predict future outcomes. That is, by comparing different past events, and by comparing events with developed rules, individuals are able to test hypotheses about how the world (not just the social world) currently operates, and to make predictions about the future. Similarly, in several studies individuals report remembering past events and the lessons they learned from them as useful in guiding present or future behavior (McCabe, Capron, & Peterson, 1991; Pratt, Arnold, Norris, & Filyer, 1999). Thus, the directive function of autobiographical memory, i.e., use of the past to make plans and decisions in the present and for the future, has also received theoretical support.

Neisser (1988b) claims that the social function of AM is the most fundamental function. The social function can be divided into three subcategories: social interaction, empathy, and social bonding. The most basic social function that AM serves is to provide material for conversation thus facilitating social interaction (Cohen, 1998). Sharing personal memories also makes the conversation seem more truthful, thus more believable and persuasive (Pillemer, 1992). Autobiographical memory also allows us to better understand and empathize with others (Cohen, 1998). For instance, sharing personal memories can engage the listener in a story and elicit empathic responses, particularly if the listener responds with their own personal memory (Pillemer, 1992). Providing others with information about one's self (self-disclosure) is another social function that memory serves in social relationships (Cohen, 1998). The importance of AM in developing, maintaining, and strengthening social bonds has been repeatedly noted (e.g., Nelson, 1993; Pillemer, 1998a) and even tied to its potential evolutionary adaptivity (Neisser, 1988b). When episodic remembering is impaired social relationships can suffer, thus highlighting the importance that autobiographical memories can serve for social bonding (Robinson & Swanson, 1990). Sharing AM's with someone who was not present at the past episode provides the listener with information about the self and the world, while sharing memories with someone who was present serves more of a social-bonding function (Fivush, Haden, & Reese, 1996).

One project has examined the functions of AM empirically (Hyman & Faries, 1992). In a first study, individuals were asked to report and describe past events that they had often talked about with others. In a second study, individuals generated autobiographical memories to cue words, and then described previous times when they had thought about or talked about the memory. The first study (32 participants provided 63 memories) revealed that individuals talk about memories in order to share experiences, provide information and advice, or to describe themselves to others. The second study (19 participants provided 152 memories), which did not require that the memory had been talked about before, showed that many memories are recalled privately and not told to others. In addition, other memories were described as being shared with others and thereby used to inform others about one's self and life.

In sum, theoretical work in the AM literature supports three functions of remembering the past: self, social, and directive. Most researchers agree that the self and AM are intimately linked, and many suggest that the social function of AM is its most important or primary function. The directive function of memory is described as a way in which individuals use the past as a resource for present and future behavior. In the empirical work, self and social functions of autobiographical memory were often mentioned, but the participants in these studies did not report the directive function often.

Functions of Reminiscence:
Theory and Empirical Evidence

As can be seen from the review above, very little empirical research exists explicitly examining the functions of autobiographical memory. In the conceptually related field of reminiscence (Bluck & Levine, 1998; Fitzgerald, 1996; Webster & Cappeliez, 1993), more empirical research on the functions of thinking about the past exists alongside theoretical formulations (see Haight & Webster, 1995). While several theoretical articles outline the potential adaptive uses and functions of reminiscence, especially in later life, (e.g., Ebersole, 1978; Kaminsky, 1984; Lieberman & Tobin, 1983), the most encompassing taxonomies are presented by Watt and Wong (1991) (see also Wong & Watt, 1991) and Webster (1997).

Through content analysis of interviews with 460 individuals ages 65–95 years, the authors (Watt & Wong, 1991; Wong & Watt, 1991) arrive at a six-category taxonomy. This includes integrative, instrumental, transmissive, narrative, escapist, and obsessive reminiscence.

Integrative reminiscence refers to life review as described by Butler (1963). Instrumental reminiscence refers to the recall of past experiences in an effort to cope with a current problem. Transmissive reminiscence refers to the retelling of past events and anecdotes as a way to pass on information to other people, especially the next generation. Narrative reminiscence refers to storytelling about the past for the pleasure of the reminiscer or the audience. Escapist reminiscence refers to daydreaming and fantasy about the past that may portray the past in an overly positive light while devaluing the present. Obsessive reminiscence refers to ongoing, uncontrollable negative memories usually accompanied by guilt or despair.

This taxonomy makes a positive contribution that is not only theory based. The outlined functions (implicit in the categories) are based on narrative accounts by a reasonably large number of individuals. However, as has been the tradition in the study of reminiscence, the studied sample were all individuals over 65 years old. In fact there is little evidence that thinking about the past is the exclusive domain of the older adult (Giambra, 1977; Thornton & Brotchie, 1987; de Vries, Birren, & Deutchman, 1990; Webster, 2001).

In order to take a lifespan perspective on the functions of reminiscence, Webster (1993, 1997) developed the Reminiscence Functions Scale (RFS). The validated scale, originally constructed from 710 individuals' (ages 17 to 91 years) responses to the sentence stems, "I reminisce because . . .", and "Others reminisce because . . .", identifies eight reminiscence function factors. These are boredom reduction, death preparation, identity, problem solving, conversation, intimacy maintenance, bitterness revival, and teach/inform. Boredom reduction involves reminiscing because the environment is understimulating or the individual is unengaged. Death preparation is using our past to create a sense of closure or calm when our own mortality is conspicuous. The identity factor refers to reminiscing that serves to solidify a sense of who we are, while problem solving provides us with past strategies that serve us in the present. The conversation factor refers to reminiscence for the sake of informally connecting with others, while intimacy maintenance is reminiscing about important relationships in order to maintain bonds. Bitterness revival is reminiscing about previous unjust experiences, thus evoking negative affective responses. The teach/inform factor is the use of reminiscence for instruction or providing information to others.

The taxonomy has gained validity through identification of meaningful correlates of the categories. For example, women tend to engage in reminiscence more for the purpose of intimacy maintenance and

conversation, older adults relate reminiscence more to death preparation, and adolescents more commonly use reminiscence for boredom
reduction (Webster, 1993). Personality correlates also validate the
reported functions (Webster, 1993). For example, people who score
high on the neuroticism subscale of the NEO Personality Inventory
tend to engage in bitterness revival. Those who score high on extrover-
sion tend to endorse reminiscing as a conversational component.

The validation of the RFS in this manner, and the fact that it was
developed using a large group and age range adds to its robustness as
a measurement tool. Conceptually, the similarities to Watt and Wong's
(1991) taxonomy provide convergent validity for the existence of several reminiscence functions. The two taxonomies replicate many of
the same functions though they discuss them and label them in different ways. In the next section, we discuss these commonalities, and
the overlap of this literature with the discussion of functions found in the
AM literature.

Overlap and Differences in AM and Reminiscence Functions

Our focus in this section is to map the two reminiscence taxonomies
onto one another and to compare them with the three theoretical functions of AM (self, directive, social). Overall, as seen in Table 4.1, the
data collected by reminiscence researchers basically supports the
functions postulated by autobiographical memory theorists. Watt and
Wong's (1991) integrative reminiscence is described in terms that map
onto the self function; instrumental reminiscence can be seen as a
directive function; transmissive and narrative reminiscence serve
social functions, the first of passing on information, and the second
largely for the entertainment of self and others. Looking at the RFS categories, again the factors fit well with the hypothesized functions of
autobiographical memory outlined above. The RFS factors can be seen
to represent self functions (death preparation and identity factors), a
directive function (problem-solving factor), and social functions (conversation, intimacy maintenance, teach/inform factors).

In looking across research and theory in both the autobiographical
memory and the reminiscence literatures we find support for autobiographical memory serving self, directive, and social functions. Note,
however, that in all three studies in which individuals actually reported
on their uses of memory, the directive function received the least support. That is, the directive function can only be seen as represented by
one factor in both Watt & Wong's (1991) taxonomy (instrumental) and
Webster's (1997) RFS (problem-solving), and was not nominated

TABLE 4.1   A Comparison of the Functions of Autobiographical Memory and Reminiscence

Functions of AM	Reminiscence Taxonomy (Watt & Wong, 1991)	RFS (Webster, 1997)
Self	Integrative	Identity Death Preparation
Directive	Instrumental	Problem Solving
Social	Transmissive Narrative	Teach/Inform Conversation Intimacy Maintenance
Other	Obsessive Escapist	Bitterness Revival Boredom Reduction

by the participants polled by Hyman & Faries (1992). Note, also, that two of the functions identified in the reminiscence literature cannot easily be mapped onto one of the three AM functions. These include factors that may tend toward the psychodynamic foundations of the reminiscence literature. That is, bitterness revival or obsessive reminiscence, and boredom reduction or escapist reminiscence may be seen to serve intrapsychic functions that have not yet been fully embraced in the AM literature (cf., Pillemer, 1992). To give this comparison of overlap in functions an empirical basis, we are currently analyzing data that compares individuals' self-reports concerning the three functions of AM with their responses on the RFS (Bluck, Habermas, & Rubin, 2001).

Our analysis of the functions that have been generated across these two fields is fruitful in two regards. First, it appears that researchers from both traditions, though speaking slightly different languages, both support three fundamental functions of remembering and thinking about the past. In both literatures the three functions are differentially weighted (the directive function receives less support). This cross-field convergence is encouraging. Second, however, is the fact that they do not match perfectly. It seems that the way that researchers approach and measure individuals' uses of memory may lead to different conclusions about the number and types of functions. Our view of this is that it serves a useful purpose. For example, researchers in the autobiographical memory literature can be advised of the importance of memory for such functions as death preparation, a topic not often considered by cognitive psychologists. On the other hand, those studying the function of the past from the tradition of the reminiscence literature may benefit from locating their work also within the autobiographical memory framework: we do not remember all that happens to us, sometimes we remember it inaccurately, and parts that we do remember may not be "worthy" of reminiscing about. Research in each of these traditions can be used to broaden the scope, or specify the limits, of those using the alternate approach.

Finally, this exercise in mapping the functions of reminiscence and AM is not intended to suggest that reminiscence researchers should now think in terms of only three functions. Instead our sense is that it has shown that self, social, and directive functions may be a foundation for the study of AM at a general level, and that reminiscence, a specific type of remembering, manifests those three basic functions in particular ways that are captured in the taxonomies presented here.

Lessons Learned: Considerations of Function in Future Investigations

Both the convergence and the divergence in views of function across the AM and reminiscence literature are useful. These two fields serve to gain from further cross pollination, and the development of both different and complementary approaches to this foundational topic. That is, whether one is a reminiscence researcher or practitioner, or an AM researcher, the question remains important: *Why* do humans remember so much of their lives and spend time thinking back over their past?

Of course, the above review partially answers that question. Humans remember a huge amount of their lives because remembering our own past serves self, directive, and social functions. So, for example, a memory of autumn may provide us with continuity in our view of self across childhood and into adulthood (self), may direct us to "get going" on projects that we want to accomplish by the end of the year (directive), or provide us with memories of harvest celebrations past that we enjoy sharing with others (social).

We have a partial answer but much work remains to be done. This review shows that there is very little empirical evidence concerning the functions of AM. We also still need to address several conceptual issues in this area. In the remainder of the chapter we identify some of the conceptual and empirical work that we feel is necessary for advancing knowledge about why people remember and think about the past. This includes a discussion of several factors that may affect how autobiographical memory is used: levels of remembering, the content of memories, and the possibility of lifespan differences in functions.

Other factors that we do not discuss here, such as culture, gender, and personality, are also likely to play important moderating roles in how AM is used in everyday life.

Does Function Vary by Level of Memory?

Conway and his colleagues (Conway, 1992; Conway & Pleydell-Pearce, in press) have developed a hierarchically nested model of the organization of AM that outlines several levels of AM. It includes basic units such as event-specific knowledge, mid-level units such as personal episodes, as well as more global units such as life themes and lifetime periods. In our recent work we have extended Conway's model to also include the most superordinate unit of thinking about the past, the life story (Bluck & Habermas, 2001; Habermas & Bluck, 2000). As a result, we suggest that there are at least three levels of analysis on which individuals look back over their lives, and that should be included in a conceptualization of AM: specific events, life periods and life themes, and the life story.

For example, when individuals reminisce they may engage in review of an entire life (the life story), one version of which (the life review) was suggested by Butler (1963). They may also, however, remember certain lifetime periods (e.g., when I lived in Berlin), or share particular personal episodes. Outside of the reminiscence framework, as part of the flow of AM in everyday life, personal episodes or even event-specific details (such as smells or image fragments) may enter consciousness due to one's inner train of thought or external cueing (Bernsten, 1998).

Accepting that there are at least three different experiential and potentially organizational levels of AM, we are then challenged to grapple with whether the functions of AM outlined above are adequate to apply to all levels of memory, or if different levels of memory might serve different sets or subsets of functions. One productive direction for future research is to use self-reports of the functions of AM and reminiscence (as Webster has done) but to vary the instructions such that participants are asked to provide functions for different levels of memory. For example, in our most recent work (Bluck, Habermas, & Rubin, 2001) we ask participants to report on the frequency with which they "think back over or talk about my life or certain periods of my life" for each of 32 reasons. This follows the instruction that, "Sometime people think back over their life or talk to other people about their life: it may be about things that happened quite a long time ago or more recently. We are not interested in the times that you think back over specific events, but in when and how you bring together and connect the events and periods of your life." Thus, in this research we cue individuals to focus on life periods, or the life story, not on the more basic level of memory, the individual episode.

Does Function Vary by Content?

Gigerenzer (1997) has pointed out that theories of memory often suffer because of a focus on structure and organization without taking the role of memory content into account. In applying his observation to the current topic, individuals may rely more or less on recalled experiences to serve current functions depending on the context (Graumann, 1986) in which they are acting (i.e., in different life domains such as health, work, love relations).

Aside from the consideration of content in terms of life domain, the more micro level content and valence of the memory may also be important. The outcome of a life review may depend on the valence of the events in the life lived (Shute, 1986). If one reason for thinking about the past is to maintain self-continuity, are people just as likely to maintain a continuous negative self-concept by recalling and rehearsing past negative episodes, or does the self-continuity function imply a bias toward self-consistency that focuses on maintaining a positive view of self (e.g., see Greenwald, 1980)? At the level of memory for individual episodes, both positive and negative memories may serve the function of guiding future behavior but in different directions (Stein & Levine, 1990; Thorne & Klohnen, 1993). In social exchanges, relationships may be differentially affected by the sharing of happy memories and sad or bitter memories, though both may serve different aspects of the social function (e.g., maintaining intimacy and eliciting empathy respectively).

A final consideration concerning the relation of function to content is the extent to which particular memories or life periods are seen by the individual as being autobiographical. That is, individuals have thousands of memories of their lives but only some of these are significant enough to them to be considered autobiographical or meaningful in the scope of the whole life (Bluck & Habermas, 2001).

In future research that aims to validate or further explore the functions of AM, content must be considered: the domain of life being studied, the valence of memories being recalled, and the centrality of those memories for an individual's sense of biography may all affect, or be affected by, the function of remembering the past. For example, can we consider a memory about a negative past health condition that threatened an individual's life having the same types of functions as a memory for a mildly positive relationship that lasted only a few weeks?

In designing measures (e.g., choosing between labor-intensive narrative methods and more quantifiable checklists or self-ratings) the ability to include the role of content in function should be kept in mind.

Does Function Vary by Life Phase?

The history of the reminiscence tradition, with its focus on late life, demands that we ask whether autobiographical memory functions differently depending one one's point in the life span (Webster, 1999). Attention to the various changing and continuous contexts in which individuals lives are embedded is central to the lifespan perspective (Baltes, 1987; Baltes, Lindenberger, & Staudinger, 1998). Within the reminiscence literature, Webster (1997) has begun this process by examining age differences in types of reminiscence used by different age groups.

Speculating about more general functions of AM from the work specific to reminiscence, Webster and McCall's (1999) findings suggest that the directive function is more frequent in younger adults while the social function of teaching and informing may be more frequent in older adults. Our assumption is that frequency reflects a necessary use or function. From their findings it also seems that both young and old adults may utilize the self function of AM, although possibly for different reasons (i.e., identity construction and death preparation, respectively). Cohen (1998) also suggests that the social function of AM may be more important in late life for maintaining social relationships. Contextual factors associated with aging may be related to changes in the functions of AM across the lifespan. In one study, individuals who were aging successfully or living in the community showed more integrative and instrumental reminiscence as compared with those who were not aging successfully or who were living in institutions (Wong & Watt, 1991). That is, not only age, but life context and adaptation, were related to memory uses. This data from the reminiscence literature provides a basis for building a larger body of empirical work on lifespan differences in AM function.

Tying together developmental thinking about early, middle, and later life may provide researchers with clues as to the way that memory function may be related to these progressive life phases. Past investigations have demonstrated that remembering the past first begins in early childhood (e.g., Fivush & Reese, this volume) and adolescence has been recognized as a phase in which memory is recruited in the service of identity-building (Habermas & Bluck, 2000; McAdams, 1985). There is some evidence that individuals recall personal episodes that are consonant with the Eriksonian goals of particular life phases.

For example, that when recalling their young adulthood people tend to recall memories concerning the developments of intimate bonds (Conway & Holmes, 2000).

Beyond these early life phases, Neugarten (1979) claims that middle age brings a change in time perspective when one realizes that there is more time behind than there is left ahead in one's life, and she characterizes late adulthood as a phase when one may focus more on what one has been in the past. In keeping with this view, de Vries and Watt (1996) have shown that older adults recount more past events, and younger adults more future events, when identifying the significant events of their lives. Thus, temporal perspective, or one's vantage point in the life span, may affect the use of the remembered past.

Butler's (1963) view, in writing of the life review, was that remembering and re-examining the past in later life was possible due to the decreased demands on one's time due to retirement, and was crucial to understanding the present, and finally to accepting one's life and death. Erikson's (1968, 1982) final life stage of integrity versus despair, involves an examination of the past, and its integration with the present in order to imbue the past with the new qualities that can only be given to it by one's current vantage point in the present.

Relating life phases, roles, and contexts to the use of memory remains a challenge for future research. Within age groups, particular contexts of retrieval may also be important to memory function (Winograd, 1996). Research might address both the theoretical claims of the adaptive role of autobiographical memory in later life, as well as trying to further map the functions that are consonant with earlier life phases. This is not to suggest that we expect that different life phases require us to use memory in completely different ways. Many continuities in AM will likely be found (e.g., Bluck, Levine, & Laulhere, 1999) due to the fundamental nature of such things as self continuity, directing future behavior, and maintaining social relationships.

SUMMARY AND CONCLUSIONS

The aim of the chapter was to identify and further explore the functions of AM by examining work across the reminiscence and autobiographical memory traditions. This analysis suggests that the various specific functions of reminiscence that have been empirically established fall fairly neatly into the three theorized functions of autobiographical memory more generally. The self and social functions are well supported and the directive function less so. There are, however, functions of reminiscence that do not fit into the larger autobiographical memory scheme and these differences offer directions for broadening the view of autobiographical memory to encompass more emotional themes.

Further investigations into the functions of remembering and thinking about the past are foundational for the development of the two literatures. An understanding of the function of memory for the personal past would provide a useful underlay both for models of autobiographical memory and for the design of reminiscence techniques. Suggestions for future research and conceptual extensions include consideration of whether the function that memory serves varies by the level of memory being accessed, the content of memories, and the individual's point in the lifespan.

5

New Meanings for Old Tales: A Discourse-Based Study of Reminiscence and Development in Late Life

Sally Chandler and Ruth Ray

In his 1963 article on life review—the article that gerontologists typically cite as the motivating force behind most reminiscence research to date—Robert Butler suggests that the repeated tellings of life stories in old age are a natural, even predictable, stage of late-life development. As a geropsychiatrist acquainted with Erikson's theory of lifelong development, Butler had observed a tendency in his patients to tell the same stories again and again. Interpreting this behavior as meaningful, Butler hypothesized that retellings represent deep psychic urgings toward a final reckoning. Butler's hypothesis, as we know, has been widely tested by gerontologists and geriatric health professionals, often in the form of therapeutic groups created to assist older adults in working through difficult experiences and relationships that have not yet been resolved. The most desirable outcome for groups of this kind is for members to reach a point in which the reminiscing is vividly expressive and personally illuminating, with all elements of their lives "confidently integrated" (Sherman, 1991a). In some cases, a group member will move from a static or foreclosed position in relationship to the past to a more flexible, change-oriented position. On the basis of his study of oral reminiscence groups, for example, Sherman concludes that, ideally, "to the extent that we are reconstructing our pasts and ourselves through reminiscence in the life review, we are 'becoming' someone in the process—someone who is a little different from the one we took for granted in the past or perhaps a very different person from one we even imagined in the past" (231). Following Butler and others, Sherman defines "reminiscence" as the simple act of thinking or telling about the past and "life review" as a more systematic and deliberate activity undertaken to create a coherent understanding of one's life in its entirety. Sherman allows that, although written reminiscence has not been adequately studied, it serves an important heuristic role in this process. Birren & Deutchman, in their 1991 book on guided life review through writing, agree that the writing process itself stimulates further recall, provides the opportunity to rehearse memories before they are shared with a group, and may prompt a more comprehensive life review than that achieved through oral reminiscence alone.

In our own work with older adults, we have conducted written reminiscence groups and developed a research agenda for studying the outcomes of these groups which is both contextually sensitive and oriented toward group dynamics and narrative patterns. As English studies scholars informed by developmental psychology and trained in the methods of ethnography and textual analysis, we consider reminiscence groups to be prime occasions for observing the social process of adult development. We are especially interested in studying how emotional resolutions—or attempts at resolution—are initiated and explored through group talk around written texts.

In this chapter, we analyze excerpts of talk from two reminiscence writing groups we facilitated for five weeks each in the summers of 1999 and 2000. We have determined that there are two types of reminiscence operating in these groups—fixed and dynamic—that generate texts which serve distinctly different functions individually and socially. Fixed reminiscence generates what we call "set pieces"—writings or oral renderings which are told the same way repeatedly and often include a moral or homily meant to affirm the values of the reminiscence group. Set pieces function normatively for the narrator, as well as the group, confirming some aspect of the past that is collectively shared. Dynamic reminiscence generates what we call "reflective pieces"—writings or oral renderings which are problematized through group talk and which go through a series of changes, often with no resolution, yet with a very positive effect. Reflective pieces function transformatively for the group, generating changes in others' thinking, as well as the narrator's. We take the term "dynamic reminiscence" from Andrew Schlarch, who distinguishes between nostalgic reminiscence which transports a narrator back to an earlier time and place, usually perceived as better than the present, and a more change-oriented, "dynamic" reminiscence which brings the past into the present, raising the possibility that multiple (even contradictory) selves might coexist in memory and experience. Schlarch (1997) suggests that "part of this dynamic is analytic and reconstructive and part of it is living in the moment, being present and witnessing the fact that we are constructing as we reminisce" (p. 23).

In the following pages, we illustrate how fixed and dynamic reminiscence function in a particular social setting (an urban senior center), noting how group dynamics, particularly gender dynamics, promote either set pieces or reflective pieces. From our data, we conclude that growth in old age requires both the ability to interact with and learn from diverse others and a willingness to engage in dynamic reminiscence. We conclude with implications for future research on written reminiscence.

Senior Writing Groups

We consider older adult writing groups to be perfect sites for the study of naturally occurring reminiscence. Unlike many reminiscence groups, which are structured as interventions by gerontologists who select participants and lead them through set periods of life (childhood, adolescence, adulthood), writing groups are created for the purpose of writing itself, membership is self-selected, and members typically generate their own topics. There is great interest among the current cohort of senior citizens (age sixty and over) in joining writing groups which emphasize life story, autobiography, memoir, and oral history. This interest is often gendered, raced, and classed: women are more likely to join than men; and white middle-class adults are more likely to join than minority and working class, although this is more likely due to lack of opportunity than to lack of interest (Ray, 2000). As feminists interested in studying all aspects of diversity, we were therefore most responsive to a request to develop a writing group at an inner-city senior center which serves primarily African-American elders. The center director, noting the fascinating oral reminiscences he had heard about life and times in the city, asked that we create a "Detroit Memories" group which would generate senior writings for publication on the center's website. The following analysis draws from the 1999 Detroit Memories group and a second group which formed the following summer as a result of enthusiastic response to the first. Data was collected among seniors who gathered at the center during July and August 1999 and 2000 to talk and write about their experiences living in and around Detroit. Three members from the 1999 group joined the 2000 group.

The Senior Memories Groups

Of the eleven participants in the 1999 writing group seven were African-American women, two were African-American men, and two were Caucasian women. Ages ranged from 65 through 86. Of the nine core participants of the 2000 group, 6 were African-American women, one was an African-American man, two were Caucasian women. Ages ranged from 66 through 80. Education among group members ranged from an eighth grade education to a doctoral degree.

During a typical meeting, participants shared writings produced during the session or at home. Although facilitators suggested prompts, participants were encouraged to follow their own interests. Readings were followed by spontaneous discussions where group members affirmed the value and importance of work brought to the group. Participant response to readings generally took the form of parallel stories, comments on ideas and values suggested by the writing, and discussions of related topics. Written pieces were autobiographical and often focused on youthful to middle-aged experiences connected to Detroit. Writers acknowledged racial and economic oppression, but in general represented their youth and the city as a good time and place to live.

This common vision of Detroit and its past provided an important point of contact across social difference. Through shared stories of place, participants articulated both personal and group identities and values. When Esta, the daughter of Polish immigrants who settled in nearby Hamtramck soon after the turn of the century, read a piece about the "schmakie"(junkman) driving his horse and wagon and tooting his tin horn to get people to come out and sell him their unwanted possessions, Mary and Hattie, African-American women who grew up in different areas, responded with stories which were both similar to and different from Esta's. Two other participants volunteered other names given to the junkman who came through their neighborhoods. Then, as a group, participants conjured a vivid image of the dirt side streets, the tired horse, and the wagon tumbling full of what any household could part with for the money it might bring. Generational values connected to frugality and the coherence of neighborhood were offered as commentary to this conversation. Through these stories, participants explored the differences between their values and experiences and those of their children and grandchildren.

While sharing stories which disclose intimate aspects of personal identity is in many ways characteristic of book groups and writing groups (Chandler, 2001; Ray, 2000), intimacy within the Senior Memories groups was particularly connected to generational identity, as well as shared memories of the city. Participants agreed they said things in this group which they could not say to their friends, to members of their church communities, or even to their families. Helen, a member of both the 1999 and 2000 groups, commented that talking to people her own age who didn't have fixed expectations of who she was made it easier to discuss some aspects of her life. Bessie, a participant in the 1999 group, made a similar observation. In a written reflection on her experience with the writing group, she says, "I feel very comfortable with a group of my senior peers. They seem to understand and know where I'm coming from. They don't prejudge or look down on me. . . . The kindness of this group of seniors—from a wide variety of backgrounds—has given me a gentler, kinder outlook on all people. Life's struggles know no color." Mary, a participant in the 2000 group put it simply: "After joining the Senior Memories group . . . I discovered an extended family with more similarities than differences."

Stories about place seemed the vehicle for building the trust and familiarity necessary for the more sensitive work of articulating, exploring, and reinterpreting the troubling and complex memories of personal relationships, particularly family relationships. We suggest that the particular nature of this group, with its focus on personal histories in and around Detroit, provided not only easy access to fixed reminiscences but also the kind of trust needed to generate dynamic reminiscences.

The Emotional Terrain of Fixed and Dynamic Reminiscence

At both the 1999 and 2000 groups, participants told stories of experiences with physical punishment at the hands of parents, of their own use of physical punishment in their roles as parents and teachers, and of the importance of physical punishment as a tool for instilling values and teaching appropriate behavior. Some stories allowed for collective contemplations of the ways physical confrontations may and may not be beneficial, while others did not.

The following discussion considers "Box Boy," a set piece told by one of two male participants in the 1999 group, and "Listening for the Light," a reflective piece told by the single male participant of the 2000 group. "Box Boy" alludes to violence between adults and children but does not generate discussion in which group members problematize or reflect upon the patterns it suggests. Rather, "Box Boy" stands as an articulation of a generational perspective regarding the importance of physical punishment as a means to discipline children. "Listening for the Light" deals with physical violence within families and frames the author's ongoing efforts to understand his relationship to his father. Though quite different in narrative form and content, both pieces offer only oblique allusions to the physical realities which drive their narration. Their focus seems to be on interpreting the complex emotional outcomes of physical confrontation between adults and children, rather than contesting circumstances and/or values which contribute to the physical punishment of children.

Conversation leading up to the first telling of "Box Boy" includes a series of stories about "discipline," particularly physical discipline imposed on participants by their parents. Bessie's story explicitly describes the meaning of "discipline" which is implicit to subsequent stories:

BESSIE: Well, my father, my stepfather worked afternoons so my mother was the disciplinarian. . . . And she would spank the old fashioned way. You'd have, she'd review what you had done. (In voice of mother) Do you remember? And then she might go back for two or three years looked like to me . . .

(laughter, talking)

BESSIE: Then she'd whip you a while. Then she'd talk a while. Then she'd whip you a while, and she had your head over the toilet so you're not going to spit up on her, you know? I don't go for that . . .

(laughing)

MARTIN: . . . and by the time he [gets done] putting it on you, boy, you have a whole lot to think about, maybe for a week (describing a beating by father)

(agreement, laughing, yeah, mm-hm)

MARTIN: . . . and in my neighborhood if I did anything wrong . . .

(voices mm-hm)

MARTIN: . . . the neighbor would . . .

(voices mm-hm, that's right)

MARTIN: . . . fetch you, switch your butt and send you home and call down, and tell your parents what you did [and] you got another whipping coming . . .

(voices, that's right).

The laughing and voices which accompany Bessie's narration indicate that her whipping was not viewed as abusive, but endorsed as a necessary strategy—shared by parents and neighbors—for shaping children into responsible adults. Head nodding and expressions of assent accompanying Martin's story indicate that disciplining neighborhood children was a commonly accepted practice within the communities where participants grew up.

These stories are followed by a brief discussion of generational differences in attitude toward physical punishment. Maggie's comment sums up perspectives expressed in conversation which follows participant testimonials regarding their childhood experiences.

> MAGGIE: The thing is, the thing of it is that we hear now how [whipping is] bad for children. They have to find their own way. (in mocking voice) They mustn't be punished or they'll have a bad attitude, of themselves. The people here, every one of us has been brought up under the same discipline.

Maggie's comments are followed by two stories, one by Bessie and one by Martin, in which the narrators are no longer on the receiving end of whippings. In these stories narrators report being favorably remembered as "disciplinarians." As in earlier stories, these narratives emphasize respect for strictness. Bessie concludes that "sometimes we learn more from a lesson of pain than from a nice compliment." At the close of Bessie's story, Martin tells "Box Boy," which affirms the importance of discipline.

> MARTIN: . . . I had ah, a nice experience, that ha, there's un, [a place] down on Erskine and on Friday evenings they ah, they, it's ah fish dinner that you could come by, come by free, and ah I happened to drop by about six or seven years back, happened to walk in, and ah, young man came up to me says, "Hi, Mr. C. . . . You don't remember me?" "No." "My name is Jim, Jim Dale." Said, "You coached me little league football." "Well, I probably coached 10 thousand kids. I really don't, you know, I don't want you to ah, hold that against [me]. You have to realize that I, all of you, like it's hard to remember everybody that you've had." He says, "You don't remember me? You used to call me Box Boy." Oh, my God, and I immediately remembered. He's he's an engineer now. And ah, person I was with he said, "Well, how did you remember when he said 'Box Boy'?" Well, there was, two little youngsters. Every kid that come out to play little league football, they want to play football. Parents want to get rid of them so they can breathe for a

while, and he, and another little kid would sit on the sideline, and they'd throw pebbles back and forth at one another. They just sat down and threw pebbles at one another. And you just block them out of your mind, all right? But any time somebody got hurt, immediately when somebody got hurt, [this one] was the first on the field with the first aid kit, so I named him Box Boy.

(laughing)

MARTIN: And, you know, thirty years later, he walked up to me. "You were such a disciplinarian, and if it hadn't been for you and your regimentive ways, I never would have finished college." And it's that time that you know, tears start to form all inside of you . . .

(voices, oh yeah, yes)

MARTIN: . . . and you say, well, maybe I have done something worthwhile. And it's those kinds of things that ha, you have to say . . . it's a continuing thing, you're continuously giving and . . .

FRANCIE: . . . you don't know where your influence is going . . .

In many ways, "Box Boy" draws together and validates perspectives expressed in the stories which precede it. Martin offers an example of a young man who has grown into a responsible adult, presumably as a result of the kind of discipline provided by Martin's generation. After several brief comments which reprise the beauty of discovering positive effects of your actions years after the fact, conversation shifts to a new topic. "Box Boy" serves to validate and summarize the group's views on discipline.

Martin tells this same story, in nearly the same form and language, two weeks later in the writing group. As in the case of the first telling, conversation preceding the second telling includes comments about the younger generation. It contains themes connected to the importance of limits and self control, and directly challenges the younger generation's transgression of those limits. Martin's second narration is the second half of an extended monologue in which he tells two "success" stories connected to his role as "disciplinarian." As with the first telling, Martin uses the story as an example of positive results which accrue from adult mentoring of young people. The connection between "discipline" and "success" is made in the story's introduction where the word "disciplinarian" resonates with the "whippings" described by both Bessie and Martin earlier in the conversation.

Following Martin's reprise of the positive results of discipline, Maggie returns to issues connected to generational difference ("a lot of young people growing up today don't get a positive approach") and offers a brief statement about the need for discipline, particularly self-discipline. When Bessie comments that discipline needs to start in the home, Maggie replies that "[if] you can't control yourself, you can't control anybody else." At this point, the conversation moves on to a new topic connected to mentoring.

On both narrative occasions, "Box Boy" was the final story told in a discussion centered on discipline and generational difference. It summarized a perspective which seemed to be held in common by group members but contested outside the group, specifically by the current generation of parents. It emphasized the positive effects of discipline by presenting an example of a young person subjected to "discipline" who had grown into an adult and become a success. At the same time, this story deemphasized the physical harshness which in some ways was emphasized in the first set of introductory stories.

Both tellings of "Box Boy" are characterized by detailed description, dialogue, and a narrative gloss which "explains" the story's content. Both have an introduction which sets the stage, a middle section in which the drama develops, and a conclusion which overtly states the "moral" of the story. While other set pieces told in the writing groups were neither so formulaic in structure nor so definite in function, set pieces tend to have a "message" which unfolds in terms of a completely articulated storyline. Set pieces are composed of sections of dialog, description, and exposition, all of which are narrated in more or less the same way at each telling. When told by older adults to younger adults or children, or to an audience presumed to hold values and experiences different from the narrator's, set pieces serve as vehicles for teaching and giving advice. For example, Alex, a member of both the 1999 and 2000 writing groups, told a set piece about his son "David the Terrible" to both writing groups, to a group of peers at an orientation for a related project, and to a mixed group of seniors and college students. In this story, Alex tells how he called his son "David the Terrible," only to reveal later that he had given him this nickname because he thought of David as "terribly smart." In each case the story was told to explain adults' power in labeling their children and to convey the message that what might seem to be a destructive label can be subverted and redirected to empower a person.

Unlike "David the Terrible," "Box Boy" was told among peers in both instances. It does not seem to function so much as a didactic story, but as an expression of generational values, as well as a validation of the narrator's positive influence on younger generations. Parallel stories told about "whipping" and group response to "Box Boy's" performance suggest that this story functions to articulate and validate individual and group values regarding discipline. That is, "Box Boy" summarizes and consolidates already established beliefs.

At the same time, even though "Box Boy" may in many ways be an accurate articulation of group values, the group may have felt some ambivalence about the story's message. More than half the participants did not tell their own "whipping" stories, and some did not endorse others' stories by nodding, smiling, or vocalizing. This suggests that, although a set piece may express a group perspective, the story can still be received in multiple ways, and participants may hold complex, perhaps conflicted positions regarding its message, however unarticulated. Some of the more unresolved aspects of participant responses to physical confrontations between parents and children emerged in the construction of Alex's reflective story, "Listening for the Light."

Unlike set pieces, reflective stories tend to take form through a series of retellings where details emerge gradually. Successive versions are often more detailed and troubling than earlier versions. Analysis of "Looking for the Light" illustrates how group response influenced subsequent versions of the story.

Alex, who participated in both the 1999 and 2000 Detroit Memories writing groups, works part time and is active with his church and the Boy Scouts of America. As a result of his busy professional and personal life, he attended only the two last meetings of the 1999 sessions, and missed two of the six meetings during the summer of 2000. Despite irregular attendance, Alex's charm and openness immediately won him a place in the group. The first meeting he attended in 1999 was the penultimate session. During this meeting he sat quietly and listened as others read and talked. At his second meeting, which was the last session in the series, Alex spoke at length about his life. His talk was animated and punctuated by repeated comments of "I've had a wonderful life, a wonderful life." He remarked appreciatively about the group's attention, and noted that he valued what group members could offer one another.

ALEX: [I think] . . . the best of the hardship and maybe that's the greatest thing that we have, each other. That we we have some insight, we have some insight, and ah, I I'm glad to see that there's some kind of ah structure, systematic way that we're going to be passing on some of this wherever we live or have lived, ah whoever we are, because there are commonalities to the journey. Well, thank you. (Alex laughs)

(clapping)

FRANCIE: Alex, I like your attitude.
ALEX: (unintelligible)
Bessie: Yes, yes.
ALEX: Thank you.
MAGGIE: I think half the problem is, everybody has (laughing quietly) bruises . . .
ELLA: I'd like to say it's—it's good to hear you say that it's a wonderful time to live . . .
MARTIN: Ah, you know, I like that, too . . .

This conversation characterizes Alex's interactions with the group. He has a gift for casting life in positive and constructive ways. His openness and enthusiasm invite other participants to reflect upon their lives in similar ways, and his combination of curiosity and excitement helps group members explore material which might be overwhelming or discouraging if considered in a more negative or conclusive manner. Alex reflects upon life's "challenges" by saying, "I've lived long enough and know enough [to know] that there's a special blessing in difficulties." The group responds to Alex's brave gesture to engage unresolved issues by sharing resonant stories of their own. It is this kind of dynamic which nourishes the elusive seeds that mature into reflective stories. These seeds are cast with great frequency and, as with literal seeds, only a few develop to maturity. The fruit borne by an incipient story depends upon the ground which receives it.

A particularly striking example of a narrative seed which took root and flourished was Alex's reflection on his problematic relationship with his father. He eventually consolidates these reminiscences into a written piece entitled "Listening for the Light." The title refers to Alex's experience as a child in the dark of his bedroom, awaiting the homecoming of his absent father, Amos Ware. Throughout Alex's childhood, Mr. Ware was in and out of the veterans' hospital. Alex repeatedly told the group that he never knew when his father would be coming home, or when he would leave. A striking dimension of Alex's written narrative is his empathetic and loving exploration of how Amos Ware might feel within this difficult situation. Unlike a set piece, where the "moral" of the story is known from the outset, Alex's dynamic reminiscence remains speculative, and seems to develop through partial tellings which are shaped into coherent narratives only through interactive group response. Reflective pieces continue to evolve even when they are presented in written form. Alex has talked with one of the authors and other members of the group since composing the "final" version, and his feelings are still evolving.

The 1999 group was presented the "seed" of "Listening for the Light" in Alex's rambling self-introduction. Alex speaks of a childhood where he was "raised with both parents, although my father was ill for 30 years and unemployed, and my mother worked as a domestic." In this introductory narrative he talks of his first marriage and divorce; the way his world was opened through his education at Wayne State University; his time in the army; his career as an educator, a teacher, a principal, and a superintendent of schools; his interests in scouting and piano; and his abiding determination to press the limits imposed by cultural prejudice. He briefly alludes to his father through a series of contrasts to explain what it was that set him up to seek out challenges: "My father never did read and write. Ah I have a doctorate from the University of Michigan. We ah my father had that bad health. I've never had a health problem." Immediately after defining himself as distinct from his father, Alex offers a direct statement of his father's positive influences: ". . . he taught me how to cope with it [bad health] and how to make something of it. He taught me how to care for the children, and how to shake them down." Together, this series of observations suggests the "seed" for Alex's reflective story. It expresses the conflicting impulses toward the man who was both present and not present in his childhood, the father who had qualities which Alex both emulated and rejected. These statements, however, remain buried inside the more fixed reminiscence about successful triumph over hardship, which is the framework for Alex's personal introduction.

At informal discussions following that meeting, stories regarding Alex's father acquired more details. Through these discussions we learned that his father's illness was tuberculosis, that he was often absent from home, and that his returns were unexpected and in some ways, disruptive. As the 1999 writing group drew to a close, these details remained vague and tantalizing, but group members did not ask direct questions. As was the case with other reminiscences which "suggested" but did not reveal more complicated stories, participants listened with interest and respectful silence as they took in what Alex chose to tell, but they did not press for explanations or justification.

The following summer, Alex attended the second writing group, which had a rotating attendance of perhaps 7 members who came to several meetings but not to all meetings, and a core membership of 9. Three of these members, including Alex, had participated in the writing group from the previous summer. At the first meeting of the year 2000 group, Alex again alluded to his father's absences and illness. His talk was characteristically positive and autobiographical, but the allusions to his father's illness and Alex's conflicted feelings about the unexpected returns were more definite than they had been the previous year. He stated directly that his father would be absent, sometimes for more than a year. He said that Amos Ware's returns were "always unannounced, and always at night." He mentioned how he recognized the sound of his father's step and the opening of the door. Group members received this information attentively and asked no questions.

This lack of questioning did not indicate lack of interest. At lunch following this meeting, four female group members talked at length about what it might mean that Alex's father returned unannounced after long absences, wondering aloud, "How could he just come and go like that? How could Alex not know when he was coming back?" When it was suggested that his father must have been "up to something," someone hypothesized that the absences were connected to being hospitalized for tuberculosis. This sent discussion in another direction, but the women remained doubtful about a family relationship where the father left and returned unannounced.

Alex missed the next meeting but returned the following week. He again talked about his father's absences and returns. In this conversation, it was as if everyone, Alex included, had been considering this improbable story line during the intervening weeks. No sooner had Alex mentioned that he never knew when his father would come home than one of the women from the lunch group suggested that maybe *he didn't know* when his father would return, but perhaps *his mother did.* This comment cast the story in a different light for the whole group. In discussion which followed, Alex again told how his father always seemed to return at night and at about the same hour. He provided more details about his father's illness: Amos Ware was periodically hospitalized when the tuberculosis became active. Alex speculated that there might be a particular release time at the sanitorium and that the public transportation schedule might have made it so that he returned at the same time.

The group gradually shifts from unraveling the mysteries of Amos Ware's departures and returns to more general discussion of relationships between parents and children. In this context, Alex describes how he and his sister Yvette learned to "stay out of his father's way." He tells a story about chasing down the street to the library with his sister, running and dodging carelessly from street to curb and how, when his father came into their presence, they immediately stopped. He mentions briefly and allusively that most children are "afraid of fathers" and tells how he received a sudden and severe physical reprimand from his father which made "the lights go out." Stories told in response report others' experiences of physical discipline. These stories are neither so graphic nor unequivocal as stories told in the 1999 group. Rather, they are tempered by the uncertainty and fear implicit to Alex's story. Although most of the stories told at this particular meeting could be interpreted as supporting physical punishment of children, the fear, confusion, and resentment implicit in Alex's story of "the lights going out" is reflected in participant comments.

The juxtaposition of Alex's story of unanticipated comings and goings with stories about physical punishment and comments about children's fear of their fathers, illustrates how group dynamics can recast a story which has been told the same way many times—an important and underexamined area of reminiscence research. As this meeting begins, Alex has told the set piece of his father's unexpected return at least three times. It is group response which turns his fixed reminiscence into something more dynamic. Open questions posed by group members lead Alex back into the story with a slightly altered perspective. Group members' stories of their own related experiences reiterate themes from Alex's story and function as implicit commentary upon it. The interactions set up through questioning and telling parallel stories serve both to validate and complicate Alex's original perspective. Differences among particular narratives offered in response suggest, but do not explicitly define, alternative interpretations within Alex's unfolding story.

It is also at this meeting that Alex tells the group of his first defiance of his father. In a particularly moving story, Alex describes the time in late adolescence when he and his father were walking together to visit relatives. Alex intentionally and relentlessly picked up the pace until Amos, who was a sick man, had to ask him to slow down. Alex places his hand over his heart as he tells us that it was "like a blow" to him when his father was forced to say, "Son, please slow down." When a group member suggests that Alex might have mixed feelings about that experience, that it might have been both a blow and a triumph, Alex emphatically replies that it was not a triumph: he felt terrible and was deeply sad and ashamed at what he had done.

Alex's defiance story links discipline, violence, and independence to the earlier story of his father's illness and separation from the family. In both stories, the family repeatedly defines and redefines itself as both dominated by a father and without a father. The stories of "the lights going out" and of Alex picking up the pace suggest an impulse to "leave" his father. They connect to themes of individuation, physical violence, and the father-son relationship embedded in Alex's initial self-presentation at the first writing group. This talk contained the "seed" of the story of him and Yvette (unnamed in the first telling) running in the street. In the previous year's version, Alex says, "He was the one when I was going to—my sister and I were going to the library off on Woodward—when we got to running into the street and playing, ah, tag and just having a grand old time, and we happened to look over our shoulder and who was just slowly walking with his hands behind his back but Amos Ware. Didn't have to say anything, ha." The story told in the second year about "the lights going out," including Alex's observations about children being afraid of their fathers, supplements and explains the earlier version. Together the two versions suggest that it was not only Amos Ware's presence and his role as a father, but the possibility of physical consequences established through earlier encounters which gave him the ability to halt his children's game of tag without saying a word.

Group members respond to Alex's reminiscences with questions, hypotheses, and stories of their own. Included in these responses are group reprises of fixed reminiscences quite similar to those generated by "Box Boy." What is different, however, is an ambivalence about and personalization of the possible "meanings" of Alex's story. Despite efforts to generate a group perspective, the evolution of "Listening for the Light" is recognized as clearly belonging to Alex. Parallel stories offered in response to Alex's stories about his father are often introduced with qualifications about being "the way it was for me." These stories generally offer the narrators' unresolved experiences with parents which are related to, but distinctly different from, what had been experienced by Alex. Like the stories about discipline offered in response to Alex's first story about the lights going out, these stories about parents and children suggest alternative interpretations of Alex's relationship to his father.

At the final meeting of the 2000 writing group, we discussed the writings to be printed on the senior center website. Alex said he had nothing to submit at this point, but he wanted to write a piece entitled "Listening for the Light." In addition, he expands upon earlier versions by commenting on his childish fears connected to the "commotion" from the next room. "And what do you think they were doing?" he asks us, laughing. "What do you think they were doing?" When a group member suggests they were making love, he laughs and says, "They were making love, but as a child I had no idea. I had no idea."

We are told that the young Alex interpreted the sounds of lovemaking as sounds of his father hurting his mother. This directs group response both to childhood efforts to interpret parental actions for which they did not have sufficient maturity or information, and to adult re-considerations of interpretations formed at younger ages. One participant picks up on the theme by telling a story about her father touching her breasts when she was an adolescent. Like Alex, she presents her original interpretation as no longer valid and reframes that interpretation with "what I know now."

This particular group contemplation of Amos Ware's long absences and disruptive returns takes place through a perspective which moves back and forth between the child and the adult who experienced the situation. As we consider Amos Ware's behavior from the perspective of a child, the departures feel like abandonment and loss. When we look at these same departures as adults and parents, someone suggests that perhaps leaving his children was the most difficult thing Alex's father ever did; that his leaving was to protect his loved ones from disease; and that the departures and the returns together were a single expression of Amos's devotion to his family. While this may not have been the first time this interpretation had occurred to Alex, it may have been the first time it was said out loud and in a group. What in solitary reflection might have felt like wishful thinking may have for the first time taken on the feeling of truth. This was an intensely emotional moment for everyone in the group. In the midst of stories about parents whose actions had been interpreted as "damaging" or "thoughtless" from childhood perspectives, but which had proved to be only human or even wise as the children grew older, Alex was momentarily speechless.

The possibility that abundant and abiding love may be unnoticed or misinterpreted was not overtly articulated in Alex's early stories about his father. Rather, this possibility posed itself gradually as his story unfolded and is articulated as "truth" in the written version. In "Listening for the Light," Alex's belief in his father's love is repeated like the refrain to a song. The second, third, and fourth paragraphs of Alex's final written version conclude with "He loved us . . . ," "He loved us," and "Yet he loved his children." Group response to Alex's ongoing reflections about his father helped to confirm and extend Alex's contemplation of fatherly love.

While this may seem like the resolution to Alex's story, it is not. Connections to violence and resentment remain present and unresolved in the final written version, where Alex alludes to Amos Ware's cruelty to his wife. In a conversation after the piece was completed, Alex commented that he had not yet explored in detail "that my father beat my mother." It remains a very real possibility that as writing group meetings continue, such explorations will take place, particularly because violence within families has been an oblique focus of stories from numerous participants, and telling these stories has allowed the narrators to acknowledge these experiences publicly.

As Alex put it, coming to the group was important to him because it "provided validation of what it is to be human. . . . You find out that other people share your experience." This sharing allows for "more opening up," particularly when related to issues culturally burdened with shame, and is facilitated by honest and positive narrators such as Alex and by supportive group dynamics.

Through our observations and discourse analysis of senior writing groups, we conclude that the gradual introduction of sensitive materials through repeated retellings, group responses which explore embedded material through oblique rather than direct questioning, and the telling of parallel stories which suggest a new "twist" on the current version of a reflective story, all lead to adult development through narrative. These occasions function to push stories forward, creating group interactions which both validate and question an unfolding story as "the truth," yet incomplete. All group members benefit from a reflective story, for it prompts listeners to fill in what is missing by reflecting on their own experience. Stories in which listener experiences were fundamentally the same on a human level, yet also laden with social differences (race, class, gender, family status), seemed to present the most productive opportunities for dynamic reminiscence.

Final Thoughts and New Directions

Lest the reader think the analysis of reminiscence a simple matter, we now turn to the complexities in our own conclusion. First, fixed and dynamic reminiscence are not static categories. A reflective story may at some point become a set piece, and a set piece is always potentially reflective. Whether or not a set piece becomes a reflective story seems both highly dependent upon the context of the telling and on the teller's level of comfort with both listeners and the material under discussion. For example, in a luncheon conversation, Martin told a story which cast doubt on his unequivocal position regarding the importance of physical discipline. While this conversation did not include another performance of "Box Boy," it did reframe "Box Boy"'s central theme, namely Martin's certainty and pride in his use of physical force to ensure compliance with certain standards of behavior. The story told in this conversation, rather than expressing moral certainty, opened painful questions about the negative consequences of using physical force to make smaller, weaker people do as they are told.

Further, fixed and dynamic reminiscence are clearly influenced by gender dynamics in writing groups. While men and women engage in both types of reminiscence, the men in our groups engaged in more extended periods of talk, and their stories were therefore more likely to garner the sustained group attention, questioning, and promptings toward self-reflection that promote dynamic reminiscence. This point merits some discussion.

Although women far outnumbered men in both writing groups, the men constituted a much larger "presence" than their numbers implied, largely because of their conversational style. At the meeting where he first told "Box Boy," Martin engaged in thirteen periods of extended talk, while Bessie, the next most frequent speaker, engaged in eight. (An extended period of talk is a story or comment which is uninterrupted in terms of subject continuity and which consists of eight or more lines in a written transcript.) At the same meeting, Martin contributed 45 instances of simultaneous speech, short questions, and comments, while Bessie contributed 71. (See Coates, 1988 and Tannen, 1994 for gendered analyses of simultaneous speech.) If the kinds of "short comments" contributed by Martin and Bessie are categorized as comments to support or enhance another speaker's talk (mm hm; oh yeah, we all sang; that's right; oh, definitely) and as "interruptions" which provide a different perspective or change topics, Bessie offers more supportive comments than does Martin, who tends to introduce new topics which lead to narration of his own stories. What is more, women in the group who were not as conversationally active as Bessie contributed an even higher percentage of supporting comments. At the meeting where Martin first tells "Box Boy," for example, more than two thirds of Helen's short comments were directed toward acknowledging and supporting other speakers. This finding is not surprising. We already know from the discourse analysis literature on both informal conversation and group talk that women engage more frequently in supportive commentary than men. While men's informal conversation typically focuses on information-giving and topic-shifting, women's focuses on metamessages (the meanings that underlie a statement of information) and the emotional content of talk (Bergman & Surrey, 1997; Canary, Emmers-Sommer, & Faulkner, 1997; Hochschild, 1990; Tannen, 1986). What we don't know is how these distinct conversational styles influence the content and purpose of reminiscence or their effects on adult development. On the basis of our evidence to date, we suggest that gender differences actually enhance emotional development in mixed-gender groups.

Women, too, engage in dynamic reminiscence, but not by holding the floor in the ways men do, and not always in the presence of men. The richest example of dynamic reminiscence told by a woman was offered at the second writing group and was contemplated primarily in sessions which Alex did not attend. What is more, the woman's reflective story began as part of a luncheon conversation, a more intimate and private setting, and was slowly developed within the group. It followed the same general patterns of development as Alex's story, although the audio tapes do not reveal an instance of Alex contributing to this story's development. We don't yet know whether, how, or to what extent men's conversational style contributes to women's dynamic reminiscence, nor do we know how race or ethnicity factors into these gendered interactions (see Webster, chapter 9, this volume).

Ultimately, of course, we need to conduct more research to determine the multiple social as well as psychological influences on fixed and dynamic reminiscence. To understand fully what can and cannot be said in communal settings, and to what developmental ends, we need more ethnographic studies of reminiscence groups which explore the many factors related to group dynamics (including subgroups within groups, as in the luncheon conversations) and the ways individual personality and storytelling styles influence the formation of group personalities and styles of talking and writing. Group interactions surrounding particular stories seem to be influenced greatly by narrative style, as in Alex's case; by the depth of participants' feelings about the subject matter; and by group perception of a prevailing cultural norm regarding the material under discussion, as in the case of "Box Boy." Factors which drive these dynamics are complex and could be greatly elucidated by qualitative research that is sensitive to the nuances of meaning-making in diverse settings.

A central research agenda for the future is to document group situations which foster dynamic reminiscence. We believe that personal change and continued growth throughout the life course require a willingness to engage with others who are both similar to and different from oneself. Engagement with difference broadens the self-concept and deepens understanding and appreciation of others. Such engagement occurs most easily when the "other" is seen, like the self, as a person "in progress," even in late life. Anthropologist Mary Catherine Bateson (2000), through her ethnographic study of an intergenerational women's study group, explains this aspect of development: "The strangeness of others is most off-putting when it is experienced as static, most approachable when it is set within a narrative of continuing development" (p. 5). This is perhaps the best argument for the value of dynamic reminiscence: as a developmental narrative, it helps us accept, with patience, humor and hope, the "strangeness" of others—and ourselves.

6

Reframing Reminiscence as a Cognitive-Linguistic Phenomenon

Joyce L. Harris and Michele L. Norman

C an the human brain differentiate clinical reminiscence, moored in the tradition of adaptive human development, from other types of memory anchored firmly in cognitive psychology? Perhaps a more scientifically interesting question is: Can we fully understand reminiscence, devoid of its cognitive-communicative essence? We believe that the answer in either case is a resounding "no." And therefore it is singularly ironic that, in general, reminiscence experts have outstripped the ability of the human brain by effectively dissociating reminiscence from its cognitive-linguistic foundation (cf., Bluck & Alea, this volume). Instead, research attention has focused primarily on the adaptive qualities of reminiscence that become increasingly more prevalent in advanced age (Birren & Deutchman, 1991; Haight & Webster, 1995; Hyland & Ackerman, 1988). Such a concentrated focus virtually ignores the cognitive-communicative processes that enable the retrieval and conversion of a personal past into a linguistic code. Fortunately, bypassed opportunities for more comprehensive investigations of reminiscence are redeemable in that new research prospects abound. The challenge of reframing reminiscence as a cognitive-linguistic phenomenon promises to extend and illuminate what we already know, as well as validate the place of reminiscence in the realm of cognitive scientific inquiry.

In this chapter, we propose that the continuing advancement of reminiscence science will depend largely on situating reminiscence research within the context of cognitive psychology, perhaps more specifically within the area of cognitive aging. Only then will *all* dimensions of reminiscence be fully available for investigation. Theories of cognitive aging promise to invigorate research by suggesting new hypotheses, research paradigms, and models that more accurately reflect the cognitive-linguistic complexities of reminiscence behavior.

We begin the chapter with a general overview of cognitive aging, believing that this discussion provides a context for understanding the mechanisms of reminiscence behavior in older adults. We then move to a brief discussion of memory processes, particularly those that are most prominently activated in the recall and expression of remote personal events. Next, we provide an overview of communication changes in aging, focusing attention on verbal expressive communication. Finally, we discuss the manifested convergence of memory and language as the essence of reminiscence behavior, and end the chapter with implications for clinical practice and future directions for research.

Mechanisms of Cognitive Aging

In psychology, *cognitive aging* is the specialty area that investigates what happens to cognitive systems as human beings age (Park, 2000). Although losses associated with advanced age are well documented, cognitive aging researchers (e.g., Rogers, Fisk, & Walker, 1996) now are turning their attention to preserved cognitive abilities in aging, particularly those most closely aligned with functional independence. Nevertheless, the existence of age-related decrements in cognitive abilities cannot be easily ignored. The most prevalent explanations for characteristic performance differences between younger and older adults center on reduced cognitive processing capacity and efficiency in old age (Park & Schwart, 2000).

Generalized slowing of the speed with which mental operations are performed is believed to be at the root of age-related decrements in memory, reasoning, and other kinds of cognitive tasks (Zacks, Hasher, & Li, 2000). The disadvantage that older adults experience is exaggerated in tasks that are more complex. In general, slower neurochemical activation reflects biological slowing throughout the central nervous system. For example, Salthouse (1996) suggested that older adults are slow to perform cognitive tasks because earlier steps in complex task-sequences clog the system, making the products of the earlier task, or the cognitive resources for processing subsequent steps, unavailable. This *speed of processing* hypothesis seems to hold up as an explanation of performance age variance whenever researchers analyze tests of individual differences between younger and older adults across behavioral domains.

Processing capacity explanations, on the other hand, suggest that performance age differences result from a reduction in cognitive resources in aging (e.g., Craik & Jennings, 1994; Park & Schwart, 2000). The presumed reduction of cognitive resources refers to a lessened ability to perform necessary mental operations for effective information processing. Thus, relative to young adults, older adults have more difficulty processing sentences with complex syntax (Bayles & Kaszniak, 1987), comprehending the relationship between pronouns and their referents (Morrow, Altieri, & Leirer, 1992), and comprehending proposition-dense sentences (Stine & Wingfield, 1990).

Working memory, a psychological construct that describes simultaneous short-term information storage and processing (Baddeley & Hitch, 1974), is the cognitive resource presumed responsible for many of the observed age differences in processing capacity (e.g., Craik & Jennings, 1994; Zacks, Hasher, & Li, 2000). Tasks such as digit span, sentence span, and computation span reveal age-related deficits that become increasingly evident as tasks more heavily tax working memory (Haberlandt, 1999; Light, 1996). For example, simple digit span is less impaired than computation span, which is a more complex cognitive task. Perhaps the increased cognitive load not only results from decreased processing capacity, but also from older adults' reduced ability to eliminate or ignore irrelevant information during task performance. Irrelevant information causes mental clutter, which overtaxes the working memory system (Light, 1996; Zacks, Hasher, & Li, 2000).

Working memory is also conceptualized as a buffer in which units of meaning are stored in short-term memory long enough for a reader or listener to derive meaning coherence between preceding and incoming information (Kintsch & van Dijk, 1978). The supposition that comprehension is dependent on working memory's storage and processing components is reflected in the work of Daneman and Carpenter (1980) who stated: ". . . in reading comprehension, the reader must store pragmatic, semantic, and syntactic information from the preceding text and use it for disambiguating, parsing, and integrating the subsequent text" (p. 459). Working memory capacity is assumed to be diminished in older adults (Zacks, Hasher, & Li, 2000; Luscz & Bryan, 1999). Tun and Wingfield (1997) suggested that relative to written text, spoken language comprehension more heavily taxes working memory. Unlike written language, spoken language is often more poorly structured, and has to be processed online, often under less than ideal listening conditions.

It may be that speed of processing and working memory are not constructs that engage the attention of reminiscence researchers, unless, of course, an elicitation task is timed or requires simultaneous encoding

and manipulation of information. In either case, one might expect to
see age-related differences in response to the elicitation stimulus. The
extent of cognitive aging's influence on reminiscence behavior has yet
to be determined. A life span approach to reminiscence research
promises to clarify the ways in which age mediates reminiscence
(Webster, 1999). In the next section, we briefly discuss basic cognitive
processes underlying the storage and retrieval of memories.

Encoding. Encoding is the process that involves the conversion of
sensory information for storage in memory. An experienced event is
typically characterized by spatial and temporal features, as well as by
other unique attributes (Tulving, 1972). These attributes are organized
and coded for storage in a manner that distinguishes them from similar
information that was encoded earlier. To-be-remembered information
is associated with preexisting general knowledge that comprises
semantic memory, maintaining the distinctive properties of new information (Haberlandt, 1999; Tulving, 1972). Semantic memory is the
term used to designate cognitive representations of concepts, schema-
ta, and world knowledge. How deeply a new experience is encoded is
dependent in part on attention and intention (Klatsky, 1988). That is,
conscious attention to an event may more deeply encode all of its
attributes than the attributes of an event given less attention (Craik &
Lockhart, 1972; Metcalfe, Mencl, & Cottrell, 1994).

Retrieval. The manner in which information is encoded also facilitates its retrieval from memory (Tulving, 1972). That is, the organization of memory traces, based on their stored attributes, facilitates the
retrieval of a particular memory. For example, memories of self within
the context of an event are also stored as an integral part of an episode.
In conjunction with spatial and temporal referents, memories of self are
encoded, organized, and associated with preexisting information. Yet,
these memories of self maintain distinctive properties allowing the
recall of specific episodes.

Retrieval processes. Retrieval of information from long-term memory
involves mentally searching through stored representations of experiences to find those that are associated with particular information (Reiser,
Black, & Kalamarides, 1986). The primary retrieval processes, *recognition* and *recall,* undergo differential age-related decline (Parkin, 1993),
meaning that older adults do not perform comparably on these tasks.
    Older adults are likely to have less difficulty with recognition memory
than recall memory tasks. A recognition task involves remembering
previously presented stimuli in the presence of new stimuli (Bayles &

Kaszniak, 1987). Recognition tasks are relatively less challenging, because, like a true-false question test, the correct answer is provided explicitly, but in the presence of one or more foils. The task then becomes one of discrimination. Recall, on the other hand, requires the recollection of previously encoded memory representations either with or without external cues. To continue the educational analogy, recall tasks are like the dreaded essay question, which requires the generation of a correct response with few, if any, supporting cues. Like many students, older adults are more likely to have a difficulty with recall tasks. The age-related dichotomy between *free* and *cued recall* is somewhat analogous.

In *cued recall,* an external stimulus triggers a recollection. The cue can be a word, picture, object, sound, smell, or any intentional sensory stimulus. To be effective, a cue must have a preexisting association with the target memory representation, or must have been stored with the target at the time of encoding (Metcalf, Mencl, & Cottrell, 1994). Cued recall protocols are commonly used to elicit reminiscences, as cues may be selected to explicitly evoke memories about personal past experiences.

Free recall refers to self-initiated retrieval from memory, and is more vulnerable to the effects of aging than cued recall (Haberlandt, 1999; Kausler, 1994; Zacks, Hasher, & Li, 2000). Tasks involving free recall require self-activation of memory representations of previously experienced events without the assistance of externally supplied cues. Free recall requires greater cognitive processing resources, resulting in older adults' poorer performance (Craik & Jennings, 1994; Park, Nisbett, & Hedden, 1999). In experimentally manipulated conditions, cognitive support is provided in the form of an associative cue, such as a category label (e.g., furniture) to evoke list generation.

Consideration of recall processes makes it clear that all reminiscence tasks are not created equal. Park, Nisbett, and Hedden (1999) state that "cued recall is intermediate between free recall and recognition in effort and cognitive resources" (p. P80). In other words, more cognitive resources and effort are required as one moves from recognition to free recall. Although spontaneous reminiscence may be less demanding than free recall, it may be more cognitively demanding than either recognition or cued recall. Whether evoked spontaneously, clinically, or experimentally, the cognitive cost imposed by reminiscence is unclear. Nevertheless, the allocation of cognitive resources would seem to be an important consideration when studying reminiscence behavior across the adult life span.

Implicit versus explicit memory.   Schacter (1996) described implicit memory as the unconscious comparison of a previously encountered situation to a current one. Explicit memory, on the other hand, is intentional and at the level of consciousness. Explicit memory tasks result in marked age-related performance deficits (Kausler, 1994), with older adults having more difficulty with explicit, as opposed to implicit, memory tasks (Haberlandt, 1999; Zachs, Hasher, & Li, 2000). For example, performance differences between younger and older adults have been observed in word recognition and cued recall tasks, which activate explicit memory. In certain situations, however, slight age-differences in implicit memory have been observed, such as when the task also requires the activation of explicit memory (Kausler, 1994; Parkin, 1993). Generally, however, explicit memory declines and implicit memory remains relatively intact, except when influenced by the deficits in explicit memory.

Expressive Language in Aging

Reminiscence behavior provides communication sciences and disorders researchers with a window on the intersection between memory and discourse-level expressive communication (Harris, 1997). Communication in aging research documents the influences of cognitive aging on language production. Older adults undergo changes in language production as a result of normal aging; however, these changes cause less functional impairment than age-related decrements in memory and comprehension. Nevertheless, at the single-word level, decreases in lexical access, or retrieval of specific words from long-term memory, result in increased word finding problems and picture naming errors. Lexical retrieval deficits also manifest as decreased word production during priming and verbal fluency tasks (e.g., Kausler, 1994; Light, 1992). Despite some age-related changes in language production ability, many expressive language abilities remain intact, and, in fact, may increase during maturation.

For example, despite an increase in naming errors and word finding problems, vocabulary *increases* across the adult life span (Light, 1992). Likewise, performance during word association tasks, free and controlled, remains comparable across age groups, providing another example of how cued word retrieval, as opposed to free recall, remains relatively spared in old age. Because most word association tasks elicit automatic responses, it is conceivable that performance on these kinds of tasks is spared because the underlying process is spared. That automatic processes are spared may explain why word association ability resists deterioration in aging (Kausler, 1994).

Discourse, or connected speech, is the unit of analysis that most interests reminiscence researchers, because instantiation of recalled episodes from a personal past requires discourse-level language production. It is here that discourse analytical procedures can best inform reminiscence researchers about the quality of expressed reminiscence. Although there seem to be few age-related changes in concept formation, particularly relative to familiar information, there are other cognitive-linguistic changes in advanced age. For example, verbosity, or an excessive amount of language expression, is associated with fewer propositions, or information content. A related finding is that the discourse produced by older adults is often off-task, tangential, or irrelevant. Researchers have also documented decreases in communicative efficiency and production rate. This behavior is best characterized as the stereotypic rambling, egocentric discourse of older adults. Yet, another possibility is that older adults who are aware of their language production problems may modify verbal output in response to their self-perceived abilities. Such adaptation based on self-efficacy expectation may in part account for differences in the self-reported frequency of, or satisfaction with, reminiscence. Again, a life span approach to reminiscence research (Webster, 1999) may shed light on age-related language accommodations in reminiscence.

In their interventions with older adults, speech-language pathologists have begun to exploit the prevalence of reminiscence in the everyday conversations of these individuals (Harris, 1997, 1998). Reminiscence sharing as a clinical activity engages older adult clients and provides the "hook" that encourages them to become active participants in a broader range of therapeutic activities. Moreover, the discourse produced during reminiscence can be recorded, transcribed, and analyzed for markers of cognitive processing (e.g., propositions, coherence) and linguistic ability (e.g., number of words; pronominal referential ability). The results of these analyses have diagnostic value for speech-language pathologists and provide targets for intervention (Harris, 1997, 1998; Shadden, 1988). The normative research amassed in the disciplines of discourse psychology and communication sciences and disorders can help reminiscence researchers gain fuller understanding of age-differences in the expressive-communicative aspects of reminiscence.

Research suggests that older adults are especially capable storytellers, particularly when the story involves a personal recollection. For example, Shadden (1988) investigated the most frequently initiated topics in a sample of 68 to 89 year olds. The 48 respondents to a survey included adults of various ages. Thirty of the respondents indicated that older adults most frequently talk about "all aspects of the past" (p. 25). In an earlier study, Weintraub (1981) characterized the topical content of the monologues of 20 older adults, ages 60 to 85 years old. Themes determined from 10-minute discourse samples centered on their daily activities and "recapitulations of highlights of their lives" (p. 55). Importantly, Weintraub noted that the scores of these older adults *did not differ significantly* from the scores of adults in other age groups. Nevertheless, he did note an increase in self-preoccupation and frequent use of the first-person singular pronoun (i.e., "I") in the older experimental group.

Widening the Lens on Reminiscence Research

There is increasing agreement that the advancement of reminiscence science requires an adult life span approach to the study of reminiscence (e.g., Hyland & Ackerman, 1988; Webster, 1999). As indicated by this brief review of the mechanisms and characteristics of cognitive aging and language, many scientifically interesting questions emerge when reminiscence is situated in a developmental cognitive-communicative framework. Additionally, many insights may materialize during system-atic reexaminations of earlier research and clinical applications, when earlier studies are situated in a cognitive-communicative context.

For example, it becomes clear that the development of a taxonomy of reminiscence elicitation procedures and their associated cognitive costs would make a valuable contribution to the science of reminiscence. Little, if any, consideration has been given to the cognitive-linguistic requirements imposed by clinical and experimental reminiscence tasks. To illustrate, Harris (1998) published a manual of reminiscence therapy activities, each centered on a different socially validated, age-appropriate theme. The activities in this manual provide a single-source illustration of the broad array of cognitive-linguistic tasks commonly used to elicit reminiscence behavior. Table 6.1 illustrates a sample of elicitation tasks suggested by Harris in her manual of reminiscence activities. The tasks were *not systematically ordered* by level of difficulty. However, when the cognitive-linguistic requirements of each task are considered, it becomes evident that the tasks are not comparable in terms of complexity.

Similarly, even a cursory review of the literature reveals the variety of cueing techniques used by reminiscence researchers to elicit personal past memories. Again, the cognitive-linguistic variance of the tasks' requirements is not considered in interpretations of the research findings, thus resulting in a major limitation of the research. Perhaps the most popular technique involves word cues. Several researchers (Jansari & Parkin, 1996; Rubin & Schulkind 1997a,b; Sperbeck, Whitbourne, & Hoyer, 1986) have used words from different grammatical categories and emotionally-laden words to determine their influence on reminis-cence behavior. Currently, we are investigating the influence of time-linked word cues on the autobiographical memories of older adults.

TABLE 6.1   A Sample of Reminiscence Elicitation Prompts and Their Cognitive-Linguistic Requirements

Elicitation Prompt	Cognitive-Linguistic Requirement
"Tell us what you wore on your first date with your future husband."	Recall and discourse-level expression of a specific autobiographical episode.
"Can you remember how you felt when you got your first pair of long pants?"	Recall and discourse-level expression of the affective aspects of a specific autobiographical episode.
"Let's think of all the occupations that no longer exist."	Recall, broad memory search, then-and-now comparison, and single-word or phrase-level verbal expression.

Adapted from J. L. Harris (1998), *The source for reminiscence therapy*. East Moline, IL: LinguiSystems.

Other less commonly used techniques include olfactory cueing (Rubin, Groth, & Goldsmith, 1984) and multiple-choice questionnaires (Rubin, Rahhal, & Poon, 1998). Huffman and Weaver (1996) and Sperbeck, Whitbourne, and Hoyer (1986) used word cues in a type of verbal fluency paradigm, where participants were required to generate sample-matched language. Huffman and Weaver (1996) studied participants rated as having either high or low visual imagery to determine the role of this factor in autobiographical recall. Because there is a paucity of research involving visual imagery, olfactory cueing, multiple-choice questionnaire, and verbal fluency as elicitation tasks for autobiographical memories, opportunities abound for additional research investigation. As initial inquiries, one might ask: Do the above-mentioned sensory cues differentially tax cognitive-linguistic abilities in the expression of reminiscences, and do these sensory cues interact with age?

A more fundamental concern, however, is the selection and characterization of the participants in reminiscence research. More meaningful interpretations of research efforts accrue when participants are fully described, using a standardized set of participant selection criteria. Only then will meaningful generalizations across studies and population samples be made possible. Given our earlier discussion of cognitive and linguistic changes across the adult life span, it follows that measures of cognitive status and language ability should be routinely provided in reminiscence research. We also know that adults vary in their innate abilities, as well as the way in which age mediates these abilities. Individual difference measures then would better inform scholars of reminiscence behavior by defining subgroups based on a set of predetermined criteria.

No longer should participants' age and sex be considered a sufficiently detailed characterization of a population sample. For example, we know that individuals do not age comparably, making "old age" a rather vague descriptor. African Americans, for example, experience earlier and more protracted disability than same-age Caucasians (Manton, Patrick, & Johnson, 1994). African Americans are also more vulnerable to cognitive impairments due to central nervous system involvement resulting from stroke, diabetes, and multi-infarct dementia (Payne, 1997). Unfortunately, few reminiscence studies have focused on adult age differences in behavior (e.g., Hyland & Ackerman, 1988; Webster, 1999). This knowledge gap is particularly limiting with regard to persons from diverse racial or ethnic backgrounds (see Webster, chapter 9, in this volume).

Demographic changes in the population characteristics of older Americans indicate increasing racial, ethnic, and cultural diversity. African American older adults account for 2.5 million persons in the United States who are 65 years or older. Similarly, older adults from culturally and linguistically diverse backgrounds are increasing at a faster rate than the same-age majority population (Satcher, 1986). The scientific significance of this demographic trend indicates that research population samples should reflect the characteristics of the general population. At the same time, inclusion of persons from racial, ethnic, and culturally diverse backgrounds means that there is a concomitant risk for cognitive-linguistic involvement due to race-linked medical conditions. The implication for reminiscence researchers is that measures of cognitive and language abilities should be routinely obtained as indices of individual differences. It may be that cultural differences will also influence reminiscence function and behavior. To explore this possibility, we are currently collecting comparative data from a sample of younger and older Caucasians and African Americans using Webster's (1997) Reminiscence Functions Scale.

We believe that we have amply illustrated the centrality of cognitive-linguistic processes to recalling and sharing personal past experiences. Hence, it seems only reasonable to suggest that reminiscence research incorporate measures of cognitive and linguistic abilities, irrespective of the demographic characteristics of the population sample. Doing so means that the scientific community will be better able to interpret the meaning of the research effort as it relates to adult human development.

The implementation of these directions for future research and clinical practice will, in many cases, require a paradigm shift for the disparate groups engaged in reminiscence work. Additionally, the suggested broadened research perspective requires the blurring of disciplinary boundaries, and in some cases, may require the dismantling of disciplinary barriers. One obvious barrier is the lack of transdisciplinary dialogue about reminiscence. Speech language pathologists, for example, are primarily interested in reminiscence as a means to an end. That is, reminiscence for them is a vehicle to elicit discourse-level language expression from adult clients (Harris, 1997, 1998). Similarly, discourse psychologists are primarily interested in analyzing the discourse features of personal narratives. Cognitive psychologists, on the other hand, are primarily interested in what autobiographical memory tells us about cognitive systems and processes across the adult life span, whereas clinical geriatricians are primarily interested in the adaptive function of reminiscence in late adulthood. In every instance, the essence of the focus is reminiscence, the genre-specific manifestation of memory and language use. Each discipline can benefit from information ostensibly owned by the others.

In order for reminiscence research to be of cross-disciplinary value, a common metric must apply. That is, regardless of the discipline or the research question, a minimum data set should be obtained and uniformly reported. Still to be determined, however, is the specific content of that data set and a rubric for interpreting the information that it yields. Despite the need to work out procedural details, we believe that the concept is sound. The advancement of reminiscence science is largely dependent upon the definition of a core data set that can be used to cross-pollinate reminiscence research. It will not surprise our readers that our recommendation minimally includes measures of cognitive status and language ability, as well as racial, ethnic, and cultural markers.

Reminiscence science provides a unique window on the complexity of cognitive-linguistic operations and behaviors across the adult life span. Viewing reminiscence through the prism of cognitive-linguistic operations provides fresh insights and the impetus for new research initiatives. Based on a review of the existing literature scattered across several disciplines—particularly cognitive psychology and communication sciences—researchers have much to learn from each other. A systematic marshaling of interdisciplinary resources promises to infuse research agendas with new life. This volume exemplifies the dialogic richness that ensues when researchers from various scientific traditions bring their expertise to a common table in the interest of a mutually compelling focus—the science of reminiscence.

III

Developmental and Sociocultural Issues

7

Reminiscing and Relating: The Development of Parent-Child Talk About the Past

Robyn Fivush and Elaine Reese

MOTHER: Do you remember when Austin came to stay and Dorothy and Uncle Nick? And where did we go? Did we go to the train station, Hamish? Did we go to the station and see the trains, the puffer trains?

CHILD: Na na (attentive, listening to Mother)

MOTHER: Puff, puff, ah. Is that what they did? And did we wave bye-bye to them on the train when they went home? They went home to Gore didn't they? And we go bye-bye, say bye-bye, uncle Nick, bye-bye, Dorothy. Did we? And what did the train say?

CHILD: Brr brr.

MOTHER: Oh, do you remember? Was it a big blue train like Thomas?

As this example of a mother and her 19-month-old child illustrates, parents and children begin sharing the past together very early in development. However, as is also evident in this conversation, early on parents provide virtually all of the content and the structure of these shared reminiscences, and children participate mainly by confirming or repeating what the parent has said. Over the course of the preschool years, children begin to participate more fully in these conversations and by the end of the preschool years, children are full partners in coconstructing their past with their parents. The dramatic changes in shared reminiscing can be seen in this example of a father reminiscing with his 8-year-old child:

FATHER: What was fun about the zoo?
CHILD: Uh, I know what I liked.
FATHER: What did you like?
CHILD: I liked the grillas.
FATHER: The gorillas?
CHILD: Yeah
FATHER: Yeah, we saw some neat gorillas, didn't we?
CHILD: What did you like?
FATHER: Well gee, I may, you know that was one of my favorite
               things. You know, what was, what kind of gorillas did you
               like best?
CHILD: Ummm, the black ones.
FATHER: The black ones. And didn't they have some different size
               gorillas?
CHILD: I didn't . . .
FATHER: But didn't they have any little babies?
CHILD: YEAH!
FATHER: What, did they have little baby gorillas?
CHILD: Yes, I like those. I like those.
FATHER: What were they doin'?
CHILD: They were, umm, eating.
FATHER: Eating?

These examples illustrate a robust finding in the literature; children are learning to tell the stories of their lives through participating in parent-guided conversations about the past (Eisenberg, 1985; Fivush, 1991; Hudson, 1990; McCabe & Peterson, 1991). But children are learning more than the requisite skills for retrieving and reporting information about their past experiences. In this chapter, we argue that children are learning the core reasons for reminiscing. Why do we talk about past events at all, and especially, why do we share these events again and again with the very people with whom we experienced them? What do we gain from shared reminiscing given that we already share the past?

Through a consideration of the forms and functions of parent-child reminiscing, we argue that parents and children are creating and recreating a shared history that maintains social and emotional relationships. Reminiscing emerges from and contributes to a need for connection to others. Moreover, it is too simplistic to state that parents are teaching children the skills and structures for recounting their past. As we will demonstrate in this chapter, children are not passive partners in this enterprise. Although it is obviously true that parents are more mnemonically skilled in these early reminiscing conversations, both parents and children are contributing to constructing a history in which their lives are intertwined.

Reminiscing Styles

Although all parent-child dyads talk about past events, there are critical individual differences in this developmental process. Research with Western middle-class samples has revealed a continuum of parental questioning strategies from less elaborative to highly elaborative (e.g., Fivush & Fromhoff, 1988; Hudson, 1990). The usual technique for eliciting reminiscing in these studies has been to first help parents select unique events to discuss, and then to encourage them to converse with their children for as long and in whatever way they wish. Conversations are transcribed and then coded for parents' elaborations (new information) and evaluative feedback (confirmations and negations) and children's participation. Parents at the high elaborative end of the continuum ask a greater number of questions containing new information about the event. They also confirm and expand upon their children's responses more often. Less elaborative parents, on the other hand, ask fewer questions containing new information. They provide fewer memory cues for their children and often seem to be after a particular piece of information rather than telling a collaborative story about the past event. The real difference between high and low elaborative parents emerges when children indicate their interest by taking a conversational turn but do not provide new memory information. In such instances, high elaborative parents are more likely to elaborate than low elaborative parents (Fivush & Fromhoff, 1988; Reese, Haden, & Fivush, 1993). In the following example, a highly elaborative mother and her 40-month-old child are discussing a treasure hunt.

MOTHER: And what else happened at the celebrations?
CHILD: I don't know.
MOTHER: We did something special with all the other children.
CHILD: What was it?
MOTHER: There was a whole lot of people over at the beach, and everyone was doing something in the sand.
CHILD: What was it?
MOTHER: Can't you remember what we did in the sand? We were looking for something.

CHILD: Umm, I don't know.
MOTHER: We went digging in the sand.
CHILD: Umm, and that was when um the yellow spade broke.
MOTHER: Good girl, I'd forgotten that. Yes, the yellow spade broke, and what happened?
CHILD: Um, we had to um dig with the other end of the yellow bit one.
MOTHER: That's right. We used the broken bit, didn't we?
CHILD: Yeah.

Notice how the mother continues to provide information about the event even when the child is not supplying memory information. When the child does provide a piece of memory information (*that was when the yellow spade broke*), the mother acknowledges and expands upon the child's response. In contrast, the next example is of a less elaborative mother and her 40-month-old child discussing a fireworks display.

MOTHER: Do you remember the fireworks?
CHILD: Yeah.
MOTHER: What can you tell me about those?
CHILD: Um, made made a light and then they fell. Then there was a blue one.
MOTHER: Mmmhmm.
CHILD: And how did they finish?
MOTHER: I dunno. You tell me.
CHILD: I don't know.
MOTHER: Oh.
CHILD: Can you remember?
MOTHER: I remember the fireworks, yeah.

The mother does not supply additional information about the event even when the child asks for her help. Instead, the goal for the mother is quite clearly for the child to recall the event independently, not to create a story together about the past event.

Children of more highly elaborative parents recall more information during shared reminiscing (e.g., Fivush & Fromhoff, 1988; Hudson, 1990), but perhaps mothers are more elaborative because their children are recalling more information or asking more questions. Several lines of evidence suggest that children are not simply eliciting parents' reminiscing style. First, parents' style of reminiscing is stable across time (e.g., Reese, Haden, & Fivush, 1993) and across different children in the same family (Haden, 1998; Lewis, 1999). Second, parents' reminiscing style is not highly related to children's language levels or cognitive skills (Harley & Reese, 1999; Welch-Ross, 1997).

Most important, longitudinal relations between parent and child are critical in assessing directionality. We have conducted two longitudinal studies in our labs, together covering an age period from 1-1/2 to 6 years of age. In both studies, mothers and children participated in conversations about shared past events at several datapoints, with a special emphasis on the preschool years. With a sample of Atlanta children, we have demonstrated that mothers' reminiscing style early in the preschool period predicted children's later reminiscing, but that children's early reminiscing did not predict mothers' later reminiscing style until between 5 and 6 years of age (Reese, Haden, & Fivush, 1993). Moreover, children's provision of memory information was not stable until they were 5 or 6 years old. Thus the direction of influence over time is clearly from mother to child early in development, although it becomes more bidirectional toward the end of the preschool years.

Farrant and Reese (2000a) replicated and extended this work with a younger New Zealand sample, starting when children were 1-1/2 years old and just beginning to reminisce with their mothers. This study also controlled for children's language abilities at each age. Mothers' use of open-ended elaborations ("What did we see at the zoo?") uniquely predicted children's later reminiscing. Children's reminiscing at these younger ages did not ever directly predict mothers' later reminiscing style in this study, although children's early interest in participating in the conversations did emerge as an additional unique predictor of their own later reminiscing.

Thus, although children play a role in their own reminiscing development, parental reminiscing style appears to be stable and is the driving force in shaping children's reminiscing. Moreover, it is not simply how much information is included in past event narratives, but what kind of information. Some parents focus on orienting information, placing the event in a spatial temporal context and providing a coherent chronology of what occurred, whereas other parents focus more on evaluating the event, emphasizing their own and others' reactions to what happened. Parents who focus on orientation have children who themselves focus on orientation, and parents who focus on evaluation have children who focus on evaluation in their own independent narratives of the past (Fivush, 1991; McCabe & Peterson, 1991). In the Atlanta sample, mothers' use of orientation terms (when, where, who) and especially evaluation terms (why, how, and mental state) in conversations when children were 3-1/2 years old uniquely predicted children's use of orientation and evaluation in past event narratives with an experimenter at nearly 6 years of age (Haden, Haine, & Fivush, 1997).

Intriguingly, gender has also been shown to play a role in early reminiscing. Although mothers and fathers do not differ from each other along the dimension of elaborativeness, both mothers and fathers seem to be more elaborative and more evaluative with daughters than with sons (Fivush, 1998; Reese & Fivush, 1993; Reese, Haden, & Fivush, 1996). In the Atlanta sample, however, girls were already producing more memory information and richer narratives at the first datapoint compared with boys (Haden, Haire, & Fivush, 1997; Reese, Haden, & Fivush, 1996). Work with other samples has at times failed to replicate gender differences in reminiscing (e.g., Haden, 1998; Farrant & Reese, 2000), but when differences are found, they have always been in the direction of parents being more elaborative and evaluative with daughters than sons.

Intriguingly, as adults, women provide more elaborate and more emotionally evaluative narratives about their past than do men, and in many studies women have an earlier age of first memory than men (see Fivush & Buckner, in press, for a review and discussion). One interpretation of this phenomenon is that, at least in Western culture, reminiscing is valued more for women than men; women are socialized to be the keepers of the family history (Ross & Holmberg, 1990). Our data suggest this gendered socialization begins very early in development. Importantly, mothers' reminiscing style seems to be specific to a memory context. Haden and Fivush (1996) found that mothers' reminiscing style did not map onto their conversational style in a free-play setting with their children, suggesting that elaborative reminiscing is not simply a function of a more general tendency to talk a lot.

Overall, then, there is clear evidence that children are learning how to construct elaborative and coherent narratives about their past experiences through participating in reminiscing with their parents. Moreover, individual differences in maternal styles of reminiscing are related to developing differences in children's autobiographical skills. But when we talk about the past, we don't simply report what happened, we discuss why the event was sad, exciting, scary, and so on. It is through discussing the emotional aspects of our past experiences that we provide our listeners and ourselves with a sense of what the event means, how it fits into our lives and our understanding of ourselves. Thus far, we have considered how parents and children come to tell their shared stories. In the next section, we extend this discussion to consider the ways in which emotions are integrated into these life stories.

Emotional Content of Parent-Child Reminiscing

Emotional aspects of the past are critical in that they provide direct links between the past and the present, and between self and other. By including one's own emotions about a past experience, one implicitly marks how a past event is related to current self conceptualizations (e.g., Dunn, Brown, & Bearsdall, 1991; Fivush, 1998), and by noting emotions of self and other, one is implicitly linking oneself to others through shared understandings of experience (Bretherton, Fritz, Zahn-Waxler, & Ridgeway, 1986; Fivush, in press).

Intriguingly, a great deal of research has documented that females disclose, discuss, and value emotional experience more than do males (see Fischer, 2000, for a review). Yet little research has addressed the question of how and when females come to discuss emotions more than males. Are females encouraged to discuss emotions differently than males in conversations initially guided by parents? And, if so, how might this process unfold developmentally? In a preliminary investigation of how mothers and their 2.5- to 3-year-old children discuss emotional aspects of the past, mothers were found to discuss sadness more with daughters than with sons, and anger more with sons than with daughters (Fivush, 1989). At this early age, children rarely referred to emotions and there were no gender differences. These findings suggest that mothers are discussing emotions with their children in gender stereotyped ways (Basow, 1992) well before children are displaying any gender differences themselves.

To explore this finding in more detail, we examined mothers and fathers discussing emotional aspects of past events longitudinally with their preschool children (Adams, Kuebli, Boyle, & Fivush, 1995). We included fathers in this study because, given previous research on gender differences in emotional disclosure, we were interested in examining how parents may discuss emotions differently according to their own gender, as well as how parents may differentially discuss emotions with daughters and with sons. Somewhat surprisingly, there were no differences between mothers and fathers, but both mothers and fathers discussed emotions differently depending on the gender of the child. At both 40 months and 70 months of age, parents discussed emotions more, especially sadness, with daughters than with sons. Although there were no differences between boys and girls at 40 months of age, by 70 months of age, girls were including more emotional talk in their reminiscing than were boys. This pattern suggests that children are learning the appropriateness of including emotion in their discussions of past events by participating in joint reminiscing. Because parents include more references to emotions with girls, girls are learning that emotions are important and appropriate aspects of their experiences to report. Boys, in contrast, are not getting this message. However, in this study, parents were not asked to discuss emotional experiences; they were simply asked to discuss distinctive events that they had shared with their children. Thus any mention of emotion was completely spontaneous. What might happen if parents were specifically focused on emotional experiences?

We asked mothers and fathers to discuss four specific emotional experiences with their 4-year-old children, a time their child was happy, scared, angry, and sad (Fivush, Brotman, Buckner, & Goodman, 2000). Under these instructions, mothers discussed emotions overall more than did fathers. So when emotions are highlighted, we find the same gender differences between mothers and fathers that have been documented in previous research (see Fivush & Buckner, in press, for a theoretical interpretation of the effects of context on gender differences in emotional disclosure). Still, both mothers and fathers discussed emotions more with daughters than with sons, and especially so for sadness. Children in this study showed no gender differences.

The results are clear. In all studies, emotions are focused on to a greater extent with girls than with boys, and this is especially true for sadness (see Fivush & Buckner, 2000, for a full discussion of gender and sadness). Although there are no differences in how boys and girls talk about emotional aspects of the past early in development, by the end of the preschool years, girls are integrating emotions into reminiscing to a greater extent than are boys. To illustrate these differences, we present two conversational excerpts. The first is a mother and her 4-year-old daughter discussing a time the child felt sad:

MOTHER: I remember when you were sad. You were sad when Malika had to leave on Saturday, weren't you?

CHILD: Uh huh.

MOTHER: You were very sad. And what happened? Why did you feel sad?

CHILD: Because Malika, Malika say, was having (unintelligible word)

MOTHER: Yes.

CHILD: And then she stood up on my bed and it was my bedroom. She's not allowed to sleep there.

MOTHER: Is that why you were sad?

CHILD: Yeah. Now it makes me happy. I also, it makes me sad. But Malika just left.

MOTHER: Uh huh.

CHILD: And then I cried.

MOTHER: And you cried because . . .

CHILD: Malika left.

MOTHER: Because Malika left? And did that make you sad?

CHILD: And then I cried (makes "aaahhhh" sounds) like that. I cried and cried and cried and cried.

MOTHER: I know. I know. I thought you were sad because Malika left. I didn't know you were also sad because Malika slept in your bed.

This conversation begins with the emotion itself—what made the child sad. Provocatively, the event causing the child to feel sad is an interpersonal one, her friend leaving. Moreover, the entire conversation focuses on the emotion itself, confirming and elaborating on what caused the emotion and how it was expressed. In contrast, here is a father and son discussing a sad event:

FATHER: Do you remember last night when you took your juice upstairs?
CHILD: Uh huh.
FATHER: What did you do with the juice? When you were going up the steps?
CHILD: I spilled it.
FATHER: You spilled it? Did you get upset?
CHILD: Uh huh. I was just sad.
FATHER: You were sad? What did you do?
CHILD: Went downstairs.
FATHER: Yeah, what did you do when you came downstairs?
CHILD: Get some more.

(10 conversational exchanges about the child getting some soda)

FATHER: You came down. What did you tell me?
CHILD: That I spilled it.
FATHER: Yeah, what kind of face did you have?
CHILD: A sad face.
FATHER: A sad face.
CHILD: Uh huh.
FATHER: What did we do?
CHILD: Clean it up.

Here, the conversation begins with an event, the child spilling juice. It is several conversational turns before an emotion is even mentioned. Note, too, that the precipitating event is a behavioral mishap, not an interpersonal event. The emotion is not elaborated on by either father or son, but rather the conversation focuses on activities. Whereas the mother-daughter conversation is clearly emotional in focus, the father-son conversation simply is not.

The emotional focus in parent-daughter reminiscing may lead girls to develop a more subjective and affectively laden understanding of their personal past. Emotions provide the glue that links us to our past and to others. By expressing and elaborating on emotional experience, parents and daughters are creating a shared history replete with self-evaluation and interpersonal connections. In contrast, parent-son reminiscing focuses on the external world, the actions that comprise the physical event, sharing objective occurrences with little mention of how these experiences influence understanding of self and other.

Overall, then, the research indicates that while all parents and children talk about the past, some parents and children continue to be more elaborative and emotional than others across the preschool years, coconstructing rich stories of their shared past. Moreover, there is some suggestion that parents may be more elaborative and more emotional when reminiscing with daughters than with sons. Why might this be so? Why do some parents and children engage in highly elaborative stories of their shared lives, studded with rich detail and emotional experience, whereas other parents and children tell sparser stories, recounting the facts with little narrative or emotional embellishment? We believe the answer to this question lies not in the mnemonic aspects of narrating the past, but in the social and emotional reasons for engaging in this behavior in the first place. Parents and children reminisce about their shared past in order to create and maintain interpersonal bonds. By jointly reconstructing the funny, caring, and poignant events of our lives, we create emotional attachments that bond us together in the present and allow us to anticipate a shared future.

Reminiscing and Attachment

If parents and children are engaging in joint reminiscing in order to maintain social and emotional bonds, then we would expect reminiscing styles to be related to attachment status. More specifically, more securely attached mother-child dyads should exhibit more elaborative and emotional reminiscing.

Attachment is a core concept in developmental psychology. Decades of research has established individual differences in mother-child attachment status, such that some dyads display a secure attachment, based on mothers' contingent, appropriate, and sensitive responses to their children. Other dyads show a less secure attachment, in which the mother and child seem less able to interact in emotionally positive ways (Ainsworth, Blehar, Waters, & Wall, 1978; see Cassidy & Shaver, 1999, for an overview). Moreover, attachment status during infancy has been related to children's continuing emotional and social competence throughout development. A secure attachment early in life provides children with a secure base, a sense of predictability in the world, which allows them to comfortably explore their environment, physically, socially, and emotionally. Most interesting, it is assumed that more securely attached dyads engage in more open and emotionally integrated communication, leading to more coherent and consistent narrative accounts of earlier interactions and relationships (Bretherton, 1990; Main, Kaplan, & Cassidy, 1985).

We argue that parent-child reminiscing is both a product of and a contributor to the dyad's attachment relationship. Dyads that are more securely attached would be better able to engage in elaborated, coherent, and emotionally integrated reminiscing as an expression of their secure relationship. Moreover, as a function of engaging in this kind of elaborated reminiscing, securely attached dyads would reinforce and extend their mutuality. Less securely attached dyads, in contrast, would display less elaborated, less coherent, and less emotionally integrated reminiscing and, in turn, less elaborated reminiscing would not allow these dyads to create as rich a shared history. Thus attachment relations should be both expressed in and contribute to parent-child reminiscing.

In order to explore this prediction, we assessed mothers and their 40-month-old children in two contexts (Fivush & Vesudeva, 2001). The first context was reminiscing, in which we assessed elaborativeness and emotional integration of the mother-child conversation. Elaborativeness was defined, as in previous research, as the provision of new information. Emotional integration was defined as a ratio of positive and negative emotions discussed. We assumed that more securely attached dyads would be more likely to discuss negative as well as positive emotions. The second context was an unstructured art activity, from which we assessed nonverbal maternal warmth, measured as number of glances towards the child, number of smiles, laughs, and positive facial expressions. We included this measure to determine whether more elaborative and/or more securely attached dyads also engaged in emotionally warmer, more positive nonverbal behaviors during ongoing interactions. Finally, mothers completed the Attachment Q-set (Waters, 1987) to determine attachment status.

As predicted, mothers who were more elaborative in reminiscing showed more secure attachment relations with their child. However, neither emotional content of reminiscing nor maternal warmth during an unstructured interaction were related to elaborativeness or attachment. Thus attachment and reminiscing style are related but these constructs seem independent of other measures of the mother-child social-emotional relationship.

A critical question that arises from these findings, of course, is the developmental process by which attachment and reminiscing are linked. We explored attachment security as a predictor of reminiscing in a longitudinal study of New Zealand primary caregiver mothers and their children from ages 1-1/2 to 3-1/2 years (Farrant & Reese, 2000b;

Reese & Farrant, in press). Our primary goal was to examine the development of communication about a shared past in securely attached and insecurely attached dyads. We asked mothers in the sample to complete the Attachment Q-set (Waters, 1987) when their children were 1-1/2 years old. Mothers reminisced with their children about shared past events when children were 1-1/2, 2, 2-1/2, and 3-1/2 years old.

Dyads were divided into securely attached (n = 39) and insecurely attached (n = 19) based on their Q-set scores at the first datapoint. In accordance with our predictions, mothers from securely attached dyads were more elaborative and evaluative with their children when reminiscing. Mothers from insecurely attached dyads were less likely to follow in on children's responses with an elaboration. Instead, they were more likely to repeat their own previous question after children's responses. Thus, mothers from insecurely attached dyads provided fewer memory cues for their children and seemed to be following their own agenda rather than collaboratively constructing a shared history. Children in securely attached dyads were somewhat more likely to participate and recall more in the conversations, but the effects for children's reminiscing were fairly weak at this young age. The strongest effects occurred in the course of reminiscing development for secure and insecure dyads. Mothers and children from securely attached dyads predicted each other's styles in the long term, with many significant correlations between mothers' reminiscing and children's reminiscing over time. In contrast, mothers and children from insecurely attached dyads showed little effect on each other's reminiscing over time. In fact, these dyads sometimes did not even adjust their reminiscing style to their partner's responses within the same conversation.

The development of reminiscing thus varies as a function of attachment security. Effective socialization of reminiscing takes place in secure dyads, with children taking on mothers' reminiscing style, and mothers adjusting to children's reminiscing over time. Within insecure dyads, however, mothers rarely respond to children's reminiscing, nor are children internalizing their mothers' reminiscing styles. These results have implications for the development of children's communication about significant events in their lives. Children from insecure dyads might eventually develop a more defensive, less open style of communicating with others about their personal past as a result of their perspective being continually negated by their mothers. At its extreme, Bowlby (1988) referred to children with this communication style as experiencing "defensive exclusion" for an event. Bowlby speculated that defensive exclusion might have its origins in a parent who negated, distorted, or inadequately elaborated upon events with their children, especially about negative and traumatic events. Children from securely attached dyads might be more open in their communication style. Ultimately, they might even develop a richer internal working model of their attachment relationship as a result of their mothers' elaborative and collaborative style of talking about their shared past (see Reese & Farrant, in press).

These initial findings are provocative but are only a first step in exploring the relation between attachment security and reminiscing. We have yet to ascertain the eventual impact of attachment security on children's reminiscing with people other than their primary attachment figure. In addition, it could be that mother-infant attachment is only a mediator of mothers' and children's reminiscing style. Mother-infant attachment security is strongly predicted by the mothers' state of mind about their own early attachment experiences (van IJzendoorn, 1995). Specifically, mothers who are coherent and collaborative in their accounts of their early attachment experiences in the Adult Attachment Interview have children who are highly likely to be securely attached themselves (Main, Kaplan, & Cassidy, 1985). It's possible that mothers with a secure orientation may also be better able to construct elaborative narratives about past events for their children and to respond appropriately to children's input (c.f., Pillemer, 1998). Speculatively, learning to reminisce could be an intergenerational phenomenon, just as adult attachment orientation has been found to cross at least three generations (Benoit & Parker, 1994).

SUMMARY AND CONCLUSIONS

Research on the origins of reminiscing demonstrates the central role that sharing the past plays in parent-child communication. Even before children are capable of verbally recalling their past experiences, parents are engaging them in jointly reconstructing the stories of their lives. Importantly, however, there are clear and enduring individual differences in this process. Some parents engage in highly elaborative, coherent, and emotionally laden reminiscing and their children come to tell richly embellished narratives of their past. Other parents ask few and sparsely detailed questions, and include little evaluative or emotional information, and their children come to tell less coherent and elaborated narratives. Most intriguing, parent-child reminiscing is linked to attachment status, such that securely attached dyads engage in more elaborated reminiscing. This finding underscores one of the primary functions of joint reminiscing, that of creating a shared history on which to base current and future relationships.

Certainly the skills for reminiscing that children are learning early in development sets the stage for a lifetime of creating personal narratives. But perhaps even more important, in learning the interpersonal functions of reminiscing, children are entering a community in which an understanding of self and other rests on creating rich stories of shared lives. Children from securely attached dyads who engage in highly elaborated reminiscing may develop into adults who value reminiscing as a way of understanding self and connecting with others. Moreover, these children may have mothers who themselves had secure relationships with parents who engaged in elaborative reminiscing. Thus, in theorizing about adult reminiscing, we need to consider the developmental history of the individual (e.g., Webster, 2001), as well as the intergenerational transmission of relationships in which reminiscing is embedded.

8

Souvenirs and Other Personal Objects: Reminding of Past Events and Significant Others in the Transition to University

Tilmann Habermas and Christine Paha

Memory is not merely an internal, cognitive process, but most often relies on external media to store, and on communication to retrieve information. Thus we rely on other people to remember and to be reminded (e.g., Edwards & Middleton, 1988). In long-established relationships such as couples there is a division of memory, so that both rely on each other for certain mnemonic activities (Dixon & Gould, 1998). At a more trivial level, talking about something makes it easier to remember (rehearsal), which is enhanced by social confirmation (Pasupathi, in press).

We also rely on material media for storing and retrieving information. We organize the environment so as to relieve our memory by distributing cues in the right locations in the environment and by designing objects so that they are self-explanatory (Norman, 1988). In the

* This chapter is based on research by the first author (Habermas, 1999a, b). Data on object-related memories are based on a diploma thesis by the second author (Paha, 1996). We only report results that proved to be significant in exploratory tests of significance. We used ANOVAS for metric data like the dimensions of uses, and mostly nonparametric tests for data with extreme distributions such as uses of objects.

course of evolution, the introduction of writing, of print, and of the computer have all offered new means of external memory (Leroi-Gourhan, 1965). But we also extensively use nonlinguistic objects as mnemonic media.

In psychological research, mnemonic functions of objects have received some attention in studies on the use of props for prospective memory (e.g., Harris, 1984). They serve to remind us of an intention to act at a specific time. Objects have also been used and studied in gerontology. They have served therapeutically to elicit memories in reminiscence groups (Brooker & Duce, 2000; Burnside, 1996) and with Alzheimer's patients (Cohen, 2000). Gerontological research has identified objects as important carriers of autobiographical memories and props for life review (Cram & Paton, 1993; Oswald, 1994; Redfoot & Back, 1988; Sherman, 1991b; Sherman & Newman, 1977). Objects are theorized to support reminiscing by authenticating memories (Grayson & Shulman, 2000), similar to souvenirs brought home from traveling that authenticate the trip (Love & Sheldon, 1998). In the face of death, leaving behind specific objects to selected others is a way of passing on social status (Lillios, 1999), of symbolically preserving one's identity (Unruh, 1983), and of achieving symbolic immortality (Price, Arnould, & Curasi, 2000).

Pierre Janet was an early advocate of an ecological and social-narrative conception of memory, which he saw as a social activity constituted in the moment of recounting an experience to someone who had been absent, oftentimes based on material props: "First memories are memories of objects and use objects as memory-aids. An individual who wants to remember takes something away with him: you bind a knot into the handkerchief, you put a pebble in your pocket, you take a piece of paper along . . . From distant towns you take along souvenirs . . .; they are your memory-aids. Memory very often is material" (Janet, 1928, p. 262).

This chapter is inspired by social-ecological conceptions of memory (Graumann, 1986; Janet, 1928; Neisser, 1982). We focus on *souvenirs* (Janet, 1928) or mementos, that is, on reminders that symbolically refer to past events, to people, or to places, and sometimes also to aspirations that point to the future. They do not stand for intentions to act at a specific time.

Souvenirs vary in the explicitness of their symbolic meaning. They may contain text, they may refer to something by picturing or resembling it, or it may be related to what is referred to merely by temporal-spatial contiguity, that is by having once been associated in time and space with that which is referred to. The latter two ways of signifying rely on the rhetorical figures of metaphor and metonymy, respectively.

In the terms of Charles Sanders Peirce, souvenirs can be (conventional) symbols, iconic signs that resemble what they refer to, or symptomatic indices that have some causal or physical relation to what they refer to (Grayson & Shulman, 2000; Mick, 1986; Habermas, 1999a). Similar to objects, music may convey emotions by characteristics inherent in the music (iconic) or by its association with emotionally colored events in the past (indexical) (see Baumgarten, 1992).

Whereas souvenirs are defined by their mnemonic use, *personal objects* are defined by their subjective value for a specific person. Personal objects are favorite things that an individual is attached to, that are important to and cherished by the individual. Some personal objects may be souvenirs, others may be more utilitarian objects. On the other hand, some souvenirs owned by a given individual may be important enough to be personal objects, while other souvenirs may be kept for other reasons and not be so personal.

In this chapter, we place souvenirs that in the past have been studied in a gerontological context specifically for their mnemonic functions, in the context of personal objects, that is in the context of other objects and of other uses of objects. Also, we present studies that are located at the younger end of the adult age range. Thus we take a lifespan perspective by relating concepts that originate in gerontological psychological research, such as reminiscing, life review, and retrospective mnemonic uses of objects to other age ranges.

Studies of the uses of personal objects show that one of their principal uses is to remind (Csikszentmihalyi & Rochberg-Halton, 1981; Dittmar, 1989). The mnemonic function of objects is not limited to reminding of past experiences. Several studies have demonstrated that objects may also remind of distant places and of significant others, usually family members or partners (Csikszentmihalyi & Rochberg-Halton, 1981; Fink & Forster, 1992; Sherman & Newman, 1977). Some evidence suggests that the use of objects for reminding is related to strong interpersonal bonds (Csikszentmihalyi & Rochberg-Halton, 1981; Sherman, 1991b; Wallendorf & Arnould, 1988). Everyday observations suggest that objects are used to remind of others when these are absent. Thus people put up pictures of their family or lovers at their workplace or take them along on trips. Studies of individuals in transitions (Joy & Dholakia, 1991; Volkan, 1999; Wapner, Demick, & Redondo, 1990) and of students who relocate to start university (Hormuth, 1990) suggest that the reminding use of objects is increased when significant others are left behind. Also personal objects more frequently serve mnemonic functions in higher social classes (Csikszentmihalyi & Rochberg-Halton, 1981; Dittmar, 1992).

Reminding uses of personal objects have been studied especially in samples of elderly individuals (Cram & Paton, 1993; Oswald, 1994;

Price, Arnould, & Curasi, 2000, Redfoot & Black, 1988; Sherman, 1991). When comparing adolescent and adult samples of varying ages, reminding uses of personal objects correlate with age (Csikszentmihalyi & Rochberg-Halton, 1981; Fink & Förster, 1992; Kamptner, 1991; Wallendorf & Arnould, 1988).

In the elderly, objects often remind of significant others who have gone forever. Thus the subscale "Intimacy Maintenance" of Webster's (1993) Reminiscence Functions Scale that has a background in gerontology, primarily regards remembering loved ones who have died. While the use of photographs may help parents to grieve and adjust to the death of their child (Riches & Dawson, 1998), the protracted use of personal relics of spouses who have died indicates pathological mourning (Field, Nichols, Holen, & Horowitz, 1999; Volkan, 1981).

Personal objects and their uses also reflect gender differences, in that women tend to be more oriented towards others and emotions, men more towards activities and achievement. Women use personal objects more frequently for reminding of others and the past and for emotion regulation such as for soothing, whereas men more frequently use them for instrumental purposes, to produce or achieve, and to present themselves. Women select more jewelry, stuffed animals, pictures and letters, and diaries, men prefer sports equipment, cars and bikes, audiovisual equipment, and trophies of past accomplishments (Csikszentmihalyi & Rochberg-Halton, 1981; Dittmar, 1992; Fink & Förster, 1992; Kamptner, 1991; Sherman & Newman, 1977; Wallendorf & Arnould, 1988; Wapner, Demck, & Redondo, 1990).

There are two ways in which objects remind, primary and secondary (Habermas, 1999a). Souvenirs primarily and explicitly serve mnemonic functions. These may be diaries and old letters (texts), photographs (iconic), trophies such as a lion's head, objects taken from a specific place, or objects that were present in an important event (indexical). Souvenirs that are indexical symbols often had originally been designed for aesthetic or other purposes and only later acquired a primary reminding function by virtue of having witnessed an important event or by having been passed on as a gift, an heirloom, or a relic. We have termed all of these souvenirs.

Many other objects primarily serve practical ends, such as clothes, cars, computers, books, or kitchen equipment. Even these objects, however, evoke memories. They too become indexical signs by reminding, in a secondary way, of all the situations, persons, and places they have been in contact with in the past. Thus a car may remind of a specific trip, an expensive pen of when it escaped theft only through a miracle, or worn out shoes of a time of intensive dancing. Once these utilitarian objects cease to be used for practical purposes, they turn into souvenirs if they continue to be used for reminding.

In adults, the overall frequency of reminiscing does not vary with age (Webster, 1993). More intensive and structured reasoning about the past, which has been termed life review or identity-related and problem-solving-reminiscing (Webster & Haight, 1995), and which we have called autobiographical reasoning (Habermas & Bluck, 2000), had been theorized to peak in old age (Butler, 1963). When measured by Webster's Reminiscence Functions Scale, however, identity-related and problem-solving reminiscing are more frequent in young than in old adults (Webster, 1993; Webster & McCall, 1999). This is not a surprise especially for late adolescence and young adulthood, since it is the life-phase in which psychosocial identity may be consciously shaped (Erikson, 1968). The emergence of the life story in late adolescence (Habermas & Bluck, 2000) provides a central means for shaping identity. The so-called reminiscence bump of personal memories of adults over age 35, that is, an overrepresentation of memories from late adolescence and young adulthood (Rubin, 1986; Rubin, Rahhal, & Poon, 1998), also points to the emergence of adult identity in adolescence.

Personal objects serve to maintain and communicate identity in a variety of ways (Habermas, 1999a). While other authors focus on self-presentational uses of objects to validate social identity, we believe that objects serve to maintain identity at least in equal measure by reminding of the past and of significant others. They integrate identity synchronically by supporting social integration and diachronically by supporting self-continuity. Indeed cross-sectional evidence suggests that reminding uses of personal objects begin to emerge only in mid to late adolescence and continue to slowly increase across adulthood (Csikszentmihalyi & Rochberg-Halton, 1981; Dyl & Wapner, 1996 ; Fink & Forster, 1992; Kamptner, 1991; Wallendorf & Arnould, 1988). This developmental pattern supports the identity function of reminding uses of personal objects. Therefore it makes sense not only to study the uses of autobiographical remembering and reasoning in older adults, but also at the other end of the adult age range, that is in young adulthood.

In this chapter we first provide descriptive data on reminding uses of personal objects. In the first section, we support the three points about remembering in an everyday context that have been highlighted in the introduction: (a) remembering is often based on souvenirs, (b) remembering often concerns not only the past, but also significant others, and (c) objects offer two modes of remembering, namely a primary, more explicit, and a secondary, more implicit, way. In the second section, we test whether reminding uses of objects vary with situational and individual differences in a meaningful way. Reminding uses of objects are measured in the situations of relocation and transition to university.

Situational differences are also tapped retrospectively by asking which events the objects remind of. Gender and sex role orientation are explored as individual differences.

We will draw on two studies of medical students of the Free University of Berlin, Germany. The first study is based on a longitudinal sample of 186 volunteers, the second study is based on a cross-sectional sample of 226 unselected students.

Reminding Uses of Personal Objects

The first study is based on a sample of 186 beginning medical students in their first week of the first semester and again eight months later. Mean age was 21.5 years, ranging from 18 to 32. The 117 female and 69 male participants were volunteers from two consecutive semesters comprising a total of about 550 beginning students with about equal numbers of women and men. Participants were asked to name their three to ten favorite objects, including pets, but excluding humans. Participants had to give detailed information about their two most important personal objects, such as the reasons why they were important (open ended). To render objects perceptually salient, participants drew a sketch of each of the two objects before providing detailed information about them. Objects were assigned to one of 18 categories of types of objects. The most frequent objects were pictures and letters (11%), vehicles and animals (each 9%), jewelry, including watches (8%), stuffed animals, musical instruments, and books (each 7%), apartments, audiovisual equipment including computers, diaries, clothes, household items, beds, and small portable and decorative objects.

Reasons provided for the importance of objects were coded with 28 categories of uses, that had been defined on the basis of a subsample of 25 questionnaires from each measurement time, with a satisfactory inter-rater agreement of Cohen's kappa 80. The 28 uses were grouped under 13 headings (see below). In addition to these open-ended reasons for the importance of objects, we also presented a series of brief, three-item scales asking directly for several uses. Below we will report only on the three scales for reminding of others, places, and the past.

Reminding and Other Uses of Objects

Obviously personal objects may be used in different ways and for diverse ends (relative frequencies are given in brackets). The most frequently named use of objects was reminding (total 21.7%), namely of others (12.1%), places (.8%), the past (7.7%), or the future (1.1%). Self-communicative uses can imply thinking, imagining, or enacting a dialogue with the object (9.7%). Objects may be also used for self-presentation by symbolizing individuality or group membership (4.3%). Objects may serve as media of communication, as a facilitating technical device, as a token that may be used together with others, or as an object that facilitates getting to know others (4.8%). Objects may be used to enhance or to symbolize autonomy or privacy (4.8%). Objects may be used for aesthetic reasons or for their sensual appeal (6.4%). Objects may be used as instruments for, or as symbols of productive activities related to creativity or achievement (3%). Objects may be used as symbolic or magical reinforcement, for instance as a charm (3.9%). Objects can be used to regulate the level of arousal, that is for relaxation or stimulation ("fun, enjoyment") (12.5%). Objects may offer security, for example by providing a familiar context (5.8%). Objects may regulate mood by enhancing mood, offering cathartic release, or by soothing (2.8%). Objects may offer an escape into daydreaming (1.2%). Finally objects may be useful and instrumental for achieving other ends than those captured by the above categories, such as a car that may simply serve for transportation (10.3%).

Reminding was named as one possible use for almost all letters and pictures and to almost all pieces of jewelry, as well as for over 50% of stuffed animals, portable objects, and decorative objects. To explore more systematically which of the 13 uses and types of objects typically occur concurrently, a three-factor solution of a nonlinear principal components analysis was calculated. The first resulting dimension replicated the symbolic-instrumental dimension found in other studies (Dittmar, 1992; Prentice, 1987). It is defined by reminding uses of jewelry and stuffed animals at the one extreme, and arousal-regulating, media, and productive uses of musical instruments and audiovisual equipment at the other extreme. The second dimension is defined by mood regulation, self-communication, and escape at the one extreme, and by autonomy and instrumental value of vehicles and apartments at the other extreme. The third dimension is defined again by reminding uses at the one extreme and by self-communication, security, and aesthetic pleasure of using pets and diaries at the other extreme.

Primary and Secondary Reminding

When asked why an object is important, individuals will provide reasons that refer to the most important and most distinct aspects of the object. Thus if reminding is named as a use that renders the object important, the object is a souvenir that serves primary reminding. To tap the less prominent and less distinct secondary reminding function, that is, the memories associated with any object by the mechanism of contiguity, it is necessary to ask directly whether an object also reminds of past, persons, and places. We did so by presenting brief scales with three items each that asked for the use of objects for reminding of others, of the past, and of places.

To explore whether open-ended questions and brief scales really tap different aspects of reminding uses of objects (primary versus secondary reminding), both relative frequencies of reasons provided for importance and scale values were z-transformed. Mean z-scores were compared for all types of objects. Reminding of significant others, for example, was never named as a reason for the importance of diaries and music, but the average value on the scale for reminding of others was half a standard deviation above the scale mean. Diaries and music are not chosen as most important because of their mnemonic functions, but for other reasons. However, secondarily and over time they do accumulate symbolic references to others by way of contiguity (secondary reminding).

In addition, if the mere passing of time increases secondary reminding uses of objects, age of object should correlate with reminding of the past as measured by the brief scale. Indeed the age of the objects did correlate moderately with the scale for reminding of the past ($r = .20$).

Reminding of Others

All explicit references to others in the reasons provided for the importance of the objects referred either to family, to sexual partners, or to friends (5.7%, 8.8%, and 14.2% of all objects, respectively). Specific others were mostly named because the object reminded of them (18.3% of all objects). Others were also mentioned, however, when objects were used instrumentally to establish or maintain a communication or connection with them such as by talking on the phone, being together in an apartment, playing instruments together, or riding a car to someone's house (7.9% of all objects).

Objects differed according to the type of relationship they referred to. Some types of objects most frequently referred to sexual partners (jewelry and stuffed animals, most of which had been given as gifts), to family (religious items), or to friends (letters and pictures, apartment, phone, musical instruments). References to family members and sexual partners were mostly symbolic in the sense of reminding of them (5.3% and 7.2% of all objects) and less often instrumental (.4% and 1.6%), whereas references to friends were either symbolic or instrumental with about equal frequency (7.5% and 6.7% of all objects, respectively).

So far, we have provided descriptive evidence that remembering may be based on material objects, that some objects primarily serve for reminding (souvenirs), whereas all personal objects also carry a wealth of associations with them which they have accrued by contiguity with events, places, and persons. Finally, objects more often remind of specific significant others rather than merely of some past experience. From these descriptive results we now turn to testing influences of situation and gender on selection and use of personal objects for reminding.

Effects of Situation, Gender, and Sex Role-Orientation

In this section the affinity of reminding uses of personal objects to specific situations will be explored first. Then we describe gender differences in reminding uses controlling for sex role orientation.

Reminding Uses in and Beyond Transitions

It has been repeatedly suggested both that objects become more important in transitions, as reported in the introduction, and that life review or autobiographical reasoning is triggered by transitional crises (Webster & Haight, 1995). The evidence for an increased importance of objects in transitions is mostly informal. Only one study is longitudinal and suggests that reminding uses are higher in a transition than six months later (Hormuth, 1990). The evidence that transitions trigger autobiographical reasoning is retrospective (Merriam, 1993b) or cross-sectional (Lieberman & Falk, 1971; Quackenbush & Barnett, 1995).

In this longitudinal study we offer three analyses of associations between situations and reminding uses of objects. We will do this (a) directly by comparing reminding uses in transitions and eight months later, (b) indirectly by analyzing which uses of objects are associated with which kinds of situations in the memories evoked by the objects, and (c) again more directly by comparing object-related memories in transitions and eight months later.

Our longitudinal sample had experienced either one or two kinds of transitions: the role-transition of becoming a student and, for 68 of the 186 participants, a relocation to another city. Both transitions involve a temporal discontinuity, but only relocation involves multiple geographical separations from significant others.

Reminding uses. Explicit reminding uses indeed did vary with both types of transition in separate non-parametric tests for group-differences and repeated measurement. Reminding uses were named more frequently in the transition to university than eight months later, and those who had relocated named reminding uses across both measurement times more often than those who had not relocated. In ANOVAS for

repeated measurement, the same effects showed for the bipolar symbolic-instrumental dimension of object uses that had resulted from a
nonlinear principal components analysis, with symbolic uses being
more frequent in the transition and after a relocation. Thus personal
objects are used for reminding more often in role transitions and when
separated from significant others. Only few nonreminding uses varied
with transition: The instrumental uses as media and for regulating
arousal increased over time.

Explicit references to others. There were no significant differences in
references to others due to relocation. There were significant changes
over time, however, both in whom objects refer to and how they refer to
others. Reference to family members decreased significantly, and there
was a trend for references to friends to increase. At the same time,
symbolic references to others decreased, particularly for family members and partners, while references to others in which the object played
an instrumental role increased, particularly for friends and partners. As
above, when objects refer to others symbolically they remind of them,
but when they refer to others instrumentally they may help establish or
maintain contact (e.g., e-mail, motor bike) or they may be used
together (e.g., sports equipment, car).

*Correlation between reminding uses and strength of interpersonal
bonds.* As mentioned above, some studies have suggested that the
use of personal objects for reminding correlates with the individual's
quality of interpersonal relationships. In our study, participants provided information about their social network by drawing significant others
and connecting them with a representation of oneself with one to three
lines to express others' importance (Lang, Staudinger, & Carstensen,
1998; Schmiedeck, 1978). Derived measures were the number of significant others for social network size and average number of connecting lines for strength of interpersonal bonds.

There were no significant correlations of network size or strength of
interpersonal bonds with reminding uses or the symbolic-instrumental
dimension of uses at either measurement time. When analyzed separately, the group without relocation showed no significant correlations
between qualities of interpersonal relationships and reminding uses. In
the relocation group, however, in the first week of the first semester,
reminding of others correlated with strength of interpersonal bonds
($r_s = .36$). The symbolic-instrumental dimension of uses also correlated
positively with strength of interpersonal bonds ($r_s = .31$). Eight months
later, no significant correlations were found in the relocation group,
whereas among those who had not relocated, strength of interpersonal
bonds correlated negatively with reminding of the past ($r_s = -.31$).

Thus there is a correlation between interpersonal bonds and uses of objects for reminding of others, but it is restricted to a situation of transition that involves separation from significant others, such as was the case in the relocation group in the first week of the first semester. When separated from significant attachment figures such as parents or lovers, young adults tend to symbolize their affective links to them with objects. When no transition is involved, however, such as in the group without relocation after eight months, strength of interpersonal bonds correlates negatively with uses of objects for reminding of the past. Weak social bonds under normal circumstances appear to imply a nostalgic use of personal objects.

Associations of Situations, Uses, and Types of Objects in Object-Related Memories

Having discussed reminding uses of personal objects in general, we now turn to the specific memories that are attached to objects. We describe characteristics of these memories and explore retrospective associations, that is, in the memories between type of object, reminding uses, and types of situations. For each of the two most important objects named at each of the two measurement times, we asked for one particular memory that the object evoked. One hundred eighty-six answers were missing, 155 were named, generalized events describing a recurring kind of situation, and 391 were specific events that were datable in time. The kinds of answers did not vary with time or relocation.

Both objects and even more so the specific memories attached to them were quite recent. Half of specific memories and a third of objects were younger than one year, 80% of memories and 70% of objects were younger than five years. Memories were coded for the principal object use in the remembered situation, for the type of situation remembered, and for the situations' valence. Almost half the situations involved either loss, interpersonal dispute, being geographically distant from someone, relocation, or traveling. These were summarized as situations involving loss or separation. Other types of situations included achievement-related situations and social interactions and relationships. The valence of situations was coded as either positive (21%), negative (23%), as being transformed by the use of the object from negative to positive (28%), as an attempt to transform a negative situation (7%), or as not classifiable (21%). Thus memories of negative situations (58%) were almost three times as frequent as memories of clearly positive situations (21%). Objects appear to remind especially of situations in which they had helped to overcome an adverse experience (28%).

We were interested in exploring concurrent occurrences of types and uses of objects with particular types of situations. Therefore we again calculated a three-factor, nonlinear principal components analysis across all objects. The first dimension replicated the symbolic-instrumental dimension and correlated substantially ($r = .71$) with the symbolic-instrumental dimension calculated on the basis of object type and current object uses reported above. The symbolic extreme was defined by reminding-uses, by situations of geographical separation, and by the object types jewelry, letters, and pictures. The instrumental extreme of the dimension was defined by object uses related to producing something, regulating arousal, and other instrumental uses, by situations related to work or learning, to being alone, and to achievement, and by the object types music, audiovisual appliances, books, musical instruments, and vehicles. The second dimension was defined by self-communicative uses of diaries and pets in times of loss and dispute versus instrumental uses of audiovisual appliances and vehicles in situations of separation and being alone. The third dimension was defined only by one extreme of autonomy- and security-providing uses of vehicles and apartments when being alone.

The effects of the remembered situations' valence and of whether they concerned loss or separation on the three dimensions were tested in separate ANOVAS. The first and third dimensions differed between loss- and separation-related situations versus other situations: Both symbolic uses of jewelry, letters, and pictures and autonomy-related uses of apartments and vehicles were remembered more frequently for situations of loss or separation. The second dimension varied with the valence of remembered situations: Memories of self-communicative use of diaries or pets more frequently refer to situations that are experienced as negative.

Thus, in the memories attached to the personal objects of this particular group of young adults, reminiscing uses of objects were typical for situations of being separated from significant others, while instrumental uses were typical for achievement-related situations. Self-communicative uses, in contrast, were typical for situations in which a relationship was dissolving or fraught with conflict, so that the object served as a (temporary) substitute partner for communication.

Object-Related Memories in and Beyond Transitions

To test differences in memories between the relocation-groups and between the measurement times, scores were averaged across both objects for each participant and measurement time. Separate ANOVAS for repeated measurement were calculated for each memory-dimension. In the transition, object-related memories scored higher on the first, symbolic-instrumental dimension of memories than eight months later.

Situations involving loss or separation were not remembered more frequently by the relocation group, but became less frequent after eight
months. Correspondingly, remembered situations became less negative after eight months.

To sum up the relation between reminding uses of objects and situations: Reminding of others and of the past tends to be increased in
negatively experienced situations of separation from others and of transition. This shows in remembered as well as in current uses of objects.
In addition, the current experience of a transition increases the likeli-
hood that personal objects elicit loss- or separation-related memories.
In a transition that involves multiple separations such as a relocation,
and only in such a situation, do strong interpersonal bonds enhance the
use of personal objects for reminding of others.

Gender and Sex-Role Orientation

Studies of personal objects have repeatedly evidenced gender differences in choice and use of objects. As noted earlier, women use objects
more for reminding themselves of significant others and of past experiences. With regard to reminiscing in general, one study of reminiscence has found that women tend to reminisce more frequently
(Webster, 1994), while another study found no gender differences in
overall frequency of reminiscing (Webster & McCall, 1999). Webster
did find, however, that women reminisced more frequently about identity issues (Webster & McCall, 1999). Gender differences are more
clear cut when looking not at frequencies of reminiscing but at qualities
of memories. Women produce more and older memories (deVries &
Watt, 1996), and they produce more childhood memories, specifically
more emotional memories (Davis, 1999). These gender differences in
adults can already be traced in young childrens' talk with their parents:
Parents' memory talk with their daughters is more elaborative and
emotional than with their sons, and girls recall more information and
provide more contextualization and evaluation than boys (Buckner &
Fivush, 2000; Fivush, 1998; Fivush & Reese, Chapter 7, this volume).

Both gender differences in personal objects and in reminiscing appear
to be related to women's stronger interpersonal orientation and men's
stronger instrumental orientation (Spence, Helmreich, & Holahan,
1979). We tried to replicate gender differences in personal objects and
their uses. In addition, we explored whether these gender differences
could be explained by differences in interpersonal versus instrumental
orientation, so-called sex-role orientation.

A second sample consisted of all medical students who participated in
eight compulsory courses of Medical Psychology in their third semester.

A total of 226 students in their third semester participated in this study, with 120 women and 106 men.

Women named significantly less audiovisual appliances and vehicles, but more stuffed animals, apartments, decorative objects, letters and pictures, jewelry, and telephones. Reminding uses were named more frequently by women, productivity- and achievement-related uses and instrumental uses less often. Women also scored higher on the symbolic-instrumental dimension of uses that resulted from a three-factor solution to a nonlinear principal components analysis also in this sample.

We also included two scales for positive instrumental and interpersonal-expressive orientation (Spence, Helmreich, & Holahan, 1979; German translation by Runge, Frey, Gollwitzer, Helmreich, & Spence, 1981). Men typically score higher on the instrumental orientation, women on the interpersonal orientation. The scale for instrumental orientation contained items such as *independent, competitive,* and *doesn't give up easily*; the scale for interpersonal orientation contained items such as *emotional, friendly,* and *sympathetic.* In addition, we added the items *male* and *female* to measure a sense of femininity and masculinity (Spence, 1984). We introduced these measures for two reasons. One was to test whether instrumental and interpersonal orientations would be able to explain gender differences; the other was to explore correlations with object types and object uses within each gender.

Men and women differed significantly, but not very much in instrumental and interpersonal orientation. Mean differences were smaller than half a standard deviation. Men and women did differ extremely on the items *feminine* and *masculine,* with very little variation on the cross-gender items and some variation on the same-gender items.

To test the relative influence of gender versus sex-role orientation on choice of object types and on object uses, instrumental and interpersonal orientation were entered as continuous variables simultaneously with gender into ANOVAS. Relative frequencies of object types and of object uses served as dependent variables.

When object preferences were the dependent variable, the inclusion of sex-role orientation did decrease some of the gender differences, but did not alter them substantially, except that the gender difference in naming jewelry was no longer significant. In these analyses, sex-role orientations had only few significant effects on the type of object named. With gender and the respective other sex-role orientation controlled for, instrumental orientation correlated with the frequency of dress as personal object, while interpersonal orientation correlated with the naming of letters and pictures, stuffed animals, and jewelry as personal objects.

When object uses were the dependent variables, adding the instrumental and interpersonal orientation reduced the gender differences in reminding uses and in productivity- and achievement-related uses, leaving significant gender differences in reminding and in instrumental uses and in the symbolic-instrumental dimension. With gender and the other sex-role orientation, respectively, controlled for, interpersonal and instrumental orientation correlated significantly only, and inversely, with reminding uses: Interpersonal orientation correlated positively, instrumental orientation negatively, with reminding uses. Additional separate analyses for reminding of others and reminding of the past revealed that while gender differences were more pronounced in reminding of the past, instrumental and interpersonal orientation correlated only with reminding of others.

Femininity and masculinity had low correlations with object types and object uses once gender was partialled out. Only the symbolic-instrumental dimension correlated positively with feminity and negatively with masculinity with gender partialled out. All partial correlations reported in this section were below .20.

To sum up, there are gender differences not only in the types of objects chosen, but also in how they are used. The main difference is that women use objects more for reminding and less instrumentally. The gender differences in reminding uses and in choice of objects that primarily serve reminding are influenced by, but not exhaustively explained by, differences in sex-role orientation, especially in interpersonal orientation.

In this second section, across a variety of specific findings, a picture emerges of situational and gender-related influences on reminding uses of personal objects. Reminding uses become most salient in major separations from significant others and in role transitions. This is reflected in current uses, in remembered uses, and in current influences on remembered uses. Reminding uses are enhanced by strong interpersonal bonds when separated from significant others. This fits nicely with the finding that women tend to use objects more often for reminding, which is partially explained by their greater interpersonal orientation. Most effects on reminding inversely affect instrumental object uses.

From Transitional Objects to Souvenirs to Heirlooms: A Lifespan Perspective

In this chapter reminding uses of personal objects have been explored in young adults. We will conclude with some speculations about the lifespan course of reminding uses of objects by going back to infancy and extending the view to old age. We propose four considerations that may influence how intensively souvenirs are used across the life span.

The first factor concerns the development of a sense of personal history and of explicit reminding during the first ten to fifteen years of life. In a way, reminding uses of personal objects evoke infants' transitional objects. Winnicott (1971) proposed that transitional objects such as soft blankets or teddy bears help the toddler with the transition from total dependency on the primary caregiver to more independent functioning by providing an intermediary between the real mother and a mental representation of her. Transitional objects provide a sense of security and serve as an inanimate secure base.

Transitional objects do not explicitly remind of the mother (or the mothering one). They are not souvenirs. They lack the quality of a symbol that stands for an absent third. Rather they resemble the mother in touch and smell and support and partially substitute her function as a secure base. The personal objects that come closest to infants' transitional objects are those that actually stem from infancy. Many of them seem to be former transitional objects, and they still provide a kind of background security not by explicit use for remembering but by sheer presence. In spite of these differences between infants' transitional objects and adults' souvenirs, the findings reported in this chapter do suggest a functional continuity. In adults, reminding uses of personal objects in times of separation and transition apparently serve to provide a sense of continuity and interpersonal relatedness that soothes.

As reported above, explicit reminding uses begin to emerge in early adolescence and increase over adolescence. This may have to do with the development of a sense of personal life story that begins to emerge in early adolescence and develops across adolescence (Habermas & Bluck, 2000; Habermas & Paha, 1999).

A second factor that may influence the use of souvenirs is how much an individual remains integrated in the relationships with significant others and the home environment. As the study reported in this chapter has confirmed, separations from significant others, relocation, and role transitions enhance the use of personal objects for reminding. Thus the increase in mnemonic uses of personal objects in adolescence may also have to do with the growing independence of the adolescent, the tying and loss of new bonds, and the slow separation from primary attachment figures. Also the process of developing a consolidated psychosocial identity which is also defined by identification with parents and parental figures and by personal relationships may engender the use of souvenirs (Erikson, 1968). Besides adolescence and young adulthood, a second time of normative separations and transition is old age.

A third factor that may contribute to reminiscing uses of objects is how much contemplation one's everyday life allows for. While at ages at which taking care of children and pursuing a career keep us busy, in adolescence and old age active role demands decrease, which provides more space for reminiscing.

Finally, a fourth factor may simply be the portion of one's life one has already lived and how much is still ahead and to be actively mastered. This final consideration implies a linear increase in reminding uses of personal objects, while the first three factors suggest a more curvilinear course of the frequency of reminiscing across the lifespan which peaks in late adolescence and late life.

These considerations do not take into account that possessing souvenirs is different from reminiscing: The advantage of the material nature of souvenirs, when compared with the immaterial nature of memories, is that they may authenticate the past and presentify the absent other. A further advantage is that they may silently store memories that need not be looked after or rehearsed, but can reemerge after many years. Thus, in middle adulthood, many souvenirs may linger in attics or other unattended corners of one's home without being actively used. Therefore, the mere possession of souvenirs may not follow a curvilinear course, while their active use probably does.

9

Reminiscence Functions in Adulthood: Age, Race, and Family Dynamics Correlates

Jeffrey Dean Webster

"Reminiscing is a pervasive part of social interaction in families . . . with parents and children beginning to converse about shared past experiences almost as soon as children start to talk." (Haden, 1998, p. 99)

The act of recalling previous experiences is a fundamental, common activity. As the opening quote suggests, the process of remembering personally experienced episodes from one's past, that is, reminiscence, may begin very early in life. Nevertheless, the bulk of reminiscence research has stemmed from a clinical, gerontological perspective with the vast majority of work carried out exclusively with elderly adults. Consequently, we have less information concerning how the process and functions of reminiscing are manifested in younger adulthood. Further, most reminiscence research has been conducted primarily with White participants. Consequently, we remain relatively ignorant concerning whether or not, and to what extent, ethnic differences may impact the frequency and uses of reminiscence behavior in adulthood. Related research on autobiographical memory has demonstrated differences among Korean, Chinese, and White American children, for instance (Han, Leichtman, & Wang, 1998). Finally, the social origins of reminiscence have not been explored systematically in adulthood, and research in this area is just emerging with young children (e.g., Fivush & Reese, 1992, chapter 7, this volume; Haden, 1998; Haden, Haine, & Fivush, 1997). Consequently, we lack insight into the early social dynamics which may foster or curtail reminiscence behavior in later life.

The purposes of this chapter, therefore, are threefold. First, by examining differences in reminiscence functions in both younger and older community-residing adults, we broaden our appreciation of reminiscence as a normative, lifespan process. Second, by comparing different ethnic groups, we can expand our understanding of individual differences in reminiscence behavior that have important implications for both theory and clinical interventions. Third, by assessing the relationship between selected family dynamics variables and adult reminiscence functions, we can begin to determine which facets of the socialization process serve as catalysts for future reminiscence behavior.

LITERATURE REVIEW

Critical reviews of the reminiscence literature (e.g., Bluck & Levine, 1998; Haight, 1991; Merriam, 1980; Molinari, 1999; Molinari & Reichlin, 1985; Thornton & Brotchie, 1987; Webster & Cappeliez, 1993; Webster & Haight, 1995) have documented several limitations in research conducted to date. A partial list of identified problems includes: (a) conceptual issues (e.g., how are related concepts such as reminiscence, life review, narrative, and autobiography, differentiated); (b) methodological issues (e.g., lack of adequate controls, poor experimental design); (c) sampling issues (e.g., virtually exclusive reliance on older, White participants); and (d) measurement issues (e.g., few standardized instruments to measure reminiscence dimensions exist with adequate psychometric properties). For our purposes, the reliance on primarily older and ethnically homogeneous participants are the important issues, which are addressed below.

Reminiscence in Adulthood

As noted earlier, the preponderance of reminiscence research has been conducted almost exclusively on elderly adults who are often institutionalized. This focus has arisen, in part, from the clinical, gerontological origins of reminiscence research (Webster, 1999). However, in the few studies where researchers have included adults of all ages, the results indicate that for simple measures of reminiscence frequency, there are more similarities than differences as a function of age. To illustrate, consider the following empirical investigations.

Merriam and Cross (1982) examined simple reminiscence frequency in a sample which included adults from 18 to 90 years of age. Findings indicated that younger and older adults were similar to each other in frequency and that the middle-aged group had the lowest reminiscence frequency relative to the younger and older participants. In a similar finding, Hyland and Ackerman (1988) found that their younger subjects reported more frequent reminiscence than did their middle-aged volunteers, and that the frequency with which the younger subjects reminisced was similar to older adults' frequency.

Romaniuk and Romaniuk (1983) reported an overall lack of age differences in several facets of the contents of reminiscence. Specifically, there were no age differences in (a) the frequency of recalled transitional or nontransitional life events, (b) the amount of positive affect in recall, (c) the primary character of the reminiscence episode, and (d) the redundancy of memories recalled.

Webster (1994) reported that gender (women scored higher) and personality traits (i.e., openness to experience), but not age, were significant predictors of simple reminiscence frequency in a sample ranging in age from 18 to 81.

de Vries, Blando, and Walker (1995) investigated the content and structure of life review protocols in a sample of young, middle-aged, and elderly participants. Results indicated that middle-aged and older adults recalled more events than did younger volunteers, but that there were no age differences in either the type or evaluation of life events recalled. Similarly, there were no significant main effects for age when analyzing the integrative complexity of recalled life events, although there were some qualifications to the above based upon complex three-way interactions.

Webster (1995) examined adult age differences in reminiscence functions in a sample of 710 adults approximately equally spread over the decades from adolescents to octogenarians. Participants completed the Reminiscence Functions Scale (RFS), a 43-item questionnaire measuring the uses, or functions, of reminiscence (see the Measures discussion for a description of the RFS). Results indicated that there were no age differences on the total RFS score, suggesting that reminiscence is a relatively common activity regardless of age. There were, however, interesting age differences on all of the individual factor scores except for one, termed "Conversation."

Reminiscence and Race

To my knowledge, there is only one published empirical study which directly examined racial differences in the uses of reminiscence in adulthood. Merriam (1993) examined 291 adults in the Georgia Centenarian Study on a 17-item uses of reminiscence scale. Results indicated that Blacks (27.8% of the overall sample) scored higher than Whites on all 9 of the 17 items which showed a statistical racial difference. In particular, Merriam notes that ". . . blacks used reminiscence more than whites to understand life and themselves and the changes that occur, and to teach others about the past and about their own accomplishments" (p. 13). She suggested that the results reflected a stronger oral tradition among Blacks in her particular sample.

In the related area of autobiographical memory, Wang, Leichtman, and White (1997) (cited in Han, Leichtman, & Wang, 1998) report that Chinese adults report earliest memories that are dated significantly later than those of White Americans. Hence, ethnic differences on certain *structural* elements (i.e., temporal distribution) of *autobiographical* memories have been demonstrated. Whether similar differences will emerge in the *functional* aspects of *reminiscence* is one of the goals of the present study.

Reminiscence and Family Dynamics

As Habegger and Blieszner (1990) note, ". . . early experience with reminiscing—how often friends, family and acquaintances reminisced or listened to reminiscing during one's childhood and young adulthood—is a part of the socialization process that may have a relationship to reminiscence frequency" (p. 23). They found that a six-item "early experience" scale (e.g., "When I was a child, my family spent a lot of time talking things over," and "When I was a young adult, my friends like [sic] to recall their school days") correlated .24 ($p < .05$) with a total reminiscence frequency score and correlated .63 ($p < .001$) with a "current opportunities" for reminiscence scale.

Recently, Webster and McCall (1999) asked participants to respond to the statement, "In your family, how important would you say sharing memories is?" on a seven-point scale, where 1 = "not at all" important to 7 = "very" important. Results indicated that this single-item measure was positively correlated with the RFS functions of Conversation, Intimacy Maintenance, Identity, and Teach/Inform (r_s = .27, .26, .15, and .40, respectively).

Summary and Hypotheses

Few reminiscence studies have included both young and old adults or investigated race as a main variable. Similarly, we remain benighted concerning early family socialization processes and their relationship to specific functions of reminiscence in adulthood. This study tests the following three hypotheses.

1. In terms of age differences, we predict that the findings of Webster (1995) reviewed above will be replicated with one exception noted below. Specifically, we hypothesize that younger adults will score higher on the RFS functions of Bitterness Revival, Boredom Reduction, Identity, and Problem-Solving, whereas older adults will score higher on the RFS factors of Teach/Inform and Death Preparation. Older adults also scored higher on Intimacy Maintenance in the Webster (1995) study, but two recent investigations (i.e., Rybash & Hrubi, 1997; Webster & McCall, 1999) found that older and younger adults did not differ on Intimacy Maintenance. The mean levels in the Webster (1995) and Webster and McCall (1999) study were virtually identical (i.e., teenagers scored approximately 14, and 80-year-olds scored approximately 16.5) but, due to the large sample size (n = 710) in the former study, these differences reached statistical significance whereas in the latter, smaller study (n = 268) they did not. Therefore, we predict that there will be no age differences on Intimacy Maintenance in the present study. Finally, Conversation has consistently been shown not to differ as a function of age and so we predict no age differences on this RFS function.

2. In terms of ethnic differences, no previously published evidence concerning Chinese versus White adult participants on measures of reminiscence functions was found upon which to base a prediction. However, if we can say that both Black Americans and Chinese Canadians share the common trait of being a visible minority, then we might expect both minority groups to score higher than Whites on some reminiscence functions. Markus and Kitayama (1991), for instance, suggest that certain Asian and African ethnic groups are characterized by interdependent self-construals, while many Western ethnic groups are characterized by independent self-construals. Han and colleagues (1998) remark that such divergent cultural forces "have the power to shape autobiographical memory at a profound cognitive level" (p. 711). Precisely how such general differences translate into specific hypotheses concerning reminiscence functions in adulthood is currently unclear, however. For this reason, unpublished pilot data (i.e., a reanalysis of previous work with the RFS) which indicated that Chinese participants scored higher than White participants on the following RFS factors: Bitterness Revival, Boredom Reduction, Death Preparation, and Teach/Inform, constitutes the basis for the present hypothesis. Specifically, we hypothesize that Chinese participants in the present study will likewise score higher than White participants on these RFS factors.

3. Finally, given that the Family Memories Index (FMI; see below for a description) is conceptually related to the single-item measure employed in the Webster and McCall (1999) study, we hypothesize that the FMI will be positively correlated with the RFS factors of Conversation, Identity, Intimacy Maintenance, and Teach/Inform.

METHOD

Participants

Ninety-nine male and 117 female volunteers, ranging in age from 18 to 81 (M age = 42.98; SD = 20.02) participated in the current study. In terms of racial composition, 130 participants (60.2%) were White, and 86 participants (39.8%) were Chinese. Overall, the volunteers in this study rated themselves as healthy (M = 5.06; SD = 1.14) on a scale of self-perceived health where scores could range from 1 = "poor" to 7 = "excellent", and had a mean education level of 13.74 years (range = 6 to 24; SD = 2.64). Older adults had a higher mean education level than younger adults (14.18 versus 13.14, respectively), $t(234)$ = –3.07, p = .002. No other age, sex, or ethnic effects were significant for either education or health variables.

Procedure and Materials

Younger participants were solicited from undergraduate psychology classes at a large, ethnically diverse community college in the metropolitan Vancouver area. Older volunteers were recruited by psychology students from the same college. Students, both participants and recruiters, received nominal course credit for their participation. Participants were asked to complete a measure of reminiscence functions and a family reminiscence questionnaire as well as provide demographic information concerning education, ethnicity, health, and marital status.

Reminiscence Functions Scale. The functions of reminiscence were measured by the Reminiscence Functions Scale (RFS; Webster, 1993, 1997). The RFS is a valid and reliable 43-item questionnaire in which subjects indicate on a six-point scale how often they reminisce with a particular function in mind. The items are presented as completions to the stem: "When I reminisce it is:". For example, an item following from the stem might read: "to pass the time during idle or restless hours." The RFS consists of eight factors which are briefly detailed below.

Boredom Reduction measures our propensity to reminisce when our environment is understimulating and we lack engagement in goal-directed activities. Death Preparation assesses the way we use our past when thoughts of our own mortality are salient and may contribute to a sense of closure and calmness. Identity measures how we use our past in an existential manner to discover, clarify, and crystallize important dimensions of our sense of who we are. Problem-Solving taps how we employ reminiscence as a constructive coping mechanism whereby the remembrance of past problem-solving strategies may be used again in the present. Conversation measures our natural inclination to invoke the past as a means of connecting or reconnecting with others in an informal way. It serves a social bonding purpose. Intimacy Maintenance measures a process whereby cognitive and emotional representations of important persons in our lives are resurrected in lieu of the remembered person's physical presence. Bitterness Revival assesses the extent to which memories are used to affectively charge recalled episodes in which the reminiscer perceives themselves as having been unjustly treated. It may provide a justification to maintain negative thoughts and emotions towards others. Finally, Teach/Inform measures the ways in which we use reminiscence to relay to others important information about life and/or ourselves (e.g., a moral lesson). It is an instructional type of narrative. RFS factor score reliabilities (i.e., Cronbach Alphas) for the present study ranged from .79 to .90 (*M* Alpha = .85). Specifically, the RFS factors of Bitterness Revival, Boredom Reduction, Conversation, Death Preparation, Identity, Intimacy Maintenance, Problem-Solving, and Teach/Inform had alpha scores equal to .85, .87, .84, .90, .87, .82, .87, and .79, respectively.

Family Memories Index. The Family Memories Index (FMI) is a ten-item measure, constructed for this study, assessing how important sharing memories in one's family of origin was perceived to be by the participants. The FMI represents an improvement over the similar measure constructed by Habeggar & Blieszner (1990) in the following ways: (1) the FMI is more comprehensive (10 versus 6 items), (2) all FMI items refer to the past, whereas one item in the Habegger & Blieszner (1990) scale (i.e., "When I was a child, my family spent a lot of time talking things over") could refer to current events as opposed to memories, and (3) no test-retest reliability information was reported for Habegger & Blieszner's scale.

For the FMI, participants were presented with the stem: "When I was growing up, my family:", and then read 10 statements such as, "enjoyed talking about the past," "shared memories often," "valued shared reminiscences," and "found discussing the past boring". Each statement was rated on a Likert-type scale where 1 = "Strongly Disagree" to 5 = "Strongly Agree". The total score could therefore range from a low of 10 to a maximum of 50. Three of the items were reverse scored to guard against response set. A Principal Component Analysis (CPA) with Varimax rotation indicated a two-factor solution to the ten-item FMI. Upon inspection, however, the second factor was composed exclusively of the three items which were reverse scored. Therefore, all items were combined into a single score. A one week test-retest correlation of .82 indicated good reliability.

RESULTS

Age, Gender, and Race Differences in Reminiscence Functions

To assess potential differences on overall reminiscence frequency, a 2 (age) by 2 (sex) by 2 (ethnicity) analysis of variance (ANOVA) was performed with the total RFS score serving as the dependent variable. Results indicated a main effect only for the ethnicity variable, F (1, 215) = 8.71, p = .004, whereby Chinese participants scored higher than White participants. Neither age, sex, nor any two-way or three-way interactions were significant.

To determine possible variation between age, sex, and ethnic groups on individual RFS factor scores, a 2 (age) by 2 (sex) by 2 (ethnicity) multiple analysis of variance (MANOVA) was conducted with the eight RFS factor scores serving as the dependent variables. Using the Wilks Lambda criterion, the overall effect for age, F (8, 201) = 23.77, p = .000, and for ethnicity, F (8, 201) = 4.08, p = .000, were significant. The overall effect for sex and the two-way and three-way interactions did not reach statistical significance at the .05 level. Table 9.1 shows the univariate F-tests for the age and race main effects for all eight RFS factor scores.

As can be seen from Table 9.1, six of eight RFS factor scores differed as a function of age. Younger adults scored higher on the RFS factors of Bitterness Revival, Boredom Reduction, Identity, and Problem-Solving; older adults scored higher on the RFS factors of Death Preparation and Teach/Inform. Five RFS factors differed as a function of ethnicity with Chinese participants scoring higher than Whites on all five of the following: Bitterness Revival, Boredom Reduction, Conversation, Death Preparation, and Teach/Inform.

TABLE 9.1   Univariate _F_ Tests for Age and Race on Each RFS Factor

RFS Factor/Variable	F	p
Bitterness Revival		
Age	6.55	.011
Race	7.61	.006
Boredom Reduction		
Age	8.60	.004
Race	7.59	.006
Conversation		
Age	1.00	.317
Race	5.45	.021
Death Preparation		
Age	16.99	.000
Race	12.26	.001
Identity		
Age	8.23	.005
Race	2.50	.115
Intimacy Maintenance		
Age	.400	.528
Race	.481	.489
Problem-Solving		
Age	13.26	.000
Race	1.82	.178
Teach/Inform		
Age	35.50	.000
Race	11.30	.001

Reminiscence and Family Memories

To assess the relationship between reminiscence functions and the importance of shared family memories, Pearson correlation coefficients were calculated between the FMI and the RFS total score as well as between the FMI and all 8 RFS factor scores. Results indicated that the FMI correlated positively ($r = .17$, $p < .05$) with the RFS total score and that the following four RFS factors were significantly correlated with the FMI: Conversation ($r = .26$, $p = .000$), Identity ($r = .14$, $p = .041$), Intimacy Maintenance ($r = .15$, $p = .025$), and Teach/Inform ($r = .25$, $p = .000$).

DISCUSSION

This study examined the underinvestigated dimensions of age, ethnicity, and family dynamics variables as they related to reminiscence functions in adulthood. The results provide some of the first empirical evidence of ethnic differences in reminiscence behavior and introduce a new, psychometrically sound measure of family dynamics (i.e., the FMI). The strong replication of age differences provides a strong foundation for further developmental work. Some implications and limitations of the present findings are discussed below.

As predicted, and consistent with prior research with the RFS, there were no age differences on the total RFS score, indicating that reminiscence is a common activity for many adults, regardless of age. This reinforces calls (e.g., Webster, 1999) to adopt a lifespan perspective on reminiscence behavior and to see it as a normative process. Clearly, reminiscing is not the exclusive province of elderly adults. Although this age invariance has been tacitly recognized by some, and explicitly acknowledged by a few, it has been given only lip service to date.

Despite invariance on the RFS total score, however, there are nevertheless, consistent differences in the frequency with which younger and older adults engage in reminiscing for *specific* purposes.

Supporting hypothesis 1, younger adults reminisced more for Bitterness Revival than did older adults. This may suggest that older adults have acquired the wisdom necessary to contextualize previous experiences and to recognize the multiple reasons for another person's hurtful behavior. In this way, they are able to place earlier episodes in perspective and realize the futility of harbouring resentments over the long term. In contrast, for younger adults, perceived slights and hurtful behaviors from others are still fresh, perhaps due to their recency. The emotional rawness, therefore, may prevent a younger person from letting go of such painful memories.

Younger adults, as expected, also scored higher on Boredom Reduction than older adults. This suggests that the present environment of younger persons is understimulating and they reminisce to relieve the tedium of the moment more so than older adults. Perhaps the older adults in this sample, the majority of whom are either approaching retirement or have retired relatively recently, find the preparations and executions of late job/retirement-related activities more engaging than the educational and/or career entry tasks confronting the younger participants.

As hypothesized, younger adults also scored higher on the related RFS factors of Identity and Problem Solving. Consistent with developmental theory, younger adults are engaged in the task of identity formation and consolidation. Part of this enterprise involves reflection upon where one has come from, who one is now, and anticipation of future selves. Reminiscing for this reason thus makes both intuitive and theoretical sense. Problem Solving, of which forming an identity is one example, is also used more frequently by younger adults. Perhaps this stage of life is characterized by more "transitional firsts," that is, novel challenges, obstacles, and problems compared with later adulthood.

Older adults, in contrast, and also as predicted, scored higher on the RFS factors of Death Preparation and Teach/Inform. As one ages, one both moves ineluctably closer to death and progressively accumulates life experiences which can be used in a mentoring context. In terms of the former, research has documented that older adults talk more about death than younger adults, but, paradoxically, are less fearful of it. The current results suggest that reminiscing about one's entire life can help achieve a sense of equanimity in the face of personal mortality. A recognition of a full life well lived, enables the older adult to achieve some sense of personal closure and existential calmness, consistent with Butler's (1963) concept of the life review. With respect to mentoring, the Eriksonian notion of generativity states that older adults care for succeeding generations, in part, by passing on valuable life lessons. This mode of reminiscing has been documented by others (e.g., Coleman, 1986; Wong & Watt, 1991) and is an explicitly social type of remembering. Recent empirical support for an explicit link between Teach/Inform reminiscence and generativity has been reported by Norman, Harris, and Webster (2001). A caution is in order here, however. Older adults most likely have children and/or grandchildren who often serve as an audience for and solicitors of reminiscence. Younger adults have fewer "targets" for their remembrances. Consequently, this age difference on Teach/Inform may have as much to do with opportunity as with skill, desire, or life-stage imperative.

Finally, as predicted, there were no age differences on the RFS factors of Intimacy Maintenance or Conversation. This suggests that both younger and older adults are similar in their need to occasionally recall important people in their lives who are no longer physically present (i.e., Intimacy Maintenance) and to emotionally bond or reconnect with someone else by invoking the past (i.e., Conversation).

As indicated, Chinese participants scored higher than their White counterparts on all five of the RFS factors which differed by race. In this sense, the present results are consistent with those of Merriam (1993) whose Black participants scored higher than Whites on all reminiscence dimensions which achieved statistical significance. This has implications for theories which posit a universal nature of reminiscence. Clearly, both Chinese and White Canadians (as groups) in this study reminisced, but at slightly different levels. Are there other racial/ethnic/religious groups which reminisce even more than Chinese or less than Whites? For example, unpublished reanalyses of aggregated RFS data show that First Nations (i.e., Native Canadians) persons scored very high on certain RFS factors, whereas East Indian participants score lower than Whites. Perhaps certain religious principles or spiritual philosophies (e.g., reincarnation) influence how frequently different groups use Death Preparation.

One of the limitations of the current results are that they are descriptive in nature and provoke many questions which the present study is unable to answer. Consequently, possible explanations are harder to come by and remain speculative. Some tentative reasons for racial differences between the Chinese and White participants may include recent immigration, differences in negative life experiences (e.g., "culture shock", exposure to racism), varying strengths of oral traditions, or differences in cultural constructions of identity between eastern and western societies (e.g., collectivist versus individualist perspectives, respectively). The findings of higher scores on some of the "negative" RFS factors such as Boredom Reduction and Bitterness Revival, are consistent with racial differences reported recently by Okazaki (1997) who found that Asian Americans scored higher than Whites on measures of depression and social anxiety. Future work should seek to replicate the present descriptive findings and seek causal mechanisms in cooperation with sociologists, anthropologists, political scientists, and other multidisciplinary partners.

Findings that reminiscing in an earlier family environment predicts aspects of reminiscence as an adult provides new and important information concerning the origins of reminiscence behavior and also helps account for individual differences in reminiscence frequency in adulthood. Taken as a group, the four RFS factors which correlated with the FMI can be thought of as social in nature. For both Teach/Inform and Conversation, at least one other person serves as a target for the reminiscer, that is, there is a direct social audience. Similarly, for Intimacy Maintenance, one's reminiscence has as its focus an important, significant other, although they are not physically present. Identity, on the other hand, does not necessarily require a focus on others, but discovering one's own identity often entails comparisons with important members of one's social network, such as family, friends, and lovers (e.g., Andersen, Reznik, & Chen, 1997).

The family is widely acknowledged as the crucible of later development. Living in a family whose members elicit, share, and value thinking and talking about the past, models a skill and teaches a value to individual members. The lesson inculcated in such families is that reminiscing, either publicly or privately, is a valuable resource which one may draw upon in many different contexts and for myriad reasons. In contrast, families which devalue reminiscence, perhaps because their individual/collective past is traumatic or because they believe reminiscence is tantamount to "living in the past," hence worthless, indoctrinate their members with a very different set of beliefs. Recent research (e.g., Hirst, Manier, & Apetroaia, 1997) has demonstrated, for example, that family members may be assigned and/or adopt particular narrative roles (i.e., narrator, mentor, monitor) as they jointly recount shared past experiences. Similarly, research on reminiscence in very young children has indicated that family interaction patterns and conversation styles influence the frequency and complexity of childrens' autobiographical narratives (see Fivush & Reese, chapter 7, this volume). As adults, then, people may reminisce more or less because these differences in family dynamics shape subsequent attitudes and beliefs about the usefulness of reminiscence.

Over a quarter century ago, Havighurst and Glasser (1972) exhorted colleagues to "study reminiscence throughout the life cycle, to describe it empirically, and to discover its functions in human development" (p. 245). Unfortunately, there is little, if any, cross-referencing between the clinical gerontological and the child developmental literatures on reminiscence. The present paper is an initial attempt to encourage dialogue between these two research domains and to seriously accept the challenge issued by Havighurst & Glasser. The ensuing results can provide handsome conceptual, methodological, and clinical dividends.

ACKNOWLEDGMENT

The excellent data entry skills of Vincent Naidu are gratefully acknowledged, as are the helpful comments offered by two anonymous reviewers.

10

Reminiscence, Personal Meaning, Themes, and the "Object Relations" of Older People

Robert L. Rubinstein

"Why does this light force me back to my childhood?" (Jane Kenyon, 1986:34)

Reminiscence suggests periodically manifest, but continuing, ties to the past. The texture of such ties can be longed for, pleasurable, desirable, compulsive, intrusive, unhappy, or ambivalent. For older people, the relentless cultural force of chronological time cannot overcome a desire to revisit the past, a visit described by some as natural and a necessary part of growing old (Butler & Lewis, 1982; Rubinstein, 1995).

While the connections to the past expressed through reminiscence clearly reflect the past, they are significantly part of the present. In gerontology, much has been made of the question of whether people, or personality, or "the self" actually change over time and the nature of the changes (McCrea & Costa, 1984; Kaufman, 1986). In my own experience in interviewing older people, aged informants have described themselves as changing in some ways and remaining the same in others. Nevertheless, it is important to note that the self (defined here as the culturally defined and individually constructed person) changes over time, both in content and structure.

While reminiscence speaks to that of the past that is germane to the present, we rarely speak about antireminiscence, or that which is forgotten when aspects of the self are sloughed off over time. This is different from personality processes such as repression that may lead to the erasure from the conscious mind of certain difficult events that are indirectly expressed through unconscious mechanisms. Rather, reminiscence expresses the unrepressed and unsloughed off and seems more a part of the socialized or cultural self.

Indeed, recent literature from the cultural sciences suggests that collective memory is culturally and historically constructed (Connerton, 1989; Thomas, 1998). So why should not the memory of the social self be similarly constituted, that is, as the object of social and cultural processes? Indeed, the self is a cultural variable, as many anthropologists have pointed out, as is the "behavioral environment" of the self. Even such basic orienting elements as time and space are cultural products (Hallowell, 1955).

I argue here that reminiscence is a cultural product and that, for elders, one of its most important roles is as an element of the present-day self. It is not that older people necessarily "live in the past" or take interaction-numbing trips "down memory lane." Rather, it is that the past becomes important for present day identity in part due to the tension between the American (or Western) construction of the self (as "independent," "active," "of agency," and "making choices") and the cultural construction of old age (as "declining," "close to death," "inactive," "sick," and the like). It has been known since the earliest work of cultural anthropologists in the realm of aging that elders must make a number of adjustments and compromises to wisely navigate the transition to later life (Clark and Anderson, 1967). But by and large these are difficult transitions to make given the narcissistic investments that are culturally necessary to be an American and the loss to self that is so much a part of how the aged are culturally defined here (Alexander et al., 1991).

In part because of this acute discrepancy in American culture, and for other reasons as well, the relation between the person and her reminiscence parallels the presence of other media used to "support" the self in later life. Media such as place, through "attachment to place" (see Rubinstein & Parmelee, 1995) and important personal objects (Rubinstein, 1987, 1989, 1990; Habermas & Paha, chapter 8, this volume) function also as buttresses to the self and indicators of cultural agency or, in other words, as part of self-identity in later life. These representations of the self (place attachment, object attachment, and reminiscence) make permeable the boundary between person and object.

Both the Western definition of the person (Morris, 1991) and the American definition of individualism highlight the relationship between the person and possessions. The relationship between person and possessions does not concern ownership as it is generally conceived per se (a legal or moral relationship), but rather concern inalienable psychosocial processes. Thus, it may be possible to sell a home, but it is impossible to divest oneself of memories of it, of its symbolism or meaning, or of a remembered or ongoing relationship with it, once it has been sold.

Similarly, personal possessions that elders are generally attached to, such as family photos, bric-a-brac, inherited family items, older objects acquired early in a marriage, travel souvenirs, household objects, or made objects, usually have little monetary value nor would anyone necessarily be interested in buying them. Their value is personalized since they derive meaning from the relationship with the owner. (Nevertheless, the recent burgeoning of flea markets and Internet auctions must be seen in some way as a possible mercantile expansion of the capture of such personalized "object relations" by consumerism. Personal meaning can now be bought!)

In this chapter I discuss reminiscence among the aged in regard to a framework of the person in cultural context. In part I suggest that reminiscence be understood as part of the disconnect between core cultural values and the social marginality of later life. Further, the self can be seen as it emerges in dialogue with objects and environments. Below, a theoretical background is described. Next, two detailed case studies are presented. The first case concerns Mr. Gardiner, a 92-year-old, once-widowed, retired corporate executive. Here, the rather plain suburban garden apartment he shared with his second wife, and that contained his possessions, embodied key personal themes that combined reminiscence and action. The second case concerns Mrs. Stein, a 78-year-old divorced woman who maintained her nearly lifelong residence in a small Philadelphia rowhouse. This residence was truly a "symbol that stands for itself" to use Wagner's (1986) term. Because so much in her life had taken place in this home and neighborhood it was the setting of, she said, most of her reminiscence. In both instances, reminiscence was clearly associated with markers of personal identity and with maintenance of the self. In a sense, reminiscence was a form of attachment, not to the past but to persons and places still germane to the present. Reminiscence was just one of several vectors that helped arrange the current-day self and was therefore similar to objects and places. Again, the whole of this arrangement of the self may be seen as attending to the inherent cultural program of the high aspirations of the American self and the lowered aspirations culturally attributed to old age.

Theoretical Background

American culture, built on assumptions of individualism, personal agency, and choice-making, views old age as problematic in these regards. While it sets up individual action as its central mode, it largely defines the aged as outside of these areas, as dependent rather than independent for example. It therefore sets up a contested area for the person, where cultural demands increasingly do not meet culturally defined status and capacities. The self thus becomes problematized in old age, not because of losses per se, but because of the cultural conflation of old age, decline and death, the increasing commercial emphasis on youth and health self-maintenance, the loss of social space and social standing, and role loss. Through a number of psychosocial mechanisms that are provided "around" the official system of cultural meaning, the aged person must manage a self that is increasingly threatened over time. The self must integrate past identities into its current-day version. As noted above, it does so through a variety of vectors of attachment.

To invest the world around her with significance, the older person uses a system of personal meaning. This system provides subjectively accountable, evidence-based categories and emphases used to locate and place new events in context. The personal meaning system consists of three components: cultural ideas, personal biography, and the act of interpretation. Thus culture sets the larger framework, subject to historical, ethnic, religious, cohort, period, and other effects. A personal biography, including consciousness of personal habits, desires, and dispositions, provides a more immediate framework for meaning. It is very difficult to understand much about how older people (indeed, anyone at all) exist without reference to personal history—the personally constructed biography. Finally, acts of interpretation by persons assign meaning to ongoing happenings. Often, for elders, personal meaning is organized into "areas" or packets of core ideas, grouped and associated together, which have been called themes (Kaufman, 1986; Shenk, 1998).

As noted above, phenomena such as reminiscence become active parts of the current self in roles as components of the currently defined biography. In contrast, little research has focused on divested selves (perhaps the opposite of Markus' possible selves) and divested objects and places. Perhaps any hope of better understanding former or divested reminiscences is distant and ephemeral.

A cultural or symbolic system can be said to construct a "self in its behavioral environment" (Hallowell, 1955). Similarly, in a symbolic system such as American culture that emphasizes radical individualism, it is also useful to speak of an individual in a behavioral environment, that is, the personal surroundings over which the individual self habitually extends. As a consequence, both objects and places become imbued with personal meaning. Reminiscence is a less material form, but one derived from similar cultural issues facing the person.

As has often been noted, the self is dialogic. While it gives the appearance, at any one time, of seeming solid and unchanging, in reality the self is somewhat more illusory and is enmeshed in continuing relations with elements external to it. Of the various representations of the self that we have mentioned here that exist both within and outside the self (homes, objects, reminiscences), reminiscence is distinctive in that it is the least material and the most internal. Indeed, some may argue that reminiscence has no externality at all, that it occurs totally within the mind of the person. Yet reminiscence, as ideation, can move towards the objectivated in several ways. For example, it may have a structure that gives it a more material form. Further, while we would not necessarily call a new memory reminiscence, reminiscence may occur in exactly the same way time after time, giving it an objectified formality. Particular episodes of memory may be triggered by the same stimuli: bodily positioning, mood, time of day, type of association, or as Jane Kenyon notes (above) particular manifestations of light. In a sense, the self hungers for these in that they bring a pleasurable sense of completion. It is not certain whether bad memories per se are reminiscence or something else, but as Erikson long ago noted, revisiting them is necessary for the work of the self.

The self has manifestations of concreteness but it is always in motion. In concreteness, the self emphasizes a more chronological, linear perspective. In motion, the self emphasizes dialogue and perspective taking. From the view of concreteness, reminiscences are about the past, about particular times, places, moods, and events. From the view of motion, reminiscences can be thought of as "virtual" or "frozen dialogue" which open the possibility of taking multiple perspectives as the "dialogues" are approached from all sides. In both cases, reminiscences are objectivated in the sense that they can be returned to, again and again, to revisit both relationship and identity.

There is another issue regarding the aged to be mentioned at this point, that elements of a personal meaning system are often organized thematically. Themes are higher order groupings of similar elements that are personally meaningful. They are often defined or identified as such by informants themselves. In what follows, I will discuss a few of the key themes of two informants who constitute cases for description. Themes have important implications for reminiscence. On the one hand, a theme is a meta-element of identity, active at the present time.

On the other hand (as we shall see), a theme may be constituted from elements of both past and present. Whether this makes a past event that is part of a theme a thing of the past or of the present, is unimportant. For many, reminiscence takes place as part of constructing the theme, which always has meaning in the present.

Case Examples

Mr. Gardiner.   When I visited Mr. Gardiner and his wife at their two-bedroom garden apartment in suburban Philadelphia, he was 92. He was a former manager at a Fortune 500 company. I was impressed that, at the time I visited him, he had been retired longer than I had been alive. I visited him weekly for about five months. He had two children, a daughter who lived in another city out west and a son who lived closer. He had many grandchildren and great grandchildren. With the exception of his daughter, to whom he felt close, none of his family members figured prominently in what he said about himself. His first wife died nearly 30 years previously, and he had been married to his current wife, in her early 70s at the time of the interview, for almost 20 years. They appeared to be close and she, a former nurse, also appeared to be the household manager, scheduler, and caregiver. When initially asked to describe his health, he replied with energy that it was "excellent," although he backed off this statement a bit eventually. Nevertheless, he was remarkably robust and had suffered little from illness of any sort during his life. He was still active and engaged with contemporary life. In many ways he was an excellent role model for living. About a year after the interview series, I received a letter from him telling me that he had moved to an assisted living facility in the state of his birth.

As part of the format for several interviews, I asked him to tell the story of his life. I was also able to inquire about the subject matter and nature of his reminiscences. In some ways, he framed his life story chronologically. He began from the time of his birth in 1892 and proceeded through his parents and early family life, his education in a rural, one-room school, university student career, officer training, participation in World War I, his own family life, his long tenure with one company, and his retirement. However, his story appeared to be organized in a more fundamentally thematic way. Many of the linear chronological events were not told as a "straight story," but were rather tied together in crosscutting, higher order frameworks, or themes. I will describe a few of these next. It is important to note that, from what he told me about his own reminiscing, his reminiscence both did and did not correspond to his themes.

One man against the powers that be.   One theme that he identified explicitly and illustrated with many stories and examples, and one that was at the core of his being, was his view of himself as engaged in a lifelong battle against those higher in power whom he viewed as incompetent, wicked, and wasteful. On one of my very first visits to his home, he told me a story about how, during World War I, he had stood up to and openly argued with a superior officer concerning what he thought was an insane battle plan. In retrospect, he clearly relished the risk of the confrontation and drew pleasure from the identification of stupidity. In his corporate career, he drew particular pleasure in an adversarial position to the Department of Defense. The corporation for which he worked was a large defense contractor. In his job he was able to see how, towards the close of the fiscal year, immense orders for unneeded military supplies were processed so that the "need" for them could be presented to Congress for the next fiscal year. In retirement, he viewed this continuing battle as his "hobby." This task was environmentally located: he had an antique desk, inherited from his family, at which he wrote a steady stream of "letters to the editor" about what he identified as public, especially military, malfeasance. Writing materials, copies of newspapers and magazines, and responses, if any, were kept there. He clearly identified this desk as the "place" where he did this work. While this activity was important to him, and helped to centrally define him, he did not appear to reminisce about it. He was proud of what he had done to oppose malfeasance in the past, and told many stories of this, but it did not appear to engender frequent reminiscence. Rather, he had found activities which he could undertake at home that substituted for those he undertook earlier in life in the military or in business. While he had grown into his role as elderly "curmudgeon," he did not need to reminisce or undertake other buttresses to a self that, despite age, expressed agency fully.

"My love of nature."   A second theme concerned his love of nature. To him, nature meant freedom and openness. He spoke of his boyhood in rural Maryland and how he was able to wander openly for miles, across anyone's property, to appreciate the natural surroundings. He described this as "a sense of complete freedom," one which he rarely experienced again in his life and one which was completely at odds with modern life.

Nevertheless, he was able to environmentally extend this theme. As part of their tenure in their apartment, Mr. and Mrs. Gardiner has taken control of a small plot of land beside one of the parking areas and at the periphery of the apartment complex campus and had turned this into an active garden. In miniature form this expressed some of the love of nature and, Mr. Gardiner openly admitted, extended a bit the sense of freedom and love of nature which were so much a part of his childhood. The garden also enabled Mr. Gardiner to thumb his nose at convention: he took pleasure that he had rescued this small plot of land from its assignment to "progress" as a sidebar to one in an endless circuit of paved parking lot.

Mr. Gardiner did reminisce a very great deal about his youth, he reported. The sense of freedom and security he experienced was unsurpassed and transcendental. In his mind, he relived this past of unfenced vistas and few limits on his hours of pleasure. As a boy he fished, swam, hiked, and made scientific collections of natural history specimens with joy. Those days were now gone, but they stayed with him actively through his garden, and mentally through reminiscence.

Mrs. Stein.   About 77 when I first met her, Mrs. Stein was of medium height, overweight, and thoroughly pleasant, with warm eyes and an engaging smile. She liked to talk and, especially, to reminisce.

She lived in a small, two-story rowhouse in South Philadelphia, an area noted as home to successive waves of immigrants. Her street was narrow and the houses clustered together. In many conversations, she traced her life for me. Born in about 1905 in Russia, she came as a very young child with her parents and siblings to America, in about 1912. While the family myth spoke of comfort in Russia, in America they were poor. Her father was a laborer, securing jobs whenever he could. They purchased their rowhouse in 1915 and, except for the several years she was married and prior to her divorce, she has lived there all her life. The youngest of seven born in Russia (of which two survived) she was the elder to six siblings born here. While no longer so, she described her neighborhood during childhood as "very Jewish" with stores and synagogues close by. Mrs. Stein went to work at an early age to support her family. She met her husband while working as a salesgirl. While she found out later that her husband was a womanizer and scoundrel, the best part of the marriage, she noted, was that she had two sons. At the time of the interviews they and their children were her main supports. While her siblings left home, she was the main support for her parents who died in 1946 and 1951. During the 30s through the 70s, Mrs. Stein worked in a variety of sales positions in and around Philadelphia, supporting her sons through college, seeing them graduate and have families of their own, and watching their children grow and begin independent lives. All this from her long inhabited home.

She was remarkably attached to her home and to the objects within it. Besides the many things she had accumulated over the years, she also had "the wall," her display of framed photos of family members, especially her children and grandchildren. Like Mr. Gardiner, she organized her life story thematically rather than chronologically. While she identified several key themes, two should be mentioned here.

"My independence is important to me." While typical of many older adults, this theme was individualized by Mrs. Stein to include her continuing battle against her specific illnesses (including diabetes, circulatory problems, and heart disease) and her lifelong tenacity in "overcoming difficulties." The latter included being a single mother when such a status was rather rare, overcoming economic problems, overcoming sexual advances of bosses at work, caregiving, and maintaining her routines in a changing neighborhood. She insisted that her health problems, while severe, did not govern her life. She kept a routine of household duties that varied daily and seasonally, which she modified when she was feeling more unwell than usual. She likes to "design my day," as she put it. Cooking, cleaning, doing the wash, and other such tasks were not only important in and of themselves, but they also enabled her to pass the time. She described a kind of sensuous aspect to these daily, repetitive chores: they enabled her to mentally "let go" and drift back in time in a kind of fugue of reminiscence, reexperiencing events that had occurred earlier in the house. Thus her "puttering," as she labeled it, sprung her loose to engage in reminiscence, she noted.

"The meaning of time." A second theme touched on in much of her discussion about her life concerned the meaning of time. She noted that she had a very hard time recognizing how old she was. She noted, "You don't think about how old you are in the normal course of events, but from time to time you come up against it." Her current-day identity appears to be constituted in such a way that the events of the past and the present are melded together. Of course, it is incorrect to think of this as the melding of the past and present, but rather it is present-day reinterpretation of the past based on the needs and issues of the present. And, of course, this is not to suggest that her reality orientation is off; she clearly understands the difference between the past and the present. And living in the same place since 1915 contextualizes this process. As she noted, some events that occurred decades ago "seem just like yesterday," as she put it. She feels the presences of her deceased parents and siblings in this home and her frequent reminiscences about them add to a sense of their being close at hand. For her, time is all bunched up.

There appears to be a place within Mrs. Stein where events just are, without much, if any, chronological ordering. Events, people, and things of the past are drawn up into consciousness through a variety of associations or cognitive networks. Key reference points to most events are her parents' and her children's lives. Dates are before and after events in their lives, rather than her own per se. While this sense of inner time is experienced in relation to the biographical time of significant others, inner time is also experienced precisely as inner time. In the processes of daydreaming, reminiscing, or just being inside the house, aspects of inner time and the fusion of past and present just "envelop" her, as she put it. She feels wrapped in memories while at the same time physically present to their setting.

"My home is important to me."   This theme was central to her selfhood. In describing her reminiscence to me, she noted that nearly all of it involved her home. This is quite understandable, because so many of her life episodes had occurred in and around her own home. She noted of her residence, "This is my world...this is where I belong. I take pride in it and in the past. This is where I feel I'm alive."

Again, she noted, "I can't conceive of the time...that so much time has passed. Those events [of the 30s and 40s], you look back, you realized that time has passed. Each day [now] is separated. I live day to day. Each day now is different. I think...what the heck did I do? It isn't conceivable that my parents are dead that long!"

For her, reminiscence is at the crux of the two forms of time she endures, the linear and chronological, versus personal, nonlinear time. Reminiscence runs parallel to her sense of environmental attachment or "object relations," that things occur both "now" and "then" for her. She noted, "When you are five years old, you are starting to get old. Time is going by, but you only see it if you look back. Where'd they go [the people and the years]? I could go for a hundred years, if my health permits. But when I think of my age, [my age] is foreign to my ears. I think, 'It's not me'."

Depending on the perspective, reminiscence can provide an ego enhancing episode of self-involvement, but viewed another way, reminiscence causes shock, since the past is so much at odds with the present. For her, there is a fine line between reminiscing and reexperiencing. Reminiscing connotes both a looking back and a tacit separation between the present day construction of the past and the present. One clearly understands that one is looking, from the perch of the present, into a version of the past. In reexperiencing, however, the boundary between the present-day version of the present and the past is muted or permeable. While one may acknowledge the difference, one is still involved in actively experiencing "the past" as part of the present. The past has not been left behind, as it were.

For Mrs. Stein, this nuanced difference between mere reminiscing and reexperiencing is made more possible by the symbolic value of her home. As with Mr. Gardiner, there is some important form of linkage between home and object attachment, the manifestation of self in themes, and reminiscence. Because of its symbolic inducements in this way, for Mrs. Stein, being physically present in her home softens the boundary between past and present, between reminiscence and reexperiencing. She avoids the shock of the recognition of change. She stated, "When I look in a mirror, I see an old lady. I think, 'It can't be . . . it's a picture, it's not really me . . . It can't be me.' But it is. It's like hearing your voice on a tape recorder. You don't think it sounds like you, but everyone else recognizes your voice." Later, she added, "When I'm in my home, it's me. When I'm away from home [it's not] . . . I don't like to be away from home. Here. It's me. I'm an old lady. I know that. Here, I don't feel like it. I don't want to be classified as it."

DISCUSSION

In this chapter I have suggested that reminiscence functions as one of a number of media that are fundamentally a part of the aging self. These media function in part to resolve two cultural (and existential) problems. The first is the conflict between agency (culturally defined individual action) and decline (the culturally defined core of aging). For many elders, this is unsolvable because "illness," a condition of many, is often culturally conflated with old age, when the two share no inherent tie. Solving this dilemma, nevertheless, is the work of the individual. As in the case of Mr. Gardiner's letter writing, an elder may adapt by adopting new forms of long-held activities. Or, this conflict may be resolved through the interpretive schema of the personal meaning system and its organization of personal issues into themes which fuse past and present and make the past still active in the present. The material from Mr. Gardiner would suggest that goals or dispositions in which one is still active do not always require reminiscence.

The second cultural conflict is between reminiscence as something "concrete" and something "in motion" or dialogical. The concrete represents a linear structure to time and a corresponding linear format to reminiscence. In contrast, reminiscence that is in motion reacts somewhat differently to the loss of key people and relationships and may include past conversations that are still reheard and rehashed, with the elder, with the passage of time, reviewing the logic of conversation from the point of view of each participant. Or, it can refer to the fusion of past and present in an unbounded way, as part of personal meaning.

Clearly, Mrs. Stein's reminiscences fit this latter format as when the past and present fused and time seemed to have no meaning for her. Now, things were "just like then," to use her words.

These cultural problems refer to the single problem of the making of the self in a culture that stresses individual action and agency, but marginalizes people on a variety of diacritics from many socially sanctioned forms of agency. I have suggested, as have many others, that elders buttress the self through attachments to place and objects. It seems likely that reminiscence, also a form of attachment, acts with a similar purpose. Further, I have suggested that reminiscence may take particular forms that make it more material or objectivating and in so doing render pure ideation into forms that may take on characteristics of "objective" entities. Attachment of reminiscence to the bundle of identity thoughts that constitute personal themes, repeated focus on similar reminiscences, and revisiting memories in the same way are some of the key objectivating mechanisms.

ACKNOWLEDGEMENT

Research on which this paper is based was carried out in Philadelphia from 1981–1985, at the Philadelphia Geriatric Center in a research project entitled, "The meaning and function of home for the elderly." I am grateful to The National Institute on Aging for its support of my research.

11

Personal Identity and Social Discontinuity: On Memories of the "War Generation" in Former West Germany

Barbara Keller

What happens, after an historical and political break with the past, to memories of our own life concerning the now discredited epoch of the former regime? How are historical and social discontinuities dealt with in personal life histories? How can personal identity be maintained or (reachieved) despite social changes? This chapter discusses such questions in the context of the dissolution and reunification of East and West Germany. One of the results of World War II, the division of Germany into West Germany and the German Democratic Republic (GDR), has vanished with the collapse of the GDR. Its symbol, the Berlin Wall, has been destroyed with Berlin serving as the capital of a reunited Germany.

In 1989 (in the former West Germany) I conducted memory-centered interviews, (i.e., interviews discussing contexts, functions, and contents of remembering), with men and women of the "war generation," that cohort who lived, suffered, and persevered through the Third Reich and World War II. When I set out to conduct the interviews, the taboo concerning discussion of the Nazi regime and the war had already started to dissolve. A growing cross-disciplinary interest in the history of everyday life had given reminiscences of ordinary people scientific recognition. Oral historians (e.g., Niethammer, 1980; Plato, 1991), ethnologists (e.g., Lehmann, 1980, 1983) and family therapists and psychoanalysts (e.g., Massing, 1991; Moser, 1996) helped to achieve a type of rapprochement between historical and behavioral sciences through the use of personal memories and individual autobiographies.

The current study, then, attempts to capitalize on this rapproach-ment (see Bornat, chapter 2, this volume). To adequately capture the complexity of the psychosocial processes involved an interdisciplinary approach is required. Consequently, I briefly detail the contributions of autobiographical memory, reminiscence research, and discourse analysis. The dynamics of memory consolidation, negotiation, and change are illustrated in the interview material which follows. I begin with a discussion of the theoretical perspective which informs the present work.

THEORETICAL FRAMEWORK

Contextual Perspective

How do individuals remember events of their lives while living in and interacting with changing social and historical worlds? A contextual perspective is needed to address this question: "The ongoing historical event is the root metaphor of the contextual metamodel," (Webster 1999, p. 33). Also, the contextual perspective on human life as well as on its biographical reconstructions is necessarily interdisciplinary. It must allow us to link approaches accounting for both individual/personal and social/historical aspects of remembering. Therefore, concepts, methods, and research results from different psychological fields of research and adjacent areas relevant to the study of remembering in context are taken up to outline a conceptual framework. Its central con-cepts are: autobiographical memory, reminiscence research, and dis-course analysis.

Autobiographical Memory

Autobiographical remembering is reconstructive. It is influenced by the social context in which it takes place and which, on the other hand, is transformed by individual remembering. In its narrower sense, social context refers to the current social environment; in its broader sense, to the current political and cultural system. To study autobiographical remembering, including these aspects, it was necessary to combine approaches and concepts from different research traditions (see Keller, 1996, 1997).

Autobiographical memory as topic of research in cognitive psychology refers to the ability to store and remember events of one's own life (Bluck & Alea, this volume). Cognitive psychological research on autobiographical memory has its roots in a tradition that studies memory as a human faculty. Structures and processes of memory are the main focus and quantitative methods are preferred. We know that the more time that has passed since an event happened, the more likely it will be remembered inaccurately or not at all. Events experienced during adolescence and early adulthood are assumed to lead to longer-lasting impressions than events from other times of the life span. Karl Mannheim already stated that "In youth . . . where life is new, formative forces are just coming into being, and basic attitudes in the process of development can take advantage of the molding power of new situations" (Mannheim, 1972/1928, 296). Inspired by Mannheim's famous essay drawing on data from sociographic survey studies with large samples suggesting generational effects for memories of public events and referring to the "reminiscence bump" (between 10 and 30 years) in the curve of the frequency of biographical memories of subjects older than 35, Conway assumes that autobiographical memory is a bedrock of one's "generational identity". Once this generational identity is formed in late adolescence or early adulthood, people may deal with it in different ways, yet ". . . the original generation-specific self remains as the self with which all later selves must be negotiated" (Conway, 1997, p. 43). Recently Conway and Haque (1999) have shown that the reminiscence bump can be "overshadowed" by memories of such changes. May this continuity of identity development then be threatened or not in the face of historical changes?

Events experienced with high emotional involvement are assumed to be remembered better than usual or trivial events. Yet, even highly stressful and emotional memories may fade as time goes by, as a study of the memories of concentration camp survivors suggests. Testimonies of witnesses at the trial of a camp guard collected from 1943–47 were given again from 1984–87. The witnesses' experiences were generally well remembered, yet there was a marked loss of details as essential as names and appearances of torturers and of events as dramatic as seeing a murder or being brutally treated (Wagenaar & Groeneweg, 1990). It has been noted that the interview methods used—defining truth in terms of correct facts and details—may have hindered the witnesses in telling their own, subjectively meaningful stories (Leydesdorff, 1992).

To study narrative truths and their subjective functions does not mean to discard factual truth. It might rather be one step toward an empirical investigation of their complex relationship. The study reported here was less concerned with the objective truth of what people said than with the subjective meanings of their narrated memories. To include these aspects, contributions were used from the gerontological study of the life review or reminiscence which focus on the contents and functions of remembering.

Reminiscence and Life Review

Reviewing and finally accepting one's past in old age has been considered a crucial step toward integrity in the face of one's mortality. Conceptualizations of the life review that aim at the integration of one's life experiences in old age and in the face of death have been challenged. Empirical investigations failed to demonstrate that the life review is a universal process (Merriam, 1993; Wink & Schiff, this volume) or that the elderly engage more often in reminiscence than other age groups. Empirical (factor analytical) evidence shows similarly frequent reminiscing over all age cohorts and age specific trends according to different factors or functions. This suggests that different functions of reminiscing change in their importance during the life span, that specific group and cohort effects in different functions are to be expected (Webster, 1995; Webster & McCall, 1999), and different functions of the life review in the sense of life reflection have been shown to be linked to different developmental tasks (Staudinger, 2001). From a lifespan orientation, techniques of remembering and ways of handling one's memories are social accomplishments that change during the life course. It has also been argued that the wider social context of social and political changes and cultural expectations should be considered in order to understand the meanings and functions of reminiscent behavior (Lamme & Baars, 1993; Webster, this volume).

Literature on the life review and reminiscence in old age has scarcely addressed how memories spanning political and social changes are dealt with. Webster has reported a factor "identity" describing how we use our past to discover and to clarify our sense of who we are (Webster & McCall, 1999, p. 76). Interestingly, there were differences between age groups: For this factor, scores of 20- and 40-year-olds have been reported to have been significantly higher than for 70-year-olds. Because of the age by cohort confound of his cross-sectional methods it is impossible to tell whether certain functions change in their frequency/importance because of age or because of specific experiences of the cohort under study—or because of some combination of both. The "formative forces" of history may influence the perceived usefulness of specific functions of reminiscence differently for different age groups or cohorts. The study by Andrews (1997) on the collapse of the

German Democratic Republic suggests that having one's national identity destroyed impacts life review processes and outcomes differently for persons of different ages, perhaps depending on their involvements with and investments in the now dismantled regime, perhaps depending on reserve capacities available. In such a case identity or the renegotiation of identity might become even more salient for an older cohort. Identity is crucial for personal as well as for historical narratives: The formation, reproduction and presentation of identity has been described as belonging to the functions of historical narratives (Straub, 1998, 128ff). The narrator/author will situate him/herself toward relevant collectives, declaring him/herself distant or belonging. By narrating he/she will position him/herself toward collectively meaningful experiences and expectations. Further important functions are the formation of orientation, and, consistent with that, moral and educational functions. It is important to note that historical narratives cannot be expected to always offer one moral solution (Straub, 1998, 131f). The alignment of one's biography and current historical narratives is an ongoing process. German life stories covering the "Third Reich" and World War II exist in multiple tensions to (alleged or manifest) contemporary conceptualizations of successful lives, of "historically correct" behavior, or expectations concerning reasonable and adequate ways of coping and narrating. To address the question of how biography and history are negotiated in the interviews, concepts from discourse analysis are used.

Discourse Analysis

The life review, as written memory or in communication with others, is dependent on language (Harris & Norman, this volume). Language, however, changes with the social systems that are construed by its use and that it describes. Especially if divided by a radical change of the political system, members of different generations do not necessarily speak the same language. It may be hard, for instance, to translate prior experiences framed by the Nazi era in terms that a younger person who has grown up in a democratic political context can fully appreciate and understand. Currently, for example, the word "lager" (camp) invokes images and meanings of the Nazi concentration camps. However, for those elder Germans who remember exciting adventures camping with a National Socialist Youth organization it carries a very different meaning. The Nazis did prescribe vocabulary, censor the news and the use of language in the media, and persecuted people listening to "enemy" broadcasting stations. They also filled the public space with propaganda and censored news of staged events,

thereby occupying discourse and leaving hardly any space to articulate diverging experiences. Therefore, the analysis of (then) prescribed vocabulary had to be complemented by methods taken from
discourse analysis.

It is likely that older persons who were more or less involved with the
now discredited regime may feel the need to account for their lives. A
reminiscer assuming that the account of his or her life arouses doubt,
criticism, or accusation may react accordingly. Passages of argumentation and reasoning, and stories with excusing and justifying functions
were to be expected.

Research on accounts, starting with the work of Sykes and Matza
(1957) studies the argumentative strategies of people reacting to
accusations. Sykes and Matza identified "techniques of neutralization"
used by juvenile delinquents, (e.g., to deny responsibility for their
crimes). Scott and Lyman have taken up that approach and defined
account as a "statement to explain untoward behavior and bridge the
gap between actions and expectations" (1968, p. 46). Types of account
phases have subsequently been presented by Semin and Manstead
(1983) and by Schönbach (1990), among others. The question of
account structures or under what conditions accounts are demanded is
illustrated in the transcript material to follow.

METHOD

Participants

Participants were 38 elder former West German citizens (24 female, 14
male) ranging in age from 70–87 years (*M* age = 77). Participants were
recruited from the wider Heidelberg area, and were interviewed during
the fall of 1989. The sample was self-selected in response to an article in the local press that invited people age 70 or older to reflect on
their memories.

Procedure

The interviews were conducted by me and took place where participants felt more comfortable: either at the psychological institute (14)
or at participants' homes (24). The interviews lasted about 1 1/2 hours
and were audiotaped. The tapes were later used for transcription, and
transcripts were then formatted and analyzed using a computer program designed for the analysis of verbal protocols (Huber, 1990). The
schedule for the memory-centered interviews was organized according

to the leading research questions: What are important memories today? Do they often dwell on memories? How do they do that? Do they share their memories with others and, if so, with whom? How do they feel toward current reports or portraits of the times they lived through?

RESULTS

Contexts and Functions of Remembering

Memories of one's own past were described as occurring mostly spontaneously. Since not all spontaneously occurring memories are desirable, tendencies and strategies of avoidance were reported. Memories may be triggered by current events or by currently available portrayals of bygone days. Social gatherings like meetings of families or of former classmates provide social contexts for the exchange of reminiscences.

People who intentionally occupy themselves with their memories write down their biographies. They settle their last will. They go on journeys that bring them to important places of their personal history. Important motives named were the wish to pass on experiences to particular loved ones or to the coming generation in general, to gain back memories or work through traumatic experiences that had been suppressed so far.

Challenges and Defenses

Half the sample, both women and men, gave reports of feeling challenged concerning their past by younger persons in general or by their own children. Twenty-seven of the 38 interviewees claimed they "knew nothing" of the Nazi crimes, defending themselves and their lives against experienced or alleged accusations. In some cases this stands in contradiction to reported acts of injustice and discrimination. A person later in the interview may, for instance, mention having watched "Jews being brought away". This shows that this claim refers strictly to knowledge of the full scale of the holocaust that is denied in favor of an unsuspecting former attitude. It should be understood as a means of distancing oneself. Its argumentative function as a "meta-account" is defining the situation as one that does not call for accounts.

Current research methodology suggests that a situation that demands to be accounted for is already defined by a given norm violation. In my view this depends on the perspective in which an action or an event is seen. Dependent on the perspective or retrospective, chosen degrees of responsibility and corrective speech acts can be negotiated. To include these aspects I have proposed a transactional account model (see Table 11.1).

Examples for meta accounts are: (1) People who have not lived during those times are not qualified to discuss how it was *(the right or power to define past actions is challenged);* (2) Younger people cannot judge the possibilities of (alternative) actions then given *(the adequacy of ascriptions of actions is doubted);* (3) The law as it was valid and applicable then led to the action in question *(rules are qualified; their retrospective validity is questioned);* (4) It is necessary to place oneself under the former conditions to be able to judge *(meta-account in its narrower sense; the acceptance of the former perspective is demanded);* (5) One hundred years from now history will judge Hitler differently *(todays norms are judged as irrelevant and futile; the norms themselves are questioned).*

Gender Differences

For a first analysis of the content of the interviews, the events mentioned were counted and grouped according to three categories: (1) Historical events are events like "World War II" which belong to the historical background; (2) Events marked by the epoch are events that link the personal and the historical-political realm and that are typical for specific cohorts or (age) groups in a specific epoch, like becoming a member of a national-socialist organization or losing one's husband in the war; (3) Personal events are events like marriage, the births of children, and the deaths of relatives that are not connected to the historical or political sphere. These categories are illustrated in Figure 11.1.

Men and women most frequently mentioned historical events. Men mentioned more events marked by the epoch than personal events. Personal events were reported more often and in greater variety by the women of the sample.

Prejudice Stories

Some events or experiences were described in detail and elaborated to form simple stories. Stories illustrate events or experiences that are considered typical, frequent, or common by a narrator accounting for his or her life. Stories that occur in memory-centered interviews are likely to carry an explaining, an argumentative, or even a justifying function. Among those are prejudice stories.

Van Dijk's (1987) research on the communication of ethnic prejudice and racism uses the narrative structures proposed by Labov and

TABLE 11.1 Transactional Account Model

		Meta-accounts	
Negotiation of the right or the power to define an action	Negotiation of the adequacy of the ascription/definition of the action	Negotiation of the rules "Meta-account"	Evaluation (of the norm)
		Account-phases	
Definition (retrospective) of an action	Ascription of an action	"Norm violation" "Failure event" "Account"	Evaluation (of the action regarding accepted norms)

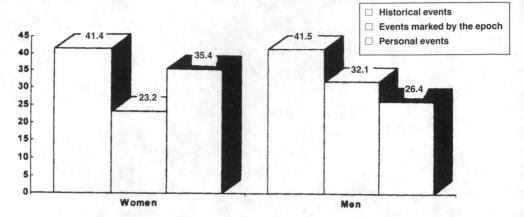

FIGURE 11.1 Percentages of historical events, events marked by the epoch, and personal events named by men and women.

Waletzky (1967) (i.e., summary, setting, complication, solution, coda) to analyze stories about immigrants. He found that stories within a prejudiced discourse do not render solutions. The behavior or the characteristics of the discriminated group is portrayed as the complication. I have used this structural analysis with stories about Jewish citizens and found structural differences between stories that do, and do not, discriminate against Germans of Jewish origin (see Figure 11.2).

In this case, the complication is the ascribed unfair behavior of a member of the discriminated group. Figure 11.3, in contrast, shows a story with a solution: The person affiliated with the discriminated group can be helped.

An Interview with an Officer's Widow

The following interview can still irritate and stimulate controversy perhaps because it somehow touches aspects of identity. I have chosen it for two reasons: To illustrate strategies to maintain continuity in a changed social context, and to suggest where further changes of context might affect these strategies. The interview with Mrs. F. was conducted in her apartment where she lived with one of her grandchildren in the fall of 1989.

At the time of the interview Mrs. F. was 74 years old. She introduced herself as a housewife, a soldier's wife, and an officer's widow. The interview presents the chronology of her life. It starts with a description of her childhood as a "soldier's daughter," it covers the First and the

"Then I had another experience, during dance lessons. I took dance lessons with students from the university. I was sorry for the boys. Some of them were studying medicine. And then it was always: We cannot get at the University Hospital. This is all Jewish. The boss is Jewish and he hires only Jewish physicians. Yes, you see, little things like that."	Summary Setting Complication (without solution) Coda

FIGURE 11.2 Prejudice story.

Second World Wars, the German Revolution after the First World War, and the economic depression. Mrs. F. compares former and contemporary life circumstances and values. She displays great skepticism regarding the changes in womens' roles, and she is worried about the depreciation of German soldiers. She discusses the time when she was a member of the "BDM," the Nazi organization for adolescent girls and explains that this was about folk songs and games and not political at all. She gives explanations of "how all this could happen," displaying antisemitic attitudes and dwells on the war and the suffering of the German people who, like her, fled from east to west to escape the Russians. She gives a short survey of her life after the war and summarizes: "I always say I was born under Kaiser Wilhelm, raised under Fritze Ebert, lived a little under Hitler, and 40 years Federal Republic" (001; 342-3451).* She links her biography to history by naming ruling figures from prewar Germany, names that stand for monarchy (Kaiser Wilhelm), the Weimar Republic (Friedrich Ebert, familiarized to "Fritze") (and the Nazi regime, leaving Hitler (or what he stands for) not much space or importance. Postwar democratic governments are reduced to "40 years Federal Republic," a term that then referred to West Germany only.

Identities are positively defined by collectives one feels one belongs to ("we") and negatively by collectives one feels different from or distant toward ("they"). What about collectives she describes herself as belonging to? For Mrs. F. the family is important: A woman with children should live as housewife and mother and she should accept no

---

* The numbers signify the number and line of the interview the quotation is taken from.

"And then we heard of those terrible things.	Summary
And where I had been delivered, that	
was a small private clinic, and that	Setting
doctor was married to a Jewish	
woman. And her brother was a lawyer.	
A doctor M. Originally their name had	
been (Name). They had it changed.	
And that lawyer disappeared	
immediately after that night.* He fled	
to (foreign country).	
And Mrs. M. came into the bank to my father.	Complication
And my father could transfer the	Solution
property to S., because Mrs. M., with	
the brother, she was not Jewish	
herself, she went to her brother to	
(other city in Germany) with her	
daughter. There nobody knew that she	
was married to a Jew, so my father	Coda
could help Mrs. M."	

FIGURE 11.3   Story with solution.

* Pogrom/Reichskristallnacht

depreciation. She herself has handed the love of her mother down to her own children. Yet, her descriptions of herself as a "soldier's daughter," "soldier's wife," and "widow of an officer" ties the female role as she has lived and interpreted it to a militaristic and nationalist tradition. This tradition has been lost and she deplores that.

Other collectives relevant to her (presented) identity can be inferred from text passages where Mrs. F. talks of "us" and "we". The collectives referred to overlap: She complains that "we" (the Germans now, that is, at the time of the interview) are not entitled to national pride, although "our" (the Germans' now and during the Nazi era)—soldiers fought for their country, "not for Adolf Hitler," that "these ten years under Adolf" are "chalked up against us (the Germans today) in such a way," reducing the Nazi regime to the person of its "leader" and decontextualizing it from German history. "And how we slipped into that. It might happen today in exactly the same way" (referring, presumably, to the Germans before, during, and after National Socialism). By this the young interviewer gets a warning message concerning possible judgments from the comfortable position after the facts—a position that might still turn out to be not so safe.

Mrs. F. refers to the educational system of West Germany: "the schools," mentioning that "they have messed up so much after the war," "they really got us down." By stating this she is distancing herself from a type of public discourse on times that she and other Germans of the war generations live. She accuses the most important institution involved in the socialization of the next generation supporting a version of recent history that is inviting the young to discount their parents and grandparents lives and characters. Constructing the "we" of the Germans of the war generation in a way that keeps the Nazi regime distant and reduced to Adolf Hitler and "these ten years" makes it possible to link this "we" to the "we" of the Germans now and to construct acceptable continuities. These continuities are defended against present affronts.

Contemporary aspirations of young women can be read by Mrs. F. as criticism of the rather conservative version of a woman's life she has lived. Her criticism of contemporary lifestyles defends her biography against such views. Complaints of neglected national pride—young soldiers are spit upon, she reports—can be read retrospectively as defense of her biography as a daughter and a wife of a soldier. It may also be interpreted as expressing a present concern, as her protest against the breaking off of a once proud tradition, a continuity that had lasted for generations. In her view West Germany of 1989 does not offer much prestige for soldiers or soldiers' mothers.

Would Mrs. F. talk differently about the experiences of her generation if asked today? Should a different interview be expected? "Germany" has changed considerably since 1989. What does that mean for German identities? An exhibition of photographs criticizing the myth of the "clean" armed forces in World War II has been shown under protest and considerable criticism, but it has been discussed widely. Meanwhile German soldiers are participating in "humanitarian activities" if not combat activities in troubled spots outside of Germany. The social context for historical narratives (especially concerning German soldiers) has changed considerably—but is it less controversial?

DISCUSSION

The social contexts of public articulation and official statements of German efforts to deal with the national past have been different in the two German states that existed until 1989. The German Democratic Republic had cultivated an official ideology of antifascism that left little or no room for differing biographical accounts (see Kohlstruck, 1997). Former West Germany offered a more pluralistic public space, yet several political scandals were motivated by the exposure of politicians' affiliations with the Nazi regime (Schwab-Trapp, 1996).

Concerning their autobiographical relation to the German past, different generations have been labelled and described: Those who are now politically active belong, if they have grown up in former West Germany, to the "second generation," to the so-called generation of 1968. This generation has taken the place of the "generation between" (zwischengeneration) and the antiaircraft gunners (flakhelfer-generation), who had, like the "war generation," although in a different way, experienced the Nazi regime and the war. Fewer and fewer people of the "war generation" are still alive and able to tell about their lives. Yet, public discussion has not lessened. It has even been supposed that it is growing and that chronological and political topicality diverge (Kohlstruck, 1997, 1998). Public discussion and official discourse have changed. Now, as the "first generation" is no longer prevalent in positions of power, it is possible to look back on "the violent aggressions and well-known self righteous productions" of the confrontations ascribed especially to the "protest generation" of 1968. (Kohlstruck, 1997, p. 285). Yet, the "inquisitorial" public discussion of the Nazi regime then is also seen as indicative of the "collective repression" that had dominated public discourse so far (Rauschenbach, 1998, p. 361). While this part of German history itself is still being discussed, the efforts to deal with this history have accumulated to a history of their own that affects different generations or cohorts in different ways.

CONCLUSION

The formation and representation of identity cannot be accounted for by individual development and age-related crises alone. It may have been underrated how pervasive historical events i.e., changes of the context, affect remembering and identity. Contextuality and, contextuality in temporal perspective, (i.e., historicity of human behavior, action, and experience), is discussed by contextualistic approaches and explored with narrative methods. A promising approach would be to register life reviews and functions of remembering separately to avoid circular reasoning from content to functions and back. These should be explored covering "ongoing historical events," that is, comparing systematically differing situative (research) and social (societal) contexts, if possible, with a longitudinal design. Also, contextualistic conceptualizations make it possible to integrate theories and concepts of adjacent cultural and social sciences and to link psychological dis-course on memory with interdisciplinary discourses. For psychologists, a look at the history of mentalities might offer interesting perspectives. Yet, there are already collaborations under way: Psychological supervi-sion of oral-history projects make new readings (interpretations) of bio-graphical interviews possible, and events rendered in clinical interviews can be understood adequately when seen in their historical context (Bornat, this volume). From a truly contextualistic perspective the reflec-tion of conceptual and historical contingencies of one's own scientific reasoning has to be included. At this point it seems important to bring together the multiple facets of remembering and narrating in complex social (political and historical) contexts and to work on the epistemo-logical fundamentals and methodological consequences involved.

IV
Special Populations

12

Themes of Continuity and Change in the Spiritual Reminiscence of Elder Catholic Women Religious

Susan Perschbacher Melia

Spiritual reminiscence, whereby people spontaneously reflect upon the importance and development of faith throughout their lives, is a valuable process. By chance I connected with this process when interviewing twenty-six elder Catholic women religious (mean age 81.5) about their prayer lives. The women described their prayers of later life in relationship to their memories of childhood religious practices and to their spiritual development during the years of religious vocation. Sister Marie, 87 years old, recited for me the night-time prayer taught to her by her mother, which she repeats each evening as she goes to bed. She also described the evolution of her faith as she became more contemplative in her spiritual practices. In her spiritual reminiscences, she demonstrates continuity and connection with her past, as well as growth and change. Time weaves throughout her narrative as she shifts her focus from the past, to the present and, on occasion, to the future. Significantly, for Sister Marie, as for the other twenty-five religious sisters interviewed, there is an overall individual motif that runs throughout her narrative reflection. The occurrence of this spontaneous spiritual reminiscence, the pattern of common themes related to continuity, change, and time, and the presence of a dominant individual motif for each of the women interviewed, leads me to conclude that spiritual reminiscence is an important aspect of late life for further study by gerontologists who seek to understand sources of continuity and of change in individual growth, the making of meaning throughout life, and the importance and function of faith in late life.

Spiritual well-being is considered to be an important component of aging successfully, along with psychological well-being, health, meaning, and peace (Ellison, 1991, Moberg, 1990). Support for this claim is based on several factors: the religious disposition of the American population, the importance of different components of religion and spirituality for older people, and a broad conceptualization of spiritual well-being (Payne, 1988). "Spiritual well-being is the affirmation of life in a relationship with God, self, community, and environment that nurtures and celebrates wholeness" (Moberg, 1990, p. 6). Most notably for older people, the spiritual domain provides an opportunity for continued growth.

Religion conveys reassurance to older people about the continued value of human life (McFadden, 1995), giving them a sense of meaning and purpose. Late life may be seen as a time for possibilities through growth of the individual, service to others, and spiritual fulfillment. Therefore spiritual well-being contributes to integration and identity, as well as to continuity of the socially constructed self. According to Ellison (1983), the spirit synthesizes the total personality and provides energizing direction and order as an integrative force. Payne (1990) links the process of life review to religious consciousness and to the ageless self (Kaufman, 1986), unifying past, present, and future on a spiritual journey of time. Nye (1993) found that religion, an important theme, with subthemes or functions, in the life stories of elderly African-Americans serves "as a bulwark of continuity" (p. 103).

McFadden (1998) emphasizes, "because religious coping can be such a significant source of comfort in difficult situations, we need to find ways to guide those persons who desire it to find a closer relation with God and as well a clearer sense of meaning in spiritual connectedness within the self, with others, and with the world" (p. 8). In working with people who receive and give care from a religious perspective, a spiritual assessment tool "can be helpful in highlighting the individual's images of the self and of the Holy Other" (p. 8). Her "Spiritual Life Review and Needs Assessment" includes questions on religious beliefs and perceptions; this information can be used to help people find sources of strength in coping.

For Magee (1988), life review is a spiritual experience providing spiritual benefit. "With this perspective they transform their life review from a developmental phenomenon enhancing 'ego integrity' to a faith-filled, ongoing give-and-take exchange with God as confidant"

(p. 69). Magee found that older adults interpret their life review in terms of three themes: God's involvement in their lives, trust in God to lead them to personal fulfillment, and God as a companion throughout life. According to Magee, this type of life review as spiritual experience focuses on the meaning of life and serves as a foundation for self-acceptance and reconciliation. Atkinson (1995), with his emphasis on life story, claims that life storytelling teaches us about our spiritual self, "about our personal quest for wholeness and authenticity" (p. xiii). He states that knowing who we are means connecting with our own spirit and with that of others.

> In seeking our spiritual selves, we seek to understand what matters most to us, what is personally sacred. Telling the stories of our life is telling our spiritual autobiography, because this helps us discover and become more aware of, what our deepest values are and what we can put our fullest trust in. We come to realize that even struggles and conflicts have their place because they have served an important purpose over time (p. xiii)

Thus, Atkinson believes that storytelling can be a transforming experience through which we can connect with the core of our lives which is spiritual.

Guided autobiography (Birren & Deutchman ,1991) helps to foster in older adults the belief that one's life is meaningful. These stories are ideal for examining the interior life because he stresses that spirituality in the later years is less focused on the external formalism of religion and more on the interpretation of life and on feelings. The inner spiritual life of an individual is important because "mature and elderly adults seek a wholeness, a meaning in life, that is more integrative of actions and emotions, but less analytical in thought" (Birren, 1990, p. 44). Birren stresses that mature individuals are very motivated to obtain an integrated picture of their lives, and that this thrust towards integration, seeing one's life as a whole, has a spiritual character.

Bianchi (1982) believes that the process of life review can aid in spiritual growth and fulfillment in late life, leading individuals to reflect on past choices and acts, injuries, and creative works. "In this attempt to create meaning for the whole span of one's life, the elderly person will encounter unhappy and unhealed memories. There will be moments of guilt, sadness, resentment, possibly even of remorse and the edge of despair" (p. 173). As an elder faces the pains, losses, and fear of death in old age, the way opens for greater faith and hope in the face of life's mysteries. Bianchi, along with the writers previously discussed, uses a broad view of religion which includes the developmental process of individuation which is aided by life review. For Bianchi, development in old age includes "interior growth through psychological and spiritual methods" (p. 190). This involves reminiscence which helps the individual to "reidentify," whereby the person both changes and becomes more authentically herself.

Because reminiscence and life review have such value for the integration of personal identity, and because spiritual well-being is an important component of aging well, it is important to learn more about the functions of spiritual reminiscence and to promote spiritual life review. Research and practice in conducting spiritual life reviews can promote an integrated and valued old age.

METHODS

This qualitative research study, formulated in the grounded theory tradition (Strauss, 1987), was undertaken to learn more about the nature and function of prayer in the lives of a sample of older Catholic women religious who have demonstrated that they are aging gracefully. The work is conducted as interpretive social science (Weiland, 1995) using narrative data to identify both the patterns and the meanings embedded in human development.

Interview Sample

The twenty-six elder Catholic women religious who were respondents for this study were drawn from a population of forty sisters from three religious orders. These forty women were part of a convenience sample I previously interviewed several years ago in open-ended interviews talking about their lives and attitudes towards aging (Melia, 1999). At that time the women agreed to the interview with the knowledge that it was an intensive (two to four hours) life review interview. Due to the nature of the life review and of the sampling technique, the results from this study portray women who have a positive outlook on aging (Melia, 1999). I recontacted the sisters for a second open-ended interview focused on their prayer and faith lives, telling them that this material would be useful to others who are interested in how to age gracefully.

The participants, ranging in age from seventy to ninety-eight (average age 81.5), were highly educated, all but one having at least a teaching or bachelors degree, over 50 percent with masters degrees or doctorates. The majority of the women had been educators. Others were nurses, administrators in their orders, and social service workers. The women were living in independent apartments, convents of varying sizes (10 to 60 women), assisted living facilities, and long-term care centers. They rate themselves as having generally good health, thus indicating positive attitudes toward health; among them they have a wide range of health conditions associated with aging, including diabetes, advanced osteoporosis and arthritis, arteriolosclerosis, stroke, cancer, blindness, and hearing loss. As in Wolf's (1990) study, the women are remarkably diverse, yet shared many of the same themes in their life stories: faith, family, education, friends, community of religious sisters, service to others, and prayer (Melia, 1999). Based on these shared individual themes and on a shared life style and common religious values and practices, these women demonstrate both continuity and generativity in their lives on into late life (Melia, 1999, 2000).

Interview Process

In interviews lasting one to two hours, the women responded to 20 open-ended questions about their prayer life. The interview schedule was developed with the help of women religious who work with the elder sisters in their orders. The interviews were conducted at a time and place chosen by the older woman religious, most often in their homes. I told them that the second interview was being conducted because the original interviews neglected to include important questions about their faith and prayer lives. While I had concerns that the women would be hesitant to talk about their prayer, a deeply personal and private aspect of their religious lives, the sisters who agreed to these second interviews answered the questions thoughtfully and at length. I believe that this second interview, approximating a spiritual life review, was possible because the women had already established a sense of connection with the interviewer.

Data Analysis

Interviews were tape recorded, transcribed, and analyzed to discover emerging themes. The data were examined two different ways: 1) the individual prayer stories of each woman in their entirety; and 2) on a question by question basis, looking at how the women collectively responded to individual questions. Through close examination of the responses, categories of responses emerged (Strauss & Corbin, 1990). These themes were identifiable because of their repetition in the data from all of the women interviewed. The "thick description" (Geertz, 1973) used to discuss this data presents an ideal type or composite picture of the group of women respondents as a whole, reporting in detail on the content of the responses categorized into the more prevalent themes.

Findings

In the structured interviews on prayer, the women spontaneously engaged in spiritual reminiscence, connecting their prayer lives in the present to their prayer stories and faith practices as children and throughout their vocational lives. When examined closely, their individual commentaries each contain a main religious or spiritual motif central to that individual's faith life. The women, who share the important overall theme of religion and faith in their life reviews (Melia, 1999), also share several subthemes (Nye, 1993) in their spiritual reminiscence: prayer as relationship and conversation with a loving God, prayer as contribution to others, changing of prayer with age, and the working of the Holy Spirit within. Running through their faith and prayer stories are also references to varying time orientations: past, present, and future. Three cases demonstrate the unique individual motifs as well as the subthemes that interweave throughout their reminiscence into the present.

For Sister Justina, who at 98 epitomizes a living spirituality and faith, the motif is "Living a Life of Prayer." She says that she learned at a young age, "from good, loving parents," about the presence of God: "God seems pretty close to me most of the time. God has been very close to me in nature. All my life, even when I was very young, I had a sense of God." This faith developed through the years: "I do have a deep sense of God's presence that has grown very much as I've grown older." She recognizes she had kind and loving teachers who "stressed a lot about the love of God for us, that God cares for us." She argues that these patterns and practices must begin when you are younger: "You can never begin this in your old age. It has to begin somewhere. I think you develop some kind of a mindset earlier on, and more and more you make God the center of your existence." Now she prays throughout the day using prayer practices she developed when she was younger: "Prayer has always been important to me. I've always loved prayer." She remembers that when she prayed her mother was always with her. In her prayer Sister Justina was influenced by her parents and by her religious sisters, but her prayer has gradually turned inward, nurturing a life of the presence of God within. She also recalls that early on she learned to pray the scriptures, and that she was influenced by spiritual writers. These practices stay with her, deepening her prayer. She uses her time to sit in chapel and to pray quietly in gratitude and thankfulness to God. "My prayer is more settling into the presence of God within me." "And I imagine the more we do prayer, the more we become conscious of the presence of God in ourselves, in others, in life, in nature, in everything. There's a great sense of companionship." She vividly described an experience she had many years ago while on retreat: "I stood for awhile looking out over a field, and suddenly a great peace came over me. I wasn't thinking about the hereafter; I was thinking about God. It seemed to me a voice said, 'This is what heaven will be like.' It was unusual. You look at something beautiful and suddenly you know God is in all this."

The central motive for 78-year-old Sister Marie is "The Family of God." Of primary importance in her spiritual development throughout her life was the formative relationship with her parents and family. Her father is a prominent figure in her spiritual landscape. "Father God is a good image for me. I have no problem thinking of God as mother too, but it's not my way of addressing God. I think of God as just father. I do have a very good father image in my own dad. Dad was the gentlest and most loving person and always smiling. He's a good image. I was very close to him, so I had no problem saying God the Father." She claims her family "planted the seed" for her religious calling, and that her sense of community and oneness with God were present in her from a very young age. "I remember being taught very young, as a child, a very young child, to pray. And prayer was very important in our family. We said the rosary together". Prayer has always been a part of her life, established in her early family life, where they recited the rosary together and said the morning prayers.

> We were taught a prayer that I still say, many times a day even, the very first prayer that I learned from my mother. Of course it's in French, cause I always prayed in French when I was younger. But I still say that prayer many, many times. So prayer's always been a part of my life. But prayers do change. The way of praying, or the type of prayer, or the method of prayer. I think it has always been important. And that's due to my parents. I saw my father kneeling on a chair saying his morning prayers before going off to work. I always had that example of father being important.

Sister Marie today is more contemplative, searching for a closer connection with God who dwells within. She describes her prayer "as relationship, and so it's simply being in each other's presence. Sometimes praying a few words; sometimes just a smile; sometimes just being, plain being, that's all." Prayer has always been part of her life, part of her relationship with God just as it was part of her relationship with her family.

Sister Ann, 75 years old, always felt a freedom of spirit in religious life which was not evidenced until the major changes in the Catholic church as a result of the Second Vatican Council (1962-64). Her central theme emphasizes that "God is a Continuous Presence." "It's a very informal, spontaneous relationship that I have". For her, God is and has always been in everything. "I would describe my prayer as relationship. It's a relationship and that can embrace just being there and let[ting] God act in me. Being called by God to be with others". This motif reflects her lifelong belief that God is everything and that her life has been an ongoing relationship with God. She has always been God centered, and chose her life to live in community with religious sisters: "They were all women who had a spiritual dimension". She has found that they are united and that they support each other, having an "esprit de corps". In her reminiscence she recalls the time of Vatican II: "I think [Vatican II] was wonderful. It was a breath of fresh air. When I entered I thought I wouldn't be able to go into a public building. I've been all over the world. I've had a glorious, I've really had a fascinating life! I think you were held down a bit before Vatican II. [Afterwards], well, for one, you could be part of the people. And be taken for another person [rather than a nun], not [set] aside with a whole set of categories before they ever had a chance to get to know you". She also realizes her relationship with God has given her great support and a sense of independence: "It gives me the courage and inspiration to move on. 'Cause I've been a trail blazer". Sister Ann values and emphasizes reminiscence in her spirituality in her late years, as she now has time to reflect. She described the type of spontaneous reminiscence that can occur. "They were singing [a hymn] which I have not sung in a long time. And all those words came to me. And I was kinda delighted. Out of the past came the words. And what I think happens is that we've got this whole treasure in us that's been building up through the years. And often it's put there and we don't have time to take it out and look at it."

As other examples demonstrate, the individual integrating motifs vary for each women, with each having a different reference in time: past, present, or future. All of the women incorporate and integrate their spiritual reminiscence into these motifs. For Sister Rhea, 74 years old, the motif, "Returning to the Prayers of Childhood" makes sense of her late life feeling that she is finally praying without formality, communicating with God at a more personal level. "[Prayer] went from formality in religious life back to what it had been when I was a kid with my mother. And it has grown from there." She told me, "When I was a kid my prayer life was more talking with God". Sister Bernadette, 77 years old, feels that her religious development is one of "Continuous Conversion" because in her life "faith is a turning that never ends." As she described, "I had in mind that I always wanted to be a nun". She recalls that she knew this ever since a very young age, and that she grew up in a very religious family. Because she was aware that her father's "faith kept him going," she finds that "in my life [prayer] was always important". Sister Mary, 82 years old, believes she is "Keeping

Spiritually Young" because she follows her prescription for spiritual youth including: trust, acceptance, versatility, adaptability, and dependence on God. As she looks back on her life she sees that she always followed God's plan. This allows her deep faith which is supported by her lifelong devotion to the Blessed Lady which started for her as a young child in her family: "I was named after our Blessed Lady". Based on her lifelong faith, she can now confidently believe: "Put [yourself] in the hands of God. Know that whatever He asks, will be accompanied with the strength to do it".

Sister Mary C., at 92 years of age, spends less time reminiscing and more time preparing for her death. The central motif for her faith life, "Preparing to Meet God," connects her past, present, and future. As she describes herself, "I [always] just accepted whatever came along". She recalls that she has always been "living for God; trying to do His will; accept[ing] the things that are a little bit difficult to accept". While her occupation in life has been prayer, she now is focused on God's grace in assisting her to die and in accepting her into heaven. She trusts that "God is very good and He's going to continue. He's watched over me all these years and He's not going to stop now. God is good. He's been very good to me all these years." Sister Ellen Marie, 86 years old, demonstrates great change in her prayer life as she focuses on the theme of "Cosmic Spirit." While this has a contemporary feel to it, she remembered that her decision to become a nun was based on the same spirit. "The call came when I was only between the ages of 12 or 13. It just struck me one day. It must have been the Lord". She also recognizes she always had a devotion to the Holy Spirit, believing: "He will help you develop your talents and lead you where you should go". Her faith life is centered on the Holy Spirit, the "breath of life". As in her past and throughout her life, she strives to become more aware of that spirit within as she raises "her heart and mind to God".

In addition to these individual motifs which connect their current religious practices with their spiritual reminiscing, the life stories of the elder sisters reveal common subthemes under the overall theme of faith. These subthemes are sources of both continuity and change in their religious lives, incorporating and integrating reminiscence with present day activities and beliefs as well as with hopes for the future.

Prayer as Relationship and Conversation With a Loving God

Frequently these women described their prayer as continuous throughout their lives: "I would say that my life is a life of prayer". They have prayed and continue to pray unceasingly: "Our life, our days are prayers" (81 years old). Their prayer is a relationship with God which is fostered by conversation with God: "Well, I formally pray every morning, but I informally pray throughout the day. Since I see prayer as relationship, then the relationship permits me to move in and out of prayer at will"(75 years old). Through continuous prayer the elder sisters feel they are never alone; they are connected to God and to other members of their community through prayer. "[I am] never alone, I know that. I'm never alone, so I can talk to Him whenever I have a problem or whenever I see something nice I say, 'Oh God, you did this.' You try to keep, have the presence of God. It is prayer, it's presence, it's connection"(78 years old). For these religious sisters this has occurred in the past as well as in the present. "As long as I've experienced God's love, I've accepted it. And let it be a touchstone in my life. Helping me. And then I've shared it with others, that others and myself can be moving towards God in love". The relationship and conversation with God was fostered in early years and developed throughout their lives.

Prayer as Contribution to Others

Through prayer the elder sisters have always believed, and continue to feel in later life, that they are able to contribute to the well-being of society:

> Hopefully He'll take my life, my prayer life, and the circumstances in my life that I offer to Him to help other people; otherwise my life would be worthless, I think. I'm not here just for myself. I think our sisters feel in aging, even though they can't physically do what they did in the past, our biggest work is prayer. It really and truly is. And I think, because we have so many people calling in for our prayer, you know, it makes us all the more, all the more aware of people and events and the suffering in the world (71 years old).

Even when they are most frail, prayers are a way to continue this form of generativity of giving to others:

> Of course I always pray for the people I love; that's very strong. But for many years I have really prayed for issues that I, justice issues. And so oftentimes I'm praying for laws to pass or not to pass, or I'm praying for the people who are hungry in our world, and the homeless, and for people in prison. And then people sometimes ask, pray for my niece, or somebody who's sick, or people that have asked for prayers. People often do. And I believe in praying for all those (93 years old).

Several women described how they were presented with models of older women religious when they were young religious. They remember and describe how they admire the strength of these elder sisters now that they themselves are older.

Changing of Prayer with Age

Prayer has changed as the sisters have aged. In part this is due to the time they have to devote to prayer now they are slowing down; in part they are preparing to meet God when they die. As one woman describes her prayer life:

> [I pray] all day long. Because every, into everything of the day you bring your prayer life. And I think as we grow older, even more so. I think your prayer life changes as you get older. It becomes more simple, and more intimate. Intimate with the Lord. I mean you become more, the curtains kinda get lifted and you're much freer in your expression of love for Him. I feel much more in love with God as I grow older. I have a much more intimate love with God than I did as younger person. And maybe I didn't have the time to just, to open up. As we grow older that is more or less where we have to find ourselves. Although I think I still have the energy and all of that. But mentally I think you find yourself there, you know, in a much closer, sincere love with God than you did as a young sister (77 years old).

Prayer, as the elder sisters describe it, becomes more meaningful, deeper, more personal, steadier, less self-centered, more important, simpler, more intimate, more familiar, and more contemplative. "You grow into, you sort of make a partnership with the Lord, see. And then, later on, you let Him take over"(78 years old). This change comes about with the opportunity for more solitude and some detachment from active daily life. "I suppose in a way you could say that prayer is more important nearer the end. It's important now too, cause you're getting older and closer to meeting God. You're getting ready to meet Him"(75 years old). As the women describe it, the prayer becomes "more a part" of them: "And then, as I told you, gradually became much more contemplative. And this whole idea of just being is something that came with, as you grow older. It's getting ready for that moment of meeting glory. I guess it's the mental attitude that's different. You can have this ability to pull away, and that's maybe what helps to maintain a certain peace, inner peace that you don't always stop to do when you're younger"(75 years old). Changing prayer is a source of growth: "I think you grow in, as you grow older you grow in prayer"(88 years old).

Working of the Holy Spirit Within

An important way that prayer has changed over the years for these women is that it has become more like meditation or contemplation, more silent. Before they often prayed to get through the day, to perform well in their teaching, to endure in the religious life. Now it is more open.

> I think it's become more focused. I would say more focused on the presence of God. As opposed to a prayer of petition, when you don't know where your life is going, when you're younger. Naturally [then] it's, 'Show me the way. What do you want me to do with my life? How can I be a blessing to this world?' And then, when you're older you don't, at least I don't have that type of prayer any more. Well, you know how when an experience is finished, and you look back and you can see a pattern in it? Well, so when your life is kind of coming to an end you look back and you can see the hand of God in it. And what position is there besides the position of thanksgiving and praise (86 years old).

As they describe their prayer now: "My prayer is more settling in to the presence of God within me. My presence, my being enveloped, my whole world being enveloped in God"(93 years old). This type of prayer represents a "letting to" or a "being in each other's presence." "I feel it's inspired by the Spirit" (86 years old). This comes from becoming more simple and spontaneous in one's prayer life. With this form of prayer often comes a sense of gratitude for all that God has done in one's life and in creation. This gratitude produces a hopeful attitude open to connection and hope, looking with faith rather than despair on the world.

Time

In each story time varies as a reference for each of the women. Do they look to the past, to the present, or to the future? Many reflect back in their spiritual reminiscence to the past and to the religious practices and experiences in their families. For some the emphasis is on the present, to the continual openness to growth and change. Sister Mary, for example, thinks that older women should "act their age," but emphasizes that openness to the Spirit can keep one spiritually young. Some, like Sister Mary Carmel, look ahead in faith and prayer in preparation for dying and death. For all of these women, whatever the time reference, continuity and change, stability and growth, are part of their prayer stories and spiritual reminiscence. An example of this occurred during the changes brought by the Second Vatican Council. The sisters adjusted to this period of church history as they did to changes in their own personal life histories; some aspects of their prayer patterns remained the same, but there were changes as well. Spiritual reminiscence reveals that faith practices throughout life and into late life are adaptable, fluctuating with continuity and change in individually unique ways.

DISCUSSION

Elder Catholic women religious, interviewed about their prayer lives, spontaneously shared their spiritual reminiscences of the past as they responded to structured questions about their current faith practices. Evidence of their process of spiritual reminiscence reveals important patterns and themes of identity and religious development with which they reidentify throughout their lives (Bianchi, 1982). As the two case studies indicate, in sharing their spiritual reminiscing they each revealed a unifying central motif characterizing the individual woman. While these motifs often appear to be very similar, each has a distinct authenticity, helping to integrate woman's life story (Birren, 1990). Analyzed as a group, responses from the women also demonstrate that there are subthemes within the encompassing theme of faith: prayer as relationship and conversation with a loving God, prayer as contribution to others, individual prayer routine incorporating devotions to saints and scripture, changing of prayer with age, and the working of the Holy Spirit within. These subthemes have elements of both continuity and change. The continuity of belief, extending throughout their lives, gives these women a great sense of integration, of meaning, and of purpose. With the strength of these beliefs they also have the potential for change and growth. As Moberg (1999) and McFadden (1995) indicate, the spiritual domain provides an opportunity for growth, particularly through service to others and spiritual fulfillment. In Payne's (1990) conceptualization, past, present, and future run together in the responses of these women, unified in the spiritual life review as a journey in time.

The findings described above support what other researchers have found true of religion or spirituality—that it helps to integrate identity (McFadden, 1995), synthesize the personality (Ellison, 1983), and unify an individual's movement through time (Payne, 1990). In support of Nye's claims (1993), the subthemes included in the main theme of religion within their life stories provide a sense of continuity for these individuals. Through their spiritual reminiscence and life review they communicate a meaningful life which has continuity and spiritual wholeness (Birren, 1990). These women provide evidence of an important late life phase of interiority (Bianchi, 1982). In addition we can see that their faith and integrated spirituality have given them strength to cope and encouragement to grow as their faith deepens. Their expressions of gratitude and their relationship with God help them to maintain a positive attitude. They approach death with hope. The themes that Magee (1988) identified, God's involvement in their lives, trust in God to lead them to personal fulfillment, and God as companion, were present for the women religious interviewed. In addition there were other subthemes within the larger theme of faith.

These spiritual reminiscences of elder Catholic women religious, shared during interviews about their faith and prayer, give us a glimpse into the souls of these women. In their lives of devotion and faith, within the same religious denomination and calling, they have fashioned personal responses to God which give us a sense of the systems of meaning and motivation in their lives, especially in their later years. Using a broader definition of religion or spirituality (Birren, 1990; Moberg, 1990), understanding this reminiscence process can inform us about how other people come to establish continuity, to change and grow, and to find meaning and integrity in their lives. According to Birren (1990), every person has an inner spiritual life, seeking wholeness, meaning, and integration. Catholic Christians may resonate with the practices of these elder sisters and with the content of their faith lives, feeling spiritually enriched when hearing their faith stories. For others who have different systems of belief and themes in their faith life, it is important to uncover, understand, and acknowledge these sources of meaning. This is a challenge for gerontologists, for caregivers, and for educators to learn through spiritual life review and reminiscence the themes of faith and belief of the individuals they care for, live with, and plan for. The unique contribution of the techniques of spiritual life review and reminiscence are to gather information or "thick description" about older people. While this information contributes to interpretive social science about individual and cultural development of meaning, it also helps us to more deeply know and appreciate the soul and spirit of the individual person, which is especially important in late life.

13

Female Survivors of Abuse and Violence: The Influence of Storytelling Reminiscence on Perceptions of Self-Efficacy, Ego Strength, and Self-Esteem

Prem S. Fry and Lisa A. Barker

A ccording to a recent study conducted by the Commonwealth Fund (1993), almost four million women are physically abused each year in the United States alone. The numbers are proportionately the same in Canada. Worldwide, between 20 and 50 percent have experienced physical violence at the hands of an intimate partner. Such statistics are frightening in their proportion and a reminder of the unique position we play as health workers and researchers in the lives of women victims and survivors of abuse (Bachman, 1994).

Over the past decade many studies (Davis & Smith, 1995; Woods & Campbell, 1993) have advanced our knowledge of the anguish and pain experienced by women who are survivors of domestic abuse and violence, and who have experienced immense ongoing trauma at the hands of male partners and spouses. The psychological literature on male violence and abuse of women abounds in clinical studies of the despair, intense anxiety, and fear experienced by women who were abused violently and at the point of death, not once, but many times over (Dunbar & Jeannechild, 1996). Clinical studies have focused on the phenomenon of learned helplessness of these women, and the loss of control, autonomy, and self-esteem following the abusive experience(s). However, little research has focused on how a significant proportion of these younger women coped with the trauma and lived to narrate the stories of how they achieved stability and solidarity in their relationships, despite their frequent and close encounters with death. If there is one common element that all female survivors and victims of abuse and violence share, it is a serious loss of self-esteem, coupled with a sense of life devalued as a consequence of social isolation, depression, and loss of status. Walker (1984) posited that battered woman's syndrome is characterized by loss of self-affirmation, guilt, and self-blame. Lately, it is becoming increasingly obvious to many professional counselors, through discussion with staff and management of women's shelters, that there is considerable room, as well as expressed need, for organizing sensitive clinical interventions (including programs of reminiscence therapy) to help the survivors of violence and abuse to resolve some of the painful, lasting dilemmas of their lives, and to help them deal with significant existential issues and questions, such as "purpose for living," "personal meaning for life," and "why hope, why pray for a better future when the present is so unbelievable, and so painfully filled with despair"? (Fry & Barker, in press).

According to the literature on identity development, these are existential questions commonly discussed in late-life functioning. Looking at one's life over a long period of time and achieving a sense of integrity about one's life in old age is what Erikson (1963) believed to be the final stage of life—or the highest level of psychosocial development that he termed "integrity versus despair". In this chapter, we pursue the question of the extent to which Erikson's notion of older adults' reconciliation with the inevitability of death due to normal human aging applies to younger women who, although at a much lower level of psychosocial development, are threatened with a form of emotional death and a struggle to achieve a reconciliation between "integrity and despair". Several theses for how younger women who have been victims of repeated trauma, abuse, and violence have recovered a positive meaning for life are proposed by the female survivors of abuse themselves. Bowker (1988) and Burnett (1996), for example, propose a religious context, and a "suffering and sanctification" concept and explanation for victims' return to a positive meaning for life. Alternate sources and origins of personal meaning for life are reflected in the reminiscences of the survivors of abuse themselves. For example, as one abused woman reminisced:

My mother lived to the ripe old age of 90 years, and when she was on the point of death, she wanted so much to share with us her struggles, her pains, and also her joys and celebrations that gave her life meaning, and gave her strength to carry on. With me it's not so different, I'm not even half my mother's age but I've already had so many near encounters with death, with violence, and have come close to understanding what violent death may have meant to other women my age who did not survive. One thing I simply do not understand is why people do not want to hear me talk about my pain, my struggles. Is it not natural for women survivors like myself that every time we've come through a near death violent experience, that like my mother, we want to look back at our whole life, to take stock of the conflicts between us and those we loved or lost or hated? Does it not make sense to you that, like my mother, I too want to grieve my losses, to think of all the "what ifs" of my life and to dwell on the pain and hurt of what others have done to me. Every time now, when I wonder if I'll ever survive another encounter with violence and death, I take time out to talk with my demons, to forgive myself, and to forgive others for taking me so close to the brink of despair. I resolve to survive one more time, if for no other reason but to let the world know that my life, painful though it is, has not been in vain. Like my mother, I too want to celebrate with my children the many ways in which my life has been complete, despite the many other ways in which it remains so hopelessly incomplete.

The preceding excerpt from the reminiscence of a 32-year-old woman who survived four horrendous physical assaults at the hands of her spouse, demonstrates her need to reminisce with others, and her strong need to recover some positive meaning for her life by telling her story to other peers and cohorts, and in return getting their sympathetic attention. It is reminiscences like these that provided the motivational basis for writing this chapter.

A Personal Perspective on Encouraging Reminiscence Among Abused Women

At the heart of this chapter is the thesis that contrary to popular notions, not all reminiscences of female victims of abuse are of an obsessive nature, or characterized by ruminations of pain, guilt, shame, or despair about the future. The purpose of the present chapter, based on narratives and reminiscences of female survivors of abuse, is to show that the need to reminisce is not restricted to old age, but is felt equally by individuals at much younger ages as well. Another equally important goal for this chapter is to demonstrate how the process of reminiscence may be immensely useful in helping individuals, at whatever age or stage of development, to achieve some sense of completion about their lives. Several excerpts from the reminiscences of younger women who were victims of abuse are provided in this chapter to demonstrate how the wisdom that these women imparted through their reminiscence, narratives, and stories not only uplifted them but permeated the whole group of survivors, and was instrumental in strengthening the resolve of other women who had similar experiences to tell their story of survival.

More than 1,500 community-based programs have been started by supporters of female victims of abuse (Stark & Flitccraft, 1996). The focus in a majority of these programs has been to teach women coping skills and how to defend against male aggression by means of cognitive-behavioral strategies and mechanisms (Walker, 1994). Generally speaking, the process of reminiscence, as a therapeutic intervention tool, has not been encouraged much among female victims of abuse, the rationale being that it elicits too many painful memories of the experience of abuse and tends to have a regressive effect on the ego strengths of the victims themselves. Furthermore, the argument is extended that encouraging survivors of abuse to reminisce on their stressful or negative experiences, leads them to become more introverted and self-absorbed as opposed to making efforts to find a concrete solution to their problem or engaging in concrete action to overcome their problems (see Brown, 1994; Whalen, 1996).

Although advocates of reminiscence (see Bornat, 1994) might claim that the reminiscence process is committed to a basic philosophy of individuality, empowerment, self-determination, and social integration for all participants, independent of any disadvantage they may be experiencing, the effectiveness of reminiscence activity in general terms has been questioned by social workers and clinical agencies who have argued that the process of reminiscence when applied to victims of abuse, trauma, and violence serves only to evoke further self-criticism, self-blame, and self-reproach among the reminiscers themselves (Walker, 1994). Social workers contend that while reminiscence may have its splendor for some older adults whose memories are embedded in earlier images of joyful times, of family relationships and interactions, and of a sense of control and autonomy in more youthful times, it may have a seriously detrimental effect on individuals who have felt alienated at a young age, and who find the struggle to confront existential isolation painful, and sometimes unendurable. The clinical implications are that the process of reminiscence may promote self-acceptance to a point that a woman loses her subversive potential and ceases to challenge the social roots of her problems. By contrast, our research results, as reported later in this chapter, will show that reminiscence had a positive effect. An increase in self-confidence became more apparent as participants began to develop their stories and creatively reconstruct them.

"Tell Us Your Story" Groups: The Basic Philosophy of Group Reminiscence

The main hypothesis of the work reported in this chapter is that when we are highly stressed and attempting to describe events and experiences which are extremely confusing, dense, and complex, reminiscence with other compassionate listeners can provide a way into understanding. Frequently, facilitators who undertake to organize the format and structure for reminiscence groups can help vulnerable reminiscers develop specific themes and sequences which help them to break their big complex life story into a series of small and intimate narratives. As Mere (1992) proposed, reminiscence, when it takes the form of a small personal story of an intimate experienced event, enables the reminiscer to narrate her story with a certain measure of safety and confidence and, in so doing, a woman may start listening to herself again, and to share herself with others.

Almost 95% of those women survivors of abuse who contacted us or who were invited or approached by us, were very keen to tell their personal story "if only they could find sensitive listeners who were genuinely concerned for them" as opposed to being concerned about "improving social policy or reducing crime against women".

It is our own convictions about the significance of the reminiscence function via storytelling that led us to form a "Tell Us Your Story" group in 1996 from among dozens of young women who had experienced severe and repeated violent physical assaults. Along with Mere (1995), as facilitators of the "Tell Us Your Story" Groups we believed fully that reminiscence is not just for the older people, nor is it just about the past. At any age, it is a dynamic process in which there is a seamless quality where past, present, and future ebb and flow, backwards and forwards. When reminiscence is used with individuals young in age, the importance of the act of reminiscence lies not in feats of memory, because memories are frequently so lucid and alive as to be detrimental to analytic discourse with the self or others. The importance of the act of reminiscence among younger minds lies in the speaking of one's own emotions, and having that voice listened to with an awareness of its unique qualities. The abused women who joined the group resolved to attend every session they could of "Tell Us Your Story" group, lest this be the last chance they had to tell of their most recent experience before the group.

Although each victim initially engaged in an analysis of fears associated with isolated episodes of abuse, over the course of a few group sessions it became apparent that reminiscing with others who had encountered similar experiences provided a kind of "comfort blanket" and conferred on them what Garland (1995) describes as a sense of security that allowed them to weave their painful recollections into a harmonious perspective. This is reflected in the evaluation of one of the participants, a survivor of abuse: "For once I felt that others were congratulating me for my courage. They were saying to me, 'you've given me the courage to keep on going, and you've given me hope that I can put my life together and put the pain behind me.' That's what I really needed to know—that others care and need me just as much as I need them, and wanted to hear my story just as much as I needed to hear their story."

As a group of reminiscers and facilitators, we had no delusions that the personal accounts of trauma and physical suffering which the young reminiscers told were of interest to anyone else beyond the boundaries of the few members of the "Tell Us Your Story" group. On the contrary, we fully accepted that the personal accounts of these survivors of abuse may have no apparent social value that needed to be recorded for posterity. Nevertheless, we encouraged each woman's reminiscence through telling her story, believing that it had *personal* value for the reminiscer, and was a "vital process" essential to keeping each member hopeful that she would return to another meeting of the group.

Reminiscence, Storytelling, and Self-Efficacy Enhancement

While there is a wealth of empirical literature describing the abused woman's depression, loss of self-esteem and loss of personal resources, there is relatively little study of the abused woman's internal resources, beliefs, and expectations that enable some women, but not others, to recover faster than others. The psychosocial model of well-being suggests that stresses arising from the experience of abuse and violence completely distort the survivor's perceptions of the self, and self-affirmation and self-esteem may not be restored unless and until the threat of violence and abuse is fully resolved. By comparison, social-cognitive theorists postulate that restoration of self-esteem and recovery from depression can be facilitated and expedited by encouraging survivors to explore in detail the self-efficacy beliefs and expectancies they held prior to the experience of abuse. Social-cognitive theorists (e.g., Bandura, 1993, 1997; Berry & West, 1993) speculate that a woman's self-efficacy beliefs in a number of domain-specific areas of functioning (e.g., interpersonal, instrumental, emotional, physical, nutritional, financial, social, and spiritual) may represent a core of factors that play a crucial role in minimizing or maximizing the negative effects that the traumatic and abusive experience has on her attempts to resolve the threats to her life. Specifically, we postulated that the abused woman's preexisting self-efficacy beliefs, prior to the abusive history, may influence the level of effort and level of perseverance a woman may exhibit in the face of threats to her well-being. For purposes of the reminiscence intervention, we postulated that women with a weak set of preexisting self-efficacy beliefs and expectancies put forth less perseverance to protect against further threats. We further posited that women's self-efficacy beliefs and expectancies would be strengthened through engagement in reminiscence. To the extent that self-efficacy beliefs are modifiable (see Bandura, 1993), our contention was that it makes them an excellent target for self-analysis and self-reflection in the reminiscence process. Hence, for purposes of the present study, we encouraged women to reminisce on their areas of strong self-efficacy beliefs and expectancies prior to their personal experiences of abuse. As the reminiscence process began to unfold and women were narrating their personal stories of struggle, pain, and strife, they were encouraged by the facilitators of the groups to reminisce on the strengths, capabilities, controls, and competencies they had earlier in their lives, and prior to the experience(s) of abuse and violence. Our prediction was that such reminiscence would also motivate them to regain the lost strengths. As seen in the excerpts that follow, the women's reminiscences of self-efficacy beliefs and controls prior to the history of abuse and violence made them more consciously aware of the strengths and efficacies they had had in their personal and behavioral repertoires.

> "Time was when I felt on top of the world . . . I had no problems making friends or being a friend to others. I simply loved people, young, old, children and adults alike." (interpersonal efficacy)
>
> "I was so proud of myself that I could stay calm most of the time, even when there was so much at stake. When my sister lost $4,000 of my money she was hysterical, but I kept my cool and together we worked it out. I was the one my mother turned to for help when things went out of hand and I was the one who was good at comforting and reassuring others that it was going to be O.K. Today, I don't know what's gotten into me . . . the slightest thing that goes wrong has me so upset. It's as if something inside me has snapped and I'm a nervous wreck most of the time." (emotional efficacy)

"I had so much self-confidence and a deep faith and trust that life would be the very best for me. I had some deep convictions inside me that said, 'I'm good, I'm strong, I'm a moral person, I'm a believer in God'. I trusted myself that I have a deep inner strength in me that would always uphold me in my hour of need . . . I felt I had a sense of balance, peace, and harmony that I got through my daily prayer. How I long to have back that faith and trust in my God and in my own inner self." (spiritual efficacy)

"Even when things were hard and money was so scarce, my family never worried. I truly believed with my mother that people are genuinely good and I had so much faith that if anything went wrong we would always know how to find some people who would help us out and support us and take care of us. I never hesitated to ask for help and I was always pleased to help others when they asked me . . . I don't know how things changed so terribly . . . I don't know who I would go to now if I needed help . . . I am afraid to ask and afraid to admit that I need help." (social support efficacy)

Before concluding a storytelling session, each woman was encouraged to talk about any small gains she felt she may have achieved in any one or more of eight domain-specific areas of self-efficacy (interpersonal, instrumental, emotional, physical, nutritional, financial, social, or spiritual) by telling her story or by listening to the stories of others. For example, as the following excerpts show, when a woman was encouraged to reflect on how her past experiences were leading her to identify the specific gains she was making toward regaining control, enhancing self-efficacy, and recovering self-esteem, she became more consciously aware of the small progress she was making toward recovering her former strengths.

"I can see how much improvement I have made in staying away from situations of conflict between Terrence and myself . . . The mere fact that I am able to walk away instead of feeling compelled to stay makes me feel better about myself." (emotional efficacy enhancement)

"I am getting better at taking care of myself . . . I am taking in more nutritious food now. I realize I have a tough battle ahead of me. I am beginning to see clearly that my health is more important now than ever before." (nutritional efficacy enhancement)

"I see now that I am gradually becoming strong . . . instead of crying and punishing myself, and denying myself any possible pleasure, I am able to block out any thoughts of suicide . . . I am able to reach into some dimensions of inner strengths I knew I had when I was single and much more self-confident. I am slowly able to sit down and work through each stressful event, reminding myself through prayer and meditation that I can make it through, one day at a time . . . One tiny little success or positive thing that happens is what I concentrate on each day. I remind myself every day that God put me on this earth with a purpose, and everyday I am creating and recreating a purpose for living." (spiritual efficacy enhancement)

"I cannot change my life as it has been in the past . . . I have to accept what happened to me, and I have to accept the pain of the past; but now I'm becoming much better at asking other persons outside my family for help, and getting their advice and encouragement . . . I'm not obsessed about keeping my painful experiences a deep dark secret, or about denying my pain. I am tired of feeling ashamed and responsible for all the things that went wrong; I've carried the self-blame for a long time . . . but no more . . . My sessions with all of you here have strengthened my beliefs that I am an important person, my life is valuable, and that it is time to cast off this emotional baggage I've been carrying around and make a fresh start on life." (interpersonal efficacy enhancement)

Does Reminiscence Intervention Have a Role to Play in Alleviating Depression and Enhancing Self-Esteem in Battered Women? Some Empirical Research Findings

As discussed earlier, research on domestic violence suggests that women who are victims of abuse experience a constellation of adverse psychological effects, especially in regard to loss of self-worth, self-esteem, and empowerment. To explain how abuse from the partner results in decreased self-esteem, some theorists (e.g., Campbell, 1990; Herman, 1992) have linked abuse with a diminished sense of the self. More recently, Licdig (1992) described a pattern of psychological consequences of abuse that includes, in addition to low self-esteem, self-imposed stigma, self-blame (Aquilar & Nightingale, 1994), and severe depression (Russel & Hulson, 1992). It is argued that abused women experience a loss of self resulting from the emotional rupture that takes place "within the self," causing a woman to perceive herself as inferior and shameful because she cannot control the violence directed toward her (Herman, 1992).

For purposes of our study, we hypothesized that the reminiscence process which unfolds through personal narrative and storytelling contributes significantly to the recovery of self-efficacy and self-esteem of women who have experienced violence. In the context of our study of the therapeutic value of reminiscence, we viewed the reminiscence process as providing a feedback loop allowing a woman to ruminate on concerns about self-esteem and self-efficacy that predisposed her to the abuse, and subsequently to ruminate on how the abuse affected her self-esteem (see Lynch & Graham-Bermann, 2000).

METHOD

Participants

Treatment Groups.   A group of 21 women ranging in age from 23 to 38 years, who had experienced domestic abuse in the previous six months or so, were invited to participate in the "Tell Us Your Story" workshops. The purpose of the intervention as explained to the participants was to afford them an opportunity to talk with the group about activity, behavior, people, events, life roles, and life attainments that had provided support and self-affirmation, and contributed to self-esteem in the past.

Controls.   Another 18 women, ranging in age from 25 to 34 years, who had experienced domestic abuse and who were attending information-giving support groups at women's shelters, volunteered to serve as controls, and agreed to complete the pre- and post-intervention measures to be administered to the treatment participants.

Measures.   Participants in the Treatment and Control Groups were administered the following paper and pencils tests:

1. *Rosenberg's* (1965) 10-item *Scale of Self-Esteem* (SES) in which scores can range between 10 and 40, with lower scores indicating lower self-esteem.
2. *Beck's* (1967) 21-item *Depression Scale* in which scores can range between 0 to 63. Total BDI scores between 14 and 21 were taken to be indicative of moderate depression, whereas scores above 21 suggested severe depression.
3. *Fry's* (2000) 25-item measure of *Global and Domain-Specific Efficacy Scale* assesses efficacy beliefs in eight domain-specific areas. Scores on this measure range from 25 to 100 with higher scores indicating higher levels of self-efficacy on subscales of instrumental, interpersonal, social, physical, emotional, nutritional, spiritual and financial efficacy.
4. The *Ego-Strength Scale* adapted from Barron (1953) and Paritzky and Magoon (1979) measures low, medium, and high levels of ego strength. High scores on the scale indicate, among other factors, the ability to share feelings, a self-image of personal adequacy, and a strong sense of reality. The 50 true-false items of the scale are worded in language that is easily understood by respondents. High scores on this scale indicate stronger levels of determination, perseverance and optimistic expectations.

5. The *Index of Spouse Abuse* (ISA, Revised) was used to measure the severity and frequency of partner abuse. Total ISA scores may range from 0 to 100 with scores above 50 indicating severe abuse.

Procedure

Depending on the severity of the abuse, women with relatively high scores, moderate scores and low scores on the ISA, BDI, and SES, respectively, were assigned to three different "Tell Us Your Story" groups. The index of abuse frequency and severity was used to determine the boundaries for the contents of the narratives, and the time limit that should be imposed on each woman's telling of her personal story. One group facilitator assumed charge of each group, and following Fry (1983, 1995), attempted to put relevant structure on the reminiscence process by offering encouragement, directing questions, and steering the contents. Other members of the group were also free to react to the narrative of the storyteller and to respond in terms of asking for clarification and offering support, encouragement, affirmation, and validation. In each of the six "Tell Us Your Story" sessions that were organized for the Storytelling Workshop, each woman was given an opportunity to narrate a story about six salient events which she experienced in the last 4 to 6 months and which she believed had the strongest impact on her self-confidence, self-esteem, and sense of self-worth. A storytelling session ranged in duration from 30 minutes to an hour and a half, depending on the individual woman's desire to provide a detailed account. Since by its very nature the reminiscence process, which unfolds through the story, represents a person's individual account of his or her own life, caution was taken to ensure that the storytelling activity was used as a method of transmission which preserved as much as possible of the authentic voice of the narrator. External interference was kept to a minimum.

Although each session of storytelling was tape recorded for purposes of data collection and analysis, we tried to make the tape recording as inconspicuous as possible so that it had the least inhibiting effect on the person recounting her story, or on the other group members who were diligently listening to the story. Following Lashley (1993, p. 139) who warns that "persons recounting painful memories may also retreat into silent reminiscing about past guilts and failures, becoming despondent and introspective," facilitators made sure that the storyteller did not engage in too much self-criticism or blame as a stick with which to beat herself. The facilitator intervened to ask questions about the progress she perceived herself as having achieved and about "wished for" events that would help her feel better, and what assurances other members of the group could give her or things they could do for her that would inspire self-confidence.

RESULTS

Salient Changes From Pre-Intervention to Post-Intervention

Table 13.1 shows mean score changes from pre-intervention to follow-up at four months, for both treatment and control participants. As reflected in the means and standard deviations of the change scores, treatment group participants made significantly greater improvement in depression than did the control participants.

With respect to "ego strength," the change scores in Table 13.1 suggest that treatment subjects, when compared with controls, made significantly greater gains in "ability to share feelings" and a significant increase in perceived "feelings of personal adequacy" and "sense of reality".

Similarly, a comparison of the change scores of treatment and control participants on the measures of "global self-efficacy" and "self-esteem" (see Table 13.1) indicate that treatment participants made significantly greater gains in perceptions of self-efficacy and perceptions of self-esteem.

The fact that the no-treatment control group participants also showed some minor improvement on measures of "feelings of personal adequacy," "global self-efficacy," and "self-esteem" suggests that not all of the improvement in depression, ego strength, self-efficacy, and self-esteem in the participants should be attributed to the reminiscence intervention procedures. It is conceivable that some of the positive changes that occurred were a function of other change-inducing variables not measured or assessed in the present study design.

Major Thematic Contents of Stories and Narratives Told by Participants

In the mini-stories, women talked about the life paths they had selected, the choices they had made, the hardships they had endured, and the many personal resources (including one's most intimate relations) they had sacrificed in the belief that through this struggle they would achieve a firm sense of self or personal identity. At the general level,

TABLE 13.1 Mean Pre-Intervention to Follow-up Change Scores for Depression, Ego Strength, Global Self-Efficacy, and Self-Esteem for Treatment and No-Treatment Control Respondents

Variables	(Treatment Group) Storytelling Intervention (N=20) Mean Change Scores		(No-Treatment Control) No Storytelling Intervention (N=18) Mean Change Scores		t	p
	M	SD	M	SD		
Beck Depression Inventory (range of change scores = 0 to 21)						
Depression Scores	−6.00	2.75	−2.1	1.65	5.36	<.001
Ego Strength Scale (ESS) (range of change scores = 0 to 25)						
Ability to Share Feelings	+3.82	0.89	+0.99	1.00	9.17	<.001
Feelings of Personal Adequacy	+5.85	1.02	+1.60	0.98	13.09	<.001
Sense of Reality	+4.69	0.94	+1.65	0.99	9.68	<.001
Global Self-Efficacy (GSES) (range of change scores = 25 to 100)						
Global Self-Efficacy	+14.22	2.01	+2.99	0.99	22.18	<.001
Self-Esteem Scale (SES) (range of change scores = 10 (Low) to 40 (High))						
SES Scores	+8.6	2.99	+2.1	0.98	9.19	<.001

t = Independent sample t - test

Note: Negative scores indicate change toward lower scores and positive scores indicate change toward higher scores after each storytelling session, women indicated not only a somewhat stronger need for stability but also a contrasting need for change in their children's lives. One poignant excerpt is worthy of attention:

> "Dear Lisa: Do not go gentle in the dark night . . . but rail and rail and rail against the light [sic]. Some day soon, I hope you will understand that others can be cruel, but you must not accept their cruelty. You must fight and be strong and remember that your mother will always be on your side fighting with you against those who want to hurt and destroy us . . ." (Doris, age 29: a survivor of abuse)

Thematic Content Analyses of Early and Later Storytelling Sessions for Six Participants: Major Changes

Two research assistants who had no previous involvement in the reminiscence workshops and were unaware of the hypotheses of the study, went over the tape recordings of the first three storytelling sessions and the last three storytelling sessions of six randomly selected participants, and noted the frequency of major themes that emerged in the stories. The purpose of studying the frequency with which certain salient themes were mentioned in the beginning and terminal storytelling sessions was to test the hypothesis that, over the course of treatment, there would be a move or shift from negative preoccupations and negative self-perceptions of functioning to more positive self-perceptions of functioning, and a corresponding reduction in themes of depression, isolation, and loneliness.

Table 13.2 presents a breakdown of the major themes that emerged in the storytelling sessions of six participants, and the raw frequency counts. Although statistical significance of the differences between the frequencies of themes that appeared in earlier sessions and later sessions cannot be validly established, the general trends are clear and support the hypothesis that with treatment (reminiscence therapy through storytelling), there would be a noticeable move in the direction of positive perceptions of efficacy, adequacy in coping with obstacles, self-confidence, and ability for social interactions.

The trends that appeared in terms of frequency of positive and negative themes from earlier to later sessions are consistent with the trends that were observed in the change scores of participants as derived from their self-reportings on measures of depression, ego strength, self-efficacy, and self-esteem (see Table 13.1).

TABLE 13.2   Salient Themes in Early and Later Storytelling Sessions of Six Randomly Selected Participants in the Treatment Group

	First Three Sessions of Storytelling (Thematic Contents of 18 Stories)	Last Three Sessions of Storytelling (Thematic Contents of 18 Stories)
	Frequencies	Frequencies
Expressions of Guilt	116	33
Expressions of Hopelessness	124	41
Confusion	129	37
Loneliness	82	31
Depression	118	51
Loss of Control	81	22
Inability to Cope With Obstacles	89	24
Life Has No Meaning	101	34
Expressions of Anxiety and Fear	97	39
Perceptions of Self-Confidence	19	67
Perceptions of Adequacy in Social Interactions	20	69
Ability to Cope with Obstacles	18	59
Plans for the Future	19	67
Perceptions of Self-Control	17	59

DISCUSSION

The findings reported in Tables 13.1 and 13.2 confirmed for us the profoundly positive effect that the reminiscence experience had in the lives of the young survivors. For many young survivors of abuse who had an opportunity to stay with the group for a period of 4 to 6 months, the "Tell Us Your Story" reminiscence group became a pathway to growth in helping build self-confidence, regaining self-esteem, and extending self-knowledge. Our qualitative analysis of the contents of narratives helped us to conclude that the storytelling sessions provided each individual narrator an important path for moving toward others, and for recognizing bonds and relationships of strong attachments.

In the early stages of telling her story, each woman revealed the abuse she had experienced, the threats to her life, and the threats to her "self" as a "good person," an "adequate person," and a "person able to control her emotions". But as the storytelling advanced, it became more apparent that each woman was making more gains in self-affirmation as she sought and gained reassurance from the group that her "self" was indeed good, competent, and able to maintain control in interactions with others. Although the sources from whom a woman obtained reassurance were completely unrelated to the sources of threats to her well-being, the affirming information she got from the "Tell Us Your Story" group appeared to have a buffering effect on her self-image as a "good," "competent," and "controlled" person.

By encouraging survivors of abuse to stay involved in reminiscence sessions we, as facilitators of the group sessions, were successful in our attempt to reposition the young survivors of abuse among a "community of the living" as opposed to a "community of almost dead" or "barely living" women. The repositioning process was taken further by our supporting the notion that survivors of abuse and injustice had a moral responsibility to relate those stories of pain and injustice "that are of personal importance" and which reveal the survivor's need to say "I am here, I survived, and so can you".

The findings of the study supported previous claims that reminiscence intervention through storytelling facilitates "the acceptance of one's life as it has been in the past, and overcoming a sense of shame and despair" (Stevens-Ratchford, 1992). Likewise it can be utilized as a viable tool for distressed individuals to enhance their future lives through what Whalen (1996) describes as "regaining a sense of a new individuality" characterized by increased feelings of personal strength, decision-making ability, and self-efficacy. Such positive feelings were frequently not connected to any behavioral change, but considerable healing may have come through positive cognitions of self-esteem and self-efficacy. As the reminiscence process unfolded, each newly vulnerable participant began gradually to look for solutions to problems that could be personally useful to her. The reminiscence activity served to support rather than supplant problem-solving solutions that she felt were appropriate for her. This perspective of the value of reminiscence reinforces or evokes Jung's (1933) view of individuation. Individuals began to engage in reminiscence and ruminations of the past as a reflex bid to regain control of the present, and to reflect on the past to resolve, reorganize, and reintegrate what was troubling or preoccupying them in the present. As proposed by Kimmel (1990), by engaging in ruminations of a painful and aversive past, participants began to reintegrate a changing physical and emotional "me" into a relatively continuous sense of "self". They began to talk about ways and means by which to improve current and future functioning.

Because of each woman's immersion in a narrative of a daily event, a description of a critical event, or the story of a new relationship, these events became laden with a storied sense. A different story told each week about an important event began to acquire the reality of "a beginning," "a climax," "a low point," "a small solution," or "an ending" leading to "another beginning" (Gergen & Gergen, 1988). Rather than seeing one's life as simply "one damned thing after another," each woman was attempting to understand the systematic relationship between and among the events she was describing. They were rendered intelligible because she was able to locate a sequence or "unfolding process" in the events she selectively described for the group. Thus, her self-identity for that one hour, or one day, or one week was not a sudden and mysterious development, but a sensible result of the mini-stories she had narrated. Each story or mini-narrative reflected a woman's sense of whether life was improving, whether a relationship was breaking down or being replaced by a new relationship, or whether there was a leveling of strife, and so on. Each woman became more adept at understanding herself in the context of her personal history. Her social capabilities were enhanced and she worked harder at presenting herself as having an enduring, integral, or coherent identity. Thus, by the end of a series of stories, each woman found that she was being immersed into a world of relationships. Out of this sense of engagement born out of telling her story, life that seemed empty a few weeks previously began to take on meaning. Furthermore, notwithstanding survivors' frequent ruminations of painful and distressing experiences and multiple wrenching losses in relationships, it is important to note that their stories frequently contained several small didactic messages of hope, trust, new resolve, and advice to other women that simply could not be ignored by group members or facilitators:

Learn to forgive: "I had to learn to forgive people who did not help me when I needed them . . . This was most important to my personal recovery and healing."

Admit your limitations: "I confess that I was not faithful to him . . . the more he hit me and struck me, the more I found myself turning to other men for comfort . . . but then it became a messy sexual affair at times and I must admit that these were my mistakes . . ."

Be sensitive to other people's understanding of your problems: "Other people have their own problems to deal with . . . I have to learn to appreciate others' problems as well . . . not get so wrapped up in my problems that I lose sight of others' problems."

Manage your goodbyes well: "I must shut the doors quietly but firmly on some relationships . . . but even with these people who were an important part of my life at one time, I must be careful to say my goodbyes with tenderness, compassion, and sorrow, not with hate, anger, or bitterness."

Learn to take each day, a day at a time: "At the break of each day, I start with a ray of hope in my heart . . . at the break of each day, I start with a word of praise in my heart . . . at the break of each day, I start with a prayer of thanks in my heart . . . at the break of each day, I start with a note of love in my heart."

Do not be afraid to ask questions about the meaning of life: "As survivors of abuse, we women must move together through time. Our pasts may have been different and our pasts may have begun at different times, and we may have survived for different reasons, but it is important that we journey into the future together, and not be afraid to dream dreams, to hope for new relationships and new meanings for our lives. We can help each other make peace with the past . . . let's not be afraid to talk about the sense of emptiness and lack of meaning that overwhelms us."

In summary, the storytelling sessions helped clients meet some psychological needs, such as gaining self-affirmation, preserving and recovering self-esteem, and overcoming constant feelings of self-blame and self-criticism for negative events they had experienced. The storytelling enabled some clients to recognize that indeed, they had powerful stories to tell. The fact that clients were given the opportunity to tell their stories to attentive listeners contributed considerably to their self-confidence, and in several small ways it revealed to them their own strengths and capabilities they had had in the past which they now felt they could regain with some effort. The storytelling enabled several clients to give order to the many chaotic events of their lives. Although their past negative experiences made little sense to many clients, the storytelling sessions motivated them to anticipate the future in a more planned way, and to work toward specific goals.

CONCLUSIONS

Storytelling as a form of reminiscence is a component of many therapeutic approaches, and perhaps because it is so embedded, specific investigation of its efficacy with distressed individuals has been relatively neglected. Based upon our observations, it is reasonable to conclude that the main functions that storytelling reminiscence therapy fulfilled for participants in our study was enhancing their sense of self-worth, helping them understand themselves in relation to others who had had similar experiences of abuse, and finally allowing them to assimilate or reintegrate a meaning for life. Based on informal interactions with participants in this study who told stories of both positive and negative events and experiences, it is reasonable to conclude that the telling of stories answered a deep human need of the survivors of abuse—the need to say "I am here, my life has not been filled with great successes . . . but it has not been in vain." These forms of expressions appeared and reappeared in both the earlier and later sessions of storytelling. Almost all of the participants were younger women. Their storytelling was about experiences in the recent past and the present. However, with some assistance from the group members and facilitators, participants were steered into linking each story of past events with personal hopes, aspirations and, sometimes, fears concerning the future. Overall, the stories provided evidence that reminiscence is therapeutic not just for older persons but for the young as well.

It is important to recognize that storytelling is a viable and powerful reminiscence tool. The emphasis is on the empowerment of the individual: It is the storyteller who sets the agenda and is therefore in a position of power regarding what is to be told and how it is told. However, a few words of caution are important for group facilitators. First, it is important to note that not all clients have experience for storytelling. Many clients may need much encouragement and support in narrating events and experiences. On those few occasions when clients had no materials for a story, the facilitator encouraged them to reminisce about events, roles, persons, and activities that the individual had found distressing, or enjoyable and satisfying. Following Steele's (1988) theory that self-affirmation comes from the availability, accessibility, and enjoyment of resources and important roles (e.g., parental role, occupational role, friendship role) that are closely tied to one's self-image and one's sense of self-esteem, the facilitator encouraged the narrator to weave into story form her major source of distress or enjoyment coming from other roles, for example: Are you a parent? If yes, how important to your self-image is being a parent? How stressful or enjoyable is it for you to be a parent at this time?

Another major risk encountered by a distressed and vulnerable client in storytelling is the possibility that she may link together painful experiences in such a way that leads her to believe that she is not making much progress or that she has suffered irreversible losses. Thus, a risk or danger to the self or evaluation of the self may result from allowing the vulnerable individual to proceed too long with a narrative that is obviously damaging to the self-image or identity (Burnside, 1995). It is important that at the close of each story session the storyteller leave with a sense of hope, a feeling that some progress has been made, and with some small goal or small plan for tomorrow (Gergen & Gergen, 1988). Therefore, one of the major responsibilities of the group facilitators is to ensure that a potentially regressive or negative "series of events" or "turn of events" in the narrative of the client is propelled, as soon as possible, in the direction of a valued goal, or valued relationship or engagement that reminds the client of a "small victory gained," "a danger withstood," "the recovery of a lost relationship," or "the fortunate demise of a destructive relationship," and so on.

Clinicians and researchers need to come together to ensure that the outcomes of reminiscence and storytelling are investigated from the client's perspectives. Using qualitative analysis and working in a much closer partnership with the clients themselves is essential to the success of the reminiscence therapy. At the end of each story narration, the narrator will invariably seek affirmation and assurance that her story made sense to the listeners. Facilitators and group members must provide this assurance regularly, and without hesitation or delay, and let the client know they look forward to her next narrative.

From our perspective, the storytelling reminiscence therapy procedure used in this study is one that captured the clients' interests and was effective in unfolding within-person processes. It also revealed individual differences in the temporal patterning of events, emotions, and coping.

Some limitations of the procedures and analytic tools we used to interpret the clients' within-person reminiscences are obvious and must be acknowledged. First, the time-intensive nature of the reminiscence process places significant burdens on both the clients and the facilitators. The reminiscence intervention places a burden on the clients who must concentrate intently on describing their experiences, while at the same time being concerned about being intelligible to their listeners. It places a burden on facilitators who must be vigilant throughout each session of storytelling and must take the lead in encouraging certain positive themes in the storytelling and restructuring any negative themes of the narratives. These and other limitations of within-person process research have been discussed elsewhere by researchers (e.g., Tennen, Eberhardt, & Affleck, 1999). However, we remain confident that reminiscence therapy (using a storytelling modality) holds the greatest promise of linking qualitatively derived data with rich clinical traditions in psychotherapy for survivors of abuse. We have presented both qualitative and quantitative data to show that reminiscence intervention, especially the storytelling mode, makes a significant contribution to enhancing self-esteem and self-efficacy and to alleviating depression in female survivors of abuse.

ACKNOWLEDGEMENTS

Grateful thanks are extended to Sharon Ali, Colleen Kasting, and Arlene Wells for their assistance in recruitment of participants and data collection at various stages of the research, some of which are reported in this chapter. Vanessa Young served as a group facilitator in several storytelling sessions. The qualitative data were analyzed by both authors of this chapter. Further work in the use of reminiscence as a therapeutic tool for female survivors of abuse and violence is currently being supported by a grant award to P.S. Fry and P.T.P. Wong from the Social Sciences and Humanities Research Council of Canada, (File No. 816-97-0009).

14

Trauma, Reconciliation, and Generativity: The Stories Told by European War Veterans

Peter G. Coleman, Airi Hautamaki, and Andrei Podolskij

M emory is a dynamic and creative force, a searching after truth by means of art as well as science. It seeks not only past under-standing but also future inspiration. This is an ancient concept. For the Greeks, Mnemosyne (memory) was the mother of the Muses. We remember for ourselves, but also, and more important, we remember for the benefit of our society (Moody, 1984). Through narrative we connect past, present, and future, creating a story which makes life meaningful by explaining the intentions, goals, and achievements that characterize both the life of individuals and that of society. Such story making typically involves judicious selection, letting go not only of the ordinary dross but all that is unhelpful to the narrative drive.

But not all that memory gives birth to is good. There is a dark side. This is illustrated by the first author's studies on reminiscence carried out in London from the late 1960s to the early 1980s (Coleman, 1974; 1986). Many of the men interviewed were veterans of World War I. The only literature on the subject of reminiscence at that time was American, and although it might deal with personal difficulties, it did not deal with shared trauma. One of the most significant pieces of early empirical research had, in fact, been carried out on war veterans of the Spanish-American War (McMahon & Rhudick, 1967). This was a war that had been won by the United States and the empirical studies emphasized the self-sustaining features of the reminiscences of these old veterans. They had witnessed action and adventure and, for the most part, celebrated their experiences.

However the World War I veterans interviewed were survivors of quite a different conflict. They had difficult experiences to tell, and they had come to terms with them to varying degrees. Some were well adjusted, some not. Some avoided the subject. Some were still struggling to find something meaningful to say from their narratives. Society is still coming to terms with the difficulty of this task. It is well illustrated in recent novels about war trauma, notably in Pat Barker's *Another World* which describes the haunting effects of continued World War I nightmares on the last days of a 101 year old man.

Recent research on resolution of war trauma suggests that over time "consummate" memories emerge from traumatic memories (Hunt & Robbins, 1998). This means that even the most emotion-laden and uncontrollable flashbacks can be replaced by memories that, although preserving the detail of the traumatic memory, become more coherent and under the control of the person. Many recorded examples of World War I memories could be described as "consummate". Others seemed still to be emerging from their traumatic form, even though more than fifty years had elapsed. What was also striking about these reminiscences was the determination of the veterans both to bear witness to the truth of what had happened, and to convey some meaningful message, whether about the nature of warfare, about human behavior under extreme stress, or about society and values, that had emerged from their experiences.

For example, Mr. R. had started his working life on the land as most Quakers did, could not make ends meet, and so enlisted in the army only to find himself caught up in the maelstrom of World War I. The war had affected him deeply. He still showed many signs of trauma-related disturbance of memory and behavior. If disturbed at night, he still tended to reach for his rifle. He had tried unsuccessfully to forget the war. Nevertheless, despite the pain of his reminiscences, he was able to articulate a powerful condemnation of the war and those who had unleashed it:

"It was a dirty business. You see each war throws people further back. You see we were practically living in the Stone Age again. We were just living in holes, covered with lice—I never slept in a bed for about three years—subjected to heavily concentrated artillery fire . . . Lloyd George, he made millions out of armaments with his 'Feed the Guns' campaign. He did very well out of the war. So did the big steel people. So did the clergy too. 'Praise the Lord, my dear Augusta, we've won a battle, such a muster. Ten thousand Germans sent below, praise God from whom all blessings flow!' There is nothing like a bit of soldiering to buck your ideas up, you see life in the raw then!"

Mr. H. had recovered somewhat better from his experiences, yet remained bewildered by the senseless waste of lives he had witnessed and also participated in. He wondered about his own survival. He remembered how he had looked down at his hands and been amazed that he had worn out the barrel of his machine gun through continuous firing. Yet he was at his happiest acknowledging that there had been a degree of shared understanding between the victims on the opposing sides.

"Along came more German prisoners. Our sergeant said to the Jerry sergeant major. 'Who's going to win the war, Jerry?' This German could speak better English than I could. He shouted out to our sergeant: 'All I know, is that whoever started this war ought to be where we've been'. I always remember that . . ."

Mr. H. had recently heard that there was a new book out on the Battle of the Somme and was determined to have a look to see whether 'he's writing the gospel about it!'

An important feature of these interviews was that the veterans were speaking to a young man. They had been given an opportunity to teach lessons from their experience. Most had stories to tell, but not all were able to construct coherent messages from their experiences. Subsequent analysis demonstrated that the reminiscences of the men with higher morale and life satisfaction were characterized by a stronger teaching element (Coleman, 1974).

Generativity and Reconciliation in Stories

Veterans' experience of World War I is a critical example of the search for meaning (Frankl, 1984). The battles on the western front in World War I were particularly senseless examples of warfare. Enormous masses of soldiers were sacrificed for little or no gains. The consequent great European struggle of World War II is easier to understand, both in terms of the well articulated ambitions of Nazi Germany to dominate Europe, and the determination of the other great powers to resist. At the same time both the greater scale of conflict and the horrors meted out to civilian populations have posed more difficult issues of reconciliation.

It is important to understand the processes at work in creating meaning after conflict. We live for generations, for centuries, and even perhaps for millennia, with the hatred stirred up by memories of ethnic and religious conflict. We recognize, but probably do not quite fully appreciate, how rooted in symbolic historical memories the conflicts of our present world are. We can see it clearly in the conflicts in Ireland and the former Yugoslavia. But I suspect that we underestimate just how much of our national, racial, and ethnic attitudes are formed in these ways, and how deep and subterranean they run.

Stories of atrocity in particular mark out dividing lines very clearly. For example the memory of the sack of Constantinople in 1204 along with other cruelties perpetrated by the crusaders created a permanent separation between Western and Eastern Christianity that has proved very difficult to heal. Such long consolidated memories may become defining elements in the culture itself and therefore even harder to change. Yet it is also possible for cultures to create healing narratives that, while recognizing the traumas of the past, are also capable of transcending them.

We believe that psychology can now make contributions not only at the level of therapy with individuals but also in addressing major social issues which call for healing. This has been made possible by developments within lifespan psychology and reminiscence studies. More attention is now being paid to the investigation of human strengths and optimal functioning including the positive transformation of post-trauma personality (Seligman & Csikszentmihalyi, 2000; Tedeschi & Calhoun, 1995). The processes of acknowledgement and acceptance which operate at the individual level also operate on a societal level. A very good example is the work of Truth and Reconciliation Commission in South Africa. As Linley states "the creation of narrative is the milestone marking the progress made since the trauma" (Linley, 2000, p. 354). Developmental theories of aging have also contributed to an understanding of the social functions of reminiscence, the place of generativity in human development, and the promotion of intergenerational transmission of memories.

Although the early writings on the functions of reminiscence emphasized such intrapsychic functions as life review and identity maintenance, it is clear that reminiscence serves social needs as well. It produces optimum effects where it has social benefits as well, particularly through the transmission of cultural values. This is a point already made by McMahon and Rhudick (1967). As David Gutmann has pointed-ed out from his studies of aging in traditional cultures, most societies the world has known have been gerontocracies (Gutmann, 1994). In those societies it is the expected role of older people to be involved at the cultural and spiritual level even though they may disengage from practical concerns.

Generativity, which Erikson defined as the marker of mature adulthood, requires the integration of earlier life experiences, especially when it concerns the transmission of commitments and values. This is not necessarily straightforward. McAdams (1996) illustrates how adults scoring most highly on generativity are not necessarily those who had the most positive early experiences, but were those who had been able to transcend difficulties. It is in the sequencing of life events that the life stories of generative adults differ from those less generative. Both tend to refer to the same mixture of positive and negative events, joy and sorrow, good and bad. But for generative adults bad scenes tend to precede and eventually give birth to good.

Life review also appears linked to generativity. A very interesting finding of the Berkeley Longitudinal Study of Ageing (Wink & Schiff , this volume) is that the strongest associates of life review activity are not subjective well-being, but developmental achievements such as creativity, generativity, and spirituality and, as one would expect, using reminiscence for purposes of identity exploration and problem solving. Considered in terms of social relevance these may be much more important outcomes than well-being. Gerontological research may have been hindered by an excess focus on individual, subjective well-being as the primary outcome variable in aging research. The objective behaviors of older people, the function they fulfill and the roles that they occupy in society, are certainly as important if not more so.

Among these roles the intergenerational transmission of memories is a key but neglected one. Evidence exists for the potential older people have. There may be a natural tendency for older people to reminisce and for their voices to gain attention (Mergler & Goldstein, 1983). Yet in many Western societies older people have become less confident about their roles, they may feel they have no natural audience to speak to, or may not even be sure they have a story to tell (Coleman, 1999). Even reminiscences of major communal importance may have become desiccated and lost their potency. Societal stories are living things, but it is the responsibility of all of us, and particularly older people, to hand them on in good shape so that they then become healthy traditions for others. The extent to which this occurs harmoniously within a society is an important marker of positive aging.

Stories Drawn From World War II Experience in Northern Europe

We would like to illustrate these concepts from research we are conducting on World War II experiences and the stories veterans tell about them. We considered that these issues would benefit from cross-national and cross-cultural consideration, and we are currently collaborating on a project examining the narration of World War II experience across

Northern Europe. The aim of these studies is not principally to examine the consequences for the individuals themselves, but to investigate how the stories are transmitted to the next generation. So far we have carried out a series of pilot studies.

In this chapter we report on studies in Finland and Russia. But our current collaborators also include British and German psychologists working in the area of war trauma (Hunt & Robbins, 2001; Kruse & Schmitt, 2000), and we hope to extend our network to include other countries as well.

War memories are particularly susceptible to social censorship in which only narratives consistent with the received view of events are socially permissible. This remains a problem in Britain as well as other countries. There is much of course for Britain to be proud of in the second world war, but the propaganda that operated in wartime to conceal failure, chaos, disorder, and insurrection still operates. Research has identified individuals who have never been able to tell their stories about Dunkirk, for example, because it was inconsistent with the standard view of glorious retreat (Coleman & Mills, 1997). A further problem for many World War II veterans is that the present state of Britain does not, in their view, measure up to the sacrifices they made to preserve it. There is insufficient continuity of meaning. Recent research has highlighted large amounts of hidden trauma (Hunt & Robbins, 2001).

The involvement of Germany is crucial to our enterprise of understanding healing of World War II memories, but German war memories remain very difficult to record. There is resistance to speaking openly about the war. Most German researchers have felt it their obligation to direct their research to those who suffered under Nazi persecution (Kruse & Schmitt, 2000). Very few studies have been conducted on ordinary German soldier and civilian experiences of the second world war (e.g., Lohmann, Heuft, & Schneider, 1999). As a result, we know relatively little about how older Germans have been able to interpret their own sacrifices during the war, given the eventual defeat and disgrace of their country (see Keller, chapter 11, this volume). It is particularly important to understand the consequences of this apparent lack of communication on younger as well as older Germans.

The Experience of Finnish War Veterans

Finland was drawn into the second world war after being attacked by the Soviet Union which aimed to occupy the country. This attack started the so-called "Winter War" (30 November 1939–13 March 1940). A strong will to defend their country sprang up among the Finns, spoken of then and now in terms of the "Spirit of the Winter War". This phase of the war in which the Soviet forces were repulsed lasted for "105 days of honour" (Jarho, 1991, p. 11). After an interval of over one year there followed the "Continuation War" (25 June 1941–4 September 1944) also against the U.S.S.R., but which involved Finland in conflict with the allies of the U.S.S.R. in association with Germany. After the negotiation of peace terms with the U.S.S.R., the "Lapland War" (15 September 1944–27 April 1945) was fought to remove German forces from northern Finland.

The immediate consequences for Finland of World War II were grave. A part of eastern Finland, i.e., eastern Karelia, was lost to the U.S.S.R. and high war reparations had to be paid as well. But the nation kept its independence. Finland was not occupied and it was saved from massive aerial bombing (Jarho & Saari, 1991, p. 14). Most of the losses were in combat at the front involving men born between 1896–1926. The final account of those involved in the war is as follows: out of 700,000 men and women serving, 200,000 were wounded, injured, or suffered chronic disease, and 86,000 perished. The figures show that almost half of those in the war were either injured or killed.

Thus, when compared with many other European countries, Finland experienced some definite advantages in regard to the psychosocial effects of World War II (Jarho, 1991, p. 13). The number of POWs as well as the number of civilian victims was rather low. The "Spirit of the Winter War" survived relatively intact, creating solidarity among the Finns and uniting a young nation that had only recently engaged from bitter civil war following independence from Russia in 1917. The wars were, in general, considered inevitable and legitimate by the Finnish people, and war veterans were paid credit as honored and honorable citizens.

Our recent interviews were drawn from a sample of thirty veterans interviewed in Finnish rehabilitation centers. War veterans and their widows are entitled to spend three weeks a year at no cost to themselves in these well equipped and furnished centers. Many of the veterans we interviewed had been very severely wounded, and were still disabled. But they seemed both capable and willing of sharing even the hardest experiences (e.g., the death of a good comrade or being themselves severely wounded). As reported in other samples of Finnish war veterans we found a very low rate of continuing post-traumatic stress disorder (e.g., compared with British prevalence rates) (Hautamaki & Coleman, 2001).

Most had overcome the pain of these memories:

"I can say that surely the war left some kind of marks in me, because more than ten years after the war, if I had drunk more than moderately, those war memories popped into my mind—I found myself always in Hatjalahti, fighting against the Russians. Or so my wife told me . . . yes, until some twelve years after the war. Since then they didn't come back . . . Nowadays when I watch war films, I watch them as an "outsider". I do like to watch them, but I feel "cool" . . . in fact without any feelings. I don't dream any more of these things. It's the past . . . and those times are gone forever."

However, difficult feelings were aroused by certain memories. These included the unintentional killing of woman soldiers used by the Soviet army. One participant commented on the surprise discovery of women's bodies among the dead enemy soldiers. At first he commented that their gender did not matter. "No, it didn't matter, not in the least . . . Of course, if I really reconsider it thoroughly, maybe the only thing that occurred to me was: 'Why do the Russians use these young and beautiful women?'" But he then hesitated in his conclusion, remembering, on the basis of a scar on one women's stomach which indicated a caesarean section, that the soldiers could have been mothers. "At least the one I just told about—probably she had been a mother. In fact, all of these three could have been mothers, they were of that age, over twenty, but definitely less than thirty years of age." The interviewer had the distinct impression that an internal conflict between two value systems, that of instrumental, rational and efficient warfare and what Ruddick (1990) terms "the politics of peace," resting on maternal thinking, was emerging in the mind of the respondent.

Our study supported two principal reasons for the low prevalence of PTSD among surviving Finnish war veterans. One was the collective nature of the war, the resulting feelings of community spirit, and the very strong supportive networks created during the war which have persisted after the war. The second was the meaning and significance given to the war. Most important, this meaning has not dulled with time. It was seen and is still seen as a deeply collective endeavor, a joint responsibility to defend Finland's independence. As one of the most wounded and still disabled veterans said:

"For our independence . . . yes. And the fact which I said before that I don't accept that any foreign state—not Sweden, not Russia—should rule us, but *we* decide on our own affairs. It is not widely known, but the Finnish nation is so different compared with other nations . . . I kept thinking in the way that we have to maintain our independence and manage ourselves the affairs of our own country. If it's not possible otherwise, then we're going to fight for these values. That's how I felt about the war."

When asked how the war had influenced their lives, these men—many of whom had been disabled since the war—could answer affirmatively, integrating their losses with meaning for society as a whole. One veteran retorted strongly to the question "What aspects of the war did you find most interesting?" "As I am a peaceful man, I did not find it interesting. You just had to be there. It was the task of our generation—to save Finland as an independent nation. And now our children and grandchildren have a good country to live in." He completed this sentence with tears in his eyes and a wavering voice. Another severely wounded war veteran—he had tripped on a landmine in the Continuation War and lost one eye, an arm, and a leg, but still had a respected leadership position in the war veteran association—was asked whether he would have liked his life to have been different. "No. This is life. This is *my* life. With me it's like that. OK! I would like to reply that this has been my destiny and my way. You can't restore that, it is so that the Lord determines the length and the quality of your days."

One of the oldest veterans interviewed was a 94-year-old man who was proud to call himself a professional soldier. He expressed well the strong sense of integrity exhibited by so many of the veterans. "I was so well prepared for the war that it has been my vocation. And I did my job so well that nobody has ever blamed me: 'You failed!' And I was always in front, always in the front line!" He had a similarly positive view of his present life at the veterans hospital:

> "I'm treated so well here—surely the others are treated well, too. But I feel so good here! The head nurse called me up recently and asked me: 'Have you got your uniform and your badges of honour here?' I said: 'As this wardrobe is so small I have not brought them here.'She responded: 'It's not! You must have your uniform and your badges of honour on you!' And that she will check personally that they will be brought here."

Looking retrospectively at his life, he summed it up:

> "I cannot say anything else, but: I have had such a good life! I've been involved in so many things, that only very few have had the possibility for. For in my life—from the beginning of this century, when I was born— and which I now have lived through as a whole—so many things have happened here in Finland!"

The Experiences of Russian War Veterans

For Russia the Great Patriotic War remains a huge subject for remembrance; with at least 28 million dead, no one was unaffected. The scale of suffering is unimaginable and affected populations of large cities such as Leningrad and Stalingrad, both of which were besieged for long periods of time. However the war is only part of a continuous series of traumatic events the Russian population has suffered in the last century.

The veteran survivors of the titanic struggle with Nazi Germany are justly the focus of each year's May 9th victory celebrations, but in recent years they have also had to come to terms with the collapse of the Soviet Union and the system of government it represented.

This makes the experience of Russia's older people similar in some respects to that of Britain's, an experience of hard-won achievement followed by, in Britain's case, the dissolution of the British Empire. In Russia the connection between victorious struggle and eventual loss of power is less evident. In fact the geographical power of the U.S.S.R. increased greatly as a consequence of the war. But the collapse of the U.S.S.R. ten years ago and the subsequent difficulties in evolving a humane capitalist system pose psychological challenges to older people's well-being. It is far less easy for them to perceive the continuous line between past sacrifice and present achievement which characterizes the Finnish veterans' view of society.

Our initial sample of ten Russian war veterans whom we interviewed in depth is small. All were traced through contact with families known to staff and students at the Department of Developmental Psychology of Moscow State University. We cannot be sure that their views are representative of surviving war veterans, nor of course, as in Finland, of those who have not survived to advanced age. The ages of our participants range from 75 to 88 years, and the sample included two women. Some were still living with spouses, some with children, while others were living alone. Their health status varied considerably from very good to poor, and the main concern of most of them centered around their health and that of their families. The morale of the sample was mainly high and was linked closely to their health status. As with the Finnish war veterans, the interviews covered in detail the participant's war experience, but also took the opportunity to explore their perception of their life as a whole from past to present.

All were prepared to speak in detail about their war experiences. A number commented that it was the kind of reminiscing they often engaged in. Like the Finnish interviewees, they were proud of their achievements during the war and many had gone on to take responsible positions in military or civilian life afterwards. Some spoke in emotional terms of their defense of their motherland, and how they had sought to perform their duties to their best ability. They described many instances of bravery they had witnessed. Some had continued opportunities to speak about the war, for example in schools, which they appreciated doing. All saw their lives in terms of a story, with the war forming either a major part of the whole or a crucial time of transition. Their war experience had been varied; one had served in the navy and another in the air forces, while the remainder had served in the land forces.

Between them they had experienced many of the most important battles in the German-Russian war, including the siege of Leningrad, the defense of Moscow, the battle of Stalingrad, operation Kutusov, the battle of Kurskarc, the liberation of Smolensk, Warsaw, Budapest, and Prague, and the capture of Berlin. Nearly all had witnessed the death of friends, and had experienced either being shot at or bombed themselves. All reported continuing examples of the unwanted intrusion of, and avoidance of, traumatic memories, although none of the sample appeared to be suffering from major disorder in this respect. Some traumatic images surfaced in their reminiscences (e.g., walking upon dead bodies; bullets racing towards them before changing course; the sight of burning pilots). One woman reported persistent dreams of horses spattered with blood that she had seen and pitied as they worked day and night through the campaigns.

One of the woman had been taken prisoner. Fortunately she had been able to escape, thanks to the efforts of a German soldier who had recognized she was a woman (an interesting parallel with the Finnish veteran's comments previously).

> "Our regiment was surrounded by enemy troops. They bombed us. We were defeated and had to run away. I went through the forest all the night and finally had to find myself in front of the enemy. So I was captured. All the Russian captives were gathered together in a big column which was guarded by German soldiers with rifles and dogs. This column was accompanied to the concentration camp. If someone cried—even if it was a woman with a child—they were killed by the German soldiers immediately. We needed to rest and to talk. All the way along I was crying quietly to myself. One young German noticed me. When we were passing through a Russian little town, he came to me and began to push me aside. I couldn't understand what he wanted to do with me. I pushed away from him. But he resolutely pulled me out of the column and pushed me behind a house near us. The column had passed and I had stayed in an unknown place, an unknown town. But I was free! So, this German soldier saved my life."

It is noteworthy that all the participants took the opportunity at the part of the interview which compared their past and present lives to comment critically on the changed situation within Russia. This was an obvious challenge to their system of values which they had to grapple with. Many of them contrasted present day social life with the solidarity they had experienced in wartime:

> "In the past everything was easier. There was friendship, mutual aid and mutual understanding. Now man is an enemy for man. There is unemployment. A lot of people can't choose their professional way. There are a lot of thieves and bandits."

"It's hard to see what is happening in the contemporary Russian navy forces that we were proud to serve in. It is hard to see stealing and other dirty things."

Of particular concern was how the collapse of public morality had affected young people:

"We loved our motherland and were always ready to defend it. There were the Pioneers' Organization, the Comsomol Organization and each child and adolescent did something useful. The level of moral development was higher than now. Now the youth is more educated, everybody can use the products of technical progress. But children and adolescents can't spend their time well, they go to basements, smoke, drink etc. And the greater part of them is scared to defend our motherland. No one does a thing unless he knows someone will pay him money for it."

Some tried to be unbiased in their comments. There were criticisms of Soviet society as well as praise, but on balance the past society had seemed better.

"I didn't like it that in those days nobody could say openly what he thought. Our government didn't value a human life. Once we got the government's order to test a new metro line. It was dangerous and killed a young man who was taking part. But the government wasn't sorry for him. There were more and more sacrifices. Nobody spoke about it . . . There are good people both then and now. But there were less gangsters and thieves. I don't like it that the U.S.S.R. doesn't exist any longer. In those days people showed more solidarity. I liked the power and the honour of the U.S.S.R. Moral behavior in families was better."

For many these issues raised an intense inner dialogue, one they were prepared to reveal to their young interviewers. The following is an example from one interview:

"During the Soviet period our life was completely ensured. It was my firm belief that the next day will come, that my family will live in peace and in happiness. The confidence in next day—that gave us the great stimulus to live and to live with interest. But now I give up my hope. There are no good perspectives for our country, for our suffering people. In the Soviet age we hoped in justice, now most people have money as their purpose in life . . . My opinion has changed greatly. Knowledge about the world and people has changed. Now we have more true information which we can trust. Earlier there were no alternatives. But today I can compare many points of view on any problem and have my own opinion in spite of the common one. In the Soviet age personality had no value for the government . . . It's impossible to throw away anything from the memory. If it happens all the image will be destroyed. How should I describe my life? It's difficult. Indeed it's easier to name the events themselves. But what I can say is that at the time life was interesting and quieter as well. Young people think that our Soviet living was dull and grey. It's not true. Our life was bright and full of life and perhaps even better than nowadays . . . . Earlier we had the faith in happiness, we had enthusiasm to help our country. I'm an old man. I can't say that these days are worse. They are different."

Many of these veterans' reminiscences were linked to themes of generativity:

"I think back on my past life every day. I make a lot of appearances in schools, colleges, institutes, and public meetings. I tell people about the war because I don't want a war again and I don't want anybody to see a war."

"The most important thing for me is to bring kindness to people. That's the main thing for me in the past as well as in the present . . . All my life I tried to do my best to bring my knowledge to other people. In other words I was a teacher all of my life. I was encouraged in teaching activity by my own teacher at school. I was taught how to fly airplanes in the war. After the war I studied in the Air Force Academy. Then I became a teacher in that academy. After demobilization I worked in the school, in the Palace of Pioneers, in the Pioneers' camps. For more than 30 years I was the leader of the radio club where the children were taught. Nowadays I'm a member of the radio club."

This last man quoted also had a remarkable story to tell of his current work of generativity and reconciliation. He recounted it in answer to a request to provide a story from his recent experience that conveyed something of the meaning of his life.

"During the war my father was killed on the front. I tried to find out where it was but with no success. Then suddenly I got the information from the TV as to where he had died. I happened near Novgorod in the village called Lesnoi Bor. From the history I know that two armies, the 2nd and the 52nd were destroyed there during a large-scale attack trying to deblockage Leningrad. It happened in a small area. Officially about 100,000 of our soldiers lie there unburied. And I knew that my father was also there. So I decided to come and to see this place myself. And now already for 13 years every Spring at the end of April and the beginning of May I go there with other people. We seek for bones, find them and bury them. They are not difficult to find. They are situated on the swamps and all the bones are situated just under the first level of ground. You just seek everywhere and find them. But we try to find not only bones but also medallions of the soldiers, on which you could read information about the man or his address. Sometimes we find letters to parents, wives and children.

Some time passed and I got a desire to inform the relatives about their heroes. For me this became very important. It's easy to find bone, it's harder to find medallions, but the hardest problem is to find relatives, because the addressee changed and administrative borders changed also. The other problem was finding a way of informing people. It is too expensive to write letters or to phone. And at the same time the quantity of medallions increases. For example I have about 1,000 of them now, more than 1,000 addresses all over the former U.S.S.R. That's why I decided to use my radio station. I call all the cities, towns, villages and some of them answer. For some time I called from my house, then I began to take the radio station to that place. Sometimes I find the relatives by radio in an hour or two after the finding of the medallion. Some of them even come to the burial procedure in three days."

He had found a new role that allowed him to continue to be generative. At the same time he had also found fresh hope in the younger generation.

"Among the people searching I am the oldest. They come from different regions of our country, sometimes even from Sakhalin. On the last number of occasions the quantity of searches has decreased because it became more and more expensive, and people did not have the financial resources. But about 500 persons are always present there at our 'meetings'. I would like to say that the youngsters who come with us have changed in the course of those trips. They became more kind, more responsible and more attentive. I think that this has been the most important work of mine during the last ten years."

Conclusion

Memory, trauma, healing, generativity, reconciliation—these are key themes for the future of all societies. For the Finnish and Russian war veterans we have interviewed the wars they have experienced have been deeply meaningful despite the trauma involved. For both groups the strong meaning has not waned with time. It is clear to them why the sacrifice was made. For the older Finns there is a continuous line between those sacrifices and the Finland of today, a prosperous member of the European Union with a strong voice of its own after centuries of Swedish and Russian domination. For the older Russians, however, the massive societal changes they have recently experienced has been disturbing, and yet they are still able to give strong witness to continuing human values.

We consider that there is much to learn from cross-national investigations into reminiscence and intergenerational transmission of memories.

Our interviews illustrate well the saying of Victor Frankl that anything can be endured if it can be made meaningful. But that meaning of course has to persist with time. Frankl himself was a survivor of the extermination camps, of the Holocaust. If anywhere in the past century, the Holocaust tests the limits of meaning making and reconciliation.

In 1999 the European Congress of Gerontology was held in Berlin and a special symposium was held on work with Holocaust survivors. In Berlin, as elsewhere, initiatives have been taken to create lasting memorials of the Holocaust. This is a very important activity as we move into a new century and millennium. In many ways the Holocaust is only now properly being recorded. There is a great fear among survivors that the start of a new millennium might be used as an opportunity to begin afresh and to forget, when for them the only meaning is to be found in continuing to remember. It is important to emphasize that the first aim of memory is to bear witness to truth. Without the search for truth, healing and reconciliation are impossible.

ACKNOWLEDGEMENT

The Finnish study was made possible by funding from the Swedish School of Social Science, University of Helsinki, during the first author's time as international reader there in 1996-99. The Russian study was made possible by a grant from the University of Southampton. The authors would also like to make special mention of the Finnish and Russian interviewers: Airi Hautamaki, Runa Reimavuo, Elena Borovaia, Alexandra Bucharskaia, Daria Druzhinenko, Sergey Molchanov, and Dmitry Podolskij.

15

Reminiscence as Reading Our Lives: Toward a Wisdom Environment*

William L. Randall and Gary M. Kenyon

W e are coming to see that development has a "biographical" dimension (Birren, et al., 1996), that experience itself has a narrative quality (Crites, 1971), and that human identity is the result of continual "storying" (McAdams, 1996; Schank, 1990) and "restorying" (Kenyon & Randall, 1997). Ontologically, it could be said, we are *homo fabulans* (Howard, 1994). Indeed, our very lives *are* stories (Randall, 1995), the medium of which is not paper and print but flesh and blood. As Mary Catherine Bateson (1989) would say, we are forever "composing a life". "A life is a work of art," echoes Jerome Bruner (1999, p. 7), "perhaps the greatest one we produce". In short, "no story, no self" (p. 8).

Claims about lives as stories and self-authoring creations figure frequently in the emerging discourse known as narrative gerontology (Kenyon, Clark, & de Vries, 2001; Kenyon, Ruth, & Mader, 1999). Together, they suggest a variation on a "contextualist" model of reminiscence (Webster, 1999) that is *poetic* in nature, where poetic derives from *poiesis,* a term associated since Aristotle with the analysis of literature, or literary theory. Such a model constitutes a distinctive

---

* Portions of this chapter have been adapted, with permission, from Randall and Kenyon (2001).

framework and starting-point for the study of reminiscence, at least of its more adaptive manifestations (Wong, 1995). Our purpose here is to present a perspective for which that starting point is key. Central to it is an understanding of reminiscence as "reading" the "text" of our life in such a way as to facilitate the expression of what we call "ordinary" wisdom (Randall & Kenyon, 2001)—both in ourselves and in the various "biographical encounters" (Kenyon, 1996b) that make up our lives.

LIFE AS LITERATURE

The origins of narrative gerontology lie in an overall "narrative turn" that has been increasingly noted within the human sciences (Hinchman & Hinchman, 1997). This significant intellectual shift has fostered wide-ranging inquiry aimed at "the narrative study of lives" (see Lieblich & Josselson, 1997) and at such specific aspects of lives as emotion (Singer, 1996; Schweder, 1994), memory (Bluck, 2001; Neisser & Fivush, 1994), and identity (McAdams, 1994; Kerby, 1991). Investigation into "the storied nature of human conduct" (Sarbin, 1986a) is being undertaken not only in established disciplines like psychology (Sarbin, 1986b; Freeman, 1993), sociology (Gubrium & Holstein, 1998), and anthropology (Turner & Bruner, 1986), but in applied fields, too including healthcare, psychotherapy, and education (see Kenyon, Clark, & de Vries, 2001).

A key factor in the emergence of a "narrative perspective" (Randall, 2001) is the conceptual potential of the "narrative root metaphor" (Sarbin, 1986a; see also Schroots, Birren, & Kenyon, 1991) and its numerous entailments (Lakoff & Johnson, 1980), such as character, point of view, and plot. Because narrative ideas have spread so widely and rapidly, however, it is difficult to point to any one notion that takes precedence over others. Yet, one around which everything revolves where narrative perspectives prevail is that, fundamentally, we are meaning-making creatures (Reker & Chamberlain, 2000; Kenyon, 1996a). Through our relationships with others and our reflections within ourselves, we habitually interpret and reinterpret the events, circumstances, and people that make up our lives, assessing their significance for our personal existence. The main process by which we do this is complex but commonplace. Among the phrases by which it has been described are "narrative knowing" (Polkinghorne, 1988), "narrative imagining" (Turner, 1996), "narrative understanding" (Polkinghorne, 1996a), "narrative thought" (Bruner, 1986), and the "narrative construal of reality" (Bruner, 1996).

Without such ways of knowing, the users of these phrases would argue, distinctively *human* life would be impossible. We would be unable to compose a life, unable to participate in the colossal work-in-progress, the "fundamental project" (Charmé, 1984), that *is* our life. Put another way, we would be unable to "textualize" our life and, in that respect, be unable to "know" it (Bruner & Weisser, 1991). We would be unable to weave our own "lifestory" (Ochberg, 1995; Kotre, 1990) that multi-levelled, multiversioned text that we not only have but, on some level, *live* or *are* (Randall, 1995). In other words, our life and *lifestory* are inextricably entwined (Kenyon & Randall, 1997). "A life as lived," insists Bruner (1987), "is inseparable from a life as told". As McLuhan might put it, the medium is the message.

Facilitating this intricate process of composing a life is a capacity we call "narrative intelligence" (Randall, 1999). One of a family of "multiple intelligences" (Gardner, 1990), narrative intelligence is a logical extension of concepts like "narrative thought". In essence, it is the capacity to formulate and follow a story—above all, the story of our own life. The processes it involves are linked to labels like emplotment, characterization, and genre-ation, or like authoring, narrating, and reading, each of which is also an entailment of story. By means of these processes, we continually fashion and refashion the accounts that we offer both to others and to ourselves as to who we are, where we have come from, and where we are bound.

Where reminiscence is concerned, one consequence of narrative intelligence is that the so-called "facts" of our lives are always, in some sense, fictionalized. This is due not just to the refractive effects or "slippage" of language itself (Spence, 1982; Gubrium & Holstein, 1998) but to the very nature of the "faculties," i.e., memory and imagination, through which we make sense of situations, interpret events, and thus—gradually, continually, and actively, not passively (Casey, 1987)—transform the *stuff* of our lives into the *story* of our lives. With such processes in mind, one psychologist proposes that we speak not of the *facts* of our lives but of the "factions" (Steele, 1986). These factions are oriented toward the past, on the one hand, as our memories, and toward the future, on the other, as our hopes and fears, or, in general, our anticipations of what is to come. Without the capacity to compose them, however, it would be impossible to maneuver through everyday life, for we would be unable to make up and make use of a continuous sequence of "likely stories" with which to explain to ourselves what is happening in our world. For this reason, narrative intelligence may be considered native intelligence, fundamental to our being in time, a mode of cognition (Bruner, 1986, 1987) that constitutes the context in which reminiscence occurs.

Taken together, our narratives of the past compose a vast, ever-expanding anthology for which the term "autobiographical memory"

(Rubin, 1996; Conway, 1990) has come to be applied. Compared with other modes of memory, which are typically viewed in terms of the metaphor of "mind as computer" (Neisser & Fivush, 1994) and seen to involve processes like "encoding," "storage," and "retrieval," autobiographical memory is intricate, fluid, multilayered, and continually changing. As the memory we have—or make—of our entire life, it is integral to our sense of "the story of my life," in relation to which it constitutes the "inside story" (Randall & Kenyon, 2001). In other words, autobiographical memory is inextricably linked to our inner self-concept. Not only does this mean that the present can thus influence the past as much as the past can influence the present, but also that it is difficult to look objectively at the operation of such memory, to measure it in empirical fashion, and to transform it into statistical terms.

Most important, for our purposes here, autobiographical memory is seen to be penetrated by narrative patterns and constructed according to narrative conventions (see Neisser & Fivush, 1994; Rubin, 1996). "Memory," argues one theorist, "is memory for stories, and the major processes of memory are the creation, storage, and retrieval of stories" (Schank, 1990, p. 16). In short, autobiographical memory is storied, and as such is the precursor to autobiography per se. It is "a mode of self-invention that is always practiced first in living and only eventually—sometimes—formalized in writing" (Eakin, 1985, p. 9). Thus, to conceptualize the ways we compile autobiographical memory, a narrative metaphor is in our view more fitting than a computer one. In essence, autobiographical memory is better conceived as *story*-memory (Randall & Kenyon, 2001), akin to the memory we employ when comprehending a novel, and our experience of it is thus characterized less by a sense of clock time than of story time (Randall & Kenyon, 2001; Kenyon & Randall, 1997). Correspondingly, many of our memories can thus seem to refer to our future as much as they do our past. This is arguably the case with nostalgia or regret: Emotions associated with reminiscence in which the future or the past is often felt in the present as a kind of "counterfactual" (Ferguson, 1997), or as a sense, painful or sweet, of "what might have been" (see Ray, 2000).

While the links between memory, emotion, and narrative merit much attention in relation to reminiscence, a corollary of likening autobiographical memory to story memory that is of interest to us here is that, just as we say about the plot of a novel, such memory continually "thickens" (Casey, 1987). More to the point, and concomitant with this thickening, autobiographical memory involves a steady accumulation of meaning*fulness* (Randall & Kenyon, 2001)—that is, where "meaning" means "*story*-meaning". In other words, the meaning both *in* and *of* our lives—or *life*story meaning—is never fixed nor final, anymore than is "the past" per se. It is open and continuously developing (Charmé, 1984), and can be appreciated on numerous levels in numerous ways. By thinking of the meaning of memory as *story* meaning, then, we are led to an additional notion: lives as the medium of "narrative truth" (Spence, 1982). This line of thinking suggests an extension of the familiar postmodern notion of "lives as texts" (Rosenau, 1992; White & Epston, 1990) to embrace lives as *literary* texts—in other words, embodied, textual constructions that are novel-like at bottom (Polster, 1987; Glover, 1988) or *literary* in essence (Charmé, 1984; Bruner, 1999). Appreciated for their "literariness" (Wyatt-Brown, 1996) or "novelty" (Randall, 1999), qualities that are connected to the narrative dimensions of autobiographical memory itself, our lives can be seen, therefore, as dynamic, coherent, aesthetic compositions which, like great works of fiction, mediate a unique and potentially unlimited meaningfulness—and, in that sense, "wisdom" (Randall & Kenyon, 2001). In sum, they are distinctively storied creations, of which we are, at once, principal author, character, narrator, *and* reader.

NARRATIVE ENVIRONMENT

Before exploring the idea of reminiscence as *reading,* we must stress an important point. Central to narrative gerontology is the conviction that we construct the stories we tell and live not in an existential void but in particular social contexts, for example, the families and communities in which we grow up. To use story language, such contexts comprise a sequence of intersecting "settings" in which our individual stories unfold. In short, our lives, plus the processes by which we remember them (Wallace, 1992; Meacham, 1995), are socially constructed—not exclusively, since personal agency is inevitably at work, but significantly all the same (Holstein & Gubrium, 2000; Gubrium, 2001). To reiterate: We do not compose ourselves—we do not tell and retell, imagine and reimagine ourselves—in a narrative vacuum. Our lives are authored both for us and with us *by others,* in a web of "larger stories we live within" (Kenyon & Randall, 1997). Accordingly, the stories we compose about our lives—as well as the wisdom of which they are the vehicles—are functions of "the company we keep" (Booth, 1988). Every exchange we have with another person, every biographical encounter, has not only an intertextual and aesthetic dimension, therefore, but an ethical and indeed political one as well.

Each of the larger stories of our lives reflects the influence of still larger stories—for example, a family story unfolds within a community story within a national story, and so on. Furthermore, each is characterized

by its own "narrative environment" (Bruner, 1990). Among the con-
stituents of a narrative environment are the implicit and explicit codes
for telling and listening that are operative within it (Kenyon & Randall,
1997). Each such environment entails a set of unspoken guidelines for
what can be told and what must be left untold, for how much air time
each person is entitled to and how they can use it. Each involves tacit
directions for revealing and concealing, for remembering and forget-
ting. Moreover, each mediates a unique set of "story forms" (Cupitt,
1991), "forms of self-telling" (Bruner, 1987), or "storying styles"
(Randall, 1995) for editing our memory and tailoring our identity.

The most important narrative environment is the family into which
we are born. As noted by Bruner and Weisser (1991, p. 141): "Early in
life . . . we learn how to talk about our lives . . . we learn the family genre:
the thematics, the stylistic requirements, the lexicon . . . procedures for
offering justifications and making excuses, and the rest of it". But narrative environments include not only a specific family. They include the
various relationships, communities, and organizations, the different institutions, ideologies, and creeds (political and religious), to which we have
belonged across the years. Each of these in turn has, tacitly or openly,
prescribed particular conventions of "narrative practice" (Gubrium &
Holstein, 1998), and thus, directly or indirectly, has steered how we
story our lives (past, present, and future), how we go about "rewriting
the self" (Freeman, 1993), and how we "read" the self as well.

One of the most critical concepts in connection with narrative environment is *coauthoring*. As we share our stories with others whom we
meet in these various environments, their reactions shape (however
subtly or slightly) both the content and form of what it is we share,
affecting how we understand ourselves thereafter, and thus how we feel,
believe, and act. "Any self-narrative," notes Sarbin (1994), "is necessarily a collaborative, negotiated enterprise" (p. 9). As an example,
Bridges (1980) notes that "to become a couple is to agree implicitly to
live in terms of another's story" (p. 71). To use a term put forward by
Kenneth and Mary Gergen (1983), our self-narratives are "interknit"
with others', meaning that, storywise, we are intersubjectively connected, or narratively linked, in countless, complex ways. Where my story
ends and your story begins is thus difficult to say. Not only this, but no
narrative exchange is ever innocent. You tell me your tale and I tell you
mine, and no matter how ordinary our meeting might be, both of us
emerge, to some degree, restoried.

Tied to this notion is the fact that listening is as critical as telling
(Kenyon & Randall, 1997); it is one half of an indivisible whole. Says
psychotherapist, Susan Baur, "there is no story without a listener"
(1994). Selves, add Holstein and Gubrium (2000, p. 124, citing

Hermitage, 1984), are "talked into being". Thus, "the machinery of everyday conversation" warrants detailed analysis, for it "provides the scaffolding that supports the discursive practice which constitutes selves" (p. 124) and, we would add, shapes the reminiscence in which selves become engaged. In sum, we may reminisce one way when interacting with one listener and quite another way with another listener. Each listener, because of their lifestory, or because of *our* sense of their lifestory, triggers in us different recollections, or invites us to wander down different memory lanes.

While *co*-authoring suggests a balanced transaction in which we exercise equal influence on the storying of each other's life, the fact is that, in many of our relationships, a less parallel process prevails. Rather than coauthoring, *coercion* is often at work, where one person assumes undue authority over another; for example, a teacher over a learner or a clinician over a client. Instead of assisting in storying a person's life, such a lopsided linkage may lead to *de*-storying it (Randall, 1995). Between certain people for certain periods, such imbalances of poetical power no doubt have their place; for example, with parents over children. The latter need the former to tell them who they are, at least until they take agency for their own autobiographical development (McAdams, 1996; Bruner, 1987). What we are proposing here, however, is a more equitable quality of coauthoring—and indeed co-*reading*; one conducive to exploring our lifestory and thus eliciting our wisdom—or our "wisdom story". Such coauthoring, of which our most intimate friendships routinely give us a taste, could be called "therapoetic" (Randall, 2001). And the kind of context in which it might naturally occur could be called a "wisdom environment," the central characteristics of which we shall consider in a moment.

So then, we are inveterate storiers of our lives; we story them within a range of relationships that are coauthoring to varying degrees and, in the process, we draw on the narrative resources of numerous larger stories in turn. But what light can such a "political-literary" or "socio-poetic" perspective shed on the processes and purposes—the "uses" (Kaminisky, 1984)—of reminiscence? In addressing this question, one entailment of the narrative metaphor that is of significant assistance is self as *reader*.

READING OUR LIVES

Extending the analogy of life as story to life as novel pushes us to appreciate the various "points of view" that each of us possesses in relation to our life, namely as its author, character, narrator, and reader.

We have already introduced the idea of self as author or, rather, as coauthor, with others, in particular environments in particular ways. While the concepts of self as character and self as narrator also deserve treatment, their relevance for reminiscence can perhaps be summarized by saying that at the heart of each life is a particular person whom the story is *about*—that is, its main character. At the same time, that person is typically the one best positioned to talk about the story and to articulate what it feels like to live it—that is, its primary narrator. Enriching this picture still more, therefore, though at the same time complicating it, is that, besides being principal coauthor, character, and narrator of our own lifestory, we are also the person best positioned to explore it, ponder it, or *read* it. In thinking about reminiscence, the idea that we can read our own life text holds great explanatory promise. This is especially true for gerontology, insofar as it can be argued that it is into the reader mode (Randall, 1995, 1999) that, with advancing age, many of us tend to move.

Self as reader and reminiscence as reading—these are beguiling concepts, but what do they mean? What really is "reading our lives"? What is the focus of such reading, and what processes does it involve? Finally, what conditions, personal and social, can best permit it and promote it? We shall turn our attention to this latter question in the final section. For now, let us reiterate that reading our lives is an essential element of "narrative intelligence," the capacity by which we make sense of our life's ever-changing circumstances. Without some measure of such intelligence, any sort of meaningful existence would be impossible to manage. But just as there can be *degrees* of narrative intelligence, ranging from basic to advanced (Randall, 1999), so, it could be argued, there can be degrees of reading, ranging from shallow or "stock response" (Bogdan, 1990) to "deep" (Birkerts, 1994), from casual to intentional, or from mere literacy to *literary* literacy (Bogdan, 1990). Obviously, there can also be different focuses of reading, such as "point driven," "information driven," or "story driven" (Beach, 1990, p. 217). For deep or intentional reading—reading that is, as it were, *meaning* driven and aimed at the material of our own lives—we propose the phrase "literary *self* literacy" (Randall, 1999).

To digress for a moment, when we think in terms of literature per se, many factors influence why one reader derives so much from a given work and another so little, or why one reads primarily for the plot (Brooks, 1985), another for the characters, the atmosphere, the themes, and so on. Levels of education, previous experiences with other works—these are the more obvious variables involved. Let us look, though, not so much at focuses of reading, levels of reading, or degrees of sophistication of reading (which can vary enormously from reader to reader) but at the *process* of reading itself. The question is: *what happens inside of us in the course of reading?* What is the nature of our emotional and intellectual experience of the story as it "unfolds" in our memory and imagination, and as we go backwards and forwards, both reflecting on the past and projecting into the future, in the course of our journey to "the end"?

As we move from the beginning of the novel through its ever-thickening "muddle" (Atkinson, 1995) toward its eventual end, and as our experience of the text steadily intensifies, a curious emotional mix can be set off inside us (Rosenblatt, 1983). Such a mix can range from nostalgia and regret to catharsis and satisfaction to a sense of yearning and loss—loss at the prospect of leaving the world of the story for the comparative flatness of "real life". Involved as well can be a peculiar sense of vulnerability, due in part to having to let down our defenses (or suspend our disbelief) and opened ourselves to the story's atmosphere, its numerous levels, and its sheer power as a literary work. In other words, we become enchanted by its words, enmeshed in its themes, and beguiled by the links between the careers of its characters and the predicaments and patterns that comprise our own existence. We become aware of the chords that it strikes with "the story of our life" (Beach, 1990), the light that it sheds on our own conflicts and issues, the questions and dreams that it awakens within us, and the reluctance and even irritation that it triggers inside us when we think about putting it down. We become enticed by the landscape of potentially limitless—or "indeterminate" (Bruner, 1996)—meaning to which the text can point: meaning we may find ourselves continuing to ponder well after the reading is done. We become attuned, as it were, to the glorious incompleteness of the story, such that although technically it ends and may even end sadly, there is no end at all to the insight it can convey.

By relating this complex yet common phenomenon (which is so central to reading a novel) to the process of thinking about our own lives, and thus to reminiscence, we begin to perceive and appreciate the subjective *experience* of aging in—literally—a *novel* way. Given an aesthetic-poetic model of reminiscence, that is, with its respect for the narrative roots to both memory and emotion, we can bring into focus aspects of the *inside* of advancing age that may otherwise be so subtle as to be easily overlooked. Moreover, we can open ourselves to topics that have until recently seemed perhaps too esoteric for the agenda of gerontology—topics such as wisdom, which we are considering here, or spirituality, which in our view a narrative perspective uniquely illuminates, insofar as we "believe," "meditate," or "pray" not apart from our lifestory somehow but *through* it (Perschbacher Melia, this volume).

To return to the notion of "literary selfliteracy," the process we envision when we invoke such a term entails not just telling our stories, as important as that activity is. It entails listening to what our stories tell us (Hampl, 1990). In short, it means *reading* those stories as if they were literary texts (Randall, 1999; Randall & Kenyon, 2001). This amounts to a significant shift in perspective, a unique way of perceiving our relationship to the material of our own lives. It means that how we understand that material is similar to how we understand the material to which we are exposed in literature or on film. (For example, we are moved by the metaphors and themes we find in such material because they resonate with, and elicit, metaphors and themes already nascent in our own narrativized experience.) It also means accepting the possibility that *lifestory* meaning is as cumulative, as multilevelled, as ambiguous or indeterminate, and therefore as inviting of endless reflection as is story meaning (Randall & Kenyon, 2001). In recommending such a perspective, we are begging the complex question not only of the relationship between literature and life but of how literature "means" in itself, and of how its meaning is decoded, discovered, or created in the course of engaging with the text (see Bogdan & Straw, 1990). Nevertheless, we are recommending that it is this very question which needs transposing into the discourse on reminiscence, taking it thus further than ever from early perceptions of reminiscence as, for example, a sign of senility (Butler, 1963). This task of transposition is clearly enormous, one we can do little more here than to flag for the future. In the meantime, an equivalent concept for literary selfliteracy that is already in circulation, certainly in fields like adult education, is "biographical learning" (Alheit, 1995) or "autobiographical learning" (Randall & Kenyon, 2001). The essence of such learning is learning from—and about—our own experience. Perhaps few have given it more passionate expression than Michael Brady (1990, p. 51): "Is this not our destiny as human beings," he asks, "to learn, to grow, to come to know ourselves and the meanings of our life in the deepest, richest, most textured way possible? If we do not know the self, what can we know? If we cannot learn from reflection upon our own lived experience, from what can we learn?" When Florida Scott-Maxwell (1968, p. 142) says that "a long life makes me feel nearer truth," it is surely such learning she has in mind.

The process of guided autobiography is one means by which autobiographical learning can occur (Shaw, 2001). Another, we would suggest, involves close inspection or deep reading of the "signature stories" (Kenyon & Randall, 1997) that can be central to our autobiographical memory—reading them for, among other things, the "truth" that they convey, where, as we have hinted, that concept is understood in narrative terms more than historical ones (Spence, 1982). "In your own story," writes Atkinson (1995) in support of this point, "is where you will find your truth." To operationalize this insight, we might ask what these stories say about *me* as a person, about my "character," about my guiding personal myth (Larsen, 1990)? What do they indicate about the genres through which I habitually interpret and experience my world (Hillman, 1975), about the combination of curiosities and issues, the "metaphors of self" (Olney, 1972) and "themes" (Csikszentimilhayi & Beattie, 1979; Kaufman, 1986), that inform my life and shape my experience of it? What clues do they contain for how I might *re*story (Kenyon & Randall, 1997) in the direction of a fuller and healthier narrative by which to live? Such questions tempt us to see the stories by which we understand our lives as ultimately "sacred texts" (Charmé, 1984), indeed as "parables" (TeSelle, 1975), as the vehicles of a unique "literary" legacy that distinguishes our life from others. They invite us to see that, deep inside, we are rich in "narrative capital" (Mader, 1996). Such a concept suggests that reminiscence can thus be viewed not as "living *in*" the past but "living *off*" it, not in a narcissistic sense but in the sense that our memory, is a resource by which we can potentially be nourished and sustained.

The question before us now, though, is what *is* wisdom and what type of "atmosphere" (Meacham, 1990) might naturally evoke it, freeing us to develop our literary selfliteracy? Against the background of our analysis of reminiscence as reading, it is to such questions that we now turn our attention, first to that of wisdom and, second, to that of a wisdom environment.

ORDINARY WISDOM

The first point to be made about wisdom is that it is a phenomenon to be handled with humility and care. Otherwise, the search for it may become a fool's errand. In other words, we do not really know what wisdom is—whether one thing or many, or even a thing at all, rather than simply a way of being in the world. Despite this dilemma, wisdom has been enjoying a resurgence of interest in contemporary gerontology and psychology (Randall & Kenyon, 2001; Sternberg, 1990; Webster, in press). Without knowing what it is, we can still imagine what it *might* be, and can point to particular persons whom we deem to be "wise"—for example, the Dalai Lama or Mother Theresa. Moreover, descriptions of wisdom and of "wise persons" can be found in various wisdom traditions. Based on such traditions, as well as on contemporary views of it as, for example, "expertise," wisdom has come to be understood as an *extra*ordinary quality, whether it be described as high virtue, specialized cognitive abilities, or insight into "the meaning of life." Behind what follows, though, is the conviction that there is also such a thing as *ordinary* wisdom, that it is intimately connected to our own lifestories, and that it is basically a way of being in the world *with* those stories.

The question, of course, is whether ordinary wisdom and *extra*ordinary wisdom differ in kind or only in degree. Is it possible that, to varying degrees, *all of us are wise,* either potentially or actually? The thesis that runs through this chapter is that we are, and that this ordinary wisdom is accessible through *reading* our lifestories. But what is wisdom that we might view it in such a way? Whatever wisdom is, and whatever tradition on which one might draw, we would venture that at least six inter-related dimensions are central to it (for more extensive treatment of these dimensions, see Randall & Kenyon, 2001).

Cognitive

Associated with wisdom must be some degree of cognitive functioning. It is difficult to argue against this claim. The question could be asked, however, as to how intelligent we need to be in order to be wise. The links between concepts like intelligence, cleverness, and expertise, on the one hand, and wisdom, on the other, require careful examination. It is laudable that there are contemporary attempts to study wisdom within the cognitive tradition (see Sternberg, 1990); however, in relation to that tradition, we need to question the atheoretical nature of psychometric notions of intelligence with which wisdom is often connected. While the cognitive tradition has made major contributions to the study of aging, it has not yet developed theory to go with its methodological narrative that would link intelligence and wisdom together. This applies both to theoretical matters and to the way in which we decide to study wisdom, or the methodological story that we adopt. For example, is it appropriate, as some have thought, to study wisdom by using hypothetical or fictive situations, such as when a priest must offer advice to a devout couple dealing with an unwanted pregnancy (Csiksenthmihalyi & Rathunde, 1990)? While this situation qualifies as an existential dilemma that might require wise counsel, in our view it lacks "ecological validity" (see, for example, Ruth & Coleman, 1996).

The point is that wisdom, if it is anything, is not only, or not most importantly, about what amounts to abstract problem solving. It is more about involvement and decision making in real-life biographical encounters. It is more about what we *did* do than what we *would* do. Wisdom requires that, in the end, we jump or leap, and whether or not an action is deemed to be wise is often not known until after the fact. This existential dimension of wisdom is difficult to capture within the psychometric story of intelligence. In any case, without prejudging what wisdom is, or whether it is one thing or many, such a dimension suggests that lifestories would complement our investigations, since it is possible that wisdom emerges only in a specific situation—by looking into people's eyes and entering their life world.

Practical-Experiential

Wisdom is, to some extent, about thoughts and ideas and mental capacities; however, not for their own sake. The type of knowledge associated with wisdom is practical, related to the world, and based on experience. Further, in most wisdom traditions, wisdom itself is a practice. Whether we look at the sweat lodges of the native tradition, the meditation practices of Buddhism and Hinduism, or the prayer regimens of Islam and Christianity, the emergence of wisdom is associated with a form of regular spiritual cultivation.

In most traditions, wisdom thus involves an element of contemplation or personal reflection. This aspect of wisdom is a basic feature of our analysis here, namely "reading" for our unique wisdom story. The difference between these wisdom traditions and postmodern life, however, is that we have left out the "receiving" side of wisdom in favor of dominance and control through technical arrogance. In the traditions we have just identified, there is a highly developed logic and a system of argumentation and debate. In Buddhism, for example, while clarity of thinking is a goal of spiritual practice, this clarity does not emerge from thinking alone, or from the manipulation of concepts and insights from books. Rather, it emerges from silence, which provides the vehicle to make "our own" whatever truths are available. From this point of view, it is the inability to "sit still" that has resulted in the contemporary spiritual malaise often associated with postmodern society. It appears, in other words, that we have lost touch with our own wisdom, which is ultimately there for the taking.

Interpersonal

In most traditions, wisdom is firmly embedded in social practice and relationships. This is the case explicitly in the West, both in Judaism and in Christianity. It is also a dominant aspect of Islam, and of Confucianism, as expressed in the cultures of China and Korea. In these traditions, the focus is on the concept of filial piety or duty to the family. Particularly in Confucianism, filial piety is said to be the main guiding moral principle, one that defines the very meaning of being in the world. For example, wisdom is derived from meaning in life as measured by the amount of good an older person does for family and society, and from serving as an example for the younger generation.

The same insights are found in the Hindu tradition. There, one progresses through a series of life stages that involve different degrees of emphasis on family and social commitments, on the one hand, and personal contemplation, on the other. The highest stage is represented by a person who, through the journey of their own story, is engaged in the world but not for solely personal ends (Chethimattam, 1982). In this regard, the Hindu tradition has important similarities with the work of Erik Erikson (Cole & Winkler, 1994).

Meacham (1990) raises an intriguing point that highlights the interpersonal dimension of wisdom. In an ageist society, he argues, we are at risk of experiencing a "decline" in wisdom, insofar as we cannot be wise unless we are free to express our doubts and insecurities. Wisdom presupposes an ability to become detached from knowledge, success, power, and importance, which are the very things that we gain as adults and try to hang onto as long as possible. What we need, however, is an environment that allows us to share our doubts and to hear the doubts of others. Accordingly, we would agree with Meacham (1990, p. 209) when he says that "it is through the supportive and sharing relationships within a wisdom atmosphere that one gains the courage to engage in confident and wise action even in the face of one's doubts". In the final section, we shall consider what such an atmosphere involves when we examine the concept of a wisdom environment.

Ethical-Moral

A fundamental aspect of wisdom concerns good intentions and appropriate actions. As the ancient Greeks would say, the wise person knows and does "good." Among other things, this means that evil is not associated with wisdom, and neither is ignorance. Further, wisdom is associated with being able to "walk the walk" and "talk the talk". In other words, though no one is perfect, wisdom is about not only insightful ideas and intellectual erudition, but the intention and courage to act appropriately, to be part of the dilemma of involvement (Kenyon, 1991).

Furthermore, wise people can treat each situation according to its own uniqueness. That is, being doctrinaire or applying universal principles does not appear to be part of wisdom, whereas contextual, ethical insight does. Thus, while we may have knowledge of various precepts and commandments, it is wisdom that brings these precepts alive. This distinction points up the difficulty of understanding wisdom on the basis of the fictive situations we discussed earlier. In agreement with the cognitive tradition, wisdom does often emerge in important matters of life. However, the matters in question are in *my* life or *your* life, and they are here and now. Donald Polkinghorne (1996b) addresses this insight in his discussion of the process of counseling. Advanced or expert practitioners, he says, employ a "narrative understanding" that is based on their accumulated wisdom in arriving at appropriate decisions concerning their biographical encounters with particular clients.

The crucial point here is that this approach goes beyond logical and intellectual modes of thinking and beyond the application of universal principles. As Polkinghorne (1996b, p. 732) notes, "the process through which these unique ideas arise for responding to different clients occurs largely outside of awareness and is not available to reflective inquiry. When questioned, expert practitioners often cannot explain why they chose to act in the way they did; the helpfulness of their response can only be determined by examination of its consequences". In our view, these practitioners are wise because they have the intention, and take the action, to allow the client to discover his or her own wisdom story.

Idiosyncratic Expression

The fifth dimension of wisdom concerns its modes of idiosyncratic expression—or, if you will, its "novelty" from person to person. Depending on the tradition under discussion, we can identify several different faces of wisdom. This is one of the features of wisdom that makes it so difficult to study. Wisdom might express itself as "cross-legged immobility" (Holliday & Chandler, 1986), such as is represented in the lives of contemporary Chinese hermits (Porter, 1993), in the late-life political activism of a Bertrand Russell, or in the eccentric behavior of a Zen lunatic. Or it might express itself in words, such as in a well-written autobiography, or in a touch, in a look, or even in silence and simply *being there*. This idiosyncratic aspect of wisdom becomes complicated even more when combined with the dimension of intentions that we just discussed, an extreme illustration of this being the psychopathic person who may behave "wisely" but be not at all engaged in doing good. As Kekes (1983, p. 286) points out, "a fool can learn to say all the things a wise man says, and to say them on the same occasions".

The point here is that more ordinary wisdom might be evident to us if we knew how to look for it and listen for it, without "storyotyping" too narrowly its many expressions (Randall & Kenyon, 2001).

Spiritual-Mystical

Wisdom is fundamentally a spiritual phenomenon since, as we have said in previous sections, it has to do with meaning—meaning of life, of relationships, of ourselves, of the cosmos. The range of meaning extends from concern with everyday judgments in the cognitive tradition to the experience of ultimate enlightenment in the Buddhist tradition, to union with God in the Christian tradition, and to everything in between. Nevertheless, it is difficult to find a wisdom tradition that is not focused on this life and this world. That is, we can speculate and wonder about death and the afterlife, and indeed some traditions possess specific mystical beliefs and views concerning the human telos. However, as esoteric as these views may be, there is usually an emphasis on how to live in the here and now.

A core spiritual characteristic of wisdom, ordinary and extraordinary alike, is acceptance (see also Kenyon, 2000). Acceptance involves a giving in but not a giving up. It is a life-affirming experience. Nevertheless, wisdom in the form of acceptance does involve loss. As evidenced in all traditions, the process of spirituality is, paradoxically, one of growth *through* diminishment. That is, life invites and indeed often pushes us to lose our old and smaller story, about both ourselves and our world, in favor of a new and larger one. The key, though, is that this diminishment has nothing to do with passivity or resignation, or with what in gerontological terms is called "disengagement". Rather, depending on the tradition, whether it be through prayer, meditation, or some other form of "reading" our lives, including ones we adopt accidentally, it is *in* and not *outside* the human condition that we find meaning and wisdom.

Having summarized, then, what we see as six dimensions of wisdom, why might we say that someone is "wise"? It may be because they know a great deal (cognitive), because they make what we think are wise judgements (practical-experiential), because they are compassionate (interpersonal), because they have special insight (spiritual-mystical), because they have high values or are courageous (ethical-moral), or because they laugh a lot or appear peaceful (idiosyncratic expression). In other words, some of these same dimensions of wisdom can be found in all of our lives. Once we focus our lens properly, then, we begin to see many more wise people around us, for wisdom is both extraordinary and ordinary at the same time. In addition, we would argue, there is a potential for *more* wisdom in the world, whether it be attained by following existing wisdom traditions, as we have just indicated, *or* by facilitating the personal and societal conditions that will enable people to see, celebrate, *and read* their lives as stories.

TOWARD A WISDOM ENVIRONMENT

Ordinary or extraordinary, wisdom cannot be forced. It arises at the intersection of the paradoxical processes of both creating and discovering, both doing and being, both making an effort and sitting still (Randall & Kenyon, 2001). Moreover, we do not know by what means it will decide to show itself to a particular person at a particular time. In addition, wisdom is intensely personal. It resides in, and arises through, our *inside* stories, which are both unique, as we have seen and, to some extent, ineffable. Having said this, we have also discussed how our lives as stories are, at the same time, inter-personal. They are not lived in isolation; they are shared. Despite the many forms of separation and alienation that can characterize our lives, there is a fundamental relatedness about us.

Practically speaking, not everyone appears to possess the same capacity to learn from their own experience, the same capacity for autobiographical learning. Not everyone appears to have the same measure of narrative intelligence and thus the same access to the meanings in the stories of their life, and thus to their wisdom. Among these are the demented. Yet even if we grant that no such differences exist, there still seem to be three main groups of people.

First, there are those who will become wise no matter what. They will grow in wisdom in spite of age, physical decline, or anything else that life may throw at them, and perhaps even *because* of such things. Such people exemplify the way of life that Ruth and Oberg (1996) call "the hurdle race," in that difficulties become challenges for them to overcome and then to continue on their journey. Second, there are those who may simply be too hardened by life to open themselves to their wisdom story. Although from a narrative perspective, we can never assume that a person is incapable of restorying, the reality is that many people die without apparently finding or even seeking their own wisdom. According to Ruth and Oberg (1996), they lead "the bitter life." However, while the lives of such people may be said to trace *tragic* stories, they still possess an integrity and can still provide a measure of wisdom, if only to the rest of us and not to themselves. Finally, though, there are those, perhaps most of us in fact, who can benefit from what we would call a wisdom environment.

Apart from certain exceptional examples, it is our belief that more opportunity to tell and listen to each other's stories in an open, non-judgmental manner can always be provided, and in any number of domains: in friendship, for instance, or marriage, or in intimate relationship of any kind. It can also be provided in the area of education and of professional caring, and in the realm of religion and of counselling—perhaps especially in models of counselling that employ a narrative approach (see White & Epston, 1990; Kropf & Tandy, 1998). And it can certainly be provided in the context of activities like life review, guided autobiography, and reminiscence (Fry & Barker, chapter 13, this volume). Perhaps most significantly, it can be provided in "ordinary" conversation.

Using the six intertwining *dimensions* of wisdom just described, we want now to sketch the broad characteristics of the narrative environment in which we can coauthor one another in the direction of our ordinary wisdom. To help us do so, we offer this passage from philosopher, Jonathan Glover (1988, p. 153), as an illustration of the mutually beneficial, telling-listening exchange that is always a possibility, even in our everyday encounters.

> Talk affects self-creation. When we talk together, I learn from your way of seeing things, which will often be different from mine. And, when I tell you about my way of seeing things, I am not just describing responses that are already complete. They may only emerge clearly as I try to express them, and as I compare them with yours. In this way, we can share in the telling of each other's inner story, and so share in creating ourselves and each other.

Glover's words capture the essence of the sort of wisdom environment that we envision, in which the processes of coauthoring and coreading converge—wherever, whenever, and however such an environment gets realized between us.

The Cognitive Dimension

You help me—as I help you—to investigate the events of my life for the patterns and themes that may be running through them. You help me to gather up my past and to re-member my life as a whole. You help me to appreciate its rich and complex unfolding over time. You help me to inquire concerning what insights have been accumulating within me across the years and what meanings might lie between the lines of my actions, gestures, and words. You help me to acknowledge how I habitually interpret the people and situations I encounter, in terms of what genres I am inclined to cast occurrences, and what conclusions I tend to draw. You help me to gain an affectionate detachment from—so that I can creatively critique—how I characteristically construe my reality and, accordingly, how I believe and feel and act.

The Dimension of Idiosyncratic Expression

You help me to tell *my* story of my life, not society's, my family's, or any one else's, story of my life, but my own, real, *inside* story, with its unique potential for discovery and adventure, meaning and truth. You help me to identify my doubts, confusions, and fears, as well as my loves, hopes, and dreams—including my lost loves, shattered hopes, and broken dreams. You help me to celebrate my own individuality, warts and all, to honor the novelty of my particular life-course, and to appreciate, even wonder at, the incomparable combination of life events, storying styles, and narrative environments that have contributed to who I am.

The Interpersonal Dimension

You help me to see how my way of seeing things has, throughout my life, been influenced by others' ways of seeing things too. You help me to appreciate how I have been continually coauthored. You also help me to notice the many ways in which, in the middle of each day, I coauthor others in turn. More to the point, you help me to see how I can influence for the good how they make sense of their lives and how I can invite them, as I have been invited by you, to discover their own wisdom and to view both themselves and their world in positive, more meaning-filled ways.

The Moral-Ethical Dimension

You help me to become more aware of the larger stories in which I have lived and by which, for better or worse, I have been shaped. You help me to identify the master narratives that are embedded in the ideologies and creeds that may surround me and that are mediated through the various institutions—educational, political, medical, and other—by which my life is bound. You encourage me to critique the authority these narratives have had over the dominant version by which I understand who I am. And, where these versions have assumed an unwarrantedly coercive and unduly destroying power over me, you empower me to be and to behave *sub*versively toward them. You also help me to see the value, the necessity even, of the conflicts, the struggles, and the "mistakes" that I have experienced in my life. You help me to appreciate the potential for learning which each of them carries.

Through your patient listening to and, with me, your creative reframing of otherwise negative events, you help me to transform the pain and regret in my life into sources of openness and compassion in my relationships with others. You help me to experience them as, fundamentally, interesting, intricate, and inexhaustible as I can experience myself.

The Spiritual-Mystical Dimension

You help me to restory a given event, or indeed my life as a whole, so as to produce more positive versions of what has happened. With respect to the loss of a job, for instance, you help me to re-genre-ate the experience in a more optimistic light, so that I can see it not as the ultimate tragedy it might seem at the time but as, conceivably, a necessary, if painful, first step in a much larger and more exciting adventure still, that of developing my deepest gifts and of exploring the mysteries of my own experience. Rather than allowing me to wallow in a story that says, essentially, "I'm incompetent," you help me to realize that in fact "I'm free," that "I finally have the impetus and opportunity to pursue what has always been my dream". With respect to my entire life, you help to coax forth and affirm a different and more liveable story of who I am. Rather than "I've been a failure," you help me to understand that in fact "I've been a survivor". Such a story puts a radically different spin on what might otherwise seem a life of inadequacy, incompetency, and loss. It increases my self-esteem and my sense of purpose on this planet, and it helps me acquire some sense of trust toward the larger and ultimately mysterious processes within which, along with your own, my existence is unfolding.

The Practical-Experiential Dimension

You help me to see that, within the context of my own particular life, I possess significant experience, insight, and wisdom. You help me to have respect for the details of my ordinary, everyday life, with its ever-changing web of relationships and responsibilities, stresses and circumstances, pleasures and pains, and to acknowledge them as invitations to continually learn—about myself, about others, about the world, about life as a whole.

CONCLUSION

Drawing on themes and concepts from narrative gerontology, we have sketched a perspective that sees reminiscence not in cognitive or ethical terms, at least not exclusively, but in aesthetic or poetic ones as well. Such a perspective places emphasis more on the "art" than on the "science" of reminiscence (Haight & Webster, 1995). Our broad agenda has been to invite analyses of adult development that appreciate memory's subtler and less measurable dimensions and that, in general, reflect a more "soul-ful" science of human life (Kenyon & Randall, 1997). In pursuing that agenda in relation to reminiscence, we have no doubt raised more questions than we have resolved, questions that future treatments of reminiscence that set off from a similar starting-point will, we hope, be able to investigate more fully.

At the core of our perspective is the concept that a life is a type of literary text, and that reminiscence can be understood as *reading* that text for the meaning that it mediates, or for its "truth". Thus, reminiscence can constitute a royal road to wisdom. We do not read ourselves in a vacuum, however, but always within a variety of environments, where the stories by which we live are continually coauthored and coread through our relationships with others. Such a line of thought leads to speculation on the nature of an environment in which reminiscence as reading might naturally occur. We call it a "wisdom environment". Its features, however, are hardly exotic. They are common and everyday, as ordinary as wisdom itself.

V
Clinical Applications

16

Transformation in Life Stories: The Canadian War Veterans Life Review Project

Muriel E. Shaw and Marvin J. Westwood

This chapter explores the transformative dimensions of autobiographical life review for Canadian World War II veterans. The life review program for Canadian World War II and peacekeeper veterans was designed as a health promotion project. The program, designed at the University of British Columbia (Westwood, 1998) was a joint venture with Veterans' Affairs Canada and the Royal Canadian Legion. Veterans' Affairs Canada has provided physical, medical, social, and financial services and support for World War II veterans. The needs of veterans relating to social support and community development are central to the commitments of the Royal Canadian Legion. However, this focus on life review, life stories, and lifespan development, provided an exciting new joint venture. The purpose of the life review project was to enhance understanding about how the experience of war impacted the veterans' life stories and lifespan development. The central question was how does the war experience impact veterans' lives? Promoting personal integration, lifespan development, and trauma repair for World War II veterans has implications for restorying (Kenyon & Randall, 1997) and transformation (Shaw, 1999) of the aging paradigm.

The war event can shape the life stories of veterans in a number of important ways. The war experience can influence life decisions, career choices, and roles in relationships, along with impacting physical and mental health. Veterans, for the most part, have not had the opportunity to integrate the war experience into their broader life stories. Some veterans have symptoms of post traumatic stress, lingering from their experience of trauma in the war. Aging World War II veterans may experience the onset of post traumatic stress for the first time. Achieving personal integration is difficult for most veterans for two reasons: (a) the nature of the war experience and the tendency not to talk about it, and (b) the lack of opportunities and programs that provide a safe, supportive, structured space to tell and share life stories. In the life review project, the guided autobiography format (Birren & Deutchman, 1991), along with an emphasis on leadership development, provided veterans a "democratic space" to tell, share, and transform their life stories.

We used a narrative approach and the guided autobiography method of life review (Birren & Deutchman, 1991) in the veterans' project. Transformative learning (Mezirow, 1991, 1998) provides an interpretive framework for this model of life review. Guided autobiography can promote personal integration and lifespan development along with bridging stories and individual and/or social change or transformation. The narrative approach highlights the inside story—the psychological and spiritual meanings in aging (Ruth & Kenyon, 1996; Ruth, Birren, & Polkinghorne, 1996). The metaphor of life as a story is central to the narrative approach (Kenyon & Randall, 1997). Focusing on the meaning and interpretations—the hermeneutics of life stories (de Vries, Birren, & Deutchman, 1995) brings the voices and the visions of the veterans into the metastory of the aging paradigm. For veterans the autobiographical life review has positive integrative potential with implications for growth in knowledge, wisdom, and self actualization. Giddens (1991) suggests that autobiography is a "corrective intervention" (p. 72). Reconstruction of the past is relevant to anticipation of the future. In Giddens' (1991) words "The self forms a trajectory of development from the past to the anticipated future. The individual appropriates his/her past by sifting through it in the light of what is anticipated for an (organised) future." (p. 75). With this in mind, we will now describe the conceptual framework of the veterans' project including transformative learning theory (Mezirow, 1991, 1994, 1998) and the guided autobiography method (Birren & Deutchman, 1991) as it contributes to a "trajectory of development". These central concepts are described and a case study is offered by way of clarification.

TRANSFORMATIVE LEARNING AS A METATHEORETICAL FRAMEWORK

Transformation Theory

In the veterans' project, Mezirow's (1991, 1998) theory of transformative learning, provides a metatheoretical framework for interpreting the guided autobiography method (Birren & Deutchman, 1991) of life review. Transformative, or emancipatory, learning is defined as "the process of effecting change in 'a frame of reference'" (Mezirow, 1997, p. 5). Mezirow's (1991, 1998) theory is an existential, meaning centred, contextual model of learning. Transformative learning focuses on the interpretation and meaning—the hermeneutics of inquiry in the veterans' life stories. Revised meanings are often more effective as "templates" for future individual and/or social action (Shaw, 1999).

Habermas' (1984) writings on communicative action provide the philosophical framework for transformative learning. Habermas (1984) identifies two major domains of intentional adult learning as instrumental action and communicative action. A third domain of learning, which affects both instrumental and communicative action, is identified as emancipatory action. Each domain is grounded in its own area of knowledge, human interest, and method of inquiry. Instrumental action focuses on technical interests, the experimental method and the causal explanation of events. Communicative action is concerned with dialogue, communication, hermeneutic inquiry, and the interpretation and understanding of experience. Emancipatory action relies on critical reflection relating to objective and subjective reframing. This is the reflexive component in research. Critical self-reflection can be emancipatory and may lead to individual and/or social action. Life review, in the veterans' project is situated in the communicative and emancipatory dimensions of learning and action.

Frames of Reference

According to Mezirow (1991, 1998) our frames of reference include two dimensions, meaning perspectives and meaning schemes. In the first place, meaning perspectives, also termed "habits of mind" (Mezirow, 1998, p.6) are habitual overarching belief systems, like personal paradigms. The second dimension, meaning schemes, also referred to as "points of view" (Mezirow, 1998, p. 6), are beliefs, attitudes, opinions, feelings, and judgments, related to a specific habitual meaning perspective. Our intentions, emotions, and cognitions are embedded in meaning perspectives that (a) affect how we interpret experience, and (b) inform our actions. We view meaning perspectives as templates for present and future actions. Meaning perspectives, often developed in early childhood, can be distorted or inadequate as an interpretative framework for adult experience. Transforming meaning perspectives or habits of mind can occur suddenly when faced with a "disorienting dilemma." Many of the veterans faced disorienting dilemmas in their war experience. There can be sudden all encompassing change in our frames of reference. However, incremental shifts in meaning schemes and points of view can ultimately contribute to transformation in meaning perspectives or habits of mind (Mezirow, 1998, pp. 6–7) and this is more common in guided autobiography and life review.

LIFE REVIEW AND TRANSFORMATIVE LEARNING

As you will see, life review (Butler, 1963) and guided autobiography (Birren & Deutchman, 1991) have integrative and developmental potential. Brown Shaw, Westwood, and de Vries (1999) suggest that the mechanism by which this potential can be realized and understood is through the framework of transformative learning. Reviewing the self and events of one's life can highlight contradictions in life stories. For example, in the veterans' stories, contradictions about success and failure, along with gains and losses, came to light. As Kegan (1998) points out "contradictions are one of the royal roads to transformative learning." Contradictions, like dilemmas (disorienting or not), trigger the self-reflections and dialogue that can contribute to participants understanding themselves, their social relationships, and their world view. This can be understood as changes in frames of meaning about the self and others, in roles and relationships. The autobiographical format promotes transformation in that internalized assumptions and self schemas are made external for comparison, dialogue, and development in the group. The desired outcome of the ten-step process toward transformation is that new meanings and assumptions will be more (a) inclusive, (b) discriminating, (c) open, (d) reflexive, and (e) integrative of experience (Mezirow, 1998, pp.5–6).

THE METHOD OF GUIDED AUTOBIOGRAPHY
The Historical Context of Life Review

Birren (1987) created the guided autobiography method of life review. Guided autobiography is defined as "a semistructured, topical, group approach to life review" (de Vries, Birren, & Deutchman, 1995, p. 166). Butler's (1963) theory of life review marks the historical turning point, emphasizing the positive integrative and developmental potential of life review. Life review can contribute to integrity and/or despair (Erikson, Erikson, & Kivnick, 1986). Birren (1987) and his graduate students at the University of Southern California (a) created the guiding themes and autobiographical format, (b) developed a course 'Psychological Development through Guided Autobiography,' and (c) established the autobiographical archives as a research database.

Guided Autobiography as Hermeneutic Inquiry

How can the method of guided autobiography facilitate hermeneutic inquiry in the narrative approach to life review and life planning? First and foremost, guided autobiography is an existential, educational, narrative approach to inquiry. Although the reflexive and communicative learning and development is often therapeutic, guided autobiography is not a therapy. However, the therapeutic potential is developed in the application of guided autobiography in the counseling context (Brown-Shaw, Westwood, & deVries, 1999). We emphasize both the therapeutic and developmental potential of guided autobiography as applied in the veterans' life review project.

The method of guided autobiography (Birren & Deutchman, 1991) provides for critical self-reflection and collaborative communication, thereby enhancing hermeneutic inquiry and the possibility for transformative learning (Mezirow, 1991, 1998). In the guided autobiography method, the structure, and the elements, along with the themes and the group process, can contribute to narrative exploration and hermeneutic inquiry (e.g., Birren & Hedlund, 1986; de Vries, Bluck, & Birren, 1993; Ruth, Birren, & Polkinghorne, 1996).

The Structure of Guided Autobiography

The structural components and the guiding themes set forth multiple roads to reflection about the self, others, and world view as embedded in life stories. de Vries, and colleagues (1995) identify two structural components that facilitate autobiographical reflection. The written component provides for personal reflection and "scrutiny of the past" (p. 166). The group component facilitates further reflection and collaborative participation in the present (p. 166). Similarly, Mader (1995) suggests that five elements together make guided autobiography an effective narrative invention. These elements include metaphors, themes, personal reflection, written reflection, and communication in the group. As

Kenyon (in press) points out, these elements in combination create the reflective space for participants in guided autobiography to stand back and look at their life as a story. This reflexive space then places the participant in the position of being a reflexive researcher, like an ethnographer of his/her own life story (Shaw, 1999). Seeing the "possibilities" in life stories can result in the discovery of new meanings and wisdom (Kenyon, in press) on the road to transformation.

The Themes that Guide Reflection

The discovery of new meaning and the wisdom in the veterans' stories can be greatly enhanced by the thematic exploration in the autobiographical life review. The thematic exploration is compared "to a nine-sided glass prism refracting the light (the life story) differently, depending on which side (theme) is showing" (de Vries, Birren, & Deutchman, 1995, p. 168). Each theme sheds light and meaning on an important part of the life story. Exploring branching points, family, career, health, money, love, sexuality, death, and meaning in life, the nine sides of the prism can bring to light new meanings and wisdom in the stories of veterans. We developed the theme "Your War Experience" for the veterans' project (Table 16.1).

The Group Process

The group process has important implications for life review. Telling the stories in the group has both risks and responsibilities. Self-disclosure can be viewed as risky by veterans. Creating group cohesion, therefore, minimizes risks and increases the responsibilities and commitment to the process. The "developmental exchange" and the leadership of the group contribute to creating group cohesion. And the "ground rules" for the group are always confidentiality and nonjudgmental communication. Kenyon (in press) refers to this as a wisdom environment. We suggest this is like Habermas' (1984) democratic public space.

According to de Vries and colleagues (1995), the "developmental exchange" relies on incremental mutual exchange of personally meaningful, emotionally laden experiences, as written in thematic stories. At first group members are tentative in risking disclosure. As trust increases in the group, the quality of shared life stories takes on an incremental increase in emotional intensity. In a cyclical manner, this increment of increased intensity and disclosure in stories contributes to building trust (p. 170). Giddens (1991) describes this as the transformation of intimacy.

TABLE 16.1   Theme Assignment: Your War Experience

The war event shapes lives in several ways. It often affects life decisions, career paths, health and emotion in critical ways. Enlisting, serving, and returning to civilian life can include experiences of adventure, failure, accomplishment, and loss. For many, the war event has been a major branching point, a life-changing event.

How has the war experience impacted you?

Think about your war experience by reflecting on the following questions. Remember, these questions are given as a guide only. You don't have to answer all of them! As thoughts come to your mind write them down or jot a few notes.

1. Think about the moment you decided to enlist. What prompted your decision? How did your family and friends react?
2. What was the first thing you did when you came home?
3. Returning to civilian life often means challenges, rewards, and difficulties. What was it like for you?
4. What changed when you came home?
5. Often people have to make important decisions when they return home. What about you?
6. What important lessons did you learn as a result of your war experience?
7. Based on your war experience, what advice or suggestions do you have for peacekeepers that are going to war or returning from war?

Source: Brown-Shaw, Hunter, Peck, & Westwood, 1998.

Guided Autobiography and Group Psychodrama

Adding the action component of group psychodrama creates a new dimension to guided autobiography. Contradictions in our life stories embedded in the internal scripts (Brooks, 1999) and schemas (Shaw, 1999) are made external in the enactments in group psychodrama. Holmes (1992) integrates role theory with object relations' theory to make internal frames of meaning external in group psychodrama. Blatner (2000a) focuses on applied role theory using methods of psychodrama and sociodrama in an integrative approach (pp. 152–153). This creates a "role distance" for reflexivity and dialogue in groups. In Blatner's (2000b) words, "techniques derived from the method called psychodrama can be applied in the service of experiencing life as a kind of story, embellished dramatically" (p. 1). This additional space adds to the reflexivity and coconstruction of meaning in life stories. The action component was added to the life review to promote trauma repair for the group of Canadian peacekeeper veterans in this project.

THE LIFE REVIEW PROJECT
FOR CANADIAN VETERANS

How does the war experience impact veterans' lives? This question was central in the life review project for six groups of World War II veterans and one group of peacekeeper veterans in the Vancouver and Victoria area of British Columbia. The case study to follow will focus on one group of veterans at a local legion in Vancouver which met in a group of seven on Monday mornings from 10:00 a.m. to 12:30 p.m., for a six-week period, through June and early July in 1998.

The narrative approach and the guided autobiography method described above were applied in the life review project. However, the sequence and selection of guiding themes was adapted to facilitate narrative exploration about the war experience and its impact on their life stories. The guiding themes selected for this exploration include: major branching points; family history; work and career; health and body image; stress and coping; and our newly developed theme "your war experience" (see Table 16.1). The guided autobiography has implications for bridging stories and transformative change.

The Benefits

The benefits for veterans imply that guided autobiography can contribute to integrity rather than despair and a "trajectory of development" (Giddens, 1991) and they are the following: recognition of contribution to your country; validation, comradeship, and support provided a sense of relief; integration of war events in terms of losses and gains; reconciliation, repair, and resolution of unresolved conflicts; new awareness of effective coping strategies; development of a future focus on life goals; and action plans for World War II veterans to serve in the re-entry of peacekeeper veterans (Westwood, 1998, pp. 27–31). These benefits were evident in the following case study of life review at the Legion. The voices and visions of veterans at the Legion highlight the importance of recognition for service to your country.

A CASE STUDY

How does the guided autobiography bridge stories and individual and/or social transformation? This case study clarifies the bridging context of guided autobiography. It suggests some answers and in turn raises more questions about the connection of the guided autobiography to transforming life stories. We suggest that the view from the bridge (the guided autobiography) can place veterans in a position of being reflexive ethnographers of their life stories. Veterans at the Legion were all leaders in their military action and they became core-searchers on the front line of the Veterans' Life Review Project. As you will see, new meanings and wisdom in stories, often coconstructed in the group, can shift the veterans' gaze to a future focus on goals and plans for action. With this in mind, we will briefly describe the context of the case study, highlighting the importance of the bridge (the guided autobiography) as a democratic space for communicative and transformative learning.

The Context

The group, organized by one of the veterans, was motivated to partici-pate in the guided autobiography to improve the life review project to benefit other veterans and peacekeepers. The group had seven partici-pants, all male of comparable age (mid-seventies to early eighties) and of different military backgrounds, with a male and a female group leader. There was an immediate sense of group solidarity and cohesion not uncommon in guided autobiography groups. Initially veterans were reluctant to self-disclose. As mentioned above, this is not surprising because veterans are often reluctant to talk about their war experiences even with other veterans. As veterans shared their stories through the guiding themes, particularly "major branching points" and "your war experience" they became increasingly committed to the life review. Unresolved issues from World War II, including the lack of recognition for service, came into sharp focus. One veteran pointed out that we were "fifty years late" in offering the life review.

The theme of recognition or lack of it, for service to your country, previously not talked about, was made salient in the telling of life stories. Two veterans gave voice to a pivotal missing frame of reference—they were not recognized by their country. Consider this unresolved issue in the framework of transformative learning. Veterans were faced with a contradiction, recognition or the lack of it for service, leading to critical reflection about the role of recognition and related assumptions of life, as revealed in the group dialogue and the reported experiences of oth-ers. The group and discussion also provided the forums for new ways of thinking and acting. Changes in "meaning perspectives" resulted in recognition of these veterans in the life review and action plans to con-tribute to the reentry and recognition of peacekeepers.

Creating the "democratic space"—the space for communicative and transformative learning—was central to the success of the life review at the Legion. Mezirow (2000) emphasizes that "values such as freedom,

equality, tolerance, social justice, civic responsibility, and education"
(p. 16) can create a space for learning that is transformative. And the
veterans' valued freedom, equality, civic duty, and democracy—these
were the very reasons they served their country in World War II. What
surprised us at the legion was the extraordinary group cohesion. The
solidarity and cohesion went beyond that ordinarily seen in guided autobiography groups. The values stated above—tolerance, equality, and
freedom, along with social justice and civic duty—defined this group.
The spirit of camaraderie and collaborative leadership, contributed
greatly to this positive outcome. Confidentiality and protection of privacy was an "ethical imperative" in this unique space. Comradeship
developed into a bond of trust, as veterans shared stories from their
war experiences and coping with tuberculosis (TB). During or after
World War II these veterans were diagnosed with TB and coped with the
trauma of long hospitalizations. This unique camaraderie and the recognition of services was particularly powerful during the final meeting.

CASE ILLUSTRATIONS

1. A Tribute to Honour and Dignity

This veteran served his country with honour—enlisting in the Royal
Canadian Naval Volunteer Reserves. He served at sea for five and one-
half years, patrolling the west coast of South America followed by
naval duty in Africa, Suez, and Sicily.

But he describes "another war when he had TB." The battle with TB
began shortly after World War II—ending with surgical removal of his
left lung. Presently he faces another battle, cancer in his right lung—
terminal cancer. He faces death with dignity, and has perfected positive thinking as an art form. In his words, "I try to keep a somewhat
positive perspective when I hear my family say, 'you have been retired
from transit for seventeen years, it's about time you really take into
consideration what retirement really means, including the support of
others around you and those trips into Vancouver by West Coast
Express for Monday sessions at the Legion.' It's no cure, but mentally it
helps the art of positive thinking."

Communicative Learning

This veteran's stories about the war experience and coping with TB
generate dialogue, hermeneutic inquiry, and communicative learning.
Stories about (1) coping with a positive attitude, and (2) support

and comradeship in survival, along with related dialogue in the group, illustrates communicative learning. First, on coping with a positive attitude, this veteran says, "Out of the critical experiences during the war, I learned to face adversity with a positive attitude. Critical moments shape a way of coping that is very positive. Turn the negative to positive. [He laughs.] I have since coped with half a swing while playing golf but doesn't everyone have a handicap when enjoying a game of golf?" A dialogue about coping with the "ongoing battle with TB," and the "shared theme of struggle with lungs," is generated. One veteran responds, "Individuals with TB struggle alone. We have a community. We are together with people in the same boat." Another veteran adds, "Every day is a gift." One of the leaders summarizes the communicative learning, "The story since you contracted TB is unique to you as a group—a joint story and each of you have a piece of it. This is a resource you share—a positive attitude."

Comradeship and Coping

Second, about support and comradeship in coping and survival, this naval veteran points out that "the most important lesson is to be trained in survival with other naval personnel, both physically and mentally, and most important, relying on each other's support during those nerve-wracking war years." Dialogue stimulated by his story, shifts to the importance of cooperation, comradeship, and common goals for peacekeepers. One veteran comments, "Comradeship is like block watch—looking after each other." Another veteran adds, "Comrades are willing to give their life for you." Conversation shifts to words of wisdom for peacekeepers and they are the following: (1) "Have a common goal, [asking] what are we here for?" (2) "Don't compete with each other, you have to stay together." and (3) "Act together for survival."

2. Leadership in the Line of Duty

As the leader of an infantry combat troop in Sicily and Italy, this veteran identified discipline, belief in yourself, and leading from the front as essential for survival. The leader sets the example. He emphasizes that, "above all never expect or ask anyone to do what you, yourself, would not do." Discipline and duty went together. This veteran was wounded in action three times. Each time he returned to combat—to the front—in the line of duty. Returning home from duty was hard. As this veteran points out, "The hardest [thing] I was faced with were the people at home—my mother and father and the civilian population. I had to find (if I could) the trust and closeness I had with my army comrades and, I must tell you, I never did find the relationship again."

Tranformative Learning

Transformative learning from the life review is evident in this veteran's written story. He is skeptical about the theme assignment "major branching points in your life" saying, "I don't have any branches." However, he learned to look at his life story in a new way. We suggest the view from the bridge (the guided autobiography) contributed to this change in meaning perspective. In his view, "As I write this, I suddenly find many avenues that have been branching points in my life and I now feel that as life goes on there will be many more because this is the way of life. Remember I said earlier that I don't have any branches and so this exercise has proven me wrong. I only regret that it has taken me 82 years to find many of these branching points, and I dare say I'll be faced with many more as life goes on. Take advantage of the opportunities that present themselves and handle them as a student willing to learn. "I've been asked by my family to write a biography of my life which would include my memory of what I know of my mother and father and their past—the biography of my life will be a serial to continue as long as I live. That will be my life story. I've commissioned _____. He names the veteran known as 'the prophet' and 'the poet'."

Life Review and Life Planning

In the life review this army veteran's story takes a pivotal turn toward a future focus on life goals and life planning. He plans to take an active role in the reentry of peacekeeper veterans. His goal is to tell them his story and the lessons he learned about leadership from his war experience as follows: "War—appreciate life, being alive, recognize the fact you were spared. It made me grow up fast. When I accepted a rank in the service along with it went responsibility and instant decision making to survive. We were trained to be combat soldiers and in time we became seasoned soldiers able to cope with combat, but most of all we learned how to stay alive, if at all possible. I learned how to relate to others in fairness and support, and was always rewarded with a good response. If you gain the trust and respect from others—they will put their trust in you as their leader. Above all never expect or ask anyone to do what you yourself would not do. If you choose to be a leader, lead, don't push from behind. Lead by example from the front." In response to these lessons about leadership one of the veterans in the group recognizes his practical wisdom. In recognition of this army veteran he emphasizes that, "real genius is the practical man with wisdom in everyday practice."

3. Valour, Honour and Heroism

This veteran, a bomber pilot in the R.C.A.F., flew 33 missions from a base in India west of Calcutta. Bombing bridges on the infamous Burma-Siam, "death railway," ships in harbour and at sea, along with Japanese troop concentrations and railway yards in Bangkok, were dangerous missions. Landing the plane safely after machine gun fire damage with low-level bombing of bridges and after loss of two engines hundreds of miles from base, were valorous acts in enemy territory. But flying at night and monsoon weather was often "more hazardous" than the enemy. This is valour and heroism.

The Democratic Space

The story of this pilot, a recognized war hero provides a catalyst for democratic participation. His story as told below sets a tone for storytelling and storylistening—a tone of honour. This was the first story told and a story told for the first time. Modelling tolerance, equality, freedom, social justice, and civic duty sets the tone and trust is transformed. In turn, listening to the stories of other veterans changes his perspective. The story of the veteran from the merchant navy inspires him. His courage in carrying out his duty unarmed and in the end without recognition, inspires him. As the story goes, "The major branching point in my life was my decision to join the Air Force which resulted in an abrupt switch in the direction of my life. I made it on my own without consulting anyone, neither family nor friends. Until now I have never really stopped to consider *why* I made that decision. There were certainly no economic pressures. I had completed one year at UBC and was intending to continue in Science. There were powerful propaganda messages encouraging enlistment, such as billboards and posters and newsreels preceding every movie in the theatres. One, which strongly affected me, was showing the bombing of London and the fires and devastation and misery which followed. London had been the home of my father and several of his family lived there."

"We lived in a small orchard community. Most of the neighbouring orchards were owned by veterans of the First World War and as youngsters we were all aware and proud of our fathers' participation. My parents had always impressed on me the importance of completing school and continuing on with higher education and I always assumed that was what I would do . . . Why have I related so much of my parents' history? Partly because their own experiences made them determined that I should be prepared for a constructive life and partly because I think I must have inherited genes that suggested I should alter course—the direction of things. Anyway, my decision to enlist was mine alone, I feel comfortable with it and have never had any regrets." The tone of honour is echoed by other veterans. One veteran responds, "I think your mother and father would be proud of you. This is admirable, you speak highly of your parents. You sit high in our eyes. And you made up your own mind to enlist and gave up a lot to do it." Another veteran concludes, "You earned a Ph.D. in living."

Words of Wisdom

For this veteran "joining the R.C.A.F. was like getting on a raft in the river and I never did get off the raft." At the end of the war circumstances influenced his choices. Due to unforeseen circumstances, his studies at UBC were interrupted for a second time by a shadow on his lung in his discharge x-ray, the diagnosis of TB, and the year of treatment at a veterans' hospital. He graduated from UBC in 1951. Words of wisdom about the life review follow: "It is difficult to describe the experiences with others who 'weren't there' and even with those gatherings of people who were there. Therefore, the relating of the experiences by the group of six over the last few weeks has been most enlightening and enjoyable. One must get on with life today and not dwell on the past. It is over. We are the lucky ones—we survived." For him, the life review would have been invaluable "if it had happened fifty years ago" and it would be important to "do it earlier for the peacekeepers." This veteran says that the war experience as a pilot was "the time of my life." But, the life review changed his perspective. Now he concludes, "Although it was an unforgettable and often exciting experience, to keep it in perspective I have to remind myself that it only lasted for about five to six percent of my lifetime so far, and life continues on."

4. Courage and Honour Behind Enemy Lines

This veteran, a Chinese Canadian, was conscripted for duty in the Special Operations Executive (S.O.E.) as an interpreter on intelligence missions. Chinese Canadians were not recognized as Canadian citizens: they were not allowed to vote in Canada until 1947. Courageously, he volunteered to take the parachute jump behind enemy lines in Malaya. Consider the danger. They were dropped at night deep in Malaya. Their parachutes got caught in trees. They could hear the enemy in the jungle. And on this mission, this veteran carried the battery pack on his back. Battery acid splashed on his back—burning him, as they hacked their way in the jungle. So why did he volunteer? He answers, "It was the thing to do to be honoured."

Capturing Courage

This veteran's story reminds us that the guided autobiography format is not for all veterans. He has second thoughts about the written component even though he wants to participate in the life review and he makes his feelings known to the leaders after the first meeting. He says, "I am a man of few words." And the written words are the source of his second thoughts. The leaders suggest that he bring photographs and they will interview him with questions from the guiding themes. He takes his courage in hand, volunteering to participate, just as he did behind enemy lines. The photographs and thematic questions prove to be an effective narrative intervention. Soon, other veterans join him, bringing photographs to illustrate their stories and service in the war. In this case, each picture was worth a thousand words.

This veteran is popular at the Legion. He is a recognized dancing instructor. "I'm a little short of breath," he says, because of the TB. We are aware of the film crew waiting in the wings to capture his story, his wisdom, in a documentary to recognize the courage of Chinese Canadians who served behind enemy lines. This is an important Canadian story and we are thankful we captured some of his wisdom in the life review. His courage and honour is recognized in the life review group.

5. Courage, Valour and Duty in the Line of Fire

This veteran served his country in the Merchant Navy. Having the courage "to conquer fear" in the line of fire, was a turning point in life for this veteran. On one trip to England, in a convoy of 40 ships, they were hit by a "wolf pack of subs" and only 13 of the ships made it to England. Ships were blown up around them. Duty meant going down a 75-foot ladder into a tunnel to oil shaft bearings to keep the engine going. When the torpedoes went off, it blew the paint off the wall. In his words, "that was a turning point in my life to conquer fear and carry on as my mates depended on me as I depended on them to survive. Besides us on the ship many comrades in the other forces depended on us to get the ammo, fuel, and food to survive." Imagine his despair. Veterans in the Merchant Navy were not recognized for their service to their country. Each member in the life review group recognized this veteran's courage.

Recognition for Service to Your Country

This veteran of the Merchant Service is recognized as "the poet" and "the prophet" in the group. He has a way with words. In poetic words he captures the essence in stories of self, of others, and of the cultural context. His writing is riveting and captures the danger, the sense of duty, and his despair about not being recognized for service to his country. About despair he writes, "When I came home on my last trip in the service, I got a rude awakening. When we came before the officer to sign off our enlistment, they never said a word of thanks or a job well done. Nothing. This was just the start of disillusionment to come. The Canadian government said, 'sorry men you are not part of the armed services and, as such, you are not included in *any* benefits.' Being rejected by the rest of the military would be comparable to the English aristocrat calling the Canadians that had been fighting in Sicily and Italy for so long, D-Day Dodgers. What a slap in the face for those troops. Amen."

This unresolved issue and the related contradictions about recognition or lack of it provided a focus for reflection and dialogue with implications for future actions. Recognition of his courage by other veterans in the group resulted in some personal resolution implying integrity rather than despair. Transformation in the life stories went both ways. His story changed the perspective about peacekeeper veterans with implications for recognizing their service.

DISCUSSION

The benefits of the life review project along with implications for future practice emerged from multiple sources of evidence. These sources include: ethnographic observations; field notes; interviews with leaders; written narratives of veterans; responses to questionnaires; and focus groups. In follow up meetings in Westwood (1998), the director of the project conducted focus groups (that were videotaped and audiotaped) with the veterans groups and the leaders to obtain reactions, feedback, and recommendations for the life review project.

Based on insights from practice, changing the selection and sequence of themes could make this a more effective narrative exploration. First, themes focusing on stress and coping, along with health and body image, could be removed from the sequence. Second, themes about death and dying, along with goals, aspirations, and meaning in life, could be added to enhance this thematic exploration. In response to the questions distributed at the completion of the life review group, veterans at the Legion indicated that they found the theme "stress and coping" the least interesting and the theme "your war experience" the most interesting in the life review.

Celebration of camaraderie is evident at the Legion in the snapshots of the veterans captured on camera. The value of the life review in terms of camaraderie, relief, and recognition was captured in voices and visions of the veterans. For veterans, it was "a relief to talk about the war" and the camaraderie and comfort in the group made this possible. Veterans valued the comradeship, comfort, and compatibility of the group. One veteran speaks of the value of life review in the following way: "The opportunity to speak freely about war experience without the fear of appearing boastful or boring. It does provide relief." Another veteran voices valuing the comradeship and compatibility in the group. In his words, "[he values] the compatibility in the group—the moderators made it easy. They brought out the best . . ." And the best is yet to come!

New meanings and wisdom about the importance of recognition for service to your country became pivotal in the implications and recommendations for peacekeepers. New meanings resulted in new "templates" for action. As you will recall, lack of recognition and related contradictions and dilemmas provided a focus for reflection and dialogue in the discussion about war experiences. Resolution of issues relating to recognition was a positive outcome at the Legion. The response of one veteran in the follow-up focus group implies resolution was the most valued outcome of the life review, since the valour and sacrifice of the merchant navy veterans were not recognized. In his words, "This is the best thing that has happened to me since the war."

In the follow-up focus group at the Legion, veterans turned their attention to action in the recommendations for improving the life review project. This is not surprising. From the outset these veterans were motivated to participate to improve the program for other veterans. What is surprising was the new awareness of the role of recognition and their suggestions and recommendations for action. They recommended that all peacekeepers be offered the life review program. They wanted to speak to the peacekeepers and serve in a mentoring role. For them it was important that the Royal Canadian Legion recognize them as peacekeeper veterans. This is evidence of guided autobiography bridging stories and individual and social transformation.

Both the war experience and the diagnosis and treatment of TB were identified as major branching points in the veterans' lives. Following the sharing of stories about the war experience the veteran known to the group as "the poet" and "the prophet" said that each veteran earned "a Ph.D. in living." And one of the leaders noted that there was "a sense of nobility"—that the veterans were all noble in their "sense of duty, honour, adventure, and loyalty" in their service to their country in World War II. All of the veterans at the Legion were recognized for their service to their country.

CONCLUSION

A photographer documenting parts of the group captures a transformative moment on camera: a veteran at the piano who has not played since the war! Eight years of piano lessons along with practising two hours a day culminated in an ATCM in music. In his words, "This came in handy when I was in the service as I played the piano and never had to buy a drink for me and my buddies." Now, he plays "We'll meet again, don't know where, don't know when . . ." The song ends, bringing to a close a remarkable life review project.

This model of life review in the veterans' project provides a lens to focus on the hermeneutics of inquiry toward restorying (Kenyon & Randall, 1997) and transformation. The narrative approach and thematic exploration brings to light many contradictions in the war experience as a focus for dialogue in the group. In the case of the Legion, contradictions about recognition or not, for service to your country, was a focus for dialogue and discussion. And the camaraderie and collaborative leadership in the group contributed to the positive outcome of relief, resolution, and recognition towards integrity rather than despair. The new meanings, wisdom, and knowledge coconstructed in the group provided new templates for future action. We interpret this as communicative and transformative learning. And the guided autobiography provided the bridge between stories and the individual and social transformation.

17

Integrating Reminiscence and Life Review Techniques With Brief, Cognitive Behavioral Therapy

John A. Kunz

There is growing interest in the use of reminiscence, life review, guided autobiography, narrative biography, and similar processes to improve the quality of life of older adults. Researchers and practitioners in this field continue to struggle with further defining these processes and substantiating the validity of such work. Natural reminiscence has occurred throughout the course of human history and is evidenced in many publications, including the Bible. When visiting long-term care facilities and other programs serving older adults, it is common to see reminiscence approaches being utilized, often without defining them as such, by family members, care givers, and professionals. Many activity professionals will tell you that almost any group activity they conduct ends up having a reminiscence focus to some degree. The very fact that reminiscence is such an ingrained part of the psychology of human development and adaptation makes it even more difficult to understand in scientific terms. The telling of one's life story is rooted in modern psychotherapy. Evaluating one's life and finding new meaning in life is a common outcome of traditional psychotherapy. Recalling solutions of past problems to address current issues has also been a common therapy technique. It is, however, difficult to pinpoint just why these techniques are so effective.

Furthermore, clinician's work is increasingly scrutinized for medical necessity by third-party payers. Reminiscence and life review techniques may be seen as superfluous, "nice" but not necessary, by reviewers of insurance claims. Third-party payers often favor the use of solution-focused or brief, cognitive behavioral therapy techniques as a method of delivering cost-effective, symptom specific therapy when medical necessity dictates. The purpose of this paper is to demonstrate that reminiscence and life review can be effectively integrated within the context of solution-focused, cognitive behavioral therapy in ways that better meet the developmental needs of older adults. This paper also proposes that the solution-focused, cognitive therapy framework can often explain the successful outcome of reminiscence and life review in community and clinical case studies of older adults across the continuum from oriented to extremely confused.

REMINISCENCE AND LIFE REVIEW

The term "life review" was coined by Butler (1963) when he began to scientifically identify life review as a normal aspect of older adult development. This led the way for society to look at the reminiscence and life review process as a part of normal human aging. He also indicated that life review was normal for anyone approaching death. At the point of death it is natural to want to put your life in perspective, resolve past conflicts, grieve losses and changes, forgive yourself and others for wrongdoings, celebrate your successes, and feel a sense of completion about your life. Erikson (1963) also discusses the older adult's reconciliation with the inevitability of death. The wisdom acquired as a result of living long enough to reach the highest level of psychosocial development is what he called "ego integrity versus despair." Looking at one's lifetime and achieving a sense of integrity about one's life is what Erikson believed to be the final stage of life.

Since Butler first introduced the term life review, there has been a great amount of discussion and investigation regarding the definition and usefulness of reminiscence and life review (see Haight & Webster, 1995, for an overview). Parker (1995) cited a number of both positive and negative outcomes of studies of the effectiveness of reminiscence and indicated that there were clearly two camps with regard to the utility of reminiscence, concluding that reminiscence itself has no influence on well-being. She hypothesized that continuity theory may best explain the adaptive process of reminiscence.

In defining reminiscence and life review, Webster and Haight (1995) synthesized the existing literature into four areas with five dimensions in each area. The four basic categories of recall were reminiscence, life review, autobiography, and narrative. They defined the dimensions of reminiscence as highly spontaneous, frequent in practice, requiring little structure, noncomprehensive and only moderately evaluative. Life review, on the other hand, was seen as highly structured and evaluative, very comprehensive, but only moderately spontaneous, and lower in frequency. Autobiography was seen as the least spontaneous, low in frequency, moderately comprehensive and evaluative, and highly structured. Narrative was seen as relatively low in evaluation and comprehensiveness, low to medium in structure and frequency, and medium to high in spontaneity.

Precise definitions are most helpful in conducting research, but become blurred when such processes are used in a clinical setting or as part of normal day-to-day life. Some older adults naturally engage in activities that enable them to accomplish the tasks of life described by Erikson and accomplish what Butler referred to as life review. Family or class reunions, annual events, and even funerals are examples of when such natural reminiscing occurs (Kunz, 1991b).

As individuals age, however, more and more significant people in their lives may die, become disabled, move, or for some other reason become unavailable. Thus, there are fewer contacts available to promote natural reminiscence and more structured approaches may be needed to promote quality of life through the facilitation of normal developmental processes. Such techniques may be particularly useful in enabling older adults to apply the wisdom acquired during their life time to current problems and issues, particularly in preventing, assessing, and treating mental health problems (Kunz, 1991b).

Reminiscence and life review approaches can be directed towards preventing, assessing, and intervening with mental health problems of older adults.

Prevention

Facilitating natural reminiscence in family and social situations, or the use of structured reminiscence in individual or group approaches, improves quality of life and prevents mental health problems. This can take place at family or other reunions, structured individual or group activities, public lectures or presentations, or facilitating the telling of an individual's life story through writing, video, other media, or the performing arts (Kunz, 1997).

Assessment

Similar approaches are useful for developing rapport and gathering social history and other information in the assessment process. For some individuals, particularly those less educated, it is helpful to ask them to describe how to carry out lifelong daily tasks (such as making bread) as part of a mental status examination (as opposed to counting backwards from 100 by sevens). Reported changes in the way an individual does or does not reminisce can be critical factors in making an assessment. For example, if an individual ordinarily enjoys talking about the past, but is now avoiding doing so they may have some unresolved grief issues. Or an individual who has recently become obsessed with some negative issue from the past that had previously been resolved and long forgotten may be depressed and/or experiencing posttraumatic stress disorder (Kunz, 1997).

Intervention

Once the initial assessment is complete and treatment deemed appropriate, reminiscence and life review approaches can and should be incorporated in the treatment plan. These approaches may be utilized at multiple levels. They may include the use of approaches described above as preventative. Individuals, their family members, and other care providers and treatment program providers may be directed to include specific approaches. Each intervention must be planned in keeping with the capabilities and limitations of the individual and family/support system.

For example, an older adult who is experiencing a sense of worthlessness may be encouraged to tell their life story in some form. Since they may be overwhelmed with depression at the time, health care professionals from a variety of disciplines can assist family members or other close friends to encourage the depressed older adult to do so. A teenager who has an interest in making videotapes may be asked to tape his/her grandfather as he is interviewed about his life. Later the teenager can edit the tape and the family can have a premiere celebrating the grandfather's life. This can be a very powerful intervention.

Beyond the creation of a therapeutic milieu that utilizes reminiscence and life review approaches, these strategies should also be incorporated with individual and group work including integrating these approaches with solution-focused, cognitive behavioral therapy. A framework for doing so includes the use of reminiscence matches, resulting therapeutic resources states, and in some cases advanced psychological directives. These terms are further defined and illustrated below (Kunz, 1997).

REMINISCENCE MATCHES

The use of reminiscence triggers, props, and themes in individual and group work is frequently cited in the literature (Osborn, 1989;

Burnside, 1995). These may be used in community presentations, and in individual and group situations (Kunz, 1990).

Bandler and Grinder (1975) studied the therapeutic communication of Milton Erikson and other noted therapists and, in what they called neurolinguistic programming, emphasized how each human being perceives and interprets the world through the five basic senses: visual, auditory, kinesthetic, olfactory, and gustatory. Most individuals also use one of the five senses in particular as their preferred or primary sense for experiencing and understanding reality. In order to develop rapport quickly and effectively, Bandler and Grinder recommended determining the client's lead sense and then matching that lead sense by using language that is similar. A depressed individual whose lead sense is visual might describe their future as dark and dim. The therapist would use language that is also visual by asking questions about what dark colors the client sees and leading them to see some variation in the darkness that might lead to some brightness. In contrast, the depressed client with a kinesthetic lead sense might say "I feel liked I'm bogged down in mud and slipping deeper and deeper." The therapist would use language laden with emotional/feeling content and eventually might help the client find a "strong, solid root to grab onto." In both of these examples the depressed individual was describing symptoms of depression and while doing so they were experiencing this deep state of depression. These types of emotional states have been described by Bandler and Grinder as "stuck states." Clients are stuck in their depression or other emotions. By using their lead system to first establish rapport and create a mood of understanding, the therapist is able to mirror or match the individual. Once this occurs, the therapist can then lead the individual to another, more positive emotional state.

Following this framework Kunz (1991b) defines a reminiscence match as a stimulation of one or all senses. These senses include visual, auditory, kinesthetic, olfactory, and gustatory. Pictures, old toys, radio equipment, music, food, flowers, bread baking in an oven, and a list of innumerable stimuli produces these matches. They happen naturally all the time, but can be developed and used clinically on a number of levels.

These reminiscence matches connect individuals to positive or negative resource states, similar to the stuck states defined by Bandler and Grinder. The stimulation of one or more of these five senses forms a match of current experience with past experience. For example, when grinding coffee in an old-fashioned grinder placed between the knees, the scent of coffee beans and the taste of the fresh coffee can elicit memories from several senses. As participants discuss their reactions to these types of experiences, they commonly discover unknown connections, and the conversation frequently goes into several unforeseen directions.

Another example is that of a reminiscence group using a wind-up phonograph and old records. The facilitator played the "Skater's Waltz" expecting a discussion of dances and romance. However, three female participants in their late 80s recalled skating to the music as young women and winning competitive skating matches. This certainly connected them to a sense of competence and success, while also bonding them together as former athletes.

Often these reminiscence matches are positive in nature. However, the more cognitively impaired an individual is, the more likely it is that negative reminiscence matches may be unintentionally stimulated. In these situations the only method the confused individual may have to communicate this negative result is through a behavioral outburst (Kunz, 1997).

THERAPEUTIC RESOURCE STATES

The successful use of a reminiscence match allows the individual to access a resource state from their past. These may include coping skills, identity, past experience, courage, security, or spiritual values or beliefs. One way to make sense of these resource states is to use Maslow's "hierarchy of needs" (1968). Resource states may include knowing that one's basic needs will be met; reassurance that one is and will continue to be safe; having a sense of connection, love, and belonging; and having a sense of self-esteem and value and a sense of self actualization. By the time an individual has reached older adulthood, the "calling in life" that Maslow refers to is usually quite evident. This core of an individual's identity that can be found through reminiscence and life review work is the key to his or her emotional well-being. Through the structured use of reminiscence matches, individuals are helped to use their uniquely developed coping skills, identity, experience, courage, security, spiritual values, sense of purpose, and inner values to cope with current issues and problems. This process is especially helpful as older adults and others face dramatic life changes. These resource states may be used in an obvious, overt, or conscious manner, or in more subtle ways with the individual less aware of the manipulation of reminiscence matches and resources states (Kunz, 1991b).

Due to a longer life history, most older adults have a large variety of resource states to draw upon. In fact, these resource states can be looked at as results of the successful resolution of each of Erikson's (1963) stages of human development. Individuals develop trust in Erikson's first stage. To know that one is loved and will be taken care of is important for everyone. Most older adults are "adult orphans" and may be facing very traumatic changes in their lives. Using reminiscence matches to help them reaffirm the trust and security they developed so long ago can be very helpful as they face these changes.

Similarly, the sense of competence developed in most individuals from the ages of 6–12 is needed throughout our adult lives. If older adults are having some physical or cognitive problems that result in their feeling a sense or inferiority, reminiscence matches can be employed to reaffirm their sense of competence through related resource states.

Reminiscence and life review approaches can be developed in order to affirm or strengthen an individual's sense of self at each of Erikson's stages, promoting increased feelings of competence, independence, initiative, competence, identity, intimacy, generativity, and integrity. This is all integral to good mental health.

Reminiscence matches can also cause an individual to access a negative resource state from the past. A simple St. Patrick's Day party may be enjoyable for many, but if an individual experienced trauma in their family on that day, participation in such a party may be too stressful. Unresolved or partially resolved issues may be reawakened. An oriented older adult in this situation would likely use avoidance to cope with this situation. Demented individuals may not be able to explain why they didn't want to attend the party resulting in their being further traumatized and have a catastrophic outburst because an unsuspecting staff member brought them to the party. Social history and the observation of physiological/emotional reactions are keys in avoiding these negative matches, as is communicating such events to family members and other care providers.

ADVANCE PSYCHOLOGICAL DIRECTIVES

The preceding example of a negative reminiscence match is a good example of what problems could be avoided by the use of an advance psychological directive. Advance psychological directives are a means of making sure that one's individual psychosocial history is best utilized in future care. Older adults without cognitive impairment are usually able to say what they want or don't want. In contrast, if depressed or having some other emotional problem, they may be less likely to apply the positive use of reminiscence and life review approaches. If older adults develop a dementing illness they will be less and less likely to apply these approaches as their disorder progresses.

The best way to start the process of identifying advance psychological directives is to use a workshop or other educational tool to sensitize older adults and their families to the value and use of reminiscence and life review approaches. Then, as follow up, individuals and their family members plan for their future by writing their own social history and developing guidelines about what activities and approaches should be avoided (such as the St. Patrick's Day party), and what activities and approaches should be emphasized. Other media besides writing can be utilized.

One example is that of macaroni soup. If an individual has fond memories of their grandmother feeding them macaroni soup as a child and records this as an advance psychological directive and that person later becomes confused and agitated, care providers could try serving the individual macaroni soup as an intervention. This may or may not help, but the goal would be to create a visual, kinesthetic, olfactory, and gustatory reminiscence match for the individual that would result in a therapeutic resource state of love and security—with the hopes that it would decrease the level of agitated behavior and improve the quality of life for the individual.

The use of advance psychological directives helps increase the chances of maintaining a higher quality of life in the event an individual can no longer effectively advocate on their own behalf and also provides guidelines for concerned family members and guardians. It provides the additional benefit for an individual facing the potential of a dementing illness to be and feel more in control of their destiny during the early stags of the disorder. These concepts also help family members and friends find more effective ways of communicating and maintaining a positive relationship with their demented loved ones (Kunz, 1997).

BRIEF THERAPY

Psychotherapy is often defined as a change in one or more of the domains of affect, behavior, or thoughts. The use of reminiscence matches to produce therapeutic resource states often results in an immediate change in one or all of these domains. Solution-focused or brief therapy (Watzlawick, Weakland, & Fisch, 1974) utilizes the client's own language and interpretation of the world to conceptualize the problems and contract for what changes the client wants to make. Fully oriented older adults are able to be verbally explicit in defining these changes. The more cognitively impaired an individual is the more the clinician needs to interpret the "poetry" of that individual and look for meaning about what they need in their verbalizations and behaviors (Kunz, 1991a). The perspective of the therapist is often broader than that of the client, and may include the input of family members, care providers, and other multidisciplinary professionals, particularly if the client has some level of cognitive impairment (Kunz, 1997). Brief therapy can result in desired changes in a single session.

COGNITIVE BEHAVIORAL THERAPY

Cognitive Behavioral Therapy (CBT; Beck, 1995) is currently considered by many to be the most researched, respected, and funded form of psychotherapy. Recent studies have shown effective use of cognitive behavioral therapy for older adults with depression (Dai et al., 1999); anxiety (Koder, 1998); intergenerational programs for cognitively impaired older adults (Camp et al., 2000), obsessive compulsive disorder (Carmin, Polland, & Ownby, 1999); pain management (Cook, 1998); and sexual dysfunction (Crowther & Zeiss, 1999).

CBT focuses on changing dysfunctional cognitions (thoughts), emotions, and behavior and includes the following three assumptions: (1) Dysfunctional behavior is the result of distorted or negative automatic thinking often based on faulty logic or errors in reasoning, (2) these underlying negative thoughts can be changed through examining the underlying core beliefs or schemas, and (3) self-affirmations and other techniques can build positive behavior and reduce problematic behavior by counteracting the negative automatic thinking with positive thinking.

Three modifications of cognitive behavioral therapy in working with older adults have been suggested (Gallagher-Thompson & Thompson, 1996): (1) The therapist should remain more active in therapy than with younger adults, (2) the process should be expected to go more slowly, and (3) efforts must be made to compensate for cognitive or sensory deficits. Interweaving life review techniques in counseling oriented to mildly confused nursing home residents is recommended by Spayd and Smyer (1996).

One specific example is provided by the work of Young (1990). The use of a time-line life review technique to assist older adults in developing more functional schemas based on a detailed evaluation of their life history was described by Young (1990) and Young, Beck, and Weinberger (1993).

INTEGRATING BRIEF, COGNITIVE BEHAVIORAL THERAPY WITH REMINISCENCE AND LIFE REVIEW

Medicare and other third-party payers are increasingly concerned about when and if psychotherapy is medically necessary for older adults. Some fear that reminiscence and life review approaches in therapy will no longer be funded at some point in the future (Butler, 1995). Solution-focused cognitive behavioral therapy is an accepted framework for individual and group therapy with older adults (Beck, 1995). Integrating reminiscence and life review processes within this framework should further substantiate and justify the use of reminiscence and life review techniques in working clinically with older adults.

The following case summaries illustrate the integration of the reminiscence and life review techniques of reminiscence matches and resource states with a brief, cognitive behavioral therapy framework.

Crisis Situation

During a reminiscence group an 82-year-old woman fell off the sofa and broke her hip. She was an avid storyteller and had many tales to tell about the community in which she lived. As she was transported to the emergency room and later for x-rays, the staff kept asking her questions and actively listened to her tales. Special emphasis was placed on eliciting reminiscence matches using all sensory modes. This approach helped her maintain identification with community leaders and changes in the community over the years. The reminiscence matches lead her to a confident, successful emotional resource state. This recaptured schema allowed her to stay connected with her rational intellectual abilities, helping her avoid her feelings of emotional and physical pain, and reduced the potential for panic or other behavioral problems at this time of crisis. Appealing to cognitive resources through reminiscence approaches reduced the potential for the development of dysfunctional behavior and/or being overwhelmed by negative emotions.

Depression

When listening and eventually dancing to Glen Miller's "Sunrise Serenade," a withdrawn, 74-year-old psychotically depressed, acute mental health patient began communicating and discussed aspects of a time in her life when she lived in a large city where she worked, dated, and danced before returning to the region where she grew up to care for her aging parents. She was able to grieve the changes and losses in her life and connect with the therapist and group members. This auditory, musical reminiscence match accessed the resource states of confidence, self-esteem, social skills, and lifelong values. Beginning in that group session, and without explicitly discussing the use of brief and cognitive behavioral therapy processes, she was able to examine her self-worth and validate a schema that supported her self-esteem and value as a single individual. This new level of self-affirmation resulted in more social behavior in other aspects of her treatment and life. These behavioral changes further supported and enhanced her improved emotional state that was also tied to her rediscovered, more functional schema. The continued use of music in subsequent therapy sessions reinforced this affirmation of her earlier identity and the more functional schema she had lost in her grief and subsequent depression. The therapist maintained individual contact during a four-year period as follow-up to this group work. This became the longest time period the patient had remained out of the hospital for 11 years.

Acute Confusion

An angry, withdrawn, 66-year-old psychotically depressed acute mental health patient receiving electroconvulsive therapy for a recurrent depression would become agitated, withdrawn, and uncooperative during the treatment process. She had reminisced about her mother's holiday sausage while attending a group with her brother one day. The next day she had no recollection of that reminiscence group and was insistent upon not eating, not bathing, and staying in bed for the day. When the therapist approached the patient with a platter of that sausage he had made from the recipe roughly described by her and her brother the day before, her affect immediately brightened and her behavior changed dramatically. She bathed, dressed, and attended the group where she enjoyed the sausage, ate other foods, and socialized with others.

This simple intervention using the visual, olfactory, gustatory, and kinesthetic reminiscence matches helped this acutely confused older adult access her resource states of attachment, love, and belonging that she developed years ago in her relationship with her mother. During this time of confusion, fear, and anger she was in desperate need of this more secure schema. The reminiscence intervention helped her find the resource of this schema. She could feel a sense of security in knowing that she was loved and belonged. Her behavior improvement followed this change in thinking and affect. Significant change had occurred in one therapy session.

Moderate To Severe Confusion

A moderately to severely confused older adult was observed pounding on the nursing station counter of the nursing home where she resided. She was demanding a train ticket immediately. She became increasingly insistent on receiving that ticket as her requests were ignored.

When approached about her needs, she immediately expressed a desire to talk about where she wanted to go. She wanted to ride the train to another community where her cousin, a teacher, lived, and where she helped her with her children. She gradually calmed during this five-minute conversation as the therapist asked simple questions and validated the significant relationship and role she had with her cousin. She became secure and confident knowing she was important to someone and needed. Her verbal and creative reminiscence helped her find these resources with the assistance of the effective communication techniques utilized by the therapist. Her affect had now changed. She was no longer frustrated, angry, and agitated. She was calm and secure thanks to the more functional schema she had found from her past. Her behavior followed suit as she then sat calmly with other residents.

Activity Group

A group of assisted living residents was assembled to create a "life quilt". The group met weekly and was provided technical assistance from the leaders. A current photo of each member was taken and printed on a fabric square. Members then embellished their square with drawings, buttons, stitching, and other representations of their life-time experiences and values. The entire individual and group process accessed a myriad of reminiscence matches and resulting resource states. Lifelong schemas became graphically apparent and shared. This process resulted in enhanced or improved affect and improved self worth.

IMPLICATIONS

Reminiscence matches, resulting resource states, and advanced psychological directives may be used to maintain and improve quality of life on a number of levels of interaction with older adults who may range from being fully oriented to extremely confused. Such techniques may be used to develop rapport and maintain group attention when meeting with groups of older adults. Using photographs and ads for businesses from decades ago with phone numbers that no longer exist, such as "Melrose 203," or "two longs and a short," stereoptic viewers from the turn of the century, or other props enable a speaker to better obtain and maintain audience attention when doing outreach education to groups of older adults. Using such an approach demonstrates the speaker's and the organization's understanding of older adult development and provides instant rapport with the audience. This primes participants to take in new information as well.

When provided this informational framework older individuals, family members, and friends are able to creatively develop a variety of plans to ensure that their quality of life is maintained and enhanced as they age, whether or not they ever become cognitively impaired. Family, community, and facility events can be fine tuned to better meet these developmental needs of older adults. The use of life history books, scrapbooks, photo albums, music, foods, smells, and other ways of stimulating the senses can be included in all activities. If trained properly, community, teenager, and children's service groups can use these approaches to develop intergenerational programs that provide deep levels of meaning and understanding for both the older and younger participants. Incorporation of these principles is very useful in architectural designs, and in planning and marketing strategies for assisted living and other programs designed for older adults. Increased use of these activities should prevent mental health problems from developing. Scientific studies as to the ongoing effect of such activities are needed. It would be helpful to establish a training protocol incorporating these ideas for individuals initially diagnosed with Alzheimer's disease and their family members and friends and then tracking both the progression of the disease, levels of caregiver and patient stress, level of care needed, and number of behavioral or mental health problems.

It seems imperative to train those caring for older adults in all capacities about the significance of these principles and approaches. Training programs that allow the care provider to experience a reminiscence match, resulting resource states, and advanced psychological directives themselves is an excellent way for them to personalize the value of such approaches and incorporate such approaches in their daily work. Professionals responsible for planning the care of older adults should include such approaches in a multidisciplinary treatment planning process. These approaches should be used both individually and in group settings. Drawings, photos, bracelets out of special beads, quilts, collages, and other techniques may incorporate this material. For example, a collage of items representing the home he built for his wife and family can connect an older adult with a schema of strength, accomplishment, and pride.

The use of an edited video life review done while an older adult is fully functioning may prove useful as they age, especially if cognitive impairment develops. This video could help the older adult maintain a connection with lifelong functional schemas. It would also be a tool to assist caregivers in better understanding the psychosocial essence of the individual for whom they are caring. This would be an excellent area for future research, particularly to determine what effect watching the edited video life review had as individuals faced various changes in their lives or progressed through the stages of Alzheimer's disease.

The use of these principles is even more crucial if an older adult has unresolved grief issues or is experiencing the most common forms of mental health problems: delirium, depression, or dementia. In these situations, the multidisciplinary treatment team should determine if and when any negative reminiscence matches may be causing or exacerbating the symptoms. They should also determine which reminiscence matches appear to improve the symptoms. A consistent treatment plan should then be developed integrating the positive reminiscence matches and resulting resource states with a brief, cognitive behavioral therapy approach. This plan should be reevaluated often and new approaches added or deleted depending on the results. Such approaches should be utilized in individual, group, couple, and family therapy. Comparative research evaluating the effectiveness of increased integration of reminiscence and life review techniques with brief, cognitive behavioral therapy should be relatively easy, since these therapies already have a well-established research base.

The expanded use of reminiscence and life review approaches in caring for or treating older adults requires a great amount of energy. Likewise, a great deal of effort must be made to personalize the approaches used for each individual. Many professionals and care providers have felt enormous satisfaction in doing so. Sometimes, however, professionals and care providers succumb to the very symptoms of depression or frustration their client's are experiencing and don't challenge themselves to work even harder at applying these principles and techniques. Further studies, if the results are positive, may increase professionals' and care providers' motivations for doing so.

18

Evaluative Research on Reminiscence Groups for People With Dementia

Toyoko Nomura

Reminiscence has been widely used in group settings both as an intervention and as an activity. Most reports on reminiscence interventions have been positive when evaluated in both an objective and a subjective manner. Reminiscence in groups is an excellent way to introduce individuals to new environments and to help them get to know other people (Haight & Dias, 1992). Often, people of the same age recall similar pasts and in this way they find a common ground to begin to forge a relationship with strangers. For example, two women new to a nursing home were invited to participate in a reminiscence group. As they discussed their childhoods, they realized they had gone to school together and had been best friends all through grammar school. As they talked about their shared past, both began to feel more comfortable with their new environment, and from that day on they were again fast friends but now in a nursing home.

Reminiscence group work for people with dementia is even more recent. Gibson (1998) was one of the first to use this modality with people with dementia. She said that reminiscence made connections between a person's past, present, and future, and encouraged sociability. She further stated that reminiscence also confirmed identity and encouraged a sense of self-worth. While facilitating the life review, reminiscence can change relationships and alter others perceptions by clarifying present functioning. Gibson (1998) has given many workshops throughout Europe to teach others how to use the modality and was largely responsible for the adoption of this modality by others, especially in Great Britain.

Just outside of London in Blackheath, there is a Reminiscence Center. In this center, people tell their stories, attend workshops, and learn to use the reminiscence modality. Working with Pam Schweitzer, through Age Exchange, Gibson and Schweitzer taught many people the value of conducting reminiscence groups. Reminiscence was adopted so quickly throughout Europe that there are now reminiscence centers in Norway and Finland as well. Additionally, Schweitzer gained funding for the European Reminiscence Network and provided oversight to eight European countries whose caregivers learned the modality and conducted reminiscence groups with people with dementia and their caregivers in their own countries (Schweitzer, 1998).

Bender, Bauckham, and Norris (1999) speak to the therapeutic purposes of reminiscence and explain why it is not therapy. They posit that people are not referred and do not perceive that they have a problem. However, when they participate in a reminiscence group it can be therapeutic. Bender, Bauckham, and Norris see the group as providing an historical identity while allowing people to rework troubling parts of their lives. People enjoy being listened to and respected. Those who are lost in dementia become socially stimulated and again become a part of a group. They can connect with others even though they have not done so for some time. Bender, Bauckham, and Norris provide a "cookbook" for those who want to learn about the uses of reminiscence for different reasons.

Most of the aforementioned work provides instruction for running reminiscence groups. However, there is another body of literature on reminiscence group work with dementia that deals with group work as an intervention and provides outcomes that result from the intervention. Youseff (1990) reported a positive effect on depression as the result of participating in a reminiscence group. Cook (1998) ran reminiscence groups with 36 women and reported a statistically significant difference between the control and the treatment group on life satisfaction. Weiss (1994) compared life review groups with cognitive therapy and found no significant differences on outcome measures between the two groups. However, he did learn a great deal about running older groups and suggested the two modalities be combined for the most effective outcomes with older people. Finally, Gatz, Fiske, Fox, Kaskie, Kasl-Godley, McCallum, and Wetherall (1998) studied the literature to list all empirically validated treatments for older adults. One of these was reminiscing groups. However, when compared with exercise, exercise had a greater effect on depression.

PURPOSE OF THIS STUDY

Most research on reminiscence group work for people with dementia has involved groups diagnosed with dementia regardless of the source of the illness. Little research, especially in Japan, has differentiated between types of dementia when delivering reminiscence interventions to groups to see, in fact, if reminiscence is more effective with one type of dementia than another. Thus, the purpose of this study is to: examine subjects in a day-care setting for people with dementia with and without reminiscence therapy; examine the differences and commonalities between reminiscence groups for people with Alzheimer's disease and reminiscence groups for people with Vascular dementia; and develop more appropriate practice frameworks for reminiscing with people who have different types of dementia.

METHODS

In order to evaluate the effectiveness of a reminiscence approach for people with dementia, two types of group practice were organized. The first group was a reminiscence group for people with Alzheimer-type dementia (AD). The second was a reminiscence group for people with vascular-type dementia (VD). Forty-four clients (Male–19, Female–25; Average age–74.8) who were diagnosed with AD (25 clients), or vascular dementia (19 clients), were divided into the following four groups:

GROUPS

Group 1—Ordinary day-care program (AD-9, VD-6)
Group 2—Ordinary day-care program and reminiscence group (AD-8)
Group 3—Ordinary day-care program and reminiscence group (VD-5)
Group 4—No participation in day care (AD-8, VD-8)

In Group 1, clients attended day care twice a week from 10 a.m. to 3:00 p.m. for 3 months. Clients of Groups 2 and 3, attended reminiscence groups in the morning for three months and then joined day care in the afternoon. Group 2 received a total of 25 reminiscence sessions, while group 3 received 24 sessions.

The program began with themes related to group members, origins, and personal experiences. A sample of the content of the program is displayed in Table 18.1.

TABLE 18.1 Content of Group 2

Group Meeting	Themes of Reminiscence
1	Memories of hometown
2	Origin of their names
3	Memories around flowers of a spring in hometown
4	What their family did for living, things they did in helping out their family
5	Memories of elementary school
6	How they kept warm in winter
7	Events in winter
8	Clothing they would wear in winter
9	Places they went on a school day trip
10	Scenes of hometown from spring to summer
11	How they would spend their time on a rainy day
12	Joyful memories of elementary school days
13	Memories of running errands
14	Memories of breakfast
15	Foods they enjoyed back then
16	Clothing they wore back then
17	Open (no particular theme)
18	Upon receiving their very first paycheck
19	Memories around hair (haircut, hairdo)
20	Things they have been careful about since childhood

Some examples of the chosen topics are schooling, clothing in winter, memory of breakfast, first salary at work, person whom they were pleased to meet in their life, words which they had easily learned, and so on. The themes were set both chronologically and occasionally, through assessment of members' life history and interests.

The flow of each session was similar across all sessions and is described in Table 18.2.

PROCEDURE

Each session was divided into two sequential parts and began by welcoming the members with background music. The first part of the session asked members for memories around particular themes.

TABLE 18.2   The Flow of Each Session for Group 2

Guiding the way to the place of group/gathering/background music

Making the most out of the time till the opening for introduction of the Group

A checkup for health—opening of group/greeting/rules

Members' introduction, guiding to unfold reminiscence and images

Reminiscing with the support of pertinent materials and tools

Closing/individually checking the attendance book/background music

Leaving/participating day-care group

The second part encouraged them to explore reminiscing with the support of one or two kinds of goods or props pertinent to the theme. These goods had been selected to promote sensory stimulation and matched each individual's life history. Since almost all members of the group came from other districts in Japan and were not born in the community where they were now living, the themes as well as the goods were rich in variety according to their original district and culture.

Group 3 (for VD)

Although the content of the program was similar for people with vascular dementia, Group 3 was more focused on the developmental stage of members and their life history. Sometimes the group began by recalling the content of the former session. Our purpose was to promote the life review of members. The flow of each session was similar to the flow in Group 2 and was the same through all sessions. We did not use as many goods or props as we did in Group 2. Rather, we put more emphasis on verbal expression and the narratives of members. The themes for Group 3 are reported in Table 18.3.

EVALUATION TOOL

We assessed the cognitive function of clients with the Mini-Mental State Examination (MMSE) and the revised Hasegawa Dementia Scale (HDS-R). We measured three times: 1 week before the start of the group, 1.5 months after the start, and 1 week after the end of the group. In order to evaluate the effect of the reminiscence group focusing on the view of the clients, we employed three approaches. The first approach was to ask the clients about the experience of reminiscence in the

TABLE 18.3   Content of Group 3

Group Meeting	Themes of Reminiscence
1	Memories of hometown
2	Origin of their names
3	Joyful memories of elementary school days
4	Memories of school events
5	Memories of their friends
6	Helping out their family
7	Seasons of autumn leaves
8	Dreams of their childhood
9	Adolescence
10	Hairstyles in their twenties
11	People they are glad to have met in their lives
12	Most memorable words from people they received
13	Getting ready for winter
14	Medical things prepared in their house, memories around being sick
15	Seeing life as the flow of river, the turning point(s) in their lives
16	Things they enjoy in their everyday life that keep them happy
17	Ways to appreciate the longer evening hours in autumn → memories of being at the hospital (for one of the members was to be hospitalized)
18	Music they would often listen to when little or when young
19	The most precious thing for them in life → stories of war
20	Things to organize in December towards the end of a year and the coming of a new year
21	Some advice they would give to the young
22	How they would spend their lives, if given another life
23	Their plans for near future, places they wish to visit

group by using the brief questionnaire of reminiscence function applied from Webster and Haight (1995). The second approach was to question their life satisfaction by using a modified Life Satisfaction Index (LSI). The LSI was employed 1 week before the start of the group and 1 week after the end of the group. The third approach was to interview the clients with their families after the end of the group.

RESULTS

Results are presented in the order of the questions asked.

1. Overall Effect of Day Care for Individuals With Dementia

Consistent with Kawada and colleagues (1998) significant improvement was found in MMSE ($p < 0.05$). In Group 4 (nonday-care group receiving no reminiscence intervention) both the MMSE and HDS-R declined (MMSE $15.8 \rightarrow 13.4$; HDS-R $12.7 \rightarrow 12.1$). On the other hand, in Groups 1, 2, and 3, the MMSE increased from 16.9 to 17.4. In the same groups, HDS-R increased from 13.0 to 14.8. When Groups 1, 2, and 3 were separately tested according to the type of dementia, the results of MMSE showed increase from 22.6 to 23.9 in vascular dementia clients. VD clients in the nonday-care group showed a decrease from 18.4 to 14.9.

2. Overall Effect of Reminiscence Groups for Persons With Dementia

Whereas Group 1 did not show an increase in MMSE nor HDS-R (MMSE $15.2 \rightarrow 15.1$; HDS-R $12.0 \rightarrow 11.0$), Groups 2 and 3 showed an increase in both the MMSE and the HDS-R (MMSE $18.2 \rightarrow 19.4$; HDS-R $14.9 \rightarrow 16.7$). As to the change of MMSE, significant differences were found between Group 4 and Groups 2 and 3 ($p < 0.01$). Significant differences were also found between Group 1 and Groups 2 and 3 ($p < 0.05$). As to the change of HDS-R, positive effects were found between Group 1 and Groups 2 and 3 ($p < 0.05$), while there were no positive effects within any group.

3. Effect of Reminiscence Group for Individuals With Alzheimer Type Dementia

Group 2 did not show any significant effect in the MMSE or the HDS-R (MMSE $14.7 \rightarrow 15.6$; HDS-R $10.7 \rightarrow 12.7$).

4. Effect of Reminiscence Group for Persons With Vascular Dementia

A significant difference was found between Group 1 and Group 3 in terms of the MMSE score ($p < 0.05$). In addition, a significant difference was also found between Group 4 and Group 3 in MMSE ($p < 0.01$). In

HDS-R score, the same result was found as MMSE which showed a significant difference between Group 4 and group 3 ($p < 0.05$) and between Group 1 and Group 3 ($p < 0.05$).

CASE STUDY

Mr. A, 72-Year-Old Man With Vascular Dementia

Upon post-group evaluation interview, Mr. A clearly articulated his view on the functions of reminiscence. He added, "Given how I had spent my childhood without my parents around and my grandmother being the one taking care of me, till today I have always believed that my mother did not want me. But looking back, now that the group sessions are over, I sense that something is changing inside me. Although I did not speak a word about it in the group sessions here, without realizing, I find myself starting to rethink over back then that maybe my mother did not treat me as bad as I thought for such a long time." Mr. A's wife who overheard this comment, was quite surprised to hear his words and said to her husband: "I have been with him ever since we got married and along our way I have believed that his mother is kind-hearted and not like the cold-hearted person he describes. And so my heart broke as he talked about his mother by pushing her away from him. My dear, I have not expected to hear such words from you. I tell you, it seems that this group was not just simply a delighted gathering but more."

From the beginning of the pregroup interview, Mr. A talked about his childhood experiences. The focus of his reminiscing of childhood experiences tended to be on his grandparents and the house of his grandparents where he had lived. Over the group sessions, he barely talked about his parents, his mother herself, nor themes related to himself. As the session went on, the tendency for Mr. A to reminiscence in an evaluative way grew more than it did for others. The focus of the evaluation spread from his teenage years to present life, and what he wishes to do in the near future. For Mr. A, it was the process of looking back on his own evaluation of his life that led him to see the unresolved issues, namely, the relationship between him and his mother. Mr. A's wife had known her husband's ongoing feeling around his relationship with his mother, but, from respect for him, had never said a word about it. When she said to him, "I am glad to hear you say so. I have been waiting for this moment," he shyly and gently smiled back to his wife with tears in his eyes.

2. 84 Year-Old Woman With Alzheimer's Disease

At the very beginning of the pregroup interview, Ms. F was hesitant to be involved in social engagement, which reflected her withdrawn personality and nervous feeling towards others. When we showed Ms. F two pictures, one of a child formally dressed and the other of a wedding ceremony, Ms. F smiled and said, "How sweet." She then took the pictures in her hands and said in a whispering voice, "I wonder who this is . . ." From her calm eye movements and gentle smile, it was clear to us that the pictures invoked joyful feelings. As the social interaction went on, Ms. F began to communicate more. When we moved on to ask her about her hometown, she wrote down her address accurately and described the scenery of her hometown in detail for us. When we commented that she was lucky to have lived in such a peaceful place with fields laying across, she proudly replied with a gentle smile, "Indeed. It is such a nice place." We considered her smiles as an inner attempt to communicate to us upon understanding the give and take flow of the ongoing social interaction. While Ms. F's score was low (9 points) on MMSE, a scale that reflects language comprehension, Ms. F impressed us with her high ability to comprehend language. At the same time, the changes in Ms. F's ways of interacting during the interview led us to believe that for her participation in the group was a positive experience, with occasions to interact with others, and a joyful stimulant of reminiscence.

DISCUSSION

Although there was no evidence to suggest a significant effect of the reminiscence group on Alzheimer-type dementia in terms of cognitive function, we qualitatively examined five members who showed an increase in the MMSE and the HDS-R. These five members showed an elevation of 5 points or more in MMSE and HDS-R. For example, one group member showed an increase in MMSE from 19 to 22 and in HDS-R from 13 to 22. Yoshiyama and colleagues found that this elevation was shown only in HDS-R, in particular, in semantic category word fluency. In comparison with HDS-R, MMSE does not include any questions in semantic category word fluency. For instance, the same member as mentioned above showed an increase in this area from 0 to 3. Other members showed increases from 0 to 4, 2 to 5, 0 to 5, and one remained static at 1 to 1.

As to the results of the brief reminiscence function question, two members of Group 2 expressed in their response that the experience was valuable and they enjoyed the group. They also stated it was fun.

In terms of Group 3 (vascular dementia group), one of the members clearly responded to the question and he answered that the reminiscence experience for him was worthwhile because he was able to integrate his past and present. While it was difficult to address these questions to people with dementia, they were able to respond to the question and to evaluate the experience.

The LSI was given to people with dementia in order to evaluate the reminiscence approach. However, the LSI seemed more difficult to answer. In particular, few members responded to abstract questions so it was difficult to assess change. We might use the LSI in an interview with clients and families in order to determine their needs in life and in their present situation. In addition to the evaluation interview with clients and families, these evaluations by clients and family themselves were important. The client evaluation informed us of their need, satisfaction, and comments.

We used the Healthy Life Scale for evaluating the social interaction aspect of the members who took part in the reminiscence group, a total of 25 sessions over 13 weeks. The results of the evaluation showed improvement in the members' ways of interacting with others. A closer look at three periods over the group sessions, (1) immediately after starting, (2) the intermediate period, and (3) near the end, reveals that while improvement in the social interaction aspect can be observed across the periods, it is most prominent around the intermediate period and from then onward. We assume that the intermediate period of the group was the key point towards which the group dynamics were formed (as a sense of group membership grew in the participants), and around which fluency of communication and social interaction among the participants was supported and facilitated.

As to the group for people with vascular dementia, what was interesting was the way in which member's reminiscence was mediated. In many cases, rather than by stimuli of materials, goods, and tools, members' reminiscing was invoked and mediated through social interaction with other members, and through looking back on a particular scene, time, or theme.

For the members of this particular group, the functional role of materials, goods, and tools in reminiscing was limited in that they were not effective in invoking diversity of memories (such as "We used this to _____." "This is how we used this." "My mother would often buy this for me. I was so happy to get this."). To be more specific, rather than expressing personal and emotional feeling around the objects, the members made factual statements about the objects. Moreover, there were few cases where reminiscence of a specific object opened the way to further reminiscing.

One source for the ineffectiveness of the objects as a mediational tool for reminiscing may be due to the fact that the members learned the pattern of using objects as mediational tools for reminiscing and got too used to it as a repetitious routine. Nevertheless, we speculate that the main source of the ineffectiveness lies in the nature of the group population, specifically, the group as a particular setting of socializing.

The group was made up of people who go to nursing day care twice a week, and who live alone or with their family. Thus, in comparison with people who are long-term residents of nursing homes, the members and their cognitive functioning level do not differ much. They also were surrounded or exposed to various stimuli in their everyday life. Knowing the how-to of their basic everyday household tasks, some of the members even take part in housework. For them, then, what has changed now and what is missing from their previous lifestyle is the occasion and setting to socialize and communicate with others. Their lack of socialization also explains why the quality of each session for this group was denser and richer in quality, in comparison with the group of elderly persons in long-term care. The members of this group expected more than the joy and pleasure of interacting with others. They also sought self-actualization and self-disclosure.

19

Cognitive-Reminiscence Therapy for Depressed Older Adults in Day Hospital and Long-Term Care

Philippe Cappeliez

After decades of underdevelopment the field of psychotherapy for older adults was given a major impetus with the publication in the mid 1980s of several studies empirically supporting the efficacy and clinical usefulness of various approaches for the treatment of depression. In 1991 the National Institutes of Health in the United States convened a panel of experts in order to formulate a consensus and guiding principles for research and services in the domain of depression in late adulthood (NIH Consensus Development Conference on the Diagnosis and Treatment of Depression in Late Life; Schneider, Reynolds, Lebowitz, & Friedhoff, 1994). After reviewing empirical evidence from controlled trials, this panel concluded that psychotherapies are moderately efficacious and demonstrate enduring effects in the treatment of depression in older adults (Niederehe, 1994). Other reviewers (Gatz et al., 1998; Karel & Hinrichsen, 2000; O'Rourke & Hadjistavropoulos, 1997; Scogin & McElreath, 1994; Teri, Curtis, Gallagher-Thompson, & Thompson, 1994; Teri & McCurry, 1994) have since concurred that a variety of psychotherapies, among them cognitive-behavioral, interpersonal, psychodynamic, and reminiscence bring about statistically and clinically significant improvements in depressive symptoms in older depressed clients and that they are all equal in terms of efficacy. However, as Karel and Hinrichsen (2000) aptly noted, one should remain cautious regarding the generalization of these results since the body of evidence about the efficacy of psychotherapeutic interventions is restricted to studies which were conducted with relatively healthy, community-residing, White older adults in their 60s and 70s.

These efforts have largely been directed at establishing the clinical utility of psychotherapy by controlled clinical trials. In this initial step it made logical sense to evaluate approaches which have been empirically supported for the treatment of younger depressed adults. Several authors have suggested adaptations to the delivery of psychotherapy (Knight, 1996; Latour & Cappeliez, 1994; Zeiss & Steffen, 1996). For instance, the need to adjust the tempo and the contents of sessions taking into account age-associated cognitive changes has been mentioned. Although more general issues such as the influence of generational differences on the meaning and scope of depression, and on the purpose and language of psychotherapy have been raised, there has been limited systematic consideration given to the specificity of older clients, in particular in the cognitive and emotional domains (Knight, 1996; Logsdon, 1995; Steuer & Hammen, 1983; Zeiss & Steffen, 1996). In this context, reminiscence therapy occupies a unique place among psychotherapies for older adults. It is the only one specifically conceived with the older adult in mind and it is not typically employed with younger populations. As Knight and McCallum (1998) wrote, clinical experience suggests that older adults tend to adopt an integrative stance (reminiscence, life review) in therapy, which makes it difficult to focus exclusively on the present in cognitive-behavior therapy with these clients. Additionally we recognize that, for a number of older adults, in particular those persons who are physically limited and live in institutions, the monotonous nature of current life experiences constitutes a real challenge for cognitive-behavioral interventions, which characteristically depend on real-life experiments for correcting cognitive and behavioral patterns. By contrast, memories constitute a large reservoir of experiences on which to effect these therapeutic changes. Unfortunately the theory supporting reminiscence interventions for depression in late adulthood had been poorly developed. We have attempted to fill that void with the goal of laying the ground for a better practice.

This chapter is organized in the following way. The first section presents the characteristic features of integrative and instrumental reminiscences, which are at the heart of the intervention, and the processes of integrative and instrumental reminiscences in the therapeutic context. The second section is devoted to research examining the efficacy and effectiveness of this form of psychotherapy integrating reminiscence and cognitive interventions for helping depressed older adults.

INTEGRATIVE AND INSTRUMENTAL REMINISCENCE FOR THE TREATMENT OF DEPRESSION

We have pursued the integration of cognitive and reminiscence approaches at the theoretical and practical level (Cappeliez & Watt, in press; Watt & Cappeliez, 1995, 1996, 2000). Our starting point was the demonstration that two types of reminiscence, namely *integrative* and *instrumental* reminiscences, appear singularly related to positive adaptation among older adults (Wong & Watt, 1991). Wong (1995) suggests the following typify integrative reminiscence: acceptance of the past as having meaning and value; acceptance of negative experiences and integration with the present; reconciliation of ideal with reality; reconciliation with conflictual events of the past; recall of experiences which contributed to the development of personal values and meaning of life; elaboration of a sense of coherence through past and present. In comparison, instrumental reminiscence is characterized by contents such as; recall of life objectives and goal-directed activities; use of past experiences for current problem solving; recall of episodes of coping with life challenges.

Our analysis of integrative and instrumental reminiscences has gone one step beyond a content-based characterization of reminiscence. We have recruited the help of contemporary cognitive theories of depression to better understand, and then facilitate, the processes by which integrative and instrumental reminiscence specifically lead to improvement of depression in older adults (Watt & Cappeliez, 1995).

THE PROCESSES OF THERAPEUTIC INTEGRATIVE REMINISCENCE

In the context of therapy for depression, integrative reminiscence provides an opportunity to re-interpret certain events of the past, their causes and their short-term and long-term consequences. The person has a chance to reappraise thoughts and beliefs concerning the self that were crystallized on the negative. In this way, integrative reminiscence directly addresses both the contents and the cognitive processes which cognitive theory and therapy consider crucial in depression. Table 19.1 presents the major processes and outcomes of the intervention.

In integrative reminiscence, negative views of the self and tacit rules for interpreting life experiences, which constitute the basic elements of depressogenic schemas, are uncovered and submitted to reappraisal and restructuring. Integrative reminiscence is different from simple narrative recall of past events. It frames an effort to determine the impact

TABLE 19.1   Processes and Outcomes in Integrative
Reminiscence Intervention

Processes	Outcomes
Constructive reappraisal of causes of losses, failures, problems in relationships, with distantiation and contextualisation	Reduction of global, internal, and stable causal attributions for negative life events
Cognitive reprocessing of successes and failures from various life periods and in various domains of functioning	Development of more constructive thoughts and beliefs about the self, the world, and the future
Review of development of personal values, commitments, and objectives through the entire life	Enhancement of self-esteem through identification of renewed and/or additional sources of personal worth
Recall of difficult experiences which were overcome	Reduction of hopelessness by increase in sense of control
Reappraisal of negative events in terms of personal meaning	Elaboration of life meaning and purpose

and meaning of events through the lens of present knowledge, perspective, and concerns, with a view of fostering adaptation. In the same
way, integrative reminiscence targets thoughts and beliefs that the
person maintains about herself or himself and attributions regarding
causes and consequences of negative personal events of the past. To
counteract the tendency of the depressed person to denigrate all positive feedback and concentrate on the negative, integrative reminiscence
intervention solicits a contextualized recall of events. This identification
and exploration of the various factors contributing to the earlier life
event enables the development of alternative perceptions and interpretations. Opening up such a new array of possibilities combats excessive self-criticism or self-blame to the extent it is accompanied by a
more balanced re-attribution of respective responsibilities among self
and others, as well as a consideration of circumstances and context.
This distantiation allows for a revision of certain actions and decisions
in more relative terms. Basic acknowledgement of the attenuating
characteristic of certain external circumstances and agents contributes
to weaken conclusions often drawn in rigid terms of personal morality
or negative comparisons with others.

Together with instrumental reminiscence, as we will see later, integrative reminiscence uses the rich repertoire of older adults' memories as vehicles for accessing personal thoughts and theories. These contents constitute a rich terrain for cognitive restructuring, and allow older adults to check negative ruminations on a closed past. This richness of contents provided by memories contrasts with the reduction in quantity and variety of physical and social stimulation experienced by a number of older adults in their current life circumstances. This is particularly relevant for older persons who experience sensory, cognitive, and physical limitations and who live in institutional settings. This reduced "surface of contact" with the physical and social environments presents a difficulty for cognitive-behavioral therapists who normally turn to current life experiences of the depressed patient for identifying and correcting negative thought patterns and attitudes. The concerted use of materials from memories in reminiscence interventions provides a way to circumvent these limitations.

A distinctive advantage of integrative reminiscence is that it addresses the entire lifespan and considers both manifestations and effects of thoughts, attitudes, and beliefs in the various domains of functioning. This focus allows for the therapeutic work to target on reevaluation of life events in terms of scale of values, purpose, and personal meaning. Given that it addresses life in a synthetic fashion, integrative reminiscence provides a means to weave cognitive threads which bring out a sense of continuity and coherence. This approach thus constitutes a useful tool for the questioning of components of depressogenic schemas.

THE PROCESSES OF THERAPEUTIC INSTRUMENTAL REMINISCENCE

Instrumental reminiscence intervention aims at fostering the recall of situations that called for adaptation. These can be specific events such as the death of a loved one, or it can be chronic situations such as problems related to physical illness. Globally, this mode of reminiscence involves the recall of actions taken in order to cope with the problematic situation, at both behavioral and cognitive levels. The therapeutic edge comes from reviewing and detailing the phases of the adaptation process using the steps of problem solving strategy as a guide. First, questions are directed at specifying the nature of the problematic situation by which the person was confronted. Second, the person is invited to recall the reactions and the plans developed for coping with the situation. For instance, this may involve constructive strategies such as seeking social support and scaling down expectations, or more passive ones such as avoiding the issue, or focusing on the worst. Finally, these responses to the critical event are analysed and discussed in terms of outcomes and consequences on the person's life, using both short- and long-term perspectives. The stance is relativist, considering both advantages and disadvantages of chosen solutions. Table 19.2 presents the major processes and outcomes of instrumental reminiscence intervention.

In addition to reevoking specific instances of adaptation and demonstrations of competence, this process allows for a review of life objectives at a more global level. From this review of adaptations from different life periods, life objectives appear clearly as the threads connecting these adaptations. This process opens the way for reframing. Indeed, the person can take the time to reflect that these life objectives have evolved through the various life stages and have been transformed by circumstances and persons. In this sense, the stressful experience that triggered the current depression can be considered as another of these moments when a revision of objectives might be in order, given the changes in needs and resources. This places the adaptive process in the context of lifespan development.

TABLE 19.2   Processes and Outcomes in Instrumental Reminiscence Intervention

Processes	Outcomes
Recall of episodes of problem-solving and positive adaptation	Increase in sense of control over life situations Change in primary appraisal of stressful events, from threat to challenge Improvement in sense of self-efficacy
Recall of specific strategic steps used to solve particular problems, including formulation, generation of alternative solutions, decision-making, and outcome assessment of chosen solution	Increase in problem-focused, and decrease in avoidance-based, coping strategies
Review of the adequacy of past and present life goals and accomplishments	Reassessment of objectives in function of sense of personal worth

Therapeutic instrumental reminiscence shares a number of features with problem-solving therapy (Nezu, Nezu, & Perri, 1989). The recall of life episodes characterized by such adaptations can help the depressed older person to rekindle a sense of self-esteem, control, and self-efficacy. At the practical level, the recall of strategies leading to adaptation, even a partial one, can facilitate the reactivation of these strategies in order to cope with current difficulties. Promoted throughout is the idea that if it has worked for you in the past, it is likely to work again now. The emphasis is placed on the crucial contribution of the person in this adaptation process (internal attribution).

This approach is grounded in a reappraisal of difficult life situations as challenges rather than threats or catastrophes. A dynamic, problem-focused orientation replaces an adaptation characterized by paralysis or avoidance. These strategies emerge from the experiences of the person and not from the repertoire of the therapist. This serves to empower the client. The person rediscovers a series of capacities and skills, which he/she did not think were available anymore. At the level of self-representation, this approach reinforces a feeling of self-efficacy and competence. In a positive feedback loop, improved self-esteem and sense of control reinforce a problem-solving approach to life difficulties. This effect contributes to increased motivation and engagement in the therapy process.

Instrumental reminiscence intervention provides an interesting complement to cognitive therapy for depression, which is typically concerned with helping the person cognitively restructure negative thoughts and attitudes (see Kunz, chapter 17, this volume). Memories associated with positive affect can be recruited in the intervention, to the extent it provides contents for cognitive work aimed at identifying and reactivating coping strategies together with the feeling of being "capable".

EMPIRICAL SUPPORT FOR INTEGRATIVE AND INSTRUMENTAL REMINISCENCE THERAPIES

On the basis of these theoretical considerations (Watt & Cappeliez, 1995), we developed standardized integrative and instrumental reminiscence interventions. Space limitations only allow a succinct description of these. Our initial format, which we submitted to empirical test, proposed six weekly sessions of 90-minute duration, and with groups constituting 2–4 clients and 1 or 2 therapists. Each session had a particular theme which served as a focal point for exchanges. The selected themes, announced one week in advance so that participants could be prepared, were: family history, life accomplishments, major life turning points, history of loves and hates, stress experiences, and life meaning and purpose. Participants were invited to write short answers to prompt questions related to the theme and bring this document as a starting point for exchange with the group at the subsequent session. Following the model of cognitive-behavioral therapy, sessions are structured and they follow a prescribed agenda. The therapist starts with a brief recapitulation of the main points of the previous session. He/she questions participants about its impact on the past week, with particular attention paid to attempts at applying cognitive and behavioral strategies previously discussed. One participant volunteers to report a memory or set of linked memories in relation to the theme. In our experience, a typical session allows for the discussion of 2 or 3 memories from as many participants. Through open-ended questioning, the therapist helps the person to reprocess the memory consistent with the therapeutic principles enunciated above. In brief, in the integrative modality, the therapist uses cognitive techniques to help the person develop a more balanced perspective on the recalled event and its consequences. Through gentle probing he/she challenges the attached negative thoughts and beliefs and tries to open up the field of interpretations. He/she steers the person to recall experiences that provide a sense of meaning and purpose, and that demonstrate a sense of continuity between the participant's sense of self in the past and beliefs now. In the instrumental modality, the therapist focuses on difficult situations which have taxed coping resources. Emphasis is placed on strategies used for coping, on processes rather than on results, and on effects in the long term. The goal of the therapist is to help the person identify the constructive strategies and apply these skills to currently challenging situations. All along the therapist reinforces the image of competence and self-trust which the person's efforts evidence. The instrumental modality also focuses on memories related to goal-directed activities, the attainment of objectives, and their revision in function of new circumstances. Typically the therapist writes down progressively the main points to capture everyone's attention. Before someone else gets an opportunity to report a memory, the therapist invites comments from participants and summarizes the key points. The last minutes of the meeting are devoted to exchanges about the affective impact of the session and the commonalities and differences in participants' experiences.

Our previous work (Watt & Cappeliez, 2000) demonstrated that, at least with a relatively small and homogeneous sample, both integrative and instrumental reminiscence interventions were successful in alleviating depression (respectively 58% and 56% of participants showed clinically significant improvement). Thus, there is initial empirical support for the *efficacy* of this form of intervention. Yet, *effectiveness* still needs to be addressed. As Lebowitz (1997) underlined, whereas efficacy studies investigate treatment in highly controlled conditions with carefully selected samples of patients, studies on effectiveness evaluate a given treatment in a variety of settings such as, for instance, community agencies, long-term care units, and primary-care services. Samples in these studies are typically heterogeneous, including individuals with coexisting physical diseases, sensory and cognitive deficits, as well as other conditions which would normally justify exclusion from standard clinical trials. Moreover, in these *effectiveness* studies, treatment outcome is not only evaluated on symptomatic relief, but broadened to include changes in overall functioning, functional autonomy, and quality of life (Schneider, Reynolds, Lebowitz, & Friedhof, 1994).

We have taken this approach in our continuing examination of the clinical usefulness of cognitive-reminiscence therapy. We report here results obtained with older participants who benefited from the intervention in a long-term care institution, either as outpatients involved in a day hospital program, or as long-term residents in this institution. We examined treatment outcome on the following variables: depressive symptomatology, psychological well-being, activity involvement, cognitive functioning, and client's satisfaction with the service. Our hypotheses were that, in addition to reducing depressive symptomatology, the intervention would increase well-being and activity involvement, improve cognitive functioning, especially attention and memory, and that the clients would consider it a useful service.

METHOD

Participants

Six health care workers in the institution showed interest in participating in the intervention program and they participated in two half-day workshops aimed at familiarizing them with depression in older adults, the adaptive functions of reminiscence, and more specifically the theory and practice of cognitive-reminiscence intervention for depression. They were invited to identify those among their clients who presented with depression and could benefit from the intervention. They further informed selected clients about the service. A clinical psychologist interviewed those who consented for a pretherapy assessment involving the variables and instruments described below.

We report here on 16 participants (13 day hospital outpatients; 3 permanent residents of the institution). Average age was 72 years (range: 55–96), with 6 patients (38%) over the age of 75. Thirty-eight percent were married, 44% widowed, and 18% divorced. In terms of education, 19% had completed elementary school, 38% secondary, and 43% had higher education. On a 4-point scale (bad, slightly bad, good, very good), 25% of the group described their health as bad, and 63% as slightly bad. The Mini Mental Status Examination average score was 27.3, indicative of good neurocognitive functioning.

Intervention

Space limitations do not allow a detailed account of the intervention. In addition to the descriptions provided above, interested readers can find further information in other writings (Cappeliez & Watt, in press; Watt & Cappeliez, 1996, 2000). Since these early developments, we have made some adaptations to the therapy format. While keeping a 60–90 minute duration for our weekly sessions in the case of outpatients, we have reduced it to about 45 minutes with institutional residents who often present with cognitive and sensory limitations. We offer ten sessions in groups of 2–4 participants led by two therapists, with the occasional involvement of health care workers of the institution. While maintaining the typical structure and thematic organization of sessions, we have blended integrative and instrumental reminiscence interventions into a single therapy, which we now refer as cognitive-reminiscence therapy. We have reduced to four the number of themes for the sessions (i.e., my family of origin, my life turning points, my personal accomplishments, what I learned about my strengths and would like to share), while systematically devoting two consecutive sessions to each theme.

Measures

Evaluations were conducted by a clinical psychologist who met with each prospective participant individually within the two weeks preceding the start of the intervention (pretherapy assessment) and during the three weeks following the end of the intervention (posttherapy assessment).

Mini-Mental Status Examination (MMSE, Folstein, Folstein, & McHugh, 1975). This instrument assesses a series of cognitive functions, such as orientation, memory, and attention for the purpose of screening for cognitive impairment. A score lower than 25 (maximum score = 30) is considered a good indication of significant cognitive deficits. It is widely used for the purpose of screening for dementia (see reviews by Tombaugh & McIntyre, 1992).

Geriatric Depression Scale (GDS, Yesavage et al., 1983). This self-report scale contains 30 items representing depressive symptoms of geriatric depression. Each item is answered by "yes" or "no" (maximum score = 30). Used for assessing the severity of depressive symptomatology, it is considered as the best all-around self-report depression scale available at present with utility across a broad range of geriatric populations (Pachana, Gallagher-Thompson, & Thompson, 1994). Scores between 0–10 are considered as indicative of no depression, 11–20 of mild to moderate depression, and 21–30 of moderate to severe depression.

Memorial University of Newfoundland Scale of Happiness (MUNSH, Kozma & Stones, 1980). This scale is a measure of psychological well-being. It contains 5 positive affect (PA) items, 5 negative affect (NA) items, 7 items of positive experience (PE), and 7 items of negative experience (NE). Each item is answered by "yes" (2 points), "no" (0 points) or "do not know" (1 point). Scores are calculated as PA + PE – (NA + NE), and range from –24 to +24, recoded in this case from 0 (lowest happiness) to 48 (highest happiness). Internal consistency, test-retest reliability, and convergent and discriminant validity are reported as satisfactory (Kop, 1993; Kozma & Stones, 1980).

Memorial University of Newfoundland Activities Inventory–Short Version (MUNAIS, Stones & Kozma, 1986, 1989). This 12-item questionnaire measures activity propensity, i.e. activities in which the respondent habitually engages in the physical, social, and cognitive domains. The response format is yes (2)/no (1). Scores range from 12 (inactive) to 24 (very active). Internal consistency and temporal stability have been reported, as well as structural analysis (Stones & Kozma, 1989). This questionnaire is appropriate for the evaluation of activity involvement of persons living independently in the community, but not for persons living in an institution. Consequently, we report here only data obtained from the 13 outpatient participants.

Cognitive Assessment Scale for the Elderly (CASE, (Geneau & Taillefer, 1995), a screening tool for cognitive impairments in old age, is designed to offer a psychometrically valid compromise between very short screening instruments and more extensive neuropsychological assessment batteries. It is a useful tool for monitoring the effectiveness of a therapeutic intervention. The CASE is composed of 103 items, grouped into ten different cognitive ability categories: (1) Temporal Orientation; (2) Spatial Orientation; (3) Attention-Concentration and Calculation; (4) Immediate Recall; (5) Language; (6) Remote Memory; (7) Judgment and Abstraction; (8) Agnosia; (9) Apraxia; (10) Recent Memory. Each set of tasks produces a score on a 10-point scale, plus an overall score varying from 0-100. The MMSE items are distributed into the above categories. The CASE was subjected to an extensive process of validation and normalization, with samples of population in various geographical locations, both in Canada and in the United States.

Client Satisfaction Questionnaire (CSQ, Larsen, Attkisson, Hargreaves, & Nguyen, 1979). In the version used here, this 8-item questionnaire assesses consumer satisfaction with health services (amount and quality, outcome, adequacy with respect to needs, general satisfaction). There are four response choices for each question, scored 1 (not satisfied) to 4 (very satisfied). Total scores range from 8–32. The good psychometric properties (validity and reliability) of the instrument have made it popular for the evaluation of satisfaction with services (Larsen, Attkinson, Hargreaves, & Nguyen, 1979; Sabourin & Gendreau, 1988).

RESULTS

Depressive Symptomatology

There was a statistically significant reduction in self-reported depressive symptoms at the conclusion of the intervention. The mean score on the GDS changed from 15.6 (SD = 5.6) pretherapy to 10.2 (SD = 4.3) posttherapy (t = 6.28, p < .001). Put in more telling terms, 10 out of the 16 participants (63%) presented a score in the nondepressed range at the end of the intervention. Before the intervention started, six participants had a score above 21, which is indicative of moderate-severe depression. After the intervention, four had scores between 10 and 14, indicative of mild depression.

Psychological Well-Being

There was a slight increase in well-being, which failed to reach statistical significance. Mean well-being score evolved from 27.9 (SD = 11.3) pretherapy to 30.7 (SD = 12.5) posttherapy (t = −1.18, p = .26), with great variability on this measure as indicated by the standard deviations.

Activity Propensity

There was a minimal increase in activity propensity, which failed to reach statistical significance. Mean activity propensity score passed from 17.0 (SD = 3.1) pretherapy, and 17.7 (SD = 2.8) posttherapy (t = −1.81, p = .10).

Cognitive Functioning

Although small, the improvement in cognitive functioning between the beginning and the end of the intervention was statistically significant.

Mean score on the full scale changed from 85.7 (SD = 6.2) pretherapy to 88.1 (SD = 7.4) posttherapy (t = −2.25, p < .05). Although a more detailed analysis of changes in attention and memory (scores on the 4 subtests of attention-concentration, immediate recall, remote memory, recent memory) did not reach significance level, it suggested that change in these processes accounted for much of the difference. Mean subtotal score on the 4 subscales was 33.3 pretherapy (SD = 4.3) and 35.0 posttherapy (SD = 4.0) (t = −2.03, p = .06).

Client Satisfaction

The level of satisfaction with the service was very high (Mean = 29.7).

DISCUSSION

The intervention had the effect of relieving depression, as evidenced by a decrease in depressive symptoms from the range of mild depression to the cut-off level. It did not have a marked influence on psychological well-being, at least at the time of assessment following the intervention. It is plausible that improvement in positive affect might occur with some delay after depressive symptoms have abated. Also it must be noted that the MUNSH contains long-term dispositional components which typically show temporal stability. This might have contributed to the lack of change observed on this measure. The intervention had little influence on the level of activity involvement. The dichotomous nature of the coding system (yes/no) appears to lack the sensitivity necessary for a measure of change. It might be useful to use a 4-point scale (never, sometimes, often, frequently) in future studies. Additionally, it might be useful to target the evaluation on the motivational component of activity involvement, rather than on pure performance. The slight increase in overall cognitive functioning may be attributed to improvements in attention and memory. Further research should refine the investigation of change in these processes as a result of reminiscence intervention. Finally the participants were very satisfied and considered the intervention highly valuable.

CONCLUSION

This research represents a modest first step in the direction of documenting the clinical usefulness of cognitive-reminiscence therapy in real-life clinical settings where presenting physical and emotional problems are complex and interventions can rarely be delivered in pure form. We are presently engaged in efforts aimed at further adaptations of these interventions for long-term care patients with more significant cognitive limitations and more severe distress.

Obviously we need more information on the processes underlying these therapeutic changes. This improved understanding would lead us to a better identification of treatment conditions/components and client characteristics associated with improvement, absence of improvement, or deterioration. Given the high prevalence of depressive conditions among some subgroups of older adults (e.g., physically ill, living in institution, caregivers), the development and delivery of better psychotherapeutic interventions should be regarded as a great priority. We believe that these efforts should be grounded in sound theoretical and empirical bases. This also includes a more complete understanding of the contributions of the various functions of reminiscence to adaptation in later life (Bluck & Levine, 1998; Cappeliez & O'Rourke, 2000; Parker, 1995, 1999).

20

The End of the Story

Barbara K. Haight and Jeffrey D. Webster

Because of changes in the field over the past few years, we have organized *Critical Advances in Reminiscence Work* slightly differently than our previous volume of 1995, *The Art and Science of Reminiscing*. The literature review stands alone. We tie new ideas together by using a conceptual issues section and, in so doing, underline the fact that our theory has still not been developed. We need good theory to guide our studies more than ever because the growth in reminiscence work is from several paradigms, adding a new richness to the field but also adding more confusion as we each try to explore reminiscence work from our own interests, stance, or belief system. Although the paradigms differ in many respects, each of the paradigms has two things in common, and we might start from there when looking at theory. One of the commonalities is the use of memory; the other is the production of a story. The story is ubiquitous throughout this volume.

When Paul Harvey shares an ending at the completion of a radio broadcast, he usually announces in a resonant tone "and now we have the end of the story." As this volume ends, we see extraordinary growth in the interest in memories and reminiscence work. With the end of this particular story, we see an opportunity for many new beginnings such as the creation of appropriate theory to guide future work. To date, most authors still use Erikson's developmental theory to provide structure to their work. Erikson's theory has been described as forward looking by some for its ability to address old age, and chauvinistic by others because it was developed around a male world. As we move into diverse age groups of storytellers, there must be other theories developed, at least for those who have not transgressed the ages of man. Bluck and Alea's chapter suggests one possible direction, namely a closer connection with the experimental area of autobiographical memory.

In section three we explore developmental and sociocultural issues. There is a tremendous amount of work in the examination of the process of life review and reminiscence. Much of the work uses Webster's Reminiscence Functions Scale to look at the process by age or gender. Although solely the purview of older people for many years, scholars now recognize that children have a story, and have the same need to tell it as a way of establishing their identity. The child may use the story to achieve closeness to a parent or to understand an event. Over time, children have always loved stories and they have learned from them. For example, the tale of the ugly duckling teaches children that we are not all beautiful in the same way. That story was probably based on fact, but embellished with imagination to develop a point and to hold the listener's attention. Some of our stories are developed the same way. The story is the teacher, it can provide a route to self-knowledge and spirituality, and it can manage self-esteem. And, best of all, everyone has a story to share.

We are looking at a narrative revolution combined with other reminiscence work. Narrative methodology has become a significant part of the social sciences. The story which is produced through the narrative process cuts across many methodological perspectives in psychotherapy and offers an alternative to positivistic paradigms in research. The use of the story is what the last half of the 90s has been about. Telling one's story is the crux of the matter from which counseling and self-learning derive. Several authors speak of the story as a way of gaining an identity because, in fact, one's story is one's individual identity. We have evolved from focusing on the process of getting the story through life review and reminiscing to the product itself.

The product provides us with large amounts of data and feelings and emotions that inform us about individuals. The evolving tale is a discourse of connected happenings with which we can relate and which we can use to learn about others. It is a way to interpret experience and gets us more involved in the research process or the counseling process as we become engaged with the teller. After hearing the narrative, we recontextualize the story to reach new understandings of an event or group of people. The story becomes the object of inquiry. The reminiscers are teachers as they make meaning of their life events and the actions surrounding them. The outcome product provides rich sources of data for qualitative analysis. A distinct and growing trend is epitomized in section four as we learn from the stories of special populations such as war veterans and survivors of abuse and violence.

Researchers and practitioners often talk of the story as retelling or restorying, thus implying that this is not the first time the story has been told but, in fact, it has been restructured to fit the occasion. We accept that the story may vary as it is informed by the present and becomes more dim in the past. Whereas we can remember being asked many times in the past, "How do you know it is true?" We accept now that the story is informed by experience and may be always changing, but still true to the teller. The outcome product can illustrate and elucidate a certain way of life such as in a case study. In this book, case studies are used to test theory, and to point out that different interpretations of the same data set are always possible.

In section five, we are exposed to the clinical applications of reminiscence work. Reminiscence or life review is espoused for people with depression, with Alzheimer's disease, and as a tool for transformation. The use of the process is surfacing in psychotherapy as counselors learn the techniques of narrative therapy and seek the story surrounding the problem that has been responsible for sending the individual to counseling. Remembering and retelling is the task of reconciliation as the telling serves the people who tell it. The process of reminiscing exposes the self, while allowing one to redo the self. In the telling of one's life story, insights are gained and integrated into the whole. The process is nonthreatening and provides a sense of intimacy through sharing. There is more give and take in reminiscence work and more sharing of emotions that are spontaneous and true. The life review or reminiscence process will provide new roads to new truths that reveal themselves to the teller and the listener as they proceed with their interchange.

Distinct changes over the last few years are many and include the greater use of longer and more introspective periods of reminiscing that are similar to life review. There is a more widespread use of descriptions of the methodologies. Now one knows what one is evaluating when one reads a clinical or research report. Certain groups are targeted to tell their story or to examine the efficacy of the process, and there are many more waiting to be targeted. The process has been used with people who have AIDS, Alzheimer's disease, and depression. Through reminiscence processes, we have learned about drug addiction, ethnicity, and younger people. The processes themselves are being applied in practice and earn third-party payment. There are numerous experts and multiple books, whereas a few years ago, few people were active in this field. Finally, as indicated in the foregoing review, people are interested in the product and realize the importance of the story for knowledge and analysis.

Qualitative studies presently outnumber quantitative studies. Qualitative analysis has its own paradigms such as ethnography, case study methodology, hermeneutical analysis, and life history analysis. These paradigms must not be ignored and should be applied properly when planning reminiscence work so that qualitative studies have the same degree of rigor as quantitative studies. There is a need for considerable clarification when discussing the process of reminiscence in terms of a qualitative analysis. For example, the life review or reminiscing is the process used to produce the product, the story, or history. Thus, the story is the outcome product. It is the body of the reported story that is available for analysis. The story can be analyzed in many ways depending on the questions asked of it and provides a rich data source. Qualitative methodology is particularly useful when we know little about the subject. With a qualitative methodology, we can learn from the subjects themselves and, again, the story is the teacher.

New Directions

Reviewing what has been written in the field should provide us with new direction. Where have we been and where are we going? We can summarize today's work by saying the work is geared toward understanding the process of reminiscence and life review, but there is so much more to do. We need to identify what factors in reminiscence work make it therapeutic and what factors are potentially harmful. Case studies should be written about unsuccessful endeavors to provide more succinct guidelines for the use of the modalities with special populations. For example, when gaining an oral history about the holocaust, is any thought given to the effect the telling of the story has on the individual historian? Each new study presents us with new questions to answer. This is an exciting time for people in the field.

Cautions include an ongoing need to differentiate our methods. We need to look at the intended purpose of the use of reminiscence and tailor our use accordingly. More outcome research is necessary to examine therapeutic efficacy with selected populations. Attention must be paid to ethnicity, for example, do all cultures like to tell their stories, or is it taboo in some? We need to marry our paper and pencil outcome measures to more accurate physiological measures such as changes in immune response. We need to continue to ask ourselves these questions: Is there a science and what is the art? What are the guiding theories? Is our process well-defined? Can the research be applied in practice? And, for practice, we need to provide interested entrepreneurs and scholars with coursework.

We then need to develop certification for practice that is agreed upon by an international body. We have the means to do that. Presently there is the International Institute of Reminiscence and Life Review, whose board, in conjunction with other disciplines, could serve as this body and enable us to join our work with the work of others. Certification would ensure a certain universal standard for delivering the intervention. A universal standard would facilitate good practice.

TABLE 20.1   Discipline-Specific Reminiscence

Discipline	Vehicle	Sample Concern/Focus
Performing Arts	Play, drama, poetry	How to express lifestories in dramatic form
Humanities	Novel, autobiography	What are the meaning and purpose of life memories?
Oral History	Documented historical memories	Whose "truth" is accepted?
Anthropology	Cultural significance of memories	Do cultural myths and personal memories interact?
Sociology	Social contexts/institutions	Does place shape memory; can memory shape institutions?
Psychology	Person variables	How do gender, age, and personality shape memory?
Psychiatry, Nursing, Clinical Social Work	Life review, narrative therapy	Is the process therapeutic?
Neurophysiology	FMRIs, CAT scans	Where is reminiscence "located"?

A final observation suggests an additional important direction for future research, namely, interdisciplinary awareness, if not coopera-tion. The chapters in this volume, as previously noted, represent many disciplines. It strikes us that reminiscence has been investigated across a breadth of levels, or hierarchy, of specificity. Table 20.1 illustrates the layers of disciplines that have investigated facets of reminiscence behavior. As can be seen, reminiscence components can be investi-gated from the levels of the performing arts to neurophysiology, an incredible range spanning Shakespeare to chemicals. We suspect that future reminiscence work will increasingly become cognizant of findings from related disciplines. This growing awareness will foster insights which may be potentially beneficial to each domain. The Bornat and Bluck and Alea chapters are examples of the fruitfulness of this interdis-ciplinary awareness.

We can speculate about a time when we have the precision to ask and answer more refined questions which connect multiple levels of analysis. For instance, do the tacit norms of a subculture (sociology) influence the types of negative emotional memories recalled in a group setting (psychology) which, in turn, reciprocally influence particular neurotransmitter activation in certain subcortical structures such as the hippocampus or amygdala (neurophysiology)?

In concluding our previous 1995 edited volume, *The Art and Science of Reminiscing: Theory, Research, Methods, and Applications,* we stated: "Given the emerging conceptual clarity, availability of assessment tools, and specific research questions, the future vitality of reminiscence research and application seems guaranteed" (p. 286). The work of the authors in the present volume provides ample justification for continued optimism.

The natural, ubiquitous, and powerful nature of personal memories continues to attract researchers and practitioners from diverse areas to the reminiscence fold. We predict that this infusion from multiple perspectives will create the type of challenges and opportunities that will ultimately strengthen the field. We look forward to participating in these critical advances in reminiscence work in the future.

References

Adams, J., Bornat, J., & Prickett, M. (1998). Discussing the present in stories about the past. In A. Brechin, J. Katz, S. Peace, & J. Walmsley (Eds.), *Care matters: Concepts, practice and research.* London: Sage.

Adams, S., Kuebli, J., Boyle, P., & Fivush, R. (1995). Gender differences in parent-child conversations about past emotions: A longitudinal investigation. *Sex Roles, 33,* 309–323.

Alexander, B., Rubinstein, R., Goodman, M., & Luborsky, M. (1991). Generativity in cultural context: The self, death and immortality as experienced by older American women. *Ageing and Society, 11,* 417–442.

Ainsworth, M. D. S., Blehar, M., Waters, E., & Wall, S. (1978). *Patterns of attachment: A psychological study of the strange situation.* Hillsdale, NJ: Erlbaum.

Alheit, P. (1995). Biographical learning: Theoretical outline, challenges, and contradictions of a new approach in adult education. In P. Alheit, A. Born-Wojciechowska, E. Brugger, & P. Dominice (Eds.), *The biographical approach in adult education.* Vienna: Verband Wiener Volksbildung.

Andersen, S. M., Reznik, I., & Chen, S. (1997). The self in relation to others: Cognitive and motivational underpinnings. In J. G. Snodgrass, & R. L. Thompson (Eds.), The self across psychology: Self-recognition, self-awareness, and the self-concept, *Annals of the New York Academy of Sciences, 818.* New York: The New York Academy of Sciences.

Andrews, M. (1997). Life review in the context of acute social transition: The case of East Germany. *British Journal of Social Psychology, 36,* 273–290.

Aquilar, R., & Nightingale, N. (1994). The impact of specific battering experiences on the self-esteem of abused women. *Journal of Family Violence, 9,* 35–45.

Ashida, S. (2000). The effect of reminiscence music therapy sessions on changes in depressive symptoms in elderly persons with dementia. *Journal of Music Therapy, 37*(3), 170–182.

Atchley, R. C. (1999). *Continuity and adaptation in aging.* Baltimore, MD: The Johns Hopkins University Press.

Atkinson, D. (1997). *An auto/biographical approach to learning disability research.* Ashgate, England: Aldershot.

Atkinson, D., Kim, A., Ruelas, S., & Lin, A. (1999). Ethnicity and attitudes toward facilitated reminiscence. *Journal of Mental Health Counseling, 21*(1), 66–81.

Atkinson, R. (1995). *The gift of stories: Practical and spiritual applications of autobiography, life stories, and personal mythmaking.* Westport, CT: Bergin & Garvey.

Bachman, R. (1994). *Violence against women.* Washington, DC: U. S. Department of Justice.

Baddeley, A. (1987). But what the hell is it for? In M. M. Gruneberg, P. E. Morris, & R. N. Sykes (Eds.), *Practical aspects of memory: Current research and issues* (pp. 3–18). Chichester, England: Wiley.

Baddeley, A., & Hitch, G. (1974). Working memory. In G. H. Bower (Ed.), *The psychology of learning and motivation* (pp. 47–89). New York: Academic Press.

Baltes, P. B. (1987). Theoretical propositions of life-span developmental psychology: On the dynamics between growth and decline. *Developmental Psychology, 23,* 611–626.

Baltes, P. B., Lindenberger, U., & Staudinger, U. M. (1998). Life-span theory in developmental psychology. In R. M. Lerner (Ed.), *Handbook of child psychology, Vol. 1* (pp. 1029–1143). New York: Wiley.

Bandler, R., & Grinder, J. (1975). *The structure of magic: A book about language and therapy I.* Palo Alto: Science and Behavior Books, Inc.

Bandura, A. (1997). *Self-efficacy: The exercise of control.* New York: W. H. Freeman and Company.

Bandura, A. (1993). Perceived self-efficacy in cognitive development and functioning. *Educational Psychologist, 28,* 117–148.

Barclay, C. R. (1996). Autobiographical remembering: Narrative constraints on objectified selves. In D. C. Rubin (Ed.), *Remembering our past: Studies in autobiographical memory* (pp. 94–125). Cambridge: Cambridge University Press.

Barron, F. (1953). An ego-strength scale which predicts response to psychotherapy. *Journal of Consulting Psychology, 17,* 327–333.

Basow, S. A. (1992). *Gender stereotypes and roles.* Belmont, CA: Brooks-Cole.

Bateson, M. (1989). *Composing a life.* New York: Atlantic Monthly Press.

Bateson, M. C. (2000). *Full circles, overlapping lives: Culture and generation in transition.* New York: Random House.

Baumgarten, H. (1992). Remembrance of things past: Music, autobiographical memory, and emotion. *Advances in Consumer Research, 19,* 613–620

Baur, S. (1994). *Confiding.* New York: HarperCollins.

Bayles, K. A., & Kasznicak, A. W. (1987). *Communication and cognition in normal aging and dementia.* Austin, TX: Proed, Inc.

Beach, R. (1990). The creative development of meaning: Using autobiographical experiences to interpret literature. In D. Bogdan, & S. Straw (Eds.), *Beyond communication: Reading comprehension and criticism* (pp. 211–235). Portsmouth, NH: Boynton/Cook Heinemann.

Beck, J. (1995). *Cognitive therapy: Basics and beyond.* New York: Guilford.

Beck, A. T. (1967). *Depression: Clinical, experimental and therapeutic aspects.* New York: Harper & Row.

Bender, M., Bauckham, P., & Norris, A. (1999). *The therapeutic purposes of reminiscence.* London: Sage.

Benoit, D., & Parker, K. (1994). Stability and transmission of attachment across three generations. *Child Development, 65,* 1444–1456.

Bergman, S., & Surrey, J. L. (1997). The woman-man relationship: Impasses and possibilities. In J. U. Jordan (Ed.), *Women's growth in diversity* (pp. 260–287). New York: Guilford.

Bernstein, D. (1998). Voluntary and involuntary access to autobiographical memory. *Memory, 6,* 113–141.

Berry, J. M., & West, R. L. (1993). Cognitive self-efficacy in relation to personal mastery and goal setting across the life span. *International Journal of Behavior Development, 16,* 351–379.

Bianchi, E. C. (1982). *Aging as a spiritual journey.* New York: The Crossroads Publishing Company.

Birkerts, S. (1994). *The Gutenberg elegies: The fate of reading in an electronic age.* New York: Fawcett.

Birren, J. E. (1990). Spiritual maturity in psychological development. *Journal of Religious Gerontology, 7*(1/2), 41–53.

Birren, J. E. (1987). The best of all stories. *Psychology Today,* May 1987. 91–92.

Birren, J. E., & Birren, B. A. (1996). Autobiography: Exploring the self and encouraging development. In J. E. Birren, G. M. Kenyon, J. E. Ruth, J. J. F. Schroots, & T. Svensson (Eds.), *Aging and biography: Explorations in adult development* (pp. 283–299). New York: Springer Publishing Company.

Birren, J. E., & Cochran, K. N. (2001). *Telling the stories of life through guided autobiography groups.* Baltimore: The Johns Hopkins University Press.

Birren, J. E., & Deutchman, D. E. (1991). *Guiding autobiography groups for older adults: Exploring the fabric of life.* Baltimore: Johns Hopkins University Press.

Birren, J. E., & Hedlund, B. (1986). Contribution of autobiography to developmental psychology. In N. Eisenberg (Ed.), *Perspectives in developmental psychology* (pp. 1–35). New York: John Wiley.

Birren, J. E., Kenyon, G., Ruth, J-E., Schroots, J., & Svensson, T. (Eds.) (1996). *Aging and biography: Explorations in adult development.* New York: Springer Publishing Company.

Blatner, A. (2000a). *Foundations of psychodrama: History, theory and practice* (4th Ed.). New York: Springer Publishing Company.

Blatner, A. (2000b). *Deepening personal meaning.* Conference Paper Presentation. "Personal Meaning in the New Millennium," An International Conference. Vancouver, British Columbia, July 13–16, 2000.

Bluck, S. (2001). Autobiographical memories: A building block of life narrative. In G. Kenyon, P. Clark , & B. de Vries (Eds.), *Narrative gerontology: Theory, research, and practice.* New York: Springer Publishing Company.

Bluck, S., & Habermas, T. (2000). The life story schema. *Motivation and Emotion, 24,* 121–147.

Bluck, S., Habermas, T., & Rubin, D. (2001). The functions of autobiographical memory. Manuscript in preparation.

Bluck, S., & Levine, L. J. (1998). Reminiscence as autobiographical memory: A catalyst for reminiscence theory development. *Ageing and Society, 18,* 185–208.

Bluck, S., Levine, L. J., & Laulhere, T. M. (1999). Autobiographical remembering and hypermnesia: A comparison of older and younger adults. *Psychology and Aging, 14,* 671–682.

Bogdan, D. (1990). Toward a rationale for literary literacy. *Journal of Philosophy of Education, 24,* 211–224.

Bogdan, D., & Straw, S. (Eds.), *Beyond communication: Reading comprehension and criticism.* Portsmouth, NH: Boynton/Cook Heinemann.

Booth, W. (1988). *The company we keep: An ethics of fiction.* Berkeley: University of California Press.

Borland, K. (1991). 'That's not what I said': interpretive conflict in oral narrative research. In S. B. Gluck, & D. Patai (Eds.), *Women's words: The feminist practice of oral history* (pp. 63–75). New York and London: Routledge.

Bornat, J. (1994). Introduction. In J. Bornat (Ed.), *Reminiscence reviewed* (pp. 1–7). Buckingham, U. K. : Open University Press.

Bornat, J. (1989). Oral history as a social movement: Reminiscence and older people. *Oral History, 17. 2,* 16–24.

Bornat, J., & Chamberlayne, P. (1999). Reminiscence in care settings: Implications for training. *Adult Education. 14. 3,* 277–295.

Bowker, L. H. (1988). Religious victims and their religious leaders: Services delivered to one thousand battered women by the clergy. In G. Hoteling, D. Finkelhor, J. T. Kilpatrick, & M. Straus (Eds.), *Coping with family violence: Research and policy perspectives* (pp. 229–234). Newbury Park, CA: Sage.

Bowlby, J. (1988). A secure base: Clinical applications of attachment theory. London: Routledge.

Brady, M. (1990). Redeemed from time: Learning through autobiography. *Adult Education Quarterly, 41*(1), 43–52.

Bretherton, I. (1990). Open communication and internal working models: Their role in the development of attachment relationships. In R. A. Thompson (Ed.), *Nebraska Symposium on Motivation, Vol. 36., Socioemotional Development* (pp. 59–113). Lincoln: University of Nebraska Press.

Bretherton, I., Fritz, J., Zahn-Waxler, C., & Ridgeway, D. (1986). Learning to talk about emotions: A functionalist perspective. *Child Development, 57,* 529–548.

Brewer, W. F. (1996). What is recollective memory? In D. C. Rubin (Ed.), *Remembering our past: Studies in autobiographical memory* (pp. 19–66). Cambridge: Cambridge University Press.

Brewer, W. F. (1986). What is autobiographical memory? In D. C. Rubin (Ed.), *Autobiographical memory* (pp. 25–49). Cambridge: Cambridge University Press.

Bridges, W. (1980). *Transitions: Making sense of life's changes.* Toronto: Addison-Wesley.

Brooker, D., & Duce, L. (2000). Well-being and activity in dementia: A comparison of group reminiscence therapy, structured goal directed group
activity and unstructured time. *Aging & Mental Health, 4,* 354–358.

Brooks, D. (1999). The meaning of change through therapeutic enactment in
psychodrama. Doctoral Dissertation. University of British Columbia,
Department of Counselling Psychology.

Brooks, P. (1985). *Reading for the plot: Design and intention in narrative.* New
York: Vintage.

Brown, L. S. (1994). *Subversive dialogues.* New York: Basic Books.

Brown-Shaw, M., Hunter, C., Peck, E., & Westwood, M. (1998). Theme assignment: Your war experience. In M. J. Westwood (Ed.), *Life review program
for Canadian veterans.* Report for Veterans Affairs Canada and The Royal
Canadian Legion. November, 1998 (pp. 1–37).

Brown-Shaw, M., Westwood, M., & de Vries B. (1999). Integrating personal
reflection and group-based enactments. *Journal of Aging Studies, 13*(1),
109–118.

Bruce, D. (1989). Functional explanations of memory. In L. W. Poon, D. C.
Rubin, & B. A. Wilson (Eds.), *Everyday cognition in adulthood and late
life* (pp. 44–58). Cambridge: Cambridge University Press.

Bruner, J. (1999). Narratives of aging. *Journal of Aging Studies, 13*(1), 7–9.

Bruner, J. (1996). *The culture of education.* Cambridge, MA: Harvard University
Press.

Bruner, J. (1990). Acts of meaning. Cambridge, MA: Harvard University Press.

Bruner, J. (1987). Life as narrative. *Social Research, 54*(1), 11–32.

Bruner, J. (1986). *Actual minds, possible worlds.* Cambridge, MA: Harvard
University Press.

Bruner, J., & Weisser, S. (1991). The invention of self: Autobiography and its
forms. In D. Olson, & N. Torrance (Eds.), *Literacy and orality.* Cambridge:
Cambridge University Press.

Buckner, J. P., & Fivush, R. (2000). Gendered themes in family reminiscing.
Memory, 8, 401–412.

Burnett, M. N. (1996). Suffering and sanctification: The religious context of
battered women's syndrome. *Pastoral Psychology, 44*(3), 145–149.

Burnside, I. (1995). Themes and props: Adjuncts for reminiscence therapy
groups. In B. K. Haight, & J. D. Webster (Eds.), *The art and science of
reminiscing: Theory, research, methods, and applications.* Washington,
DC: Taylor and Francis.

Burnside, I. (1990). Reminiscence: An independent intervention for the elderly.
Issues in Mental Health Nursing, 11, 33–48.

Butler, R. N. (1995). Foreward: The life review. In B. K. Haight, & J. D. Webster
(Eds.), *The art and science of reminiscing: Theory, research, methods, and
applications.* Washington, DC: Taylor and Francis.

Butler, R. N. (1963). The life review: An interpretation of reminiscence in old
age. *Psychiatry Journal for the Study of Interpersonal Processes, 26,* 65–76.

Butler, R. N., & Lewis, M. (1982). *Aging and mental health* (3rd ed.). St. Louis:
C. V. Mosby.

Camp, C. J., Judge, K. S., Bye, C. A., Fox, K. M., Bowden, J., Bell, M., Valencic, K., & Mattern, J. M. (2000). An intergenerational program for persons with dementia using Montessori methods. *American Journal of Psychiatry, 157,* 1915–1924.

Campbell, J. D. (1990). Self-esteem and clarity of self-concept. *Journal of Personality and Social Psychology, 59,* 538–549.

Canary, D. J., Emmers-Sommer, T. M., & Faulkner, S. (1997). *Sex and gender: Differences in personal relationships.* New York: Guilford.

Cappeliez, P., & O'Rourke, N. (2000). *Personality traits and existential concerns as predictors of the functions of reminiscence in older adults.* Manuscript submitted for publication.

Cappeliez, P., & Watt, L. M. (in press). L'apport de la rétrospective de vie à la thérapie cognitive de la dépression. In L. Bizzini, & C. Favre (Eds.), *Thérapies cognitives de la personne âgée: Aspects psychothérapeutiques, psychogérontologiques, et neuropsychologiques.* Paris: Masson.

Carmin, C. N., Pollard, C. A, & Ownby, R. L. (1999). Cognitive behavioral treatment of older adults with obsessive-compulsive disorder. *Cognitive and Behavioral Practice, 6,* 110–119.

Casey, E. (1987). *Remembering: A phenomenological study.* Bloomington, IN: Indiana University Press.

Cassidy, J., & Shaver, P. R. (1999). *Handbook of attachment: Theory, research and clinical applications.* New York: Guilford.

Chandler, S. (2001). *Theorizing interpretation in context: A feminist ethnographic study of an elder women's writing group.* Unpublished Ph. D. dissertation. Wayne State University, Detroit, MI.

Charmé, S. (1984). *Meaning and myth in the study of lives: A Sartrean perspective.* Philadelphia: University of Pennsylvania Press.

Chethimattam, J. (1982). The place and role of the aged in the Hindu perspective. In F. Tiso (Ed.), *Aging: Spiritual perspectives.* Lake Worth, FL: Sunday Publications.

Clark, M., & Anderson, B. (1967). *Culture and aging: An anthropological study of older Americans.* Springfield, IL: C. C. Thomas.

Clayton, V. (1975). Erikson's theory of human development as it applies to the aged: Wisdom as contradictive cognition. *Human Development, 18,* 119–128.

Coates, J. (1988). Gossip revisited: Language in all-female groups. In J. Coates, & D. Cameron (Eds.), *Women in their speech communities.* London and New York: Longman.

Cohen, G. (1998). The effects of aging on autobiographical memory. In C. P. Thompson, D. J. Hermann, D. Bruce, J. D. Read, D. G. Payne, & M. P. Toglia (Eds.), *Autobiographical memory: Theoretical and applied perspectives* (pp. 105–123). Mahwah, NJ: Erlbaum.

Cohen, G. (1989). Memory in the real world. Hove, England: Erlbaum.

Cohen, G. D. (2000). Two intergenerational interventions for Alzheimer's disease patients and families. *American Journal of Alzheimer's Disease, 15,* 137–142.

Cole, T., & Winkler, M. (Eds.) (1994). *The Oxford book of aging*. New York: Oxford University Press.

Coleman, P. G. (1999). Creating a life story: The task of reconciliation. *The Gerontologist, 39,* 133–139.

Coleman, P. G. (1986). *Ageing and reminiscence processes: Social and clinical implications*. Chichester: Wiley.

Coleman, P. G. (1974). Measuring reminiscence characteristics from conversation as adaptive features of old age. *International Journal of Aging and Human Development, 5,* 281–294.

Coleman, P. G., & Mills, M. A. (1997). Listening to the story. Life review and the painful past in day and residential care settings. In L. Hunt, M. Marshall, & C. Rowlings (Eds.), *Past trauma in late life: European perspectives on therapeutic work with older people* (pp. 171–183). London: Jessica Kingsley.

Commonwealth Fund (1993). *First comprehensive national health survey of American women finds them at significant risk*. New York: Author.

Connerton, P. (1989). *How societies remember*. New York: Cambridge University Press.

Conway, M. A. (1997). The inventory of experience: Memory and identity. In J. W. Pennebaker, D. Paez, & B. Rime (Eds.), *Collective memory of political events. Social psychological perspectives* (pp. 21–45). Mahwah, NJ: Lawrence Erlbaum.

Conway, M. A. (1996). Autobiographical knowledge and autobiographical memories. In D. C. Rubin (Ed.), *Remembering our past: Studies in autobiographical memory* (pp. 67–93). Cambridge: Cambridge University Press.

Conway, M. A. (1992). A structural model of autobiographical memory. In M. A. Conway, D. C. Rubin, H. Spinnler, & W. A. Wagenaar (Eds.), *Theoretical perspectives on autobiographical memory* (pp. 207–221). Dordrecht, The Netherlands: Kluwer Academic Publishers.

Conway, M. A. (1990). *Autobiographical memory: An introduction*. Philadelphia: Open University Press.

Conway, M. A., & Haque, S. (1999). Overshadowing the reminiscence bump: Memories of the struggle for independence. *Journal of Adult Development, 6*(1), 35–44.

Conway, M. A., & Holmes, A. (2000). *Psychosocial stages and the availability of autobiographical memories*. Manuscript submitted for publication.

Conway, M. A., & Pleydell-Pearce, C. W. (in press). The construction of autobiographical memories in the self-memory system. *Psychological Review*.

Cook, A. J. (1999). Cognitive-behavioral pain management for elderly nursing home residents. *Journals of Gerontology: Series B: Psychological Sciences and Social Sciences, 53B*(1), 51–59.

Cook, E. A. (1998). Effects of reminiscence on life satisfaction of elderly female nursing home residents. *Health Care for Women International, 19,* 109–118.

Craik, F. I. M., & Jennings, J. M. (1994). Human memory. In F. I. M. Craik, & T. A. Salthouse (Eds.), *The handbook of aging and cognition* (pp. 51–109). Hillsdale, NJ: Lawrence Erlbaum Associates.

Craik, F. I. M., & Lockhart, R. S. (1972). Levels of processing: A framework for memory research. *Journal of Verbal Learning and Verbal Behavior, 11,* 671–684.

Cram, F., & Paton, H. (1993). Personal possessions and self-identity: The experiences of elderly women in three residential settings. *Australian Journal on Aging, 12,* 19–24.

Crites, S. (1971). The narrative quality of experience. *Journal of the American Academy of Religion, 39*(3), 291–311.

Crowther, M. R., & Zeiss, M. (1999). Cognitive-behavior therapy in older adults: A case involving sexual functioning. *Journal of Clinical Psychology, 55*(8), 961–975.

Csikszentimihalyi, M., & Beattie, O. (1979). Life themes: A theoretical and empirical exploration of their origins and efforts. *Journal of Humanistic Psychology, 19*(1), 45–63.

Csikszentimihalyi, M., & Rathunde, K. (1990). The psychology of wisdom: An evolutionary interpretation. In R. Sternberg (Ed.), *Wisdom: Its nature, origins, and development* (pp. 25–51). New York: Cambridge University Press.

Csikszentmihalyi, M., & Rochberg-Halton, E. (1981). *The meaning of things: Domestic symbols and the self.* Cambridge, UK: Cambridge University Press.

Cupitt, D. (1991). *What is a story?* London: SCM Press.

Dai, Y., Zhang, S., Yamamoto, J., Ao, M., Belin, T. R., Cheung, F., & Hifumi, S. S. (1999). Cognitive behavioral therapy of minor depressive symptoms in elderly Chinese Americans: A pilot study. *Community Mental Health Journal, 35*(6), 537–542.

Daneman, M., & Carpenter, P. A. (1980). Individual differences in working memory and reading. *Journal of Verbal Learning and Verbal Behavior, 19,* 450–466.

Dannefer, D. (1984). Adult development and social theory: A paradigmatic reappraisal. *American Sociological Review, 49,* 100–116.

Darlington, R. B. (1990). *Regression and linear models.* New York: McGraw-Hill.

Davis, P. J. (1999). Gender differences in autobiographical memory for childhood emotional experiences. *Journal of Personality and Social Psychology, 76,* 498–510.

Davis, R., & Smith, D. (1995). Domestic violence reforms: Empty promises or fulfilled expectations. *Crime and Delinquency, 4*(4), 541–552.

de Vries, B., Birren, J. E., & Deutchman, D. E. (1995). Method and uses of the guided autobiography. In B. K. Haight, & J. D. Webster (Eds.), *The art and science of reminiscing* (pp. 165–177). Washington, DC: Taylor and Francis.

de Vries, B., Birren, J. E., & Deutchman, D. E. (1990). Adult development through guided autobiography: The family context. *Family Relations, 39,* 3–7.

de Vries, B., Blando, J., & Walker, L. (1995). An exploratory analysis of the content and structure of the life review. In B. K. Haight, & J. D. Webster (Eds.), *The art and science of reminiscing: Theory, research, methods, and applications.* Washington, DC: Taylor and Francis.

de Vries, B., Bluck, S., & Birren, J. E. (1993). The understanding of death and dying in a life-span perspective. *The Gerontologist, 33*(3), 366–372.

de Vries, B., & Watt, D. (1996). A lifetime of events: Age and gender variations in the life story. *International Journal of Aging and Human Development, 42,* 81–102.

Dittmar, H. (1992). *The social psychology of material possessions.* New York: St. Martin's Press.

Dittmar, H. (1989). Gender identity-related meanings of personal possessions. *British Journal of Social Psychology, 28,* 159–171.

Dixon, R. A., & Gould, O. N. (1998). Younger and older adults collaborating on retelling everyday stories. *Applied Developmental Science, 2,* 160–171.

Dunn, J., Brown, J., & Beardsall, L. (1991). Family talk about feeling states and children's later understanding of others emotions. *Developmental Psychology, 27,* 448–455.

Dunbar, D., & Jeannechild, C. (1996). Stories and strengths of women who leave battering relationships. *Journal of Couple Therapy, 6*(1–2), 149–173.

Dyl, J., & Wapner, S. (1996). Age and gender differences in the nature, meaning, and function of cherished possessions for children and adolescents. *Journal of Experimental Child Psychology, 62,* 340–377.

Eakin, J. (1985). *Fictions in autobiography: Studies in the art of self-invention.* Princeton, NJ: Princeton University Press.

Ebersole, P. P. (1978). A theoretical approach to the use of reminiscence. In I. Burnside (Ed.), *Working with the elderly: Group processes and technique* (pp. 139–154). North Scituate, MA: Duxbury Press.

Edwards, D., & Middleton, D. (1988). Conversational remembering and family relationships: How children learn to remember. *Journal of Social and Personal Relationships, 5,* 3–25.

Eisenberg, A. (1985). Learning to describe past experience in conversation. *Discourse Processes, 8,* 177–204.

Ellison, C. G. (1991). Religious involvement and subjective well-being. *Journal of Health and Social Behavior, 32,* 80–99.

Erikson, E. H. (1982). *The life cycle completed.* New York: Norton.

Erikson, E. H. (1968). *Identity, youth, and crisis.* New York: Norton.

Erikson, E. H. (1963). *Childhood and society* (2nd ed.). New York: Norton.

Erikson, E. H., Erikson, J. M., & Kivnick, H. Q. (1986). *Vital involvement in old age.* New York: W. W. Norton and Company.

Farrant, K., & Reese, E. (2000a). Maternal style and children's participation in reminiscing: Stepping stones in children's autobiographical memory development. *Journal of Cognition and Development, 1,* 193–225.

Farrant, K., & Reese, E. (2000b). *Attachment security and early mother-child reminiscing: A developmental exploration.* Submitted manuscript.

Ferguson, N. (Ed.) (1997). *Virtual history: Alternatives and counterfactuals.* London: Papermac.

Field, N. P., Nichols, C., Holen, A., & Horowitz, M. J. (1999). The relation of continuing attachment to adjustment in conjugal bereavement. *Journal of Consulting and Clinical Psychology, 67,* 212–218.

Fink, B., & Forster, P. (1992). Die Bedeutung materieller Dinge in der häuslichen Lebensumwelt [Meaning of things at home]. *Zeitschrift für Pädagogische Psychologie, 6,* 115–131.

Fischer, A. (Ed.) (2000). *Gender and emotion*. New York: Cambridge University Press.

Fitzgerald, J. M. (1996). Intersecting meanings of reminiscence in adult development and aging. In D. C. Rubin (Ed.), *Remembering our past: Studies in autobiographical memory* (pp. 360–383). Cambridge: Cambridge University Press.

Fivush, R. (in press). Owning experience: The development of subjective perspective in autobiographical memory. In C. Moore, & K. Skene (Eds.), *The development of a temporally extended self.*

Fivush, R. (1998). Gendered narratives: Elaboration, structure and emotion in parent-child reminiscing across the preschool years. In C. P. Thompson, D. J. Herrmann, D. Bruce, J. D. Read, D. G. Payne, & M. P. Toglia (Eds.), *Autobiographical memory: Theoretical and applied perspectives* (pp. 79–104). Hillsdale, NJ: Erlbaum.

Fivush, R. (1998a). The functions of event memory: Some comments on Nelson and Barsalou. In U. N. E. Winograd (Ed.), *Remembering reconsidered: Ecological and traditional approaches to the study of memory* (pp. 277–282). Cambridge: Cambridge University Press.

Fivush, R. (1993). Emotional content of parent-child conversations about the past. In C. A. Nelson (Ed.), *The Minnesota symposium on child psychology: Memory and affect in development* (pp. 39–77). Hillsdale, NJ: Erlbaum.

Fivush, R. (1991). The social construction of personal narratives. *Merrill-Palmer Quarterly, 37,* 59–82.

Fivush, R. (1989). Exploring sex differences in the emotional content of mother-child talk about the past. *Sex Roles, 20,* 675–691.

Fivush, R., Brotman, M., Buckner, J. P., & Goodman, S. (1997). *Gender differences in parent-child emotion narratives*. Submitted manuscript.

Fivush, R., & Buckner, J. P. (in press). Constructing gender and identity through autobiographical narratives. In R. Fivush, & C. Haden (Eds.), *Autobiographical memory and the construction of a narrative self: Developmental and cultural perspectives*. Hillsdale, NJ: Erlbaum.

Fivush, R., & Buckner, J. P. (2000). Gender, sadness and depression: Developmental and socio-cultural perspectives. In A. H. Fischer (Ed.), *Gender and emotion: Social psychological perspectives* (pp. 232–253). Cambridge: Cambridge University Press.

Fivush, R., & Fromhoff, F. (1988). Style and structure in mother-child conversations about the past. *Discourse Processes, 11,* 337–355.

Fivush, R., Haden, C., & Adam, S. (1995). Structure and coherence of preschoolers' personal narratives over time: Implications for childhood amnesia. *Journal of Experimental Child Psychology, 60,* 32–56.

Fivush, R., Haden, C., & Reese, E. (1996). Remembering, recounting and reminiscing: The development of memory in a social context. In D. Rubin (Ed.), *Remembering our past: Studies in autobiographical memory* (pp. 341–359). Cambridge: Cambridge University Press.

Fivush, R., & Reese, E. (1992). The social construction of autobiographical memory. In M. A. Conway, D. C., Rubin, H. Spinnler, & W. A. Wagenaar (Eds.), *Theoretical perspectives on autobiographical memory*. Dordrecht, The Netherlands: Kluwer Academic Publishers.

Fivush, R., & Vesudeva, A. (2000). *Reminiscing and relating: Correlations among maternal reminiscing style, attachment and emotional warmth.* Manuscript in preparation.

Folstein, M., Folstein, S., & McHugh, P. (1975). A Mini-Mental State: A practical method for grading the cognitive state of patients for the clinician. *Journal of Psychiatric Research, 12,* 189–198.

Frankl, V. E. (1984). *Man's search for meaning: An introduction to logotherapy.* New York: Touchstone/Simon and Schuster.

Freeman, M. (1993). *Rewriting the self: History, memory, narrative.* London: Routledge.

Frisch, M. (1998). Oral history and Hard Times: a review essay. In R. Perks, & A. S. Thomson (Eds.), *The oral history reader* (pp. 29–37). London: Routledge.

Frisch, M. (1990). *A shared authority: Essays on the craft and meaning of oral and public history.* Albany, NY: State University of New York Press.

Fromholt, P., & Larsen, S. F. (1991). Autobiographical memory in normal aging and primary degenerative dementia (dementia of Alzheimer type). *Journal of Gerontology: Psychological Sciences, 46*(3), P85–91.

Fry, P. S. (2000). Validation of a "Global Self-Efficacy Scale" with eight domain-specific efficacy subscales. Unpublished scale. Langley, BC: Trinity Western University.

Fry, P. S. (1995). A conceptual model of socialization and agentic trait factors that mediate the development of reminiscence styles and their health outcomes. In B. K. Haight, & J. D. Webster (Eds.), *The art and science of reminiscing: Theory, research, methods, and applications* (pp. 49–60). Washington, DC: Taylor and Francis.

Fry, P. S. (1983). Structured and unstructured reminiscence training and depression among the elderly. *Clinical Gerontologist, 1,* 15–37.

Fry, P. S., & Barker, L. A. (in press). Female survivors of abuse and violence: Their regrets of action and inaction in coping. *Journal of Interpersonal Violence.*

Gallagher-Thompson, D., & Thompson, L. W. (1996). Applying cognitive-behavioral therapy to the psychological problems of later life. In, S. H. Zarit & B. G. Knight (Eds.), *A guide to psychotherapy and aging* (pp. 61–82). Washington DC: American Psychological Association.

Gardner, H. (1990). *Frames of mind: The theory of multiple intelligences.* San Francisco: Basic.

Garland, J. (1993). What splendour, it all coheres: Life review therapy with older people. In J. Bornat (Ed.), *Reminiscence reviewed* (pp. 21–31). Buckingham, England: Open University Press.

Gatz, M., Fiske, A., Fox, L. S., Kaskie, B., Kasl-Godley, J. E., McCallum, T. J., & Wetherell, J. L (1998). Empirically-validated psychological treatments for older adults. *Journal of Mental Health and Aging, 4,* 9–46.

Geertz, C. (1973). *The interpretation of cultures.* New York: Basic Books.

Geneau, D., & Taillefer, D. (1995). Le Protocole d'Examen Cognitif de la Personne âgée (PECPA-2). Communication presented at the 1er Colloque de Psychogériatrie du C. C. F. P., St-Hyacinthe, Québec.

Gergen, K. J., & Gergen, M. M. (1988). Narrative and the self as relationship. *Advances in Experimental Social Psychology, 21,* 17–56.

Gergen, K. J., & Gergen, M., M. (1983). Narratives of the self. In T. Sarbin, & E. Schiebe (Eds.), *Studies in social identity* (pp. 254–273). New York: Praeger.

Giambra, L. M. (1977). Daydreaming about the past: The time setting of spontaneous thought intrusion. *The Gerontologist, 17,* 35–38.

Gibson, F. (1998). *Reminiscence and recall: A guide to good practice.* London: Age Concern.

Gibson, F. (1993). What can reminiscence contribute to people with dementia? In J. Bornat (Ed.), *Reminiscence reviewed: Perspectives, evaluations, achievements* (pp. 46–60). Buckingham England: Open University Press.

Giddens, A. (1991). *Modernity and self-identity: Self and society in the late modern age.* Palo Alto, California: Stanford University Press.

Gigerenzer, G. (1997). Memory as knowledge-based inference: Two observations. In N. L. Stein, P. A. Ornstein, B. Tversky, & C. Brainerd (Eds.), *Memory for everyday and emotional events* (pp. 445–452). Mahway, NJ: Lawrence Erlbaum.

Glover, J. (1988). *I: The philosophy and psychology of personal identity.* London: Penguin.

Gluck, S. B., & Patai, D. (1991). *Women's words: The feminist practice of oral history.* New York and London: Routledge.

Goodall, H. (1994). Colonialism and catastrophe: Contested memories of nuclear testing and measles epidemics at Ernabella. In K. Darian-Smith, & P. Hamilton (Eds.), *Memory and history in twentieth century Australia.* Melbourne, Australia: Oxford University Press.

Graumann, C. F. (1986). Memorabilia, mementos, memoranda: Toward an ecology of memory. In F. Klix, & H. Hagendorf (Eds.), *Human memory and cognitive capabilities* (pp. 63–69). Amsterdam: Elsevier.

Grayson, K., & Shulman, D. (2000). Indexicality and the verification function of irreplaceable possessions: A semiotic analysis. *Journal of Consumer Research, 27,* 17–30.

Greenwald, A. (1980). The totalitarian ego: Fabrication and revision of personal history. *American Psychologist, 35,* 603–618.

Grinder, J., & Bandler, R. (1976). *The structure of magic: A book about language and therapy II.* Palo Alto: Science and Behavior Books, Inc.

Gubrium, J. (2001). Narrative, experience, and aging. In G. Kenyon, P. Clark, & B. deVries (Eds.), *Narrative gerontology: Theory, research, and practice.* New York: Springer Publishing.

Gubrium, J., & J. Holstein (1998). Narrative practice and the coherence of personal stories. *The Sociological Quarterly, 39,* 163–187.

Gutmann, D. (1994). *Reclaimed powers: Men and women in later life* (2nd ed.). Evanston, IL: Northwestern University Press.

Habegger, C. E., & Blieszner, R. (1990). Personal and social aspects of reminiscence: An exploratory study of neglected dimensions. *Activities, Adaptation & Aging, 14,* 21–38.

Haberlandt, K. (1999). *Human memory: Exploration and application.* Boston: Allyn and Bacon.

Habermas, J. (1984). *The theory of communicative action. Volume one: Reason and the rationalization of society.* Translated by T. McCarthy. Boston: Beacon Press.

Habermas, T. (1999b). *Uses of personal objects during and after the transition to university: The impact of relocation and interpersonal bonds.* Unpublished manuscript.

Habermas, T. (1999a). *Geliebte Objekte: Symbole und Instrumente der Identitätsbildung* [Personal objects: Symbols and instruments of identity-formation]. Frankfurt am Main, Germany: Suhrkamp.

Habermas, T., & Bluck, S. (2000). Getting a life: The development of the life story in adolescence. *Psychological Bulletin, 126,* 748–769.

Habermas, T., & Paha, C. (1999). *The development of causal coherence in life narratives across adolescence.* Unpublished manuscript.

Haden, C. A. (1998). Reminiscing with different children: Relating maternal stylistic consistency and sibling similarity in talk about the past. *Developmental Psychology, 34,* 99–114.

Haden, C. A., & Fivush, R. (1996). Contextual variation in maternal conversational styles. *Merrill-Palmer Quarterly, 42,* 200–227.

Haden, C. A., Haine, R., & Fivush, R. (1997). Developing narrative structure in parent-child conversations about the past. *Developmental Psychology, 33,* 295–307.

Haight, B. K. (1991). Reminiscing: The state of the art as a basis for practice. *International Journal of Aging and Human Development, 33,* 1–32.

Haight, B. K., & Dias, J. K. (1992). Examining key variables in selected reminiscing modalities. *International Psychogeriatrics, 4*(2), 279–290.

Haight, B. K., & Webster, J. D. (Eds.) (1995). *The art and science of reminiscing: Theory, research, methods, and applications.* Washington, DC: Taylor and Francis.

Hallowell, A. I. (1955). *Culture and experience.* Philadelphia: University of Pennsylvania Press.

Hampl, P. (1990). Memory and imagination. In J. McConkey (Ed.), *The anatomy of memory* (pp. 201–211). New York: Oxford University Press.

Han, J. J., Leichtman, M. D., & Wang, Q. (1998). Autobiographical memory in Korean, Chinese, and American children. *Developmental Psychology, 34,* 701–713.

Harley, K., & Reese, E. (1999). Origins of autobiographical memory. *Developmental Psychology, 35,* 1338–1348.

Harris, J., & Hopkins, T. (1993). Beyond anti-ageism: Reminiscence groups and the development of anti-discriminatory social work education. In J. Bornat (Ed.), *Reminiscence reviewed: Perspectives, evaluations, achievements* (pp. 75–83). Buckingham, England: Open University Press.

Harris, J. E. (1984). Remembering to do things: A forgotten topic. In J. E. Harris, & P. E. Morris (Eds.), *Everyday memory: Actions and absent-mindedness* (pp. 71–91). London: Academic Press.

Harris, J. L. (1998). *The source for reminiscence therapy.* East Moline, IL: LinguiSystems.

Harris, J. L. (1997). Reminiscence: A culturally and developmentally appropriate language intervention for older adults. *American Journal of Speech-
Language Pathology, 6,* 19–26.

Hautamaki, A., & Coleman, P. G. (2001). Explanation for low prevalence of
PTSD among older Finnish war veterans: Social solidarity and continued
significance given to wartime sufferings. *Aging & Mental Health, 5,*
165–174.

Havighurst, R., & Glasser, R. (1972). An exploratory study of reminiscence.
Journal of Gerontology, 27, 245–253.

Herman, J. (1992). *Trauma and recovery.* New York: Basic Books.

Hillman, J. (1975). The fiction of case history: A round. In J. Wiggins (Ed.),
Religion as story (pp. 123–173). New York: Harper & Row.

Hinchman, L., & Hinchman, S. (1997). *Memory, identity, community: The idea
of narrative in the human sciences.* Albany, NY: SUNY Press.

Hirst, W., Manier, D., & Apetroaia, I. (1997). The social construction of the
remembered self: Family recounting. In J. G. Snodgrass, & R. L. Thompson
(Eds.), *The self across psychology: Self-recognition, self-awareness, and
the self-concept, Annals of the New York Academy of Sciences, 818.* New
York: The New York Academy of Sciences.

Hochschild, A. R. (1990). Ideology and emotion management: A perspective
and path for future research (pp 117–142). In T. Kemper (Ed.), *Research
agendas in the sociology of emotions.* Albany, NY: State University of New
York Press.

Holliday, S., & Chandler, M. (1986). *Wisdom: Explorations in adult competence.* Basel, Switzerland: Karger.

Holmes, P. (1992). *The inner world outside: Object relations theory and psychodrama.* London and New York: Tavistock/Routledge.

Holstein, J., & Gubrium, J. (2000). *The self we live by: Narrative identity in a
postmodern world.* New York: Oxford University Press.

Hormuth, S. (1990). *The ecology of the self: Relocation and self-concept
change.* Cambridge, England: Cambridge University Press.

Howard, G. (1994). The stories we live by: Confessions by a member of the
species *homo fabulans* (man, the storyteller). In J. Lee (Ed.), *Life and story:
Autobiographies for a narrative psychology* (pp. 247–273). Westport, CT:
Praeger.

Huber, G. L. (1990). AQAD, Analyse qualitativer Daten mit Computerunter-
stützung. In *Grundlagen und Manual des Softwarepaketes AQAD.*
Schwangau: Verlag Ingeborg Huber.

Hudson, J. A. (1990). The emergence of autobiographic memory in mother-
child conversation. In R. Fivush, & J. A. Hudson (Eds.), *Knowing and
remembering in young children* (pp. 166–196). New York: Cambridge
University Press.

Huffman, C. M., & Weaver, K. A. (1996). Autobiographical recall and visual
imagery. *Perceptual and Motor Skills, 82,* 1027–1034.

Hunt, L., Marshall, M., & Rowlings, C. (Eds.) (1997). *Past trauma in late life:
European perspectives on therapeutic work with older people.* London:
Jessica Kingsley.

Hunt, N., & Robbins, I. (2001). The long-term consequences of war: The experience of World War II. *Aging & Mental Health, 5,* 183–190.

Hunt, N., & Robbins, I. (1998). Telling stories of the war: Aging veterans coping with their memories through narrative. *Oral History, 26,* 57–64.

Hyland, D. T., & Ackerman, A. M. (1988). Reminiscence and autobiographical memory in the study of the personal past. *Journal of Gerontology, 43,* P35–39.

Hyman, I. E., & Faries, J. M. (1992). The functions of autobiographical memory. In M. A. Conway, D. C. Rubin, H. Spinnler, & W. A. Wagenaar (Eds.), *Theoretical perspectives on autobiographical memory* (pp. 207–221). Dordrecht, The Netherlands: Kluwer Academic Publishers.

Janet, P. (1928). *L'Evolution de la mémoire et de la notion du temps* [The evolution of memory and the notion of time]. Paris: Cahine.

Jansari, A., & Parkin, A. J. (1996). Things that go bump in your life: Explaining the reminiscence bump in autobiographical memory. *Psychology and Aging, 11*(1), 85–91.

Jarho, L. (1991). Psychosocial aspects of war disabilities. Paper presented at the 20th General Assembly of the World Veterans Federation, Special Session: Psychosocial Effects of War and the Maintenance of Peace, October 20–24, 1991, Helsinki, Finland.

Jarho, L., & Saari, J. (1991). 50 years of medical care for disabled war veterans in Finland—still more than 20 years of work ahead. *WISMIC Newsletter, 3,* 14–15.

Joy, A., & Dholakia, R. R. (1991). Remembrances of things past. *Journal of Social Behavior and Personality, 6,* 385–402.

Jung, C. G., (1965). Memories, dreams, reflections. New York: Vintage.

Jung, C. G. (1933). Modern man in search of a soul. New York: Harcourt Brace Jovanovich.

Kaminsky, M. (1984). The uses of reminiscence: Discussion of the formative literature. *Journal of Gerontological Social Work, 7,* 137–156.

Kaminsky, M. (Ed.) (1984). *The uses of reminiscence: New ways of working with older adults.* New York: The Haworth Press.

Kamptner, N. L. (1991). Personal possessions and their meanings: A life-span perspective. *Journal of Social Behavior and Personality, 6,* 209–228.

Karel, M. J., & Hinrichsen, G. (2000). Treatment of depression in late life: Psychotherapeutic interventions. *Clinical Psychology Review, 20,* 707–729.

Kaufman, S. (1986). *The ageless self: Sources of meaning in late life.* New York: New American Library.

Kausler, D. H. (1994). *Learning and memory in normal aging.* San Diego: Academic Press.

Kawata, M., et al. (1998). Cognitive effects of day care and reminiscence group therapy on demented elderly. *Japanese Journal of Geriatric Psychiatry, Vol. 9,* 943–948.

Kegan, R. (1998). Transformation and development. Paper presentation at First National Conference on Transformative Learning: Changing Adult Frames of Reference. Teachers' College, Columbia University, April 16, 1998.

Kekes, J. (1983). Wisdom. *American Philosophical Quarterly, 20*(3), 277–286.

Keller. B. (1997). Memories of war and conflict: A theoretical frame for an interview study of men and women remembering the Third Reich and the Second World War in West Germany. *European Journal of Women's Studies, 4*(3), 381–387.

Keller, B. (1996). *Rekonstruktion von Vergangenheit.* Opladen, Germany: Westdeutscher Verlag.

Kenyon, G. M. (2000). Philosophical foundations of existential meaning. In G. Reker, & K. Chamberlain (Eds.), *Exploring existential meaning: Optimizing human development across the lifespan* (pp. 7–22). Thousand Oaks, CA: Sage.

Kenyon, G. M. (1996a). The meaning-value of personal storytelling. In J. E. Birren, G. M. Kenyon, J. E. Ruth, J. J. F. Schroots, & T. Svensson (Eds.), *Aging and biography: Explorations in adult development* (pp. 21–38). New York: Springer Publishing.

Kenyon, G. M. (1996b). Ethical issues in aging and biography. *Ageing and Society, 16*(6), 59–675.

Kenyon, G. M. (1991). *Homo viator:* Metaphors of aging, authenticity and meaning. In G. M. Kenyon, J. E. Birren, & J. J. F. Schroots (Eds.), *Metaphors of aging in science and the humanities* (pp. 17–35). New York: Springer Publishing.

Kenyon, G. M., Ruth, J.-E., & Mader, W. (1999). Elements of a narrative gerontology. In V. Bengston, & W. Schaie (Eds.), *Handbook of theories of aging* (pp. 40–58). New York: Springer Publishing.

Kenyon, G. M. (in press). Guided autobiography: In search of ordinary wisdom. In G. Rowles, & N. Schoenberg (Eds.), *Qualitative gerontology: Second Edition.* New York: Springer Publishing.

Kenyon, G. M., Clark, P., & de Vries, B. (Eds.) (2001). *Narrative gerontology: Theory, research, and practice.* New York: Springer Publishing.

Kenyon, G. M., & Randall, W. L. (1997). *Restorying our lives: Personal growth through autobiographical reflection.* Westport, CT: Praeger.

Kenyon, J. (1986). Evening sun. In *The boat of quiet hours: Poems by Jane Kenyon.* St. Paul, MN: Graywolf Press.

Kerby, A. (1991). *Narrative and the self.*

Kimmel, D. (1990). *Adulthood and aging: An interdisciplinary view.* New York: John Wiley.

Kintsch, W., & van Dijk, T. A. (1978). Toward a model of text comprehension and production. *Psychological Review, 85,* 363–394.

Klatsky, R. L. (1988). Theories of information processing. In L. Light, & D. M. Burke (Eds.), *Language, memory, and aging* (pp. 1–16). New York: Cambridge University Press.

Knight, B. G. (1996). *Psychotherapy with older adults* (2nd ed.). Thousand Oaks, CA: Sage.

Knight, B. G., & McCallum, T. J. (1998). Adapting psychotherapeutic practice for older clients: Implications of the contextual, cohort-based, maturity, specific challenge model. *Professional Psychology—Research & Practice, 29,* 15–22.

Koder, D. (1998). Treatment of anxiety in the cognitively impaired elderly: Can cognitive-behavior therapy help? *International Psychogeriatrics, 10*(2), 173–182.

Kohlstruck, M. (1997). *Zwischen Erinnerung und Geschichte, Der National-sozialismus und die jungen Deutschen.* Berlin: Metropol.

Kop, J.-L. (1993). La mesure du bien-être subjectif chez les personnes âgées. *Revue Européenne de Psychologie Appliquée, 43,* 271–277.

Kotre, J. (1990). *Outliving the self: Generativity and the interpretation of lives.* Baltimore, MD: Johns Hopkins University Press.

Kozma, A., & Stones, M.J. (1980). The measurement of happiness: Development of the Memorial University of Newfoundland Scale of Happiness (MUNSH). *Journal of Gerontology, 35,* 906–912.

Kropf, N., & Tandy, C. (1998). Narrative therapy with older clients: The use of a "meaning-making" approach. *Clinical Gerontologist, 18*(4), 3–16.

Kruse, A., & Schmitt, E. (2000). *Wir haben uns als Deutsche gefuhlt. Lebensruckblick und Lebenssituation judischer Emigranten und Lagerhaftlinge.* Darmstadt, Germany: Steinkopff.

Kunz, J. (1997). Enhancing quality of life for older adults. *Ed-Cetera, 2*(2), 6–7.

Kunz, J. (1991a). Case reports: Counseling approaches for disoriented older adults. *Illness Crisis and Loss, 1*(2), 91–96.

Kunz, J. (1991b). Reminiscence approaches utilized in counseling older adults. *Illness Crisis and Loss, 1*(4), 48–54.

Kunz, J. (1990). Reflections and memories: A counseling program for older adults. *Caring, 9,* 44–46.

Labov, W., & Waletzky, J. (1967). Narrative analysis. Oral versions of personal experience. In J. Helm (Ed.), Essays on the Verbal and Visual Arts. *Proceedings of the annual spring meeting, 1966.* Seattle and London: University of Washington Press.

Lakoff, G., & Johnson, M. (1980). *Metaphors we live by.* Chicago: University of Chicago Press.

Lamme, S., & Baars, J. (1993). Including social factors in the analysis of reminiscence in elderly individuals. *International Journal of Aging and Human Development, 37*(4), 297–311.

Lang, F. R., Staudinger, U. M., & Carstensen, L. (1998). Perspectives on socio-emotional selectivity in late life: How personality and social context do (and do not) make a difference. *Journals of Gerontology: Psychological Sciences, 53B,* P21–P30.

Larsen, D. L., Attkisson, C. C., Hargreaves, W. A., & Nguyen, T. D. (1979). Assessment of client-patient satisfaction: Development of a general scale. *Evaluation and Program Planning, 2,* 197–207.

Larsen, S. (1990). *The mythic imagination: Your quest for meaning through personal mythology.* New York: Bantam.

Lashley, M. E. (1993). The painful side of reminiscence. *Geriatric Nursing, 14,* 138–141.

Latour, D., & Cappeliez, P. (1994). Pretherapy training for group cognitive therapy with depressed older adults. *Canadian Journal on Aging, 13,* 221–235.

Lebowitz, B. D. (1997). Depression in the nursing home: Developments and prospects. In R. L. Rubinstein, & M. P. Lawton (Eds.), *Depression in long term and residential care: Advances in research and treatment* (pp. 223–233). New York: Springer Publishing.

Lehmann, A. (1983). *Erzählstruktur und Lebenslauf. Autobiographische Untersuchungen.* Frankfurt and New York: Campus.

Lehmann, A. (1980). Rechtfertigungsgeschichten. *Fabula, 21,* 56–69.

Leroi-Gourhan, A. (1965). *La geste et la parole.* Paris: Éditions Albin Michel.

Levine, L., Stein, N., Liwag, M. (1999). Remember children's emotions: Sources of concordant and discordant accounts between parents and children. *Developmental Psychology, 35,* 790–801.

Lewin, K. (1926). Untersuchungen zur Handlungs- und Affektpsychologie: I. Vorbemerkungen über die psychischen Kräfte und Energien und über die Struktur der Seele. *Psychologische Forschung, 7,* 294–329.

Lewis, K. (1999). Maternal style in reminiscing: Relations to child individual differences. *Cognitive Development, 14,* 381–399.

Leydesdorff, S. (1992). A shattered silence. The life stories of the Jewish proletariat in Amsterdam. In L. Passerini (Ed.), *Memory and totalitarianism.* Oxford: Oxford University Press.

Lieberman, M. A., & Falk, J. (1971). The remembered past as a source of data for research on the life cycle. *Human Development, 14,* 132–141.

Lieberman, M. A., & Tobin, S. S. (1983). *The experience of old age: Stress, coping and survival.* New York: Basic Books.

Lieblich, A., & Josselson, R. (Eds.) (1997). *The narrative study of lives, Vol. 5.* Thousand Oaks, CA: Sage.

Liedig, M. W. (1992). The continuum of violence against women: Psychological and physical consequences. *Journal of American College Health, 40,* 149–155.

Light, L. L. (1996). Memory and aging. In L. Bjork, & R. A. Bjork (Eds.), *Memory* (pp. 443–490). San Diego: Academic Press.

Light, L. L. (1992). The organization of memory in old age. In F. I. M. Craik, & T. A. Salthouse (Eds.), *The handbook of aging and cognition* (pp. 111–165). Hillsdale, NJ: Erlbaum.

Lillios, K. T. (1999). Objects of memory: The ethnography and archeology of heirlooms. *Journal of Archeological Method and Theory, 6,* 235–262.

Linley, A. (2000). Transforming psychology: The example of trauma. *The Psychologist, 13,* 353–355.

Lockhart, R. S. (1989). Consciousness and the function of remembered episodes. In H. L. Roediger, & F. I. M. Craik (Eds.), *Varieties of memory and consciousness* (pp. 423–430). Hillsdale, NJ: Erlbaum.

Logsdon, R. G. (1995). Psychopathology and treatment: Curriculum and research needs. In B. G. Knight, L. Teri, P. Wohlford, & J. Santos (Eds.), *Mental health services for older adults: Implications for training and practice in geropsychology* (pp. 41–51). Washington, DC: American Psychological Association.

Lohmann, R., Heuft, G., & Schneider, G. (1999). Biographical reconstruction of World War II experience: An exploration of German remembrances.

Paper presented at the IVth European Congress of Gerontology, 7–11 July, 1999, Berlin, Germany.

Love, L. L., & Sheldon, P. S. (1998). Souvenirs: Messengers of meaning. *Advances in Consumer Research, 25,* 170–175.

Lowenthal, M. F., Thurnher, M., & Chiriboga, D. (1975). *Four stages of life.* San Francisco: Jossey-Bass Publishers.

Luszcz, M. A., & Bryan, J. (1999). Toward understanding age-related memory for discourse. *Journal of Gerontology, 40,* 2–9.

Lynch, S. M., & Graham-Bermann, S. A. (2000). Woman abuse and self-affirmation. *Violence Against Women, 6,* 178–197.

Mader, W. (1996). Emotionality and continuity in biographical contexts. In J. E. Birren, G. Kenyon, J-E. Ruth, J. Schroots, & T. Svensson (Eds.), *Aging and biography: Explorations in adult development* (pp. 39–60). New York: Springer Publishing.

Mader, W. (1995). Thematically guided autobiographical reconstruction: On theory and method of 'guided autobiography' in adult education. In P. Alheit, A. Bron-Wojciechowska, E. Brugger, & Dominicé (Eds.), *The biographical approach in adult education.* Vienna: Verband Wiener Volksbildung.

Magee, J. J. (1988). *A professional's guide to older adults' life review: Releasing the peace within.* Lexington, MA: Lexington Books.

Main, M., Kaplan, K., & Cassidy, J. (1985). Security in infancy, childhood and adulthood: A move to the level of representation. In I. Bretherton, & E. Waters (Eds.), Growing points of attachment theory and research. *Monographs of the Society for Research in Child Development, 50*(1–2, Serial No. 209), 66–104.

Mannheim, K. (1972). The problem of generations. In *Essays on the sociology of knowledge* (orig. 1928). London: Routledge & Kegan Paul.

Manton, K. G., Patrick, C. H., & Johnson, K. W. (1994). Health differentials between blacks and whites: Recent trends in mortality and morbidity. In D. P. Willis (Ed.), *Health policies and Black Americans* (pp. 129–199). New Brunswick, NJ: Transaction.

Markus, H. R., & Kitayama, S. (1991). Culture and the self: Implications for cognition, emotion, and motivation. *Psychological Review, 98,* 224–253.

Maslow, A. H. (1968). *Toward a psychology of being.* New York: D. Van Nostrand Company.

Massing, A. (1991). Die Reinszenierung nationalsozialistischer Weltbilder im psychotherapeutischen Prozeß. *Forum der Psychoanalyse, 7,* 20–30.

McAdams, D. (1996). Narrating the self in adulthood. In J. E. Birren, G. M. Kenyon, J-E. Ruth, J. Schroots, & T. Svensson (Eds.), *Aging and biography: Explorations in adult development* (pp. 131–148). New York: Springer Publishing.

McAdams, D. (1994). *The stories we live by: Personal myths and the making of the self.* New York: William Morrow.

McAdams, D. (1985). *Power and intimacy.* New York: Guilford.

McCabe, A., Capron, T., & Peterson, C. (1991). The voice of experience: The recall of early childhood and adolescent memories by young adults. In C.

P. A. McCabe (Ed.), *Developing narrative structure* (pp. 137–173). Hillsdale, NJ: Erlbaum.

McCabe, A., & Peterson, C. (1991). Getting the story: A longitudinal study of parental styles in eliciting narratives and developing narrative skill. In A. McCabe, & C. Peterson (Eds.), *Developing narrative structure* (pp. 217–253). Hillsdale, NJ: Erlbaum.

McCrae, R. R., & Costa, P. T. (1984). *Emerging lives, enduring dispositions: Personality in adulthood.* Glenview, IL: Scott, Foresman.

McFadden, S. H. (1998). Emotions and spirituality in caregiving: An attachment theoretical perspective. Paper presented at the annual meeting of the American Society on Aging, San Francisco, CA.

McFadden, S. H. (1995). Religion and well-being in aging persons in an aging society. *Journal of Social Issues, 51,* 161–175.

McMahon, A. W., & Rhudick, P. J. (1967). Reminiscing in the aged: an adaptational response. In S. Levin, & R. J. Kahana (Eds.), *Psychodyamic studies on aging: Creativity, reminiscing and dying* (pp. 64–78). New York: International Universities Press.

Meacham, J. (1995). Reminiscing as a process of social construction. In B. K. Haight, & J. D. Webster (Eds.), *The art and science of reminiscing: Theory, research, methods, and applications* (pp. 37–48). Washington, DC: Taylor and Francis.

Meacham, J. (1990). The loss of wisdom. In R. Sternberg (Ed.), *Wisdom: Its nature, origins, and development* (pp. 181–211). New York: Cambridge University Press.

Mere, R. (1995). Arthos Wales: Working his hospitals. In J. Bornat (Ed.), *Reminiscence reviewed* (pp. 126–134). Buckingham, England: Open University Press.

Mere, R. (1992). Travelling on: Life story in a psychiatric day hospital. *Oral History, 20*(1), 75–76.

Mergler, N. L., & Goldstein, M. D. (1983). Why are there old people: Senescence as biological and cultural preparedness for the transmission of information. *Human Development, 26,* 72–90.

Merriam, S. B. (1995). Reminiscence and the oldest old. In B. K. Haight, & J. D. Webster (Eds.), *The art and science of reminiscing: Theory, research, methods, and applications.* Washington, DC: Taylor and Francis.

Merriam, S. B. (1993a). Butler's life review: How universal is it? *International Journal of Aging and Human Development, 37*(3), 163–175.

Merriam, S. B. (1993b). Race, sex, and age-group differences in the occurrences and uses of reminiscence. *Activities, Adaptation and Aging, 18,* 1–18.

Merriam, S. B. (1980). The concept and function of reminiscence: A review of the research. *The Gerontologist, 20,* 604–609.

Merriam, S. B., & Cross, L. H. (1982). Adulthood and reminiscence: A descriptive study. *Educational Gerontology, 8,* 275–290.

Metcalfe, J., Mencl, W. E., & Cottrell, G. W. (1994). Cognitive binding. In D. L. Schacter, & E. Tulving (Eds.), *Memory systems 1994* (pp. 1–38). Cambridge, MA: The MIT Press.

Mezirow, J. (2000). Learning to think like an adult. In J. Mezirow & Associates (Eds.), *Learning as transformation.* (pp. 3–33). San Fransciso: Jossey-Bass.

Mezirow, J. (1998). *Transformation theory of adult learning—core propositions.* Paper presented at First National Conference on Transformative Learning: Changing Adult Frames of Reference. Teachers' College, Columbia University, April 15–17, 1998.

Mezirow, J. (1997). Transformative learning: Theory to practice. In P. Cranton (Ed.), *Transformative learning in action: Insights from practice* (pp. 5–12). San Franscisco: Jossey-Bass.

Mezirow, J. (1994). Understanding transformation theory. *Adult Education Quarterly, 44*(4), 222–232.

Mezirow, J. (1991). *Transformative dimensions of adult learning.* San Francisco: Jossey-Bass Publishers.

Mick, D. G. (1986). Consumer research and semiotics: Exploring the morphology of signs, symbols, and significance. *Journal of Consumer Research, 13,* 196–213.

Molinari, V. (1999). Using reminiscence and life review as natural therapeutic strategies in group therapy. In M. Duffy (Ed.), Handbook of counseling and psychotherapy with older adults (pp. 154–165). New York: John Wiley and Sons, Inc.

Molinari, V., & Reichlin, R. E. (1985). Life review reminiscence in the elderly: A review of the literature. *International Journal of Aging and Human Development, 20,* 81–92.

Moody, H. R. (1988). Twenty-five years of the life review: Where did we come from? Where are we going? *Journal of Gerontological Social Work, 12,* 7–21.

Moody, H.R. (1984). Reminiscence and the recovery of the public world. In M. Kaminsky (Ed.), *The uses of reminiscence: New ways of working with older adults* (pp. 157–166). New York: Haworth Press

Morris, B. (1991). *Western conceptions of the individual.* New York and Oxford: Berg.

Morrow, D. G., Altieri, V., & Altieri, P. A. (1992). Aging, expertise, and narrative processing. *Psychology and Aging, 7,* 376–388.

Moser, T. (1996). Dämonische Figuren. *Die Wiederkehr des Dritten Reiches in der Psychotherapie.* Frankfurt: Suhrkamp.

Neisser, U. (1988a). Time present and time past. In M. M. Gruneberg, & R. N. Sykes (Eds.), *Practical aspects of memory: Current research and issues, Volume 2: Clinical and educational implications.* Chichester, England: Wiley.

Neisser, U. (1988b). Five kinds of self-knowledge. *Philosophical Psychology, 1,* 35–59.

Neisser, U. (Ed.) (1982). *Memory observed: Remembering in natural contexts.* San Francisco: Freeman.

Neisser, U. (1978). Memory: What are the important questions? In M. M. Gruneberg, P. E. Morris, & R. N. Sykes (Eds.), *Practical Aspects of Memory* (pp. 3–19). London: Academic Press.

Neisser, U., & Fivush, R. (1994). *The remembering self: Construction and accuracy in the self-narrative.* New York: Cambridge University Press.

Nelson, K. (1993). The psychological and social origins of autobiographical memory. *Psychological Science, 4,* 7–14.

Neugarten, B. L. (1979). Time, age and the life cycle. *American Journal of Psychiatry, 136,* 887–894.

Nezu, A. M., Nezu, C. M., & Perri, M. G. (1989). *Problem-solving therapy for depression: Theory, research, and clinical guidelines.* New York: Wiley.

Niederehe, G. (1994). Psychosocial therapies with depressed older adults. In L. S. Schneider, C. F. Reynolds, B. D. Lebowitz, & A. J. Friedhoff (Eds.), *Diagnosis and treatment of depression in late life: Results of the NIH consensus development conference* (pp. 293–315). Washington, DC: American Psychiatric Press.

Niethammer, L. (1980). Über Forschungstrends unter Verwendung diachroner Interviews in der Bundesrepublik. In L. Niethammer, & W. Trapp (Eds.), *Lebenserfahrung und kollektives Gedächtnis. Die Praxis der "Oral History".* Frankfurt: Syndikat.

Nomura, T. (1998). *Reminiscence and life review: Therapy and skill.* Tokyo, Japan: Chuohoki Publication.

Norris, A. (1989). Clinic or client? A psychologist's case for reminiscence. *Oral History, 17*(2), 26–30.

Norman, D. A. (1988). *The psychology of everyday things.* New York: Basic Books.

Norman, M. L., Harris, J. E., & Webster, J. D. (2001). Psychosocial correlates of reminiscence functions in African and Caucasian American adults. Poster presented at the 17th World Congress of Gerontology, July 1–6, Vancouver, Canada.

Nye, W. P. (1993). Amazing grace: Religion and identity among elderly black individuals. *International Journal of Aging and Human Development, 36,* 103–114.

Okazaki, S. (1997). Sources of ethnic differences between Asian American and White American college students on measures of depression and social anxiety. *Journal of Abnormal Psychology, 106,* 52–60.

Ochberg, R. (1995). Life stories and storied lives. In A. Lieblich, & R. Josselson (Eds.), *Exploring identity and gender: The narrative study of lives, Vol. 2.* (pp. 113–144). London: Sage.

Olney, J. (1972). *Metaphors of self: The meaning of autobiography.* Princeton, NJ: Princeton University Press.

Olsen, K., & Shopes, L. (1991). Crossing boundaries, building bridges: Doing oral history among working class women and men. In S. B. Gluck, & D. Patai (Eds.), *Women's words: The feminist practice of oral history* (pp. 63–75). London: Routledge.

O'Rourke, N., & Hadjistavropoulos, T. (1997). The relative efficacy of psychotherapy in the treatment of geriatric depression. *Aging & Mental Health, 1,* 305–310.

Osborne, C. L. (1989). Reminiscence: When the past eases the present. *Journal of Gerontological Nursing, 10,* 6–12.

Oswald, F. (1994). Zur Bedeutung des Wohnens im Alter bei gesunden und gehbeeinträchtigten Personen [The meaning of dwelling in healthy and walking-disabled elderly]. *Zeitschrift für Gerontologie, 27,* 355–365.

Pachana, N. A., Gallagher-Thompson, D., & Thompson, L. W. (1994). Assessment of depression. *Annual Review of Gerontology and Geriatrics, 14,* 234–256.

Paha, C. (1996). Persönliche Objekte in der Adoleszenz: Bewältigung von Entwicklungsaufgaben. [Personal objects in adolescence: Coping with developmental tasks]. Unpublished Diplom-Thesis. University of Heidelberg, Germany.

Paritzky, R., & Magoon, T. (1979). Human potential seminar outcomes as measured by the personal orientation inventory and goal attainment inventories. *Journal of Counseling Psychology, 26,* 30–36.

Park, D. C. (2000). The basic mechanisms accounting for age-related decline in cognitive function. In D. C. Park, & N. Schwarz (Eds.), *Cognitive aging: A primer* (pp. 3–21). Philadelphia: Psychological Press.

Park, D. C., Nisbett, R., & Hedden, T. (1999). Aging, Culture, and Cognition. *Journal of Gerontology: Psychological Sciences, 54B*(2), P75–84.

Park, D. C., & Schwarz, N. (Eds.) (2000). *Cognitive aging: A primer.* Philadelphia: Psychological Press.

Parker, R. G. (1999). Reminiscence as continuity: Comparison of young and older adults. *Journal of Clinical Geropsychology, 5,* 147–157.

Parker, R. G. (1995). Reminiscence: A continuity theory framework. *The Gerontologist, 35,* 515–525.

Parkin, A. J. (1993). *Memory: Phenomena, experiment, and theory.* Cambridge, MA: Blackwell.

Pasupathi, M. (in press). The social construction of the personal past and its implications for adult development. *Psychological Bulletin.*

Payne, B. P. (1988). Religious patterns and participation of older adults: A sociological perspective. *Educational Gerontology, 14,* 255–267.

Payne, J. C. (1997). *Adult neurogenic language disorders: Assessment and treatment.* San Diego, CA: Singular.

Pillemer, D. B. (1998a). *Momentous events, vivid memories.* Cambridge, MA: Harvard University Press.

Pillemer, D. B. (1998b). What is remembered about early childhood events? *Clinical Psychology Review, 18,* 895–913.

Pillemer, D. B. (1992). Remembering personal circumstances: A functional analysis. In E. Winograd, & U. Neisser (Eds.), *Affect and accuracy in recall: Studies of "flashbulb" memories* (Emory symposia in cognition, 4th ed., pp. 236–264). New York: Cambridge University Press.

Plato, A. von (1991). Oral History als Erfahrungswissenschaft. Zum Stand der "mündlichen Geschichte" in Deutschland. BIOS Zeitschrift für Autobiographieforschung und Oral History, 97–119.

Plaza, D. (1996). Family structure and social change of Caribbeans in Britain: An exploratory study of elderly Caribbean males. Paper prepared for the Caribbean Studies Association XXI Annual Conference.

Polkinghorne, D. (1996a). Narrative knowing and the study of lives. In J. E. Birren, G. M. Kenyon, J-E. Ruth, J. Schroots, & T. Svensson (Eds.), *Aging and biography: Explorations in adult development* (pp. 77–99). New York: Springer Publishing.

Polkinghorne, D. (1996b). Use of biography in the development of applicable knowledge. *Ageing and Society, 16*(6), 721–745.

Polkinghorne, D. (1988). *Narrative knowing and the human sciences.* Albany, NY: SUNY Press.

Polster, E. (1987). *Every person's life is worth a novel.* New York: Norton.

Portelli, A. (1997). *The battle of Valle Giulia: Oral history and the art of dialogue.* Madison, WI: The University of Wisconsin Press.

Porter, B. (1993). *Road to heaven: Encounters with Chinese hermits.* San Francisco: Mercury House.

Pratt, M. W., Arnold, M. L., Norris, J. E., & Filyer, R. (1999). Generativity and moral development as predictors of value socialization narratives for young persons across the adult life span: From lessons learned to stories shared. *Psychology and Aging, 14,* 414–426.

Prentice, D. A. (1987). Psychological correspondence of possessions, attitudes, and values. *Journal of Personality and Social Psychology, 53,* 993–1003.

Price, L. L., Arnould, E. J., & Curasi, C. F. (2000). Older consumers' disposition of special possessions. *Journal of Consumer Research, 27,* 179–201.

Quackenbush, S. W., & Barnett, M. A. (1995). Correlates of reminiscence activity among elderly individuals. *International Journal of Aging and Human Development, 41,* 169–181.

Randall, W. (2001). Storied worlds: Acquiring a narrative perspective on aging, identity, and everyday life. In G. Kenyon, P. Clark , & B. de Vries (Eds.), *Narrative gerontology: Theory, research, and practice.* New York: Springer Publishing.

Randall, W. (1999). Narrative intelligence and the novelty of our lives. *Journal of Aging Studies, 13*(1), 11–28.

Randall, W. (1995). *The stories we are: An essay on self-creation.* Toronto: University of Toronto Press.

Randall, W., & Kenyon, G. (2001). *Ordinary wisdom: Biographical aging and the journey of life.* Westport, CT: Praeger.

Rauschenbach, B. (1998). Politik der Erinnerung. In J. Rüsen, & J. Straub (Eds.), *Die dunkle Spur der Vergangenheit. Psychoanalytische Zugänge zum Geschichtsbewußtsein. Erinnerung, Geschichte, Identität 2* (S. 354–374). Frankfurt: Suhrkamp.

Ray, R. E. (2000). *Beyond nostalgia: Aging and life-story writing.* Charlottesville, VA: University Press of Virginia.

Redfoot, D. L., & Back, K. W. (1988). The perceptual presence of the life course. *International Journal of Aging and Human Development, 27,* 155–170.

Reese, E., Haden, C., & Fivush, R. (1996). Mothers, fathers, daughters, sons: Gender differences in reminiscing. *Research on Language and Social Interaction, 29,* 27–56.

Reese, E., Haden, C. A., & Fivush, R. (1993). Mother-child conversations about the past: Relationships of style and memory over time. *Cognitive Development, 8,* 403–430.

Reese, E., & Farrant, K. (in press). Social origins of reminiscing. In R. Fivush,

& C. A. Haden (Eds.), *Connecting culture and memory: The social construction of an autobiographical self.* Hillsdale, NJ: Erlbaum.

Reese, E., & Fivush, R. (1993). Parental styles of talking about the past. *Developmental Psychology, 29,* 596–606.

Reker, G., & Chamberlain, K. (Eds.) (2000). *Exploring existential meaning: Optimizing human development across the lifespan.* Thousand Oaks, CA: Sage.

Reiser, B. J., Black, J. B., & Kalamarides, P. (1986). Strategic memory search processes. In D. C. Rubin (Ed.), *Autobiographical memory* (pp. 100–121). New York: Cambridge University Press.

Riches, G., & Dawson, P. (1998). Lost children, living memories: The role of photographs in processes of grief and adjustment among bereaved parent. *Death Studies, 22,* 121–140.

Robinson, J. A. (1986). Autobiographical memory: A historical prologue. In D. Rubin (Ed.), *Autobiographical memory* (pp. 19–24). Cambridge: Cambridge University Press.

Robinson, J. A. (1976). Sampling autobiographical memory. *Cognitive Psychology, 8,* 578–595.

Robinson, J. A., & Swanson, K. L. (1990). Autobiographical memory: The next phase. *Applied Cognitive Psychology, 4,* 321–335.

Rogers, K. L., Leydersdorff, S., & Dawson, G. (Eds.) (1999). *Trauma and life stories: International perspectives.* London: Routledge.

Rogers, W. A., Fisk, A. D., & Walker, N. (Eds.) (1996). *Aging and skilled performance: Advances in theory and applications.* Mahwah, NJ: Erlbaum.

Romaniuk, M., & Romaniuk, J. G. (1983). Life events and reminiscence: A comparison of the memories of young and old adults. *Imagination, Cognition, and Personality, 2,* 125–136.

Rosenau, P. (1992). *Postmodernism and the social sciences: Insights, inroads, and intrusions.* Princeton, NJ: Princeton University Press.

Rosenberg, M. (1965). *Society and the adolescent self-image.* Princeton, NJ: Princeton University Press.

Rosenblatt, L. (1983). *Literature as exploration.* New York: The Modern Language Association of America.

Rosenthal, G. (1993). Reconstruction of life stories. In R. Josselson, & A. Lieblich (Eds.), *The narrative study of lives.* London: Sage.

Ross, M., & Holmberg, D. (1990). Recounting the past: Gender differences in the recall of events in the history of a close relationship. In M. P. Zanna, & J. M. Olson (Eds.), *The Ontario Symposium: Vol. 6, Self-inference processes* (pp. 135–152). Hillsdale, NJ: Erlbaum.

Rouverol, A. J. (1999). 'I was content and not content': Oral history and the collaborative process. *Oral History, 28*(2), 66–78.

Rubin, D. C. (Ed.) (1996). *Remembering our past: Studies in autobiographical memory.* Cambridge: Cambridge University Press.

Rubin, D. C. (Ed.) (1986). *Autobiographical memory.* Cambridge: Cambridge University Press.

Rubin, D. C., Groth, E., & Goldsmith, D. J. (1984). Olfactory cuing of autobiographical memory. *American Journal of Psychology, 97,* 493–507.

Rubin, D. C., Rahhal, T. A., & Poon, L. W. (1998). Things learned in early adulthood are remembered best. *Memory & Cognition, 26,* 3–19.

Rubin, D. C., & Schulkind, M. D. (1997a). Distribution of important and word-cued autobiographical memories in 20-, 35-, and 70-year-old adults. *Psychology and Aging, 12*(3), 524–535.

Rubin, D. C., & Schulkind, M. D. (1997b). The distribution of autobiographical memories across the lifespan. *Memory and Cognition, 25*(6), 859–866.

Rubinstein, R. L. (1995). The engagement of life history and the life review: A research case study. *Journal of Aging Studies, 9,* 187–203.

Rubinstein, R. L. (1990). The environmental representation of personal themes by older people. *Journal of Aging Studies, 4,* 131–148.

Rubinstein, R. L. (1989). The home environments of older people: A description of the psychosocial processes linking person to place. *Journal of Gerontology, Social Science, 44,* S45–53.

Rubinstein, R. L. (1987). The significance of personal objects to older people. *Journal of Aging Studies, 1,* 225–238.

Rubinstein, R. L., & Parmelee, P. (1992). Place attachment among the elderly. In I. Altman, & S. Low (Eds.), *Place attachment.* New York: Plenum.

Ruddick, S. (1990). *Maternal thinking: Towards a politics of peace.* London: The Women's Press.

Runge, T., Frey, D., Gollwitzer, P., Helmreich, R., & Spence, J. T. (1981). Masculine (instrumental) and feminine (expressive) traits. *Journal of Cross-Cultural Psychology, 12,* 142–162.

Russel, R. J. H., & Hulson, B. (1992). Physical and psychological abuse of heterosexual partners. *Personality and Individual Differences, 13,* 457–473.

Ruth, J. E, Birren, J. E., & Polkinghorne, D. E. (1996). The projects of life reflected in autobiographies of old age. *Ageing and Society, 16*(6), 677–699.

Ruth, J.-E., & Coleman, P. (1996). Personality and aging: Coping and management of the self in later life. In J. E. Birren, & K. W. Schaie (Eds.), *Handbook of the psychology of aging Fourth edition* (pp. 308–322). San Diego, CA: Academic Press.

Ruth, J. E., & Kenyon, G. M. (1996). Biography in adult development. In J. E. Birren, G. M. Kenyon, J. E. Ruth, J. J. F. Schroots, & T. Svendsson (Eds.), *Aging and biography: Explorations in adult development* (pp. 224–247). New York: Springer Publishing.

Ruth, J.-E., & Oberg, P. (1996). Ways of life: Old age in a life history perspective. In J. E. Birren, G. M. Kenyon, J-E. Ruth, J. Schroots, & T. Svensson (Eds.), *Aging and biography: Explorations in adult development* (pp. 167–186). New York: Springer Publishing.

Rybash, J. M., & Hrubi, K. L. (1997). Psychometric and psychodynamic correlates of first memories in younger and older adults. *The Gerontologist, 37,* 581–587.

Sabourin, S., & Gendreau, P. (1988). Assessing client satisfaction with mental health treatment among French-Canadians. *Applied Psychology: An International Review, 37,* 327–335.

Safranski, R. (1990). *Schopenhauer and the wild years of philosophy.* Cambridge, MA: Harvard University Press.

Salthouse, T. A. (1996). The processing-speed theory of adult age differences in cognition. *Psychological Review, 103,* 403–428.

Sarbin, T. (1994). Steps to the narratory principle: An autobiographical essay. In J. Lee (Ed.), *Life and story: Autobiographies for a narrative psychology* (pp. 247–273). Westport, CT: Praeger.

Sarbin, T. (Ed.) (1986a). *Narrative psychology: The storied nature of human conduct.* New York: Praeger.

Sarbin, T. (1986b). The narrative as a root metaphor for psychology. In T. Sarbin (Ed.), *Narrative psychology: The storied nature of human conduct* (pp. 3–21). New York: Praeger.

Satcher, D. (1986). Research needs for minority populations. *American Speech-Language-Hearing Association Reports, 16,* 89–92.

Schacter, D. L. (1996). *Searching for memory: The brain, the mind, and the past.* New York: Basic Books.

Schank, R. (1990). *Tell me a story: A new look at real and artificial memory.* New York: Scribner's.

Schlarch, A. (1997). "Response to Kathleen Woodward's 'Telling Stories'." In *Telling Stories,* Doreen B. Townsend Center for the Humanities Occasional Papers, 9. Berkeley, CA: University of California.

Schmiedeck, R. (1978). *The personal sphere model.* New York: Grune & Stratton.

Schneider, L. S., Reynolds, C. F., Lebowitz, B. D., & Friedhoff, A. J. (1994). *Diagnosis and treatment of depression in late life: Results of the NIH Consensus Development Conference.* Washington, DC: American Psychiatric Press.

Schroots, J., Birren, J. E., & Kenyon, G. M. (1991). Metaphors and aging: An overview. In G. M. Kenyon, J. E. Birren, & J. Schroots (Eds.), *Metaphors of aging in science and the humanities* (pp. 1–16). New York: Springer Publishing.

Schönbach, P. (1990). *Account episodes. The management or escalation of conflict.* Cambridge: Cambridge University Press.

Schwab-Trapp, M. (1996). *Konflikt, Kultur und Interpretation. Eine Diskursanalyse des öffentlichen Umgangs mit dem Nationalsozialismus.* Opladen, Germany: Westdeutscher Verlag.

Schweder, R. A. (1994). "You're not sick, you're just in love": Emotion as an interpretive system. In P. Ekman, & R. Davidson (Eds.), *The nature of emotion: Fundamental questions* (pp. 32–47). New York: Oxford University Press.

Schweitzer, P. (Ed.) (1998). *Reminiscence in dementia care.* London: Age Exchange Theatre Trust, The Reminiscence Center.

Scogin, F., & McElreath, L. (1994). Efficacy of psychosocial treatments for geriatric depression: A quantitative review. *Journal of Consulting and Clinical Psychology, 62,* 69–74.

Scott, M. B., & Lyman, S. M. (1968). Accounts. *American Sociological Review, 33,* 46–62.

Scott-Maxwell, F. (1968). *The measure of my days.* New York: Penguin Books.

Seligman, M. E. P., & Czikszentmihalyi, M. (2000). Positive psychology: An introduction. *American Psychologist, 55,* 5–14.

Semin, G., & Manstead, A. S. R. (1983). *The accountability of conduct. A social psychological analysis.* London: Academic Press.

Shadden, B. B. (1988). Perceptions of daily communicative interactions with older persons. In B. B. Shadden (Ed.), *Communication behavior and aging* (pp. 12–40). Baltimore, MD: Williams & Wilkens.

Shaw, M. E. (2001). A history of guided autobiography. In G. M. Kenyon, P. Clark, & B. de Vries (Eds.), *Narrative gerontology: Theory, research, and practice.* New York: Springer Publishing.

Shaw, M. E. (1999). A model for transformative learning: The promotion of successful aging. Doctoral Dissertation. University of British Columbia in Interdisciplinary Studies.

Shenk, D. (1998). *Someone to lend a helping hand: Women growing old in rural America.* Amsterdam: Gordon and Breach.

Sherman, E. (1991a). *Reminiscence and the self in old age.* New York: Springer Publishing.

Sherman, E. (1991b). Reminiscentia: Cherished objects as memorabilia in late-life reminiscence. *International Journal of Aging and Development, 33,* 89–100.

Sherman, E., & Newman, E. S. (1977). The meaning of cherished personal possessions for the elderly. *International Journal of Aging and Human Development, 8,* 181–192.

Shute, G. E. (1986). Life review: A cautionary note. *Clinical Gerontologist, 6,* 57–58.

Singer, J. (1998). Applying a systems framework to self-defining memories. *Psychological Inquiry, 9,* 161–164.

Singer, J. (1996). The story of your life: A process perspective on narrative and emotion in adult development. In C. Magai, & S. McFadden (Eds.), *Handbook of emotion, adult development, and aging* (pp. 443–63). San Diego: Academic.

Singer, J. A., & Salovey, P. (1993). *The remembered self: Emotion and memory in personality.* New York: Free Press.

Spayd, C. S., & Smyer, M. S. (1996). Psychological interventions in nursing homes. In S. H. Zarit, & B. G. Knight (Eds.), *A guide to psychotherapy and aging* (pp. 241–264). Washington, DC: American Psychological Association.

Spence, D. (1982). *Narrative truth and historical truth.* New York: Norton.

Spence, J. T. (1984). Gender identity and its implications for masculinity and feminity. *Nebraska Symposium of Motivation,* 60–95.

Spence, J. T., Helmreich, R., & Holahan, C. (1979). Negative and positive components of psychological masculinity and feminity. *Journal of Personality and Social psychology, 37,* 1673–1682.

Sperbeck, D. J., Whitbourne, S. K., & Hoyer, W. J. (1986). Age and openness to experience in autobiographical memory. *Experimental Aging Research, 12*(3), 169–172.

Stark, E., & Flitcraft, A. (1996). *Women at risk: Domestic violence and women's health.* Thousand Oaks, CA: Sage Publishers.

Staudinger, U. M. (2001). Life reflection: A social-cognitive analysis of life review. *Review of General Psychology, 5,* 148–160.

Steele, C. (1988). The psychology of self-affirmation: Sustaining the integrity of the self. *Advances in Experimental Social Psychology, 21,* 261–302.

Steele, R. (1986). Deconstructing history: Toward a systematic criticism of psychological narratives. In T. Sarbin (Ed.), *Narrative psychology: The storied nature of human conduct* (pp. 256–275). Westport, CT: Praeger.

Stein, N. L., & Levine, L. J. (1990). Making sense out of emotion: The representation and use of goal-structured knowledge. In N. L. Stein, B. Leventhal, & T. Traban (Eds.), *Psychological and biological approaches to emotion* (pp. 45–73). Hillsdale, NJ: Erlbaum.

Sternberg, R. (Ed.) (1990). *Wisdom: Its nature, origins, and development.* New York: Cambridge University Press.

Steuer, J. L., & Hammen, C. L. (1983). Cognitive-behavioral group therapy for the depressed elderly: Issues and adaptations. *Cognitive Therapy and Research, 7,* 285–296.

Stevens-Ratchford, R. G. (1992). The effect of life review reminiscence activities on depression and self-esteem in older adults. *The American Journal of Occupational Therapy, 47*(5), 413–419.

Stine, E. A. L., & Wingfield, A. (1990). The assessment of qualitative age differences in discourse processing. In T. M. Hess (Ed.), *Aging and cognition* (pp. 33–92). New York: Elsevier.

Stones, M. J., & Kozma, A. (1989). Multidimensional assessment of the elderly via a microcomputer: The SENOTS program and battery. *Psychology & Aging, 4,* 113–118.

Stones, M. J., & Kozma, A. (1986). Happiness and activities as propensities. *Journal of Gerontology, 41,* 85–90.

Straub, J. (1998). Geschichten erzählen, Geschichte bilden. Grundzüge einer narrativen Psychologie historischer Sinnbildung. In J. Straub (Ed.), *Erzählung, Identität und historisches Bewußtsein. Die psychologische Konstruktion von Zeit und Geschichte. Erinnerung, Geschichte, Identität 1.* Frankfurt: Suhrkamp.

Strauss, A. L. (1987). *Qualitative analysis for social scientists.* Cambridge, UK: University of Cambridge Press.

Strauss, A. L., & Corbin, J. (1990). *Basics of qualitative research* (2nd ed.). Thousand Oaks, CA: Sage Publications.

Sykes, G. M., & Matza, D. (1957). Techniques of neutralization: A theory of delinquency. *American Sociological Review, 22,* 664–670.

Tannen, D. (1986). *That's not what I meant! How conversational style makes or breaks your relations with others.* New York: William Morrow.

Tannen, D. (1994). *Gender and discourse.* New York and Oxford: Oxford University Press.

Tedeschi, R. G., & Calhoun, L. G. (1995). *Trauma and transformation: Growing in the aftermath of suffering.* Thousand Oaks, CA: Sage.

Tennen, H., Eberhardt, T., & Affleck, G. (1999). Depression research methodologies at the social-clinical interface: Still hazy after all these years. *Journal of Social and Clinical Psychology, 18,* 121–159.

Teri, L., Curtis, J., Gallagher-Thompson, D., & Thompson, L. (1994). Cognitive-behavioral therapy with depressed older adults. In L. S. Schneider, C. F.

Reynolds, B. D. Lebowitz, & A. J. Friedhoff (Eds.), *Diagnosis and treatment of depression in late life: Results of the NIH consensus development conference* (pp. 279–291). Washington, DC: American Psychiatric Press.

Teri, L., & McCurry, S. M. (1994). Psychosocial therapies. In C. Coffey, & J. Cummings (Eds.), *Textbook of geriatric neuropsychiatry* (pp. 662–682). Washington, DC: American Psychiatric Press.

TeSelle, S. (1975). *Speaking in parables: A study in metaphor and theology.* Philadelphia: Fortress Press.

Thomas, M. (1998). *Place, memory and identity in the Vietnamese diaspora.* Sydney: Allen and Unwin.

Thompson, P. (2000). *The voice of the past* Third edition. Oxford: Oxford University Press.

Thorne, A. K., & Klohnen, E. (1993). Interpersonal memories as maps for personality consistency. In D. C. Funder (Ed.), *Studying lives through time: Personality and development* (pp. 223–253). Washington, DC: American Psychological Association.

Thornton, S., & Brotchie, J. (1987). Reminiscence: A critical review of the empirical literature. *British Journal of Clinical Psychology, 26,* 93–111.

Tombaugh, T. N., & McIntyre, N. J. (1992). The Mini-Mental State Examination: A comprehensive review. *Journal of the American Geriatrics Society, 40,* 922–935.

Tulving, E. (1984). *Elements of episodic memory* (pp. 62–63). New York: Oxford University Press.

Tulving, E. (1972). Episodic and semantic memory. In E. Tulving, & W. Donaldson (Eds.), *Organization of memory* (pp. 382–403). New York: Academic Press.

Tun, P. A., & Wingfield, A. (1997). Language and communication: Fundamentals of speech communication and language processing in old age. In A. D. Fisk, & W. A. Rogers (Eds.), *Handbook of human factors and the older adult* (pp. 125–149). San Diego, CA: Academic Press.

Turner, M. (1996). *The literary mind.* New York: Oxford University Press.

Turner, V., & Bruner, E. (Eds.) (1986). *The anthropology of experience.* Chicago: University of Illinois Press.

Unruh, D. R. (1983). Death and personal history: Strategies of identity preservation. *Social Problems, 30,* 340–351.

Van Dijk, T. A. (1987). *Communicating racism. Ethnic prejudice in thought and talk.* Newbury Park, NJ: Sage.

Van IJzendoorn, M. H. (1995). Adult attachment representations, parental responsiveness, and infant attachment: A meta-analysis of the predictive validity of the Adult Attachment Interview. *Psychological Bulletin, 117,* 387–403.

Volkan, V. D. (1999). Nostalgia as a linking phenomenon. *Journal of Applied Psychoanalytic Studies, 1,* 169–179.

Volkan, V. D. (1981). *Linking objects and linking phenomena.* New York: International Universities Press.

Wagenaar, W. A., & Groeneweg, J. (1990). The memory of concentration camp survivors. *Applied Cognitive Psychology, 4,* 77–87.

Wagner, R. (1986). *Symbols that stand for themselves.* Chicago: University of Chicago Press.

Walker, L. E. (1994). *Abused women and survivor therapy: A practical guide for the psychotherapist.* Washington, DC: American Psychological Association.

Walker, L. E. (1989). Psychology and violence against women. *American Psychologist, 44,* 695–702.

Walker, L. E. (1984). *The battered woman syndrome.* New York: Springer Publishing.

Wallace, J. B. (1992). Reconsidering the life review: The social construction of talk about the past. *The Gerontologist, 32*(1), 120–125.

Wallendorf, M., & Arnould, E. (1988). My favorite things: A cross-cultural inquiry into object attachment, possessiveness, and social linkage. *Journal of Consumer Research, 14,* 531–547.

Walmsley, J., & Atkinson, D. (2000). Oral history and the history of learning disability. In J. Bornat, R. Perks, P. Thompson, & J. Walmsley (Eds.), *Oral history, health and welfare* (pp. 180–202). London: Routledge.

Wapner, S., Demick, J., & Redondo, J. P. (1990). Cherished possessions and adaptation of older people to nursing homes. *International Journal of Aging and Development, 31,* 299–315.

Waters, E. (1987). *Attachment Behavior Q-set (Version 3.0).* Unpublished instrument. Department of Psychology, State University of New York at Stony Brook.

Watt, L. M., & Wong, P. (1991). A taxonomy of reminiscence and therapeutic implications. *Journal of Gerontological Social Work, 16,* 37–57.

Watt, L. M., & Cappeliez, P. (2000). Integrative and instrumental reminiscence therapy: Theoretical models and intervention strategies. *Aging and Mental Health, 4,* 166–177.

Watt, L. M., & Cappeliez, P. (1996). Efficacité de la rétrospective de vie intégrative et de la rétrospective de vie instrumentale en tant qu'interventions pour des personnes âgées dépressives. *Revue Québécoise de Psychologie, 17,* 1–14.

Watt, L. M., & Cappeliez, P. (1995). Reminiscence interventions for the treatment of depression in older adults. In B. K. Haight, & J. D. Webster (Eds.), *The art and science of reminiscing: Theory, research, methods, and applications* (pp. 221–232). London: Taylor and Francis.

Watzlawick, P., Weakland, J. H., & Fisch, R. (1994). *Change: Principles of problem formation and problem resolution.* New York: W.W. Norton.

Webster, J. D. (in press). An exploratory analysis of a self-assessed wisdom scale. *Journal of Adult Development.*

Webster, J. D. (2001). The future of the past: Continuing challenges for reminiscence research. In G. Kenyon, B. de Vries, & P. Clark (Eds.), *Narrative gerontology: Theory, research, and practice.* New York: Springer Publishing.

Webster, J. D. (1999). World views and narrative gerontology: Situating reminiscence behavior within a lifespan perspective. *Journal of Aging Studies, 13,* 29–42.

Webster, J. D. (1997). The Reminiscence Functions Scale: A replication. *International Journal of Aging and Human Development, 44,* 137–148.

Webster, J. D. (1994). Predictors of reminiscence: A lifespan perspective. *Canadian Journal on Aging, 13,* 66–78.

Webster, J. D. (1993). Construction and validation of the Reminiscence Functions Scale. *Journals of Gerontology: Psychological Sciences, 48,* 256–262.

Webster, J. D., & Cappeliez, P. (1993). Reminiscence and autobiographical memory: Complementary contexts for cognitive aging research. *Developmental Review, 13,* 54–91.

Webster, J. D., & Haight, B. K. (1995). Memory lane milestones: Progress in reminiscence definition and classification. In B. K. Haight, & J. D. Webster (Eds.), *The art and science of reminiscing* (pp. 273–286). Philadelphia: Taylor and Francis.

Webster, J. D., & McCall, M. (1999). Reminiscence functions across adulthood: A replication and extension. *Journal of Adult Development, 6*(1), 73–85.

Weiland, S. (1995). Interpretive social science and spirituality. In M. A. Kimble, S. H. McFadden, J. W. Ellor, and J. J. Seeber (Eds.), *Aging, spirituality, and religion: A handbook* (pp. 589–611). Minneapolis: Fortress Press.

Weintraub, W. (1981). *Verbal behavior adaptation and psychopathology.* New York: Springer Publishing.

Weiss, J. C. (1994). Group therapy with older adults in long-term care settings: Research and clinical cautions and recommendations. *The Journal for Specialists in Group Work, 19*(1), 22–29.

Welch-Ross, M. K. (1997). Mother-child participation in conversation about the past: Relationships to preschoolers' theory of mind. *Developmental Psychology, 33,* 618–629.

Wengraf, T. (2000). Uncovering the general from within the particular: From contingencies to typologies in the understanding of cases. In P. Chamberlayne, J. Bornat, & T. Wengraf (Eds.), *The turn to biographical method in social science: Comparative issues and examples* (pp. 140–164). London: Routledge.

Westerman, W. (1998). Central American refugee testimonies and performed life histories in the sanctuary movement. In R. Perks, & A. S. Thomson (Eds.), *The oral history reader* (pp. 224–234). London: Routledge.

Westwood, M. J. (1998). Life review program for Canadian veterans. Report for Veterans Affairs Canada and the Royal Canadian Legion. November, 1998, (pp. 1–37).

Whalen, M. (1996). *Counseling to end violence against women: A subversive model.* Thousand Oaks, CA: Sage.

Whitbourne, S. K. (1986). *The me I know: A study of adult identity.* New York: Springer-Verlag.

White, M., & Epston, D. (1990). *Narrative means to therapeutic ends.* New York: W. W. Norton.

Wink, P. (1999a). Addressing end-of-life issues: Spirituality and inner life. *Generations, 23,* 75–80.

Wink, P. (1999b). *Relation between life review and acceptance.* Paper presented at the 3rd Reminiscence and Life Review Conference, New York, October, 1999.

Wink, P., & Dillon, M. (in press). Spiritual development across the adult life course: Findings from a longitudinal study. *Journal of Adult Development.*

Winnicott, D. W. (1971). *Playing and reality.* London: Penguin.

Winograd, E., & Rivers-Bulkeley, N. T. (1977). Effects of changing context on remembering faces. *Journal of Experimental Psychology: Human Learning & Memory, 3,* 397–405.

Wolf, M. A. (1990). The crisis of legacy: Life review interviews with elderly women religious. *Journal of Women and Aging, 2,* 67–79.

Woods, S. J., & Campbell, J. C. (1993). Posttraumatic stress in battered women. *Issues in Mental Health Nursing, 14,* 173–186.

Wong, P. T. P. (1995). The processes of adaptive reminiscence. In B. K. Haight, & J. D. Webster (Eds.), *The art and science of reminiscing: Theory, research, methods, and applications* (pp. 23–35). Washington, DC: Taylor and Francis.

Wong, P. T. P., & Watt, L. M. (1991). What types of reminiscence are associated with successful aging? *Psychology and Aging, 6,* 272–279.

Wyatt-Brown, A. (1996). Literary gerontology comes of age. In T. Cole, D. van Tassel, & R. Kastenbaum (Eds.), *Handbook of the humanities and aging* (pp. 331–351). New York: Springer Publishing.

Yesavage, J. A., Brink, T. L., Rose, T. L., Lum, O., Huang, V., Adey, M., & Leirer, V. O. (1983). Development and validation of a geriatric depression scale: A preliminary report. *Journal of Psychiatric Research, 17,* 37–39.

Yoshiyama, Y. (1999). Comparative investigation between improved patients and not improved patients with Alzheimer's disease by reminiscence group therapy in day care. *Japanese Journal of Geriatric Psychiatry, 10,* 53–58.

Young, J. E. (1990). *Cognitive therapy for personality disorders: A schema focused approach.* Sarasota, FL: Professional Resource Exchange.

Young J. E., Beck, A. T., & Weinberger, A. (1993). Depression. In D. Barlow (Ed.), *Clinical handbook of psychological disorders* (pp. 240–277). New York: Guilford Press.

Youssef, F. A. (1990). The impact of group reminiscence counseling on a depressed elderly population. *Nurse Practitioners, 15*(4), 32–38.

Zacks, R. T., Hasher, L., & Li, K. Z. H. (2000). Human memory. In F. I. M. Craik, & T. A. Salthouse (Eds.), *The handbook of aging and cognition* (2nd ed., pp. 293–357). Mahwah, NJ: Erlbaum.

Zeiss, A. M., & Steffen, A. (1996). Treatment issues with elderly clients. *Cognitive and Behavioural Practice, 3,* 371–389.

Index